FIELD OF FIRE

Diary of a Gunner Officer

JACK SWAAB

SUTTON PUBLISHING

First published in the United Kingdom in 2005 by
Sutton Publishing Limited · Phoenix Mill
Thrupp · Stroud · Gloucestershire · GL5 2BU

British Library Cataloguing in Publication Data
A catalogue record for this book is available from the British Library.

ISBN 0-7509-4275-4

For my family

Typeset in Photina MT 10/14pt
Typesetting and origination by
Sutton Publishing Limited.
Printed and bound in England by
J.H. Haynes & Co. Ltd, Sparkford.

Contents

LIST OF MAPS

FOREWORD

For whom are diaries written? Are they personal records, only for the purposes of private recollection? Or do we secretly hanker for the day when our innermost thoughts and reflections will be read by others? And, if the latter, do we adjust what we say accordingly?

Jack Swaab's diaries raise these questions precisely because he asked them of himself. They are so well written, so full, and – not infrequently – so lyrical as to suggest that he had an audience in mind. When one of his many correspondents during the war suggested that his letters be published, he liked the idea. The end of the Second World War found him penning short stories. And yet, at the beginning of his active service, he was recording his contempt for some comrades in terms that he would later repent, and maintaining liaisons with girl friends that were not just successive but – at least as this story begins – simultaneous. Anybody who was seriously looking to posterity might have been more circumspect. The fact that Jack Swaab was not is what makes *Field of Fire* such an immediate and powerful record, one of the great personal narratives of the experience of war to come out of the British Army in the years 1939–45.

Edmund Blunden prefaced *Undertones of War*, his reflections on the western front in a previous war, with the thought that no one would read it or would understand it who had not 'gone the same journey'. Swaab, consciously or un-consciously, reflected Blunden when he wrote in 1943, 'can anybody who has not travelled these roads be expected to understand that?' 'That' was not the horrors of war, which those who are caught up in them often do not feel need specific description, but the restorative powers of a cup of tea (on which score these pages provide plenty of testimony). Swaab may not have cited Blunden but he refers to Siegfried Sassoon and quotes Rupert Brooke and Julian Grenfell. It may be that the proximity to the literary legacy of what was still to his generation the Great War was what kept the authors of the Second World War silent for so long. Blunden published *Undertones of War* ten years after the event. With one or two exceptions the classic personal accounts of the experience of the Second World War, such as this, have appeared in the last ten years, since the fiftieth anniversary of VE day.

Swaab was a field gunner in the 51st Highland Division. For much of the war he was a forward observation officer (F.O.O. in these pages). It was a dangerous job, requiring him to be up with the infantry, directing the guns of his battery on to targets it could not see but he very often could. Their 25-pounder field guns were one of the great artillery pieces of all time, their bombardments the epitome of industrialised war, with batteries firing up to 1,000 rounds a time in the closing battles in north-west Europe. Indeed, Swaab uses the word 'work', not fighting, firing or shooting, to describe what he and his fellow gunners were doing.

When he joined the 51st Highland Division, it had just become a household name in Britain. Originally raised from Territorial Army battalions based in the north-east of Scotland, it was re-formed after the first division was overrun at St Valery in France in 1940. On 23 October 1942 it advanced into action at El Alamein, its pipes playing and, crucially for this story, its artillery giving it the sort of support which the infantry had not enjoyed since the final battles of 1918. Swaab was with it as it drove the Afrika Korps back to Tunisia. For the rest of the war, the 'HD' of its divisional shoulder flash marked the progress of the British Army as it crossed into Europe. In July 1943 the division landed in Sicily, an operation which Swaab rightly described at the time as the greatest ever combined operation. The lessons from Husky were applied in an even bigger one eleven months later, when the division, which had been brought back to Britain, took part in the D Day landings. The fighting of the bitterly cold winter of 1944/5 would have been recognisable to Sassoon and Blunden, as infantry and artillery slogged it out in attritional battles in the Ardennes and the Reichswald. Swaab was in it all, and was an F.O.O. when the division finally crossed the Rhine. By then there were some who felt that the division's morale had become the casualty of too much combat, too little rest, and too many deaths. Although there is much in Swaab's diary to contradict that view, his tone changes as he moves into north-west Europe, the sense of fear and danger increasing as the possibility of surviving the war grows.

Keeping a diary such as this was itself in breach of regulations. But keep it Swaab did. The reader needs constantly to remember that many of these entries were written under fire, particularly after D Day. Frequently they are preoccupied with the minor horrors of war, with flea bites, sore teeth, malaria, headaches and simple exhaustion. Veganin and whisky were as important as tea in sustaining morale. But possibly more vital than both was the flow of letters from home. As well as writing this diary, Swaab was corresponding daily with his loved ones. Mixed in with all his other reactions was the growing sense of professional ambition, the pride in being a front-line soldier, the contempt for 'base-wallahs', the frustration with staffs for changing plans, the admiration of

Montgomery. His desire for a third 'pip' to signify his promotion to captain was rewarded. These diaries do not reveal whether his hope that he might be awarded a Military Cross was answered, but the portrait which accompanies this book shows that distinctive and rightly coveted white and purple ribbon.

Hew Strachan
Chichele Professor of the History of War
University of Oxford

PREFACE

I suppose that it must have been the summer of 1936. Down to the last two for the annual reading prize, I approach the brass eagle in the school chapel. The large bible is open at Ecclesiastes. Loudly, and (looking back) I now suspect rather theatrically, I began to intone: 'Remember now thy creator in the days of thy youth . . .'.

Alas, I have long since ceased to believe in my creator, but with that tiresome nostalgia which seems to mark one's increasing years, I do look back on the days of my youth; and lately on the seven closely written diaries which – against all orders – I kept as a not very senior front-line officer.

The odd thing I find is that although I am the person who wrote them, what I read there doesn't seem to be me at all. Of course, I recognise certain characteristics, recall certain incidents (but have totally forgotten certain others), but the whole thing has an air of unreality; as though it all happened to someone I used to know very well.

Above all, I note the rather embarrassing ordinariness of much of what I recorded. I wince slightly at the undeniably commonplace nature of many observations. Yet, dammit, I do feel a sneaking admiration for this chap – me? – who seems to have done battle for 110 hours without getting his boots off; and who apparently coped variously with temperatures ranging from 118 °F in the shade to 40 degrees of frost, with sandstorms, snow, mud and rain; with lack of food and lack of sleep, not to mention toothache, malaria and love.

The fact is that this was such an ordinary creature who, by and large, had such an ordinary war. Not for him the terrors of Odette or the White Rabbit. Did he know of the hell of the Burma railway, the Arctic convoy or the unimaginable interior of Auschwitz? When I read of such things long after the war had ended, I felt almost ashamed of my minuscule contribution. Could it really be of interest to young people now? Or to the old who shared so much of it? Or, indeed, to anyone except perhaps myself and my family?

I try to recall why I actually wrote those diaries – often half-dead with fatigue and fear, sometimes elated, more often, it seems, depressed. There are hints that I always intended to use it in some printed form if I survived the war, but I'm not sure of this. I know that the diaries remained in an old ammunition box in the loft, untouched and unread for a quarter of a century. Then one day a young friend of mine in publishing asked to borrow them for possible extracts for a book he was editing. Later, he told me that he'd read them at a sitting and found them 'riveting – better than a novel', and urged me to publish them if I could.

It was then, that – once again, I suspect – I began to wonder whether my little war might interest the many others who had had the same kind of experience. For of one thing I have no doubt: that the old clichés about comradeship are well founded. Spared as we were the appalling carnage and squalor of the First World War, we did share hardship and privation, pleasure and plunder, and the 'red, sweet wine of youth'. And no one who lived that life with all its profit and loss will ever be quite the same.

2005

Ten years ago, my family's birthday present was a computer printout of the 140,000 words of my diaries, which I was able to read for the first time. Now, thanks to my enterprising great-nephew Simon, I am to see them published. Many of the people mentioned are now dead and I myself near the end of the road. I read again my distant words. 'Old men forget; yet all shall be forgot / But he'll remember . . .'

ACKNOWLEDGEMENTS

I am very grateful to a number of people who have helped to make this book possible: Emily Lincoln, who deciphered and typed the seven original diaries; Roderick Suddaby of the Imperial War Museum, for his guidance through the museum's resources; Jane Cochrane, Bill French and Moira Stevenson, for photographs; my nieces Ann Louise Luthi and Monica Parkhurst; my great-nephew Simon de Bruxelles, who – unknown to me – sent the manuscript to Sutton Publishing; my son Richard, an unfailing source of cogent advice and constructive criticism; my son Peter, himself a battle-hardened author, who has been my (unpaid) agent and guided me through unknown territory; Elizabeth Stone; and, perhaps above all, my editor Nick Reynolds, for taking a chance on me.

NOTE ON THE TEXT

The occasional references in *Field of Fire* to the original Diary numbers could be confusing for the reader in that they don't necessarily correspond to one of the four parts into which this book is divided. It may, therefore, be helpful to point out that Part 1 of the following text is covered by Diaries 2 and 3 (Diary 1 has not survived); Part 2 by Diaries 4 and 5; Part 3 by Diary 6 and Part 4 by Diary 7.

AUTHOR'S INTRODUCTION

T hese diaries don't start until June 1942, by which time I was just over 24, and had already been in the army for two and a half years. By way of brief background, and (I suspect) of justifying some of the more callow comments they contain, I should provide a little additional information.

I was born on the Ides of March 1918, just before the black days of the German offensive which destroyed Gough's Fifth Army. My parents were born in Holland but had come to England around the turn of the century and were nationalised British. We – my parents, two older sisters and a younger brother – lived in Sydenham, a pleasant but unfashionable London suburb, and my childhood was happy and unmemorable. We were, I suppose, totally middle class, but comfortably well off. I went to a minor but, I've always thought, rather good, little public school at Weymouth – alas an early casualty of the war. Being poorly endowed, it closed down.

After school I went to Oxford. A year later I was sent down – but not for anything criminal! After Oxford I worked as a reporter, and later went to London University where I behaved better, and would have been the gold medallist (the Principal told me) except that a year before that could happen, Hitler invaded Poland. On 10 September I enlisted – at Oxford, where a desire to be able to ride a horse had been my reason for joining the University OTC in the horse artillery. And finally, on the 10th of that icy December of 1939, I was called to the colours as (I still remember) 928547 Gunner Swaab, earning two shillings a day. Down at the training barracks at Dover I was put in the 'potential officers' squad. We were drilled and disciplined by a bunch of regulars from the British Army in India, and I remember that we had to polish the studs under our boots and the back of our cap badges. All wooden brushes had to be scraped shiny clean with razor blades for Saturday morning inspection. And woe to the man whose folded blankets showed an edge, or whose Brush, tooth, did not align exactly with the other twenty Brushes, tooth, on the barrack-room beds. I spent happy leisure hours eating bacon, egg and chips at the hospitable Salvation Army hostel in Dover. Two of us were rejected as potential officers. I recall that the Colonel (Rendell was his name) felt that we had no qualities of leadership (I met the other reject quite by chance in the Western Desert when we were both Eighth Army officers. He was even in the RHA). At the time we just felt that our faces didn't fit, though we had very different faces.

It's odd that many names in my diaries produce absolutely no visual recall. Yet from the distant 5th Training Regt RA, I clearly remember two of my early disciplinarians. Sergeant Dawnay: a big mournful face like a badger. In lugubrious tones he would warn of the perils of walking backwards at gun drill to fall squashed under the wheels of our ancient howitzers. 'I seen men killed by gun wheels, I seen men killed by G.S. waggons . . .' Sgt Dawnay had evidently seen so many men killed by accident that I sometimes wondered how they manned the army in India. Or at Bren gun dismantling: 'This 'ere 'ole we calls the happerture.'

Then there was Sergeant Chadwick, an Irishman of unbelievable ferocity, said to have been broken three times only to rise like a three-striped phoenix from the horrors of the glasshouse. Chadwick at rifle drill: 'I want to see your hands *bleeding* from hitting those rifle bolts . . .'

I spent the next year or so as a very unimportant subaltern 'Training' with two regiments in Aldershot and Dorset. I can't remember much about it, but suspect that my irreverent attitude and occasionally insubordinate tongue did not endear me to my superiors. In fact, I also suspect that I was a pain in the ass. Anyway, whatever the reason, I finally found myself drafted to Woolwich en route – at last – for some theatre of war. After twenty-four more or less reprehensible and wasted years I was, I hoped, about to do something useful.

As it happened, I didn't do anything of very much value at all until I was a couple of days beyond my twenty-fifth birthday. Or perhaps, to be a little charitable – a quality which I find disconcertingly lacking in myself in the early diaries – until January 1943, when I finally joined the Field Regiment with whom I was to fight my real war. Little could I guess then that, as its last Adjutant, I should supervise its virtual dissolution in Germany three and a half years later. When I started to re-read those long-since-written scribbled pages, I was astonished to find that I was at first unhappy in that unit with which I was later to experience a life of much self-fulfilment in the company of people I came to trust and admire. I also find I made cruel, superficial and (not infrequently) inaccurate initial judgements which now rather disgust me. Accordingly I have occasionally identified some people by initials only, though where possible I have avoided this.

My love life – if it can thus be dignified – also appears to be a very good reason for omitting the early part of the diaries. My propensity for falling in love (as well as merely satisfying my more strictly physical needs) appears to have been marked. It wasn't until later in 1943 that I fell genuinely in love, and this lasted until not too long before I married – someone else – in 1948.

So: back to 1942.

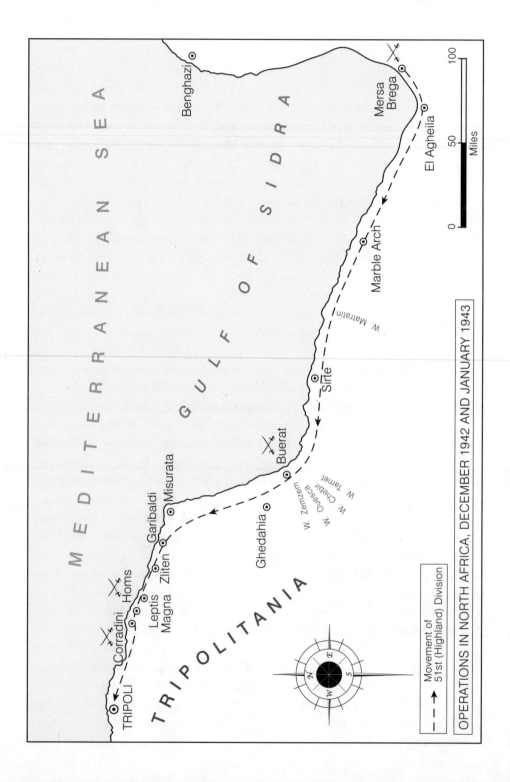

OPERATIONS IN NORTH AFRICA, DECEMBER 1942 AND JANUARY 1943

 PART ONE

20 December 1942 – 19 May 1943

J ust as Alamein was, in Churchill's words, 'the end of the beginning', so in its own small way was it the end of my beginning to learn to be a soldier.

Exercises in England gave way to fatigue and fighting over hundreds of arid miles; well-fed army life to dry tack, vitamin pills and a couple of mugs of water a day; and a bed in Britain replaced by a cold bed of sand under starlit desert nights. We marched westward. Lessons were gradually learned: earning the respect of your soldiers; coping with blood and loss; the acid tests of self-control (or at least the pretence of it) and leadership under fire.

The Axis army finally crumbled and surrendered in Tunisia. The Highland Division was, although we didn't yet know it, destined to cross a storm-swept Mediterranean Sea, and win a hard-fought battle for Sicily. The end of *my* beginning had taught me pride and confidence in my Division.

And a little in myself.

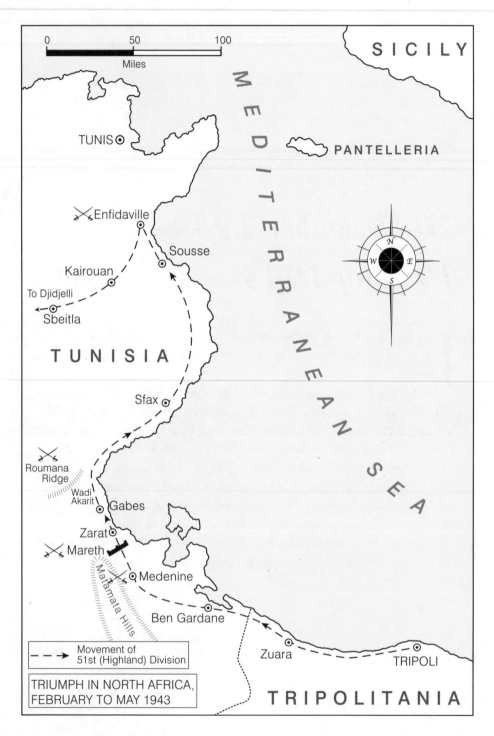

SICILY

PANTELLERIA

MEDITERRANEAN SEA

TUNIS

Enfidaville

Sousse

Kairouan

To Djidjelli

Sbeitla

TUNISIA

Sfax

Roumana Ridge

Wadi Akarit

Gabes

Zarat

Mareth

Medenine

Matmata Hills

Ben Gardane

Zuara

TRIPOLI

TRIPOLITANIA

0   50   100

Miles

- - -> Movement of 51st (Highland) Division

TRIUMPH IN NORTH AFRICA, FEBRUARY TO MAY 1943

20 December 1942

The course yesterday included a rather Diehard Colonel on 'Traditions-Regimental', and an indignant but fluent Czech on The Hun. The latter was very good though nothing he said was new to me. Unfortunately however a good many of our officers don't read very much and still have the idea that the Germans are good chaps. My fear is that when we've won the war we shall allow some militarist to take over and let the Germans give in while they are, so to speak, intact. Then we shall have another war before 1980. 1980 – what years it seems away. Yet I remember getting my *Tiger Tim's Annual* for 1926 (I particularly remember the cover for that year – very black and yellow it seems in my memory) and writing down nineteen thirties and forties and thinking how impossibly remote they seemed.

We have to give ten minute lectures. I have chosen as my subject 'An urgent draft is required. . .' As it's just about 6 months since it was, the subject and tone of the lecture should speak for itself. I am about to prepare it.

I have just finished rather a good Diary-narrative called *The Road to Bordeaux* by two Englishmen who enlisted in the French ambulance service. It's quite astonishing the way the French people panicked – though in view of the way the post services and news broke down perhaps not so very. I still can't believe the British would have cluttered up the roads and allowed such complete chaos to reign, all the same. I'm sure the army would have taken over; though one is inclined to forget that our own army had a good many shortcomings in 1940.

Went to tea with the W.A.A.F.s yesterday. They were all there except Annette (on duty) also D., Owen Lowless, and two chaps from the Niew Amsterdam. One we always called Miniver because he looks a bit like 'Viv' in the film. Real name Minchin, and not so stand-offish as he looks; the other Ian Shaw, who is one of those subalterns you always think of as being nicknamed Toby and holding a mug of beer. Rather cheerful. They are both in the 1st Surrey Regt. I am not going on the church parade 'The Brigadier likes all officers to attend' (nor is Frank Neary; as the little attendance role is apparently not presented at the porch, it shouldn't matter).

Later: Gave the lecturette. The Brigadier, criticising later, said 'Humour shouldn't be attempted unless you can get away with it. Now Lt. Swaab kept us in fits of laughter; I should think he'd always be able to make the men laugh; a very good lecture.' I only quote at such length because it wasn't as funny as all that, though it has a few rather shrewd cracks.

I rather like lecturing and find words come to me easily enough and only make out a few headings to guide me. Today we had Air V.-Marshall Lloyd of Malta, a dry, quiet, and effective speaker. Course ends at one o'clock tomorrow and it really has been rather interesting and enjoyable.

21 December

Back in Almaza with the worst cold in the head, of all things, I think I've had. As I rarely get such things, I suppose that's not much to go on. Anyway, combined with a complete lack of any mail it's put me in a depressed and irritable frame of mind. Back here my main source of annoyance apart from the lack of mail is the complete lack of any sign of a posting. So much so that I really think I shall go after all to P.R. with a view to landing this job as a front line reporter, which certainly for me has many advantages. Anything's better than this demoralising sitting around and waiting for something which never does seem to happen. I've just written a rather inadequate letter to B. I wish she were here; she's just the person I want to see tonight. Drew a princely £12 from the field cashier today, which has actually got to last rather a long time. Gordon Sudworth, and Jackie Cleughs, two squadron leaders from England and Durban whom you'll find mentioned in Diary I are here in Cairo. D. has seen them, and I certainly must.

I'm afraid Xmas here is going to be, besides being unusually nostalgic, unusually dull. However this is one of those statements I'm always inclined to make – particularly when depressed – and which may prove entirely wrong.

22 December

Went into Cairo this morning with D. to do some shopping. Our shopping included a large, and elaborately iced Xmas cake for the W.A.A.F.s. You see some very repulsive sights in Cairo where poverty and riches are so closely linked. My cold is bloody awful and I've been feeling lousy. Still no mail; it's been held up somewhere. D. and King are explaining in some detail exactly what performances they could give with the female supplied at the moment. King discussing the N.A. says 'That fucking boat, I was fucking glad to see the end of the fucking thing', the same epithet being ubiquitously used in each case. As he was supplied with $1/6$ of a cabin, even more lavishly endowed with bed bugs than our tent, I can sympathise with him. There is nothing doing here, and no sign of a posting. It is even rumoured that no more postings to the desert will take place, but this seems unlikely.

23 December

By candle: Two diverse letters today. One from Val in S.A. Long and chatty but I had the feeling she felt she had to fill space so that she could know she'd written me a long letter. Consequently it made rather dull reading.

Second from Jock Cochrane, my quondam B.C. in 132. A very pleasant note, in which he promises to rope me in if possible. He's with the 51st Highland Div.

somewhere west of Agheila now. I'd rather like to join him; can't make up my mind whether to go for this reporting or not. I think I'll wait till after Xmas to decide as I'm feeling absolutely bloody with this cold anyway at the minute. No letter from home, B., or Pam. There seems to be a general hold-up so I'm not alone in this, but it certainly has an effect on morale; the first thing people mention is lack of mail. It'll be too bad if nothing turns up for Xmas. The last para. of yesterday proved a correct surmise, as 'Big' Anthony, Bob Root, and two others have got postings for after Xmas.

I wish I could join them. It's a pity all my pals are in the A/T on this draft. I've been missing B. particularly much during the past two days. Perhaps the full moon is responsible . . . Wrote home and to Pam and sent via England a long letter to the family in Long Island.

24 December

So at last, suddenly, it came. My posting, I mean, which arrived just in time to catch me with all my stuff at the laundry, where it's likely as far as I can see, to stay till after I've gone. Bloody hell. Strange coincidence – I am going to Jock Cochrane's very Regiment (127) and thus to the Highland Division. As a posting this might be a lot worse, but not so good, we have to leave early on Boxing Day morning. One thinks wistfully of Boxing Days of the past . . . I shall miss D. very much. Tonight we're going to a party with the W.A.A.F.s, which, truth to tell, I'd give much to miss, as I'm feeling bloody with my cold and very depressed to boot. I am going after all with Nob Sutton though I doubt if we'll be in the same Battery. Outside it is a cold, dark night with the moon not yet up and searchlights all round the horizon.

Xmas Day

And now it is ending, this rather miserable, rather nostalgic Xmas Day. It has been a terrible rush. I nearly went mad when the B.Q.M.S of the Unit Kit Store refused to accept my tin box – saved from the rubbish heap – on the grounds that it was 'govt. property'. Some men love the letter of the law. I had to go out and buy a suitcase, which D. is very kindly having painted up for me and will hand in. In the afternoon all the officers in the mess listened to the King's speech. We all stood bolt upright for the National anthem, and it was all vaguely impressive. We go out at 0630 tomorrow morning. I have a batch of men to look after. It means getting up very early, before it's light. D. (who is going on a gas course to Palestine next week) has given me a damn nice torch. I've met two old friends. Gordon Sudworth at the party last night which I left just before midnight, and Mike Liddle who was with me from the first day I joined till the day we both received our commissions.

Last night a grotesque and interesting picture was provided by the men (drunk and cheerful) lurching into camp, singing like tipsy shadows as they rolled off to bed. Tonight, on the eve of leaving for the front, I have been a prey to many memories and longings. Perhaps this is a feeling common to most soldiers on such occasions. I expect Mom and Dad were feeling a little sad with the family scattered all over the earth. I can picture them sitting listening to the radio just as all of us were, this afternoon. I could go to my unit feeling fitter. This cold is still bad. Most people seem to have had it; it must be some climatic freak. So far this evening is very sober here with officers sitting looking pensive and listening to 'Cinderella' on the radio. Xmas dinner is in about half an hour. So I close for now.

Boxing Day

We are now (it is 1700 hours) at a transit camp near Alex. Very bleak and windswept but there are hot – they were never hot — showers, a YMCA for the men, and quite a passable mess with a radio. Got up at 5am to a chilly, windy morning with a dying moon. Felt envious as I bade goodbye to the other 3, warm in bed for several hours. After a lukewarm breakfast, the train, and a somewhat desultory journey here. We had two quite pleasant Anzacs in our compartment (Bob Root and 'Big' Arthur and I comprised 'we') who'd been out here $2^1/2$ and $3^1/2$ years respectively. Also I met Jock Cochrane's battery captain – one Arbuthnot, a very nice chap who promised to see the Colonel and try and wangle me into the Bty. I hope Jock won't feel I'm trying to take any advantage; I don't think he will, as he always was v. nice to me, and said he'd try and get me in if a chance occurred. We <u>may</u> move on tomorrow morning to Tobruk (in cattle trucks the informed say) but this is not definite. The 92 men I share with Stewart Hampton are a rather scruffy looking bunch and some are definitely inclined to be bolshy. It was a tedious job shepherding them here without knowing their names, particularly as we only had 2 sergeants and only one of those is useful; one Lawson – a rather tough specimen who looks like Wally Patch but does at least give orders not to make suggestions. But hell, when you think of it, what a Boxing Day; we certainly do undergo some strange and miserable experiences for England. Moreover, should I survive this war I shall never regret those experiences. The different moods and discomforts one undergoes teach one to value the small comforts of life so infinitely more. I believe my regiment to be is right up front, so I'll certainly go into everything without much of a preamble. In a way I'm glad; also slightly afraid of being afraid. Last night I had a bloody good Xmas dinner of traditional make up and completed by some excellent Xmas pudding and brandy cream. But I went to bed early and after talking for a few minutes went to sleep. I slept badly and woke up a number of times before 5 when I arose. At 6 a bugle sounded reveille over the still camp and I stood and looked at the wild sky and the wind blew gusty and cold . . . we were leaving indeed.

27 December

Still in camp. I think we shall leave tomorrow, and by boat seems a good bet as all I.R.S. have been warned to have canvas shoes ready. I think I shall remember much of my military service by a series of rather dreary transit camps, which have a character all of their own. About a mile from this one is a large belt of very green trees. It's surprising how much more you appreciate them out here; I suppose it's the contrast to the waste of stony desert. Last night, without my bed (for I haven't brought mine tho' quite a number of officers have) it was quite hard on the torso, but I had a pretty good night's sleep and quite a long one as I was asleep by half past nine and didn't get up till 7.30. Officers here spend nearly all day mooching round the mess, reading, playing cards, darts, or ping pong with the usual rush on the bar whenever it opens – tho' the place is reasonably sober. There is also a radio which plays from morning till night – just now rather appropriately in the presence of so many Highland Div. officers 'Loch Lomond' with Deanna Durban singing it. She has a rich and somehow youthful voice which I like very much. One officer (Black Watch) turns to another (Gordons) and says 'Remember this time George!' George does. We have occupied Sirte, the 1st Army is 12 miles from Tunis, and the Russians are crashing on in the middle Don. Often in these bleak places – and how much bleaker they may be soon – I daydream of pleasant places and people with whom I'd like to be. I recall whole stretches of conversation . . . Is it foolish I wonder, this nostalgic attempt to recapture the past, and plan the future we none of us can see; should one live in the present? I never could. Today I realised with great surprise that it is Sunday – I'd never have guessed. Incidentally I managed to get the laundry I mentioned on 24 Dec. after all. At breakfast today I had the smallest egg I've ever seen – I can't think what could have laid it. Perhaps this place etc. is best summed up by an officer sitting just behind me: 'Each place you go to is just a shade worse than the last; it's an old army rule.' He may be right.

28 December

We are going at 6 tomorrow by ship (cattle boat?). Today has been spent in the usual desultory way. The 'ping – pong' of the table tennis has become rather irritating but otherwise we are all fairly contented – or should I say resigned? I managed to scrounge a couple of EverReady batteries from the Q stores this morning, which gives me a reserve of 6 batteries. I feel rather dull as very little has occurred anyway, I'll close for the moment.

29 December

Had 8 very refreshing hours sleep before I rose at 0415 this morning under a diminutive but bright moon. The wind was blowing steadily from the SE and it was very cold. Breakfast was lukewarm and scarce as usual so we were not unduly fortified when we marched off to the 40 odd cattle trucks which comprised one train. This, after much squeaking and shunting set off at 0715. The wheels acted in a most octagonal fashion. We reached Alexandria docks at about 0900 and are now on board (and at sea) the *Princess Kathleen*, a comfortably suburban little steamer of about 6,000 tons, once the pride and joy of the C.P.R. The men – poor buggers – are as usual uncomfortably crowded; we have two-berth cabins – small it is true but unexpectedly comfortable (i.e. bed, running water) – I share no. 336 with 'Nob' Sutton. I am missing, perhaps expectedly, D. most at this juncture. The O.C. Tps. gave the officers a little pep talk ending with the rather amusing sentiment: 'I want everybody to get rid of the holiday spirit now and remember we're getting back to business.' A fine looking Major he is, in the Gordon Highlanders.

Alexandria is a city whose waterfront made me want to explore it more closely. As we left, we saw the 5 or 6 heavy cruisers of the now mutilated French fleet, lying at anchor. They were a fine but rather depressing spectacle. I am sitting in the lounge where most people are sitting about reading or playing Bridge. I am glad I'm not playing because I want to be alone with my rather sad thoughts. Now as it seems on the verge of battle, I can think of so many things I want to live for that I am surprised I sometimes feel indifferent about my fate. The sea is calm, and flanked by Destroyers we are steaming towards the sunset and Benghazi. I think much of B. and every now and again I take out the little St Christopher she gave '. . . to J.S. from B.B. . . .' What a torment of memory those few letters evoke; I remember her tears in that early morning when I left her, the warmth of her arms around my neck, and that cold ride back in the jolting taxi an hour before dawn. I miss Pam too, but less poignantly because perhaps I know that should I be killed she will recover fairly quickly because our intimacy was new and had not gone deep enough to give us that inter-dependence and co-happiness I found with B. (Again with Sheila who was my lover for a year her mind never reached out and interwove with mine.)

But with B. the flame that we lighted, flared up and devoured me in physical delight, and left the warm glowing embers of mental harmony. How lucky I was with B.

The men – I like to think encouraged by the two talks I gave them on discipline and by the fact that I have shared their discomforts as far as possible – have responded well, are much more disciplined and nearly all sulkiness has disappeared. Their longing for home runs very deep. Today I was jokingly saying in view of 7 men short at roll call that I'd have to report them as fallen overboard (they lined up a moment later) when a gunner said quite passionately to me 'I'd do that if it meant freedom Sir.' It's rather pathetic the way they seem to expect the war to end daily. We try to tell them not too pessimistically that it won't be yet awhile but they still cling to their hopes.

Later: I have been out on deck. The night is very blue and full of stars. I have a foreboding that we shall soon be in some very large battle. My feelings are mixed; excitement and apprehension. It appears that this route is Priority Danger 1 which means it is the most dangerous sea voyage you can make as 1942 enters its last 48 hours. I suppose we may be attacked by planes from Crete tomorrow. Hm.

30 December

We all slept clothed last night, I not very well. Sentimentally I keep the first letter B. wrote me in the inside pocket of my battledress. I was reading it over again last night. She ends 'I sent you this letter with a love that is limitless.' This morning it is calm and sunny and we are bowling along at a good pace, flanked as I said by our agile destroyers. The food is marvellous; fish AND eggs and bacon for breakfast and lovely white bread. It is really too luxurious when we are about to be shovelled straight into Benghazi and the line. Also hot water for shaving. It will be rather exciting to see Benghazi, that much exchanged town. I believe it has been considerably smashed up by war. This morning we have been in sight of the sprawling, ominous coast – it seemed somewhere near the Egyptian border. A solitary plane keeps a watch on us. No sign of enemy interference – yet.

Later: It is sundown, and on our left, quite close, is the barren looking and unfriendly shore of Libya. We disembark at 0800 tomorrow. Perhaps renewed activity will disperse the mood of sadness and introspection which has been hanging over me for the last few days. We have had a cigarette issue; one always receives some obscure brand like 'V' (packed in India). This time it is 'Two Aces' to which, thank God, I've not yet been reduced. This is said to be the most dangerous part of the voyage – we've had to wear our lifejackets all the time which is exceedingly tedious. And tomorrow will be New Year's Eve!

31 December

Benghazi: Approached from the sea the town looks almost intact but once ashore not a house is inhabited, or intact, and marching through the dusty streets one encounters little except battered British M.T. on various errands and arabs selling completely useless 'mementoes'. The docks are full of sunken ships, and the jetties show evidence of bombs, with great chunks of concrete blasted out of the sides. We marched three weary miles in full kit to this transit camp; the men – as always with drafts – arriving tired and dispirited. A meal cheered them up.

Benghazi cathedral, a well proportioned building with 2 steep domes, is more or less intact though the walls are pitted. Other buildings have not been so fortunate and I noticed several houses with their inevitable W Duce on the side, reduced to slag heaps. In the mess one hears historic names bandied about: 'Sirte, Agheila, Beninva, Marble Arch . . .' I believe the 51st bunch are going on westwards in the morning. I share a small tent with Big and Bob Root, an

ANZAC, and a pleasant Czech major in the Tank Corps. He is out here to gain experience of mech. warfare; was wounded at Martuba and is just back from hospital. Unassuming man and very congenial. The Anzac is rather morose and spends most of his time swotting the numerous flies. Wrote two shortish letters, to B. and the W.A.A.F.s, but one hardly knows what to put in them at this stage. I have filled other diaries on New Years Eve with reflections on the year to come, but this time I do not feel there is much to say. I approach 1943 as a year in which I shall see and learn much, I hope emerge unscathed and if not – well, others have gone before me and others will come after; in such things we can only trust to fate, or God, or whatever it is that ordains how we shall live – or die.

So ends 1942, the sun setting over Benghazi and voices sounding in the twilight as officers exchange memories of the past, and hazards at the future in the deepening gloom around my tent.

1 January 1943

Evening finds us north of Agedabia. A large convoy is laagered in the middle of the desert and inside the lorry in which 11 of us live, move and have our being, I am writing this. We have driven all day along the one narrow road which runs from Benghazi and which was full of M.T. driving westward after Rommel. Broken and burned out wrecks of tanks, trucks and planes litter the side of the road in places – particularly near and on the landing field at Magrum. Our rations are scanty and mainly of bully, but we managed a couple of brews midday and morning. In the truck some of the boys played bridge; an amazing sight with them lurching and swaying as the truck bumped and lurched along. During last night I was awoken by gunfire but I was informed at breakfast in the mess (one of Benghazi's 14 ex-brothels) that people were just greeting the new year. Our Czech major is still with us; a very nice man. Our truckload is very cheerful and pleasant. Nob, Big and Bob are all included. I washed my feet yesterday and am glad of it as water is very scarce now and certainly not to be used on such luxurious necessities as foot washing. We are all quoting Eliot . . . 'Let us go then you and I when the evening is spread out against the sky . . .'. Action is beginning to banish introspection. I shall go to bed (under the stars) now; we are reduced to primitive man again; sleeping at darkness and rising in the dawn.

2 January

Spent a rather erratic night as the wind blew cold and strong in the latter half of it. However as the sky grew lighter we got a petrol-and-sand fire going and had some tea and biscuits and jam – breakfast. That was 0715 and it is now 1715 and we have yet to eat a meal. We're in a very hurried camp near Agheila completely devoid (as far as one can ascertain) of any sort of water. It was a bloody trip here jolting and lurching along a road crammed with transport going Westward. I have a bad headache from petrol fumes etc. We move on probably to our units somewhere about 20 miles West of A. tomorrow morning. I think I am getting hold of a bottle of whisky which may prove useful sometime. At each stage the discomfort grows more acute, God knows what the front will be like! Several large American DC IIs and Lockheeds flew over us on the way west so they must be supplying troops by air. Agh. is a sea of desert with salt marshes to the flank, and very desolate. We found a crashed Hurricane with a lot of cannon ammo near Agedabia, a collection of white buildings, not much marked by bombs. Generally speaking we are still cheerful tho' one or two people – notably Roland Toller – a young rather Rupert Brookeish type who's going to 127 – are apt to fly off the deep end. He's not been in the army long and then straight from Cambridge to a commission. Which should indicate something or other. Water has now arrived – one waterbottle full per day!

3 January

I am writing in a terrific sandstorm (in a truck). We are 7 miles West of A. and I've got to Jock Cochrane's Bty. Not a good day to arrive, but they managed to scrape up 2 cold sardines and a cup of tea for lunch which we ate under a tarpaulin since carried away by the gale. This sand is simply terrible, gets in everything and one's eyes mouth and nose are choked right up with it. It's bloody. This is said to be about the worst they've ever had, so it's a good introduction.

Towards evening the sand died down a little and finally altogether. I have managed to get a little tent so I shall at least sleep under cover. It is rather cold, so that's just as well. I am attached to B.H.Q. for the moment, more or less as a stooge tho' this is to be expected. The other officers seem rather a good bunch but one feels very lonely at first knowing nobody else and having no particular friend. The C.P.O. seems a nice lad and has been very helpful. My batman – Turner – is a rather villainous but quite efficient individual. Jock is the same as ever and was pleasantly unimpressed at my appearance! Besides sand today we have heavy rain; it is rather difficult to say which is worse. All said and done I think sand. I am still bunged up with it and my eyes are very sore. They issue Vit. C tablets instead of fruit here – an unusual piece of enterprise. They are passed around the mess (tarpaulin over a large hole, tables pieces of planking etc. – all carried away by the sandstorm) with the cry 'Will you have an orange.'

4 January

Today similar to yesterday except that the sandstorm was smaller. Also to my delight, this evening a letter from home (2 Nov) and also 2 lovely long ones from B. rather disconcertingly 'censored' by her husband, being Embassy mail. Apparently he knows about me and 'doesn't mind'. It was so grand to hear from her, the ink phrases of the letter seemed to come to life as I read them. I am now lying in my minute tent with a very wavering candle burning beside me and the hankie she sent me (soaked in 'Caprice', the perfume I liked so) seems to bring her here to me. Oddly enough I wrote to her today.

It is strange to be in Tripolitania lying utterly alone in a little oasis of light in the darkness, with the wind blowing outside. I think I can hear the sea, just over the ridge north of our bivouac area. A dog barks, two rather torpid flies poise on the canvas roof just over my head. It appears Gen. Montgomery was here a couple of days ago to watch the Regt. shoot. Have now sewn our Div. Signs once again. They look like this: (HD). It is rather pleasant to 'belong' again. I have just written home and partly to B., which has made me feel sort of in touch and better, ages though the letters will take to reach their destinations. My pen grates sandily on this paper. My ablutions this morning were conducted effectively in one and a half mugfuls of water which wasn't I thought too bad for a novice. Actually one's teeth don't get very dirty; one doesn't eat enough! On account of this I sent to Anne the W.A.A.F. for some chocolate. However my hair feels simply foul; I must do something about it. Tonight we had a canned peach apiece which went well with an excellent bully beef stew. So far I find the meals adequate though of course I'm doing no fighting on them – or very much work. I'm now beginning to know the others by name. They seem quite pleasant. Arbuthnot I've already mentioned and like less; he's too boisterous. Wagstaff the Battery Capt. is quite civil but rather hard to know I think. Cowie – very cheerful – the C.P.O. and Buchanan – droll – the A.C.P.O. are pleasant lads and have been quite helpful explaining codes etc. Cameron who commands F Tp. is rather pleasant in a quiet and unobtrusive way. He seems one of the most intelligent members. Moncur rather country but quite friendly. Gegan – a bit of an oaf with a red face. The Buffoon – not much imagination I'd say. Rather like a fat cockatoo. Forshaw: a recent importation and too cocky by about five eighths. Another subaltern, Boys, who thinks he has jaundice but is a nice lad. 24 and with me the youngest member of the mess I believe (not certain, Buchanan is probably younger). The other Tp. Comd., whose name I can't recall,* is large, moustached and reliable looking; I believe he shoots well. Jock, his usual saturnine and unruffled self ('That's just too bad . . .') presides, dropping in an occasional crack. They all talk of past events etc. just now so I am rather out of it but this was to be expected and they are quite kind to me. I am senior to all subalterns but 3 as far as I can reckon.

Wrote to Pam earlier in the day.

---

* Gillanders 5/1/43.

5 January

I am now dug in and am much more comfortable and have more room. Turner is after all rather lazy and needs kicking tho' his work is good enough when he does it. I think I am going to be rather happy in this battery. Jock says we shall be going into action very soon and I am rather pleased at the prospect, tho' perhaps foolish to be so. I introduced the 'Convoy Cutey' with some success. Jock's comment was: 'H'm, a bit better than your stuff used to be,' but I think he was amused. Wrote to Debroy whom I still miss, and exchanged a few words with Nob Sutton whom I saw at R.H.Q. He and Toller don't seem very contented in 304 (I am in 491) the latter apparently not having recovered from the sandstorm yet! The wind has now changed from W to SE from the sea and it was quite warm today, bringing swarms of flies with the sun. Going to bed at nightfall is all very well, but becomes a bit of a bore. I suppose in a week or two, I'll be glad of the chance. The Egyptian Mail for 1 Jan, its usual sanguine self, rolled in today, but we usually get the gist of the news on a No. 11 set so it was out of date as well as out of tune. Did two 406 inspections today, which helps to get to know people's names. I now find I know quite a lot. Luckily I usually find names fairly easy to remember. I sold my bottle of whisky (to Cameron) two days ago as it really is too bulky to lug about. A flask, yes, but a bloody great bottle no. And I have now no flask.

Also I gave Cowie and Buchanan one of my bars of chocolate which seemed to cause unusual joy. It appears it's very scarce up here so I hope Anne does her stuff. A canteen ration is rumoured tomorrow which means cigarettes and cans of fruit etc. We've had our money changed to British Military Currency – rather natty notes; the first of their kind I've ever seen. I lent Moncur my *Rubayat* which Val gave me. He's been rather pleasant to me today (telling me about his conjunctivitis!). He knows the part of Dorset I was stationed in quite well. So does Cameron who dines with the Div. Commander occasionally I am told. Among the N.C.O.s Sgt. Evans is the best. Bloody efficient and helpful. The B.S.M. is also pleasant and quite youthful. He reminds me of B.S.M. Garrett my Troop B.S.M. in C/183. Hutton and Seed are also pretty reliable I should say and the Bty. Clerk Bdr. Worrall seems a good one of his type. The Q. is genial at times but by no means anxious to part with anything; I've managed an identity disc so far! One of the staple forms of diet here is all-embracingly called 'M & V' – meat and veg! But it's surprisingly nice (or possibly one meal a day makes one feel that way about it).

6 January

I am writing by candle in my bivouac again. Went practice shooting today and did a G.F. target. Colonel's comment: 'handled it very adequately'.

We are going into action; advance parties are leaving on the Sun. and the main body follows two days later. Place reputed to be the coastal strip near Buent along the Wadi Zem Zem. It is said there are 40 German guns there. I am excited.

The wind has fallen almost completely now and at night I can hear the sea booming away beyond the ridge. Dug in about 2 feet down as I am it is very comfortable and warm, and the L shape of my dugout makes coming in and out positively luxurious . . . you have to mind the front pole however which is supported on a petrol can filled with sand and liable to collapse if you bang against it. The other officers are increasingly friendly and I hope and think they are inclined to approve generally. I have been careful not to talk too much – apt to be a failing of mine – specially the first two days when I was very respectful to everybody, as befits a new arrival! Discovered today that Boys knows (and was in the 61 Field with) Denny, my best friend, in England. I must write and tell Denny tomorrow. I am just going to write B. a little letter. It is 1920 hours which will give me a little over 12 in bed!

7 January

Money ceases to have much meaning in the desert. The Arabs barter eggs for tea and sugar and among troops, cigarettes seem the only staple form of currency. Naafi today; I drew a tin of peaches and a tin of beans and 40 Players and some matches. I am just going to eat some peaches in my dugout. Some magnificent jaffa oranges for lunch. Adv. parties have been put back 24 hours. The place we're going to seems quite a hot spot as we are near to coast and Jerry holds the high ground on the left. He has nearly 300 guns behind it. It looks like developing into quite a party. Wrote to Denny and Dorothy and finished my last night's letter to B. It's a lovely soft night full of stars and was a hot day. The men went to bathe this afternoon and the B.C. found a large German petrol tank – full of petrol. We are now using it. I see in the paper that Sassoon has just written some more memoirs; I wish I could get hold of them. I am rapidly settling down and feeling nice and happy inside; that pleasant feeling that I'd rather be in this bty. than any other.

8 January

Friday: Advance parties – Sandy Cowie and Gillanders – left today and we expect to go on Sunday morning. A great rumour went the rounds today that Zem Zem had fallen but there is no confirmation. It takes 3 days to get there.

Wrote to George Long from whom I've not heard since he went off to P.-Force. We are getting army biscuits now, not bread; they are curiously more satisfying but bloody hard on the teeth. However, a big improvement on even my O.T.C. days; my god how we played at soldiers. The real thing is about as far divorced from O.T.C. camp as a Sherman tank to Boadicea's chariot. I am bitten to hell again; this time I think it must be fleas. They itch maddeningly when I get warm in my aptly named fleabag at night. I have a headache.

Mist – new moon rising. Rather cold. Heard them bombing what sounded like 'Marble Arch' for about 2 hours this morning. As to the others, to amend or confirm first impressions. Cowie ('Sandy') and Buchanan I like and they call me Jack and are always very decent. So does Gillanders whom I usually only see at meals. He also is a good sort. Cameron as before. Boys I know and like better; he is a trifle lugubrious and fond of telling me how awful it is in action! Forshaw, a bit better but as before – Wagstaff I like much more; he has thawed. Also Moncur. And Gegan tho' still slightly oafish is always genial enough. Arbuthnot as before; he's also rather selfish I find. Jock, who is very decent to me, I like serving with as much as I knew I should.

9 January

I was to have attended a court martial today but now it's been post-poned till tomorrow – the day we move – so I shall have to try and catch the column by nightfall or the day after. Rumour still persists Z-Z has fallen. More sand today though nothing like as bad as the first day I got here. All and every day bombers and transports fly over here westwards. Chiefly I have noticed, Hudsons, P12 and P14s, DC IIs, Tomahawks, an odd Spit Vc, a Lysander or two, Mitchells, Marylands, Baltimores and Bostons, and Bombays. Some-times they fly about 100 feet up, mostly higher. Xmas tele-gram from home dated 22/12. The Crusader, an 8 Army weekly published in the field, came in today; very worth reading as is 8 Army News, a daily dishout.

10 January

We are in Brigade Bivouac near Agheila. Move west tomorrow 1100 and stop tomorrow night at Marble Arch. Thence we move before dawn and bivouac at dusk for 2 days so I may not be able to write this up. Also, hot meals for that period seem out. At the court martial we only sentenced a driver who'd said 'so what' to his C.S.M. to 35 days stoppage of pay. I am changing my batman – none too soon as 50 '555', a very special purchase, has dis-appeared today. Jock has a poisoned foot. A splendid gunner who has been very attentive (Findlay or Tadman, I forget which but they pitched my tent between them) has just brought me a lovely mug of tea – 'it's nae tou gude' he says,* bless his heart; it's marvellous! Some of these lads are real gems.

12 January

We are halted near Marble Arch. It is 0730 and an icy wind is blowing. The sun has just risen. We slept the night on this bit of the desert after a long cold drive made worse by intermittent showers, and got here about 2000 last night. Up again at 0530 and jees it was cold. Shaving was pretty average misery. Breakfast was cold bacon but mercifully hot tea as last night when the first course consisted of a tin of cold Maconochie – filling but it fell to the bottom of the stomach like lead. The drive over the desert in Brigade Colm was very bleak. Relics lie about; a boat, a petrol tin, a crashed plane or burned out tank and here and there a clump of sweet-smelling purple flowers vaguely like honeysuckle. Jock is driving; I haven't taken a spell yet. We are due at Sultan tonight – 106 miles; I suppose we'll arrive after dark again.

14 January

We are on the eve of battle. We are in Wadi el Chebir and this afternoon move up 16 miles to our battle positions – unfortunately overlooked by the enemy.

It is a tremendous army; 51 Div., part of 50 Div., nearly 500 tanks (many Shermans amongst them) which we heard rumbling and clanking forward last night. We had to do over 200 miles to get here, the last 100 or so in blinding sandstorms; that was yesterday.

It was an amazing sight watching an entire army moving up in this pall of dust. The objective is Tripoli. An order of the day from Monty was read out today just after our light bombers – 18 as usual – had unloaded. We have heard quite a bit of bombing but his planes have been very quiet. I had a bloody night last night with no bedding as I had been detailed to go 20 miles back at sun-up to find some lost vehicles. All my stuff was on the B.C.'s truck so I was cold as hell with two overcoats; also I couldn't shave or wash till he got in this morning. We are now on ½ a gall. a day and feeding will be very doubtful for the next day or two. I gave Boys some cigarettes and some of my precious remaining chocolate for which he nearly bowed down and worshipped me. He is very worried and apprehensive. Everybody else is cheerful and completely unruffled. I feel a subdued excitement but at times a feeling as in the dentist's waiting room – 'for God's sake let it begin and get it over.' But not afraid – yet. It is 1230 and the last hot meal we'll get for a bit is in preparation. Going to be a good one I think, tho' the bad water here makes the tea pretty bloody. I have never seen so much stuff. Light A.A. 25 Pdrs., mediums, 6 Pdrs., 2 Pdrs., everything one has read about in the pamphlets all gathered

---

* It was Findlay; he became my batman, as you'll see.

together and marshalled for battle. We shall be digging all night and lying doggo by day till the attack which is planned for 1500 tomorrow. Our armour is taking the left flank and should we break through the 51 Div. Arty. is going straight on down the road to Tripoli. All the sappers are with us, and the 4 Light Armd. Brigade is going overland for the same destination. A good thing is that everybody down to the humblest gunner knows these plans. It gives one confidence to know what's on, and also helps to bear bloodiness knowing a town is the objective.

I wonder how many of us will get through . . . it's rather a sobering thought but it doesn't actively worry me – again yet. I am thinking of home and Pam and my god how much of B. These things must be so remote to them yet here we sit in the desert, the sand blowing and an occasional m.g. chattering, stacking our cigarettes and the odd tin of bully we've managed to hang on to – and waiting . . . This Diary has been very inadequate but it's difficult to write when I feel like it now; just when a chance occurs.

1500: Waiting to move off. I am in 'Y' which is loaded with everything in the world. Sandstorm blowing. A Grant has just shot by doing about 30 mph by the look of it. The battery is lined up all over the place and should be starting soon. Wonder how Bob Root and Big are doing in 128. Also Dave Roberts in 3 R.H.A. whom I bumped into last night in the moonlight. Just starting.

Dusk: We are halted waiting to move to battle stations. Over the ridge to the west behind a red sunset the rumble of guns and bombs. The Regt. spread out in the settling dusk, last fires dying, cigarettes beginning to glow, a machine gun tapping in the North.

15 January

0845: I am in the Command Post well dug down with a cover over the top. I got to bed about 0245 just as the moon went down. Very cold and also bitter this morning but now improving with sun-up. A goodish bit of m.g. fire last night and some shelling this morning but not very near. Also some planes flew over and the AA opened up. Generally however pretty quiet. Dug myself a slit trench by my bed before turning in; a good way to keep warm on a cold night – I was positively sweating. Cowie is a good C.P.O. Doesn't flap and has things well organised. Our guns (128 I think) are firing a few stray shells but generally it is quiet.

Later: Quite a bit of stuff flying about later. Found my mirror broken in my shaving outfit: so what? Food very short, also water, but had a cup of tea for breakfast and watercart is reported on way. Jerry seems to be using those 210mm guns.

1430: Minor irritations. (1) The B.C. has borrowed my watch. I could hardly refuse him but it's bloody being without it; also there's a good chance it won't reappear as he's gone forward with the other two F.O.O.s. It's the last time he or anybody else has it. (2) A large filling has come out of one of my teeth and with biscuits only it makes things difficult. I am therefore in a bad temper. Sporadic shelling from the Jerries. We are doing a barrage tonight.

Evening: In the C.P. again about to work out the barrage which begins at 2300. About 1730 four shells landed fairly near with a spiteful whistle and bang. When you hear that whistle, the old stomach curls up for a moment but quite frankly I'm already getting used to it; you can usually hear when it's really near and get down. It's curious in a way to think we may be in Tripoli by 22 Jan – the date reported to have been set by the Army Commander. Also Dick's birthday. The Regt. fired 3 rds. salvo with great gusto during the afternoon. Today's half gallon is bloody and tastes of petrol. Wagstaff has come up to the Bty. but is being rather officious. Is it my imagination or does he duck rather promptly at that whistle? I have heard 51 Div. is to garrison Tripoli, but I must say I hope we aren't stuck there for long as – comfortable as it may be – I've no desire to stay in Africa but want to be in the party that land in Europe. Also, as far as I can see, the prospects of promotion here are almost non-existent as the Regt. is actually overstrength in officers. But maybe I'm thinking too far ahead; there's still tonight, the battle, and a 200-mile drive to Tripoli to come before one need worry about lesser things. I wish I had my watch. It's such a beauty and I feel absolutely lost without it. Blast the B.C. I've been terribly thirsty all day and still am. I'm keeping a tin of beans I got from the canteen to eat after the barrage.

2130: One hour to go as Zero hour is now 2230. The ammo – 160 rds. per gun – is stacked and we are working hard in the C.P. against the clock. One meteor came in at 2100 and another is expected any minute. The Jocks (ours are Gordons and Black Watch) are I suppose forming up, and somewhere a few thousand yards ahead, Germans and Italians know something is in the wind but not that an hour from now a curtain of steel and an armoured wall will move in to destroy them. The enemy guns are nervously banging away all the time. We are completely silent.

Planes overhead.

16 January

a.m.: In truck. Barrage crashed out till midnight. Up at 2.30 for orders and moved at dawn. Action about 0830. Now sitting in truck waiting to advance again. Frantic hurry everywhere; breakfast cooked and served in about 20 minutes; eaten in about 20 seconds. Fighters about . . . identity uncertain. Suspect Kittyhawks.

Later: In action again some miles nearer the Tripoli road. No rations, water or petrol or ammo have so far come up so the smallest amount of each is vital. The sky is again rather monopolised by German planes.* So far we have not

---

* Later this reversed.

been attacked. We have just brewed up. It is about 1315. People are getting tired and irritable from lack of food and sleep. I find Sgt. Sherrat our Sig. N.C.O. the worst offender but there are several others. Buchanan and Cowie are keeping going well, and so is Wagstaff – somewhat ostentatiously. 12 of our fighters just going over. At least they're probably ours but rather high to be sure. Nobody knows anything tactical. Came up through a minefield on which some of our tanks had been blown up. Lots of enemy trenches, some very deep. Flies are bloody here. Cleaned teeth and shaved at this posn. in 1/4 of a pint of water.

1730: As usual in the middle of our evening stew panic order from R.H.Q. Equally as usual we are still waiting for the preceding part of the column to come through. B.C. (and my watch) back. A 5.9 is shelling the ridge about 11/2 miles forward.

2030, by moonlight: We've just received orders. Rommel has gone North fast and this time we're not sending armour only but 152 (H) Brigade and all the Div. Arty. with mediums, bofors and what have you. It means driving all tonight, all tomorrow and maybe tomorrow night. We have no food in hand (Regt. has it I believe) and hardly any water – a bottle full each. Cross country it certainly looks like being a tiring pursuit, specially as most of us have only had from none to 4 hours sleep during the last 3 days. We are at present lined up in bright moonlight waiting to go.

17 January

1420: Last night in column word suddenly came to go into action and we dug hard. But it appears to have been a false alarm for now in several enormous columns flanked by armour we are going northwest towards Tripoli. We were shelled once so far about an hour ago – or it may have been mines; I'm not certain as it was two miles to my left.* Our bombers have just been over; you could hear the rumbling fusillade as they unloaded. Only about 2 hours sleep and bitterly cold. Food came up for a very late and scanty breakfast but no water except for one brew of tea today. The columns are an impressive sight stretching for miles across the undulating desert about a mile west of the road to this Misurata. Everybody dog tired and rather irritable.

0900: I nearly ran onto some mines by driving into a badly marked minefield. This is reasonably common.

18 January

1000: Halted on a ridge. Can see what looks like Misurata about 10 miles ahead. Leaguered last night and whacked out bully and tea. Moved on 10 miles by night

* Mines.

(2115) – leaguered again (2400), up again at 6.30 dished out breakfast and have moved on. Radio says we were 70m from Buerat last night moving over 'bad country'. I'll say. Tempers ran thin last night as all were hungry but have recovered well as we (I am in charge of M.6, rations, water and cooking for B.H.Q. forward party) managed a grand breakfast with hot porridge, bacon, beans and tea. My Driver is Mealings, a typical cockney, cook 'Danny' Laing a Scot. Both goodish chaps, and have worked hard. I was pretty well all in by 0700 when I got to bed, but feel OK again now. More when chance occurs.

1115: Halted again. I've just had a magnificent shave in <u>hot</u> water! Am feeling like 1,000,000 dollars now. Rumour has it we have taken Misurata and are pushing on to Homs. Bright moonlight last night but extremely cold. I slept like a child. Yesterday my tongue was sore through smoking on an empty belly I'm told. Cigarettes are running very short with no prospect of more. I must write to D. if he's still in Cairo. I've thought of B. from time to time but mostly there's been rather too much to do. I now always carry some bully (2 tins) and tea and sugar and biscuits as a personal emergency reserve.

1320: Still halted in hot sunshine. We've had a couple of brews and some cheese and biscuits. Everybody is rather gorged and contented. Tea is the great solace in the desert; it bears little resemblance to the genuine article, is brewed in any tin in a strange variety of ways – and never fails to satisfy. Values alter out here as the following conversation between Forshaw and Moncur a few days – or was it weeks? – ago illustrates:

> F: I've a present for you Monty – what would you like most in all the world?
> M: (after several seconds weighty consideration) A tin of fruit?

Actually it was bully beef! It's bloody cold at night as we move forward in ghostly white columns of guns and vehicles, always steering a little to the left of the plough, bumping and shaking over the many wadis. 30 or 40 miles a day is good going and the equivalent physical effort of about 120 on going as we have known it in the past. The vehicles stand up to it remarkably well though broken springs are in vogue, and you see a good few trucks on tow, a quad towing 3 trailers, and similar sights. The brigade is in Misurata and we are now switching brigades and turning west across country to Zliten – said to be our next objective before Homs – and Tripoli.

1605: Orders have just come to be prepared to move. We were just in the throes (as usual) of getting some food ready.

1750: Apparently lack of petrol has been holding us up. It is now announced that we have a 50 (or up to 80) mile drive to Zliten before us, as soon as petrol comes up which may not be till dark. Radio announces that our leading elements were

948 miles from Tripoli last night. Jerry seems to have vanished – not even a plane in the sky today. I wonder if he plans a 'reculer pour mieux sauter'. The sun is going down and a cold Westerly wind is blowing. The prospect of yet another nightdrive is not at all pleasing. Everybody has almost exhausted his cigarettes. I gave the B.C. 8 today. Yet another officer is coming to the battery who has been away with jaundice. One Jack Wilson ex E Tp.-G.P.O. and Gillanders' (E Tp. Comd.) brother in law . . . Boys was telling me last night promotion is practically a closed book to non-Scots and I certainly have gone back a good 2 years in utility. Which reminds me it's 2 years today I was commissioned with hopes which have since been rather damped. It seems to me promotion all depends either on giving yourself the hell of a build-up or sucking up successfully to somebody in a position to help you on. The chance of getting G.P.O. here, for example, seems almost nil which is completely discouraging – and I am really rather depressed when I have time to consider it.

19 January

1610: Leaguered on an ex Italian colonial farm near Zliten about 90 miles from Tripoli. There are many scraps of evidence as to its former occupants; the very well tended vegetable garden – now being gleefully looted by the men – at their most disgusting I think on such occasions. I noticed the officers who joined in – Arbuthnot at his most beefy and mundane – Forshaw (whose truck I dispersed while he was at it so I hope he had a good long walk back!) – and, rather surprisingly – Cameron. Boys told me all these people are cut-throat and untrustworthy and at times I wonder if he isn't right. Wagstaff and Arbuthnot for example are always smilingly trying to knife each other in the back. I think the latter is in the wrong nearly each time – extra rations is his speciality – or extra anything – but the former is also selfish, ambitious, and sometimes objectionable; does things with a worried efficiency which makes them appear twice as difficult, and is something of a tell-tale (to the B.C.). To sum up our arrival here. We eventually left about 2100 last night after some sort of mg attack by an enemy fighter. We drove all night — and it was hellishly cold, and drew to a halt at about 0900. We dished out a quick meal which was inevitably interrupted by a move. By then it was raining hard just to add to the fun. To our right we could see these white clusters of farm dwellings all alone along the rather hilly coastline. I remember as day broke there was a glorious sunrise over the orchard in which we were halted for a few minutes. My eyes were hot and if I sat still I had that horribly exhausted feeling when your hands seem to dissolve and grow large. We drove all night as I said and everybody was tired as we covered about 50–60 miles. It is spotting with rain again now which is a pity as we are otherwise very comfortable.

A child's shoe is lying beside me and a packet (empty) of German biscuits – a sort of Italian decline and fall in symbols.

2045, bed: Wonderful supper: bully stew and stewed apricots in syrup. Then I washed, and washed my feet, and now – out of my clothes for the 1st time in over a week as I prepare to sleep like the dead. Ready to move 0830 tomorrow. Radio says 8th Army 50 miles from Tripoli with the NE coast road thrust in the Zliten area – that's us; it's funny when you hear it on a No. 11 set from thousands of miles away. Plane overhead so I must put my torch out. No air-raid warnings here . . .

20 January

0845, near Homs: At 2330 last night to me – in deep sleep – the unwelcome cry 'Prepare to Advance!' We were all ready in about 40 minutes and set out along the main coast road, a splendid, typically Italian effort, all avenues and palms. We had to leave the road occasionally as it was liberally mined by the retreating Boche. We are leaguered in a lovely sort of vineyard of palms with grottoes etc. around. I saw the sun rise again gloriously golden over the nearby Mediterranean and hell it was good to be alive, tired as I was after driving 30 miles all through the night. A full moon which didn't set till 0640 – the sun rose about 8. The place is full of friendly natives – and I've bartered my tea for two small eggs so I'll have eggs and bacon! A mine has just exploded loudly up the road. And another. And so now – on to Tripoli (in the words of Montgomery's order of the day for 14 Jan). But one man won't go. I saw him lying by his shattered jeep early today. He looked quite peaceful lying there curled on his right side. I suddenly understood Sassoon's line 'When you lie like that you remind me of the dead.' He seemed so utterly lonely lying there on the sandy grass of Tripolitania.

1125: Still here but expecting move fairly soon as recce parties have gone forward. Have had a glorious shave and a most excellent meal: egg, bacon, beans, porridge, and tea, biscuits and marge. Could a man ask for more? In connection with this I was rather gratified by the following (unsolicited) testimonial from Sgt. Evans: 'Since you taken over messing Sir, the men say they've never eaten so well.' Sundry banging a mile or less away sounded like Jerry shelling but we had the idea they'd already cleared out some way away. A magnificent thing about this area of oases is the water; wells everywhere and we have even had baths in petrol tins (discarded) washed feet, and what have you, ever since getting here. Also things grow which after the barren infertility of the desert is marvellous. Raw carrots are in great vogue.

1830: The sun has just set. Over what is, I believe, usually called an 'opalescent sea'. A full white moon is rising behind the palm trees and green plots which fringe the beach. It is all almost unnaturally 'right'. Our medium guns are banging from Homs (now in our possession) at the enemy on some high ground beyond. I am going to bed soon tho' in full expectation of another night drive and action. I am rather tired and a little shorter of temper than is usual. Sometimes on the march (when driving) I nod over the wheel and I hear all sorts of conversation usually addressed to me and see strange images and colours. Then a real voice suddenly but with very rapid crescendo breaks in, and I wake with a horrible start. At first it was hard to distinguish which voices were real, but now I know, and a second subconscious leans happily back and listens. Usually neither is the case as I am standing up. Perhaps this is what T.S.E. meant by: 'Till human voices wake us – and we drown.' There was something depressing about driving by moonlight past the white villas of Mussolini's Imperial dreams. The thing looks as if it's been done jolly well and these gardens etc. are well stocked and tended, tho' the Arabs and soldiers now trample them at will. Cigarettes are desperately short: all hopes centre on our 'V' ration tomorrow and a possible Naafi as we saw their vans going towards Homs today. Strange war. I wish to God the post would come again soon, but I suppose we can hardly expect it till Tripoli.

Later, by moonlight: You know I'm lonely in this Bty. Except for Boys none of the officers ever talks anything but shop and I am now convinced Wagstaff dislikes me. I find it hard to reply civilly to his rather arrogant cockney-ish voice. 'One of the low on whom assurance sits like a silk hat on a Bradford millionaire.' He also has the objectionable habit of ticking one off or ranting at one in front of troops, which is perhaps why this Bty.'s discipline is so bad. All the men and the N.C.O.s talk back. Some of them are grand chaps tho'. Ready to move 0800 tomorrow. It is now 2015 and I'm going to bed dog tired.

Objective – Tripoli.

I am seriously thinking of putting in for a transfer. I am tired of Field Arty with its lack of promotion, opportunity for some, closed doors, and lack of command; always going back about 2 years on joining a new unit. I think Tanks may suit me better, or reporting. In short, tho' it may be tiredness and my mood, I am not as happy as I thought I should be in 491 Field Bty. RA.

21 January

1200: I suppose after a wonderful night's sleep under the stars, I should be in a good temper today, but black depression still hangs around me. We haven't moved after all as we are still waiting for the petrol to go on. Lovely weather. I hear we are missing quite a decent little scrap the other side of Homs and wish to god we could go up to where something is happening.

1510: I am just going to take a couple of petrol lorries and ammo up to the Bty., now reported about 15 miles beyond Homs. Thank heavens for something to do.

22 *January*

First light: Went right up to the front, past the two enormous craters the Boche had made by blowing bridges in front of Homs, the little town itself, quite a near harbourage on the Mediterranean and so on through rather hilly country with many gullies and ravines. Masses of tanks – actually I suppose about 200 of all types. Reached the Bty. about 6.15 and got back about 2315 chiefly by getting the M.P.s at all the diversions to get me through on vague talk of Brigadier's priority. Luckily the moon was very bright as all the armour was coming up the other way – enormous Shermans loomed out of the dark amid clouds of dust, and the low slim Crusaders snaked noisily out at us. When I got back I was told to stay with a party of 12 till next day and a truck would come back and pick us up. With great difficulty I collected their rations – nobody had thought of it – and we settled down for a long night's sleep. At 0415 I was told the truck was present and I was to be ready to move at 0430. We moved off – 14 in the end, god knows where the other 3 came from! – and reached here – about 10 miles west of Homs – at about 0545. And now as the moon sinks in the west and the sky once again glows bright opposite, I have Laing on the breakfast (we are at 5 minutes notice) and sit here writing this. A nasty sight yesterday; an 's' minefield with about 4 violently dead Tommies and a leg with gaiter and boot attached lying about it. Managed to scrounge some cigarettes in Homs on the way back and dished out 5 apiece among the grateful populace. Bdr. Worrall has been a great help and is potentially about the best N.C.O. in the Bty.

1135: Since about 0845 the armour and its various appendages has been rolling and clanking through. We shall not move probably for several hours yet. Odd thing: I've just been having quite a long conversation with Arbuthnot and find he expresses v. similar sentiments to those entered here last thing on 20 Jan. The more I hear about this Regt. the greater the foreboding with which I face the future in a more or less static role of garrison troops. Incidentally there is always the possibility that a div. as good as this may go back to England and be used for second front. Transfer to Tanks is still high up among my thoughts. Last night I dreamed of Sheila and felt a sort of sense of loss when I awoke. She was kind to me and we were really very happy. I hear mail is at R.H.Q. and (if only they've got through) there should be plenty for me. I'm almost certain I shall hear from B., which will be a good thing, and some news from home would be welcome too.

1700: Slightly further up the road. Mail came up – and not a single one for me although I know so many must be on the way. This lack of mail is mental torture of a high order. A little story to illustrate comradely tact as displayed by Tovarich Buchanan:

B: 'Any mail?'
Me: 'No.'
B: 'I've got 7 letters, a bank statement, 2 telegrams etc. etc. . . .'
Me: 'Oh.'

Later Buchanan comes over and taking his mail ostentatiously out of his pocket says: 'Now let me see; just how many have I got?' Counts each one 'One, Two, Three Four etc.' and wanders off to read them. I am tired and dispirited. Persistent rumours that Tripoli has fallen or is about to fall. The S. Africans came through us. First time we've seen them; political gesture.

Tonight looks like being cold. We are on a bit of ground where the Seaforths have had casualties.

23 January

1130: Orders to move at 1800 last night. Further instructions made it 0030 so after 3 hrs broken sleep, we were once again lined up by then. By about 0700 all movement stopped and has not been resumed since.

Cause: heavy demolition up the road. I've been doing traffic control this end which has proved rather interesting as I've had all types from Navy to Admin Officers trying to push on. Latest is a possible move round 1300. Bloody awfully cold night and I sat and shivered in the front of the truck, being R.H.Q. Liaison Officer (Stooge). Met a machine gunner/ AT/ Infantryman from 7 Argylls whom we met on the ship from Dubai and at Clairwood.

Talking to 'Knob' and Toller; they are fed up for much the same reasons as myself and are also considering a transfer. Wilkinson (now in 126) broke his leg on a mine of all things. Fall of Tripoli not yet official but latest rumours make it hourly more imminent and say it is in flames. Navy chap told me a convoy is our way from Benghazi.

Looks as if Rommel has got all his stuff away and is heading for Tunis to await the 1st Army – yet another job for us I suppose. In a way he has won this on points tho' Tripoli if made usable can be extremely valuable as a future base for our use.

1230: Last night during my 3 hours sleep I had a curious dream which I can only vaguely remember. I know I got married to Pam and we were to go to Paris for a honeymoon. Anyway we set out in one of those sort of sail-cars with rollerskate wheels, but the weather got very bad and eventually we had to cross a large girdered bridge over which heavy seas were breaking making it roll like a ship. So Pam (who by now was confusingly like a chap I knew at school called Lionel Wells) said we should stop and we got into a jeep to continue. I was just going to get a docket for using a W.D. vehicle from Somebody High Up, when I awoke. I remember the increasing realisations throughout that I should not have married Pam, and woke up wondering whether it is really so. Dick's 22nd birthday yesterday. Laing ('Danny') has a son called Dan whose letter he persisted in reading me yesterday: 'Dear Dad I hope you are fine, I am fine, the bike is fine etc.'. Laing persists in giving me enormous helpings of everything and I haven't felt really hungry for some time. Mealings is quite useful, a trifle familiar in a cockney friendly fashion and sings or hums sentimental tunes most of the time; 'So when I said goodbye love something something my love' you hear as he cleans his plugs.

1710: We are approaching Castel Verde on the road to Tripoli which has now officially fallen. The enemy has blown the road tremendously effectively and we are moving dead slow. Either we shall drive all yet another night or shan't be there till tomorrow. 51 Div. is to be the first (except the armour) into the city. Rommel is escaping rapidly westwards.

24 January

First light: Leaguered last night 62 miles west of Tripoli and 25 miles of Castel Verde to which we are now on the road. Jerry had blown two enormous holes in the mountain road post here but they were extremely efficiently and rapidly repaired by the sappers. Just after we passed through they blasted out another bit with a vast explosion that caused a miniature fog of fumes and dust. Y.M.C.A. canteen provided us all with 40 Capstans, a packet of sweets, bar of choc, and 3 chocolate biscuits. Very welcome particularly cigarettes. Slept a wonderful sleep. The last thing I remember is an orange moon climbing the hills from which we'd come and the crowd of stars above my head, and remembering from sheer force of habit to locate the North Star before I slept. Also the wonderfully sweet cup of tea my 'crew' – now including Howell, another cockney and quite a good worker – managed to conjure up somewhere in spite of the ban on fires. Passed some 90mm Italian guns on portees with quite a number of dead of all three parties a mile or two back. We may be in Tripoli today I believe.

1420: We leaguered for breakfast about 1300 after passing a couple of very blown up bridges and several senussi villages. All these arabs carrying bundles varying in size consisting of loot from the armies. We got 3 lemons from one after assuring him the 2 English pennies we gave him were 'quatro lire'. Tripoli today now seems unlikely. Findlay, who drove X2 till it went to F Tp., has been batting for me for the last week. A Scot, a good lad, and I'll try and keep him as he seems anxious to stay.

25 January

1000 hours: Leaguered 15 hours from Tripoli which according to reports is about as near as we'll get as we are supposed to be living on this bit of desert till further notice. This is our reward for recent weeks tho' the staff are naturally comfortable installed in the city.

We drove till about 2330 last night to get here; no moon till after 2100 made things a little difficult. With civilisation comparatively near I am again becoming restless. I'd rather be 100 miles from a house than 10.

Chief points of interest yesterday evening were 5 large clouds of locusts flying past at about 1500 and an Italian lorry blown up by one of his own mines – a Double Teller I should think. The thing was completely destroyed and scattered, and a pair of trousers were hanging from the telegraph wires about 40 yards away. I scoured the wreckage, found bits of uniform etc and an intact letter beginning 'Mio amato Pero' which I intend to translate later (Damn, I have just burned a hole in my f.-pen cap). We are just moving, to the Bty area I think.

1930: Bivouacked in same area – a pretty bloody one. A cold NE wind is blowing, made worse by the fact that my tent was removed today and given to Wilson. I now have a very ramshackle little thing lent me by Wagstaff. I am Bty Messing Officer! I asked the B.C. today about a transfer but he advised me to be patient. I am wondering whether I wrongly read into his words a half promise of a decent job as soon as possible. Findlay, good fellow, has dug me well in so it's not as cold as it might be but a nasty draught whistles around my head and bits of sand come with it. Tripoli so far is completely out of bounds and has hardly any troops in it. The men are disappointed and disgruntled. No 'V's this week – 100 next – or rather this – I forgot it's Monday – or is it? Tomorrow I must write home and to Pam and of course to B., whom I'm missing like hell tonight. This wind is getting on my nerves; I must be tired; I do feel rather done up. I am not happy here; it's the first unit I've been in where I feel out of tune, tho' I get on well enough with the men.

26 January

Evening: Grand mail today. Letters from Joan Mary, Anne, Debroy, Sybil – George's cousin, Roden Parry the S.C.R.A. 45 Div. and an oldish one [8 November] from home. Nothing however from Pam or B. Also Airgraphs from Peggy Hale and Denny – now astonishingly an instructor at 123 O.C.T.U. Wrote and telegraphed home and to B. and also wrote to Roden, Pam, Sybil, J-Mary; will finish my arrears of correspondence tomorrow. Also a chequebook from Barclays in Cairo and the rather gratifying information that my balance at the end of last month was £16.12.6. As I've drawn no pay from the field cashier this month my overdraft should be almost clear. Went today on a vegetable collecting party for the men's mess. I collected 45 cauliflowers, cabbages and peas from a farm called 'Nicolini' run by an old harridan who spoke rather good French. I must get hold of an Italian phrase book somewhere and try and get back a small measure of fluency. It's rather cold here and I have bites of an obscure but exceedingly irritating variety. They are most prevalent on my fingers. It looks like rain tonight, which is about all it needs to finish me off. Gillanders has come to full Lieut., Wagstaff has gone to E Tp. and the irrepressible Buthy becomes Bty. Capt once again. Well well.

27 January.

2000, by candle: Cannot write much as my candle is nearly finished. It started raining soon after I finished last night and has only just (I think temporarily) stopped. My tent of course let nearly everything in which was bloody miserable. Findlay – more excellent as he proves daily – has shored the sides up but it is still far from weather proof. A nasty wind is blowing it violently about at the moment. A letter from B. today which I am reserving till I've written this – as something to sleep on.

Jock called me Jack in public today for the first time since I joined 491; it gratified me absurdly. Yet another officer – Kinnaird – arrived today. He is pretty junior. I find I am still 4th Senior Subaltern. Must close now as my light is shining out of this bloody transparent tent.

28 January

2000: Tonight I am installed in tremendous comfort; the ever increasingly indispensable Findlay, with 4 sheets of corrugated iron I managed to scrounge this morning, has made me a wonderful 'house' so deep down I can almost stand upright, thus removing the necessity for going outside to put on my trousers. Wooden shelves adorn the sides and I lie in great luxury by candlelight in clean pyjamas with a clean pillowcase; and tomorrow I shall have a completely clean set of clothing. Pep-talk for subalterns from the Colonel today; nothing special. The degree of spit and polish to which this division goes is astonishing. For example all brass will be polished in spite of an A.C.I. to the contrary and now I hear a church parade is to be provided – but no man must be less than 5'10"! Fantastic. More mail today; one from Pam who has had 'flu twice; she got my nightdress in time for Xmas, which is rather good. Also from George Long who doesn't seem to be liking Iraq very much. Wrote today to Debroy and Anne enclosing a cheque for some cigarettes (we got our 100 'V' this week but how bloody they are). One day leave to Tripoli starts tomorrow. 10% haversack rations to be taken and clear of the city by 1800. Not exactly an orgy. I am rather worried about my stuff at base as it includes my cigarette case and Diary I, a replica of this. I think I'll write and ask D. to send them on to me. B.'s letter dated Jan 7 was rather short and she doesn't seem to have had my two or three written since Xmas Eve which is odd. I believe our mail was held up here at Benghazi during the push as it is coming through well enough now. I wonder how many of my letters got home safely. Nobody has told me yet. It seems almost certain now that Tripoli will only be a halt for us, tho' for how long is a matter purely for speculation. I hear Jock has been cited for the MC which doesn't surprise me in the least as he seemed to me always the sort of man who was bound to collect one; also he has just little enough imagination and feeling to worry about personal security. I have many bites again – and simply must go to a dentist as I have several teeth urgently requiring filling, including my 2 canines – top. Tripoli will chiefly benefit me if I can buy a writing case, a notebook like this, and get a decent haircut and shampoo; I'll be lousy if it gets any longer and dirtier. It has just started to rain; pattering loudly on my c.-iron roof. It is 2030.

29 January

Spent a bad night; my itchy bites woke me up all the time. Today has chiefly been occupied by routine checks and vegetable seeking. I collected 180 lbs of french new potatoes which is a good addition. Not very good weather and I'm not in a very good temper.

30 January

Rather quiet day. I am Battery Orderly Officer and got the chance to write to Ian again, George Long, and my school padre E.V. Tanner who got 2 M.C.s in the last war. Lunch warmer. I had a frightful headache till about 1600 when I took a couple of veganin. Also I kept getting up during the night in positive torment from my bites. I've had all my bedding smothered in Keating's and W.D. Anti-Louse powder today so I hope to high heaven that forms a protective barrier! Jock is unusually friendly which helps and I am now beginning to get used to the other officers a bit. Gegan is the surprise. He has been unusually cordial and started telling me about his wife tonight. We've been having a bit of bread in the ration now, which reminds me poor old Findlay's got a boil on his arm so I've advised a bread poultice and given him some zinc oxide B. gave me in Cairo. I'm just going to write again to B. Forshaw, the first of our daily officers to go into Tripoli reported the place empty and miserable and said you're almost glad to get out again at 1730! The fruits of victory look more like crab apples daily! Incidentally I heard on the radio tonight speeches by Goering and Goebbels which sounded an unusual note of desperation. 'Fighting to the finish' etc. Can it possibly be that Germany is beginning to crack as silently and swiftly as she did in 1918? I rather doubt it myself, but how any thinking German can fail to see that (with America's growing output and ourselves as resolute as ever) we must win I can't understand.

31 January

Sunday afternoon even in Tripolitania retains its atmosphere. Today was devoted to 'personal maintenance' which means washing clothing and self, and scrubbing and polishing equipment, haircutting etc. and, if you have done all these things, sleeping. I was finishing a court of Inquiry.

Two letters today. One from Pam – a long A.M.L.C. which service is really excellent – and a nice letter from Anne the W.A.A.F. telling me she's sent some chocolate and will send some more – most excellent news and if only my cheque gets back rapidly, cigarettes should soon be on the way – hooray. Today I also wrote to Dick in Gib. sending him a 25/- cheque for his birthday – and asking him to send me cigarettes too! It has been very hot today and in the drowsy afternoon sunshine it was quiet, with only an occasional aeroplane droning overhead, and distant soldiers' voices to disturb the hundreds of lizards running in and out of the sandhills. I got my laundry from a neighbouring farm where the withered old woman who runs the place wouldn't take money, so I gave her the sugar I'd saved up in my ration bag. They did the laundry magnificently with the soap I provided – and certainly seem to live near starvation by their appearance. Some of the males about the place look to me like deserters. It goes around that Rommel has now 60,000 men and 200 tanks in Tunisia which makes me wonder just how long we'll be as comfortable as this . . . I start a 5 alternate days Signal Course at R.H.Q. tomorrow. The day after I hope to get in Tripoli, and am making preparations to have my only pair of b.d. trousers pressed tomorrow night! Also the shoes I (rather wisely I think) brought with me, are being repaired by the Bty. equipment retainer. We have been eating dates galore which lie like lead on the stomach. Last night I was up at 0230 smothering my bites with iodine, but I don't think I have any new ones today. Have also had headaches again today, tho' not as bad as yesterday.

1 February

It is a very hot afternoon and oddly enough I have nothing to do. In a few days there is to be a parade in Tripoli for a 'very important' person (Gen. Alexander? or Winston?) and frantic spit and polish of guns has started. This is literal as they are to be scraped and burnished! With this new order about scrubbing equipment, some of the gaiters are now dazzling white; I understand ointment A/G is being used! (illegally). All the subalterns in this Regt. seem to be utterly browned off according to remarks I've heard at the Sigs. class today. I've never seen such a state of affairs before. Kinnaird who I mentioned the other day is one of these; he was with the Regt. before, has apparently disagreed with the powers that be, and is in for transfer. The B.C. did not demur in his case which is perhaps a pointer.

Incidentally the Colonel said the other day how much he hated the word bullshit and that it must cease to exist. This reminds me of Hitler's repeated liquidation of the Russian armies. Findlay has made an ingenious wire frame and Pam's photo complete in leather frame now adorns the wall of my dwelling. I slept with the end open last night and had no headache this morning. Also no more bites so far.

2 February

Went into Tripoli today. The place, which looks exactly as you'd expect, is still pretty dead, with arabs hawking stolen goods, dates, oranges etc. in the streets and a few staff and 'intelligence' officers skimming the fat off a pretty lean city. Troops everywhere, some of them pretty scruffy, particularly the New Zealanders and R.A.F. The H.D. for all its bullshit certainly looked decently turned out. Tripoli harbour and Mole are still pretty well u.s. owing to extensive demolition carried out by Jerry. Tonight we had 3 air-raids, one after the other, and were treated to a fairytale display of flak, chiefly from the numerous Bofors guns around the harbour and waterfront. Officers are catered for by what once must have been the very comfortable Grand Hotel (how these Grand Hotels crop up) where you get army rations for lunch and lunch vino and black coffee. I think it is likely to become a second Shepheards if we stay in Tripoli long enough. The 'important person' sounds like Churchill now, as he is reported in Cairo at the moment. How he gets about at 60-odd . . . in Casablanca a week or two ago and now here again. Had my haircut and shampoo but alas no hot water at the public baths. Another Captain D.B. Grant from the H.Q.R.A. has come to our battery. The thing is fast becoming a farce. I remember seeing him one night this side of Homs. He used to be with 304 and seems quite likeable. Met Big Arthur and Bob Root at the Grand and had some interesting exchanges. They seem quite happy in 128 but would be anywhere I think. Jock is super-genial these days and always calls me Jack which has made the other officers also more genial, probably because they think the B.C. is the sort of person to whom a former acquaintance might be able to lead them; in which they are wrong. I may be wronging them however. Jimmy Gegan is now always very friendly; I am becoming the mess jester again, a position I always seem to occupy eventually. It is pleasant to laugh again. 'I'm entitled to no rations' is the laugh producer these days as food is very scarce. We get 1/3 monkey nuts in lieu of biscuits in lieu of bread now!

Still no news from B. tho' I'm sure she must have been writing to me. I suppose it's being held up somewhere.

3 February

Got up this morning with an eyeshutting headache. The walk to the Sigs. class and back – about $5^1/2$ miles – didn't do it any good, and by the time I got back here I also felt sick and could hardly stand up. Took 2 Veg. and put in a useful afternoon buying vegetables and scrounging 28 galls. of petrol – the Regt. again being in the state where every pint counts. I feel bloody again tonight and shall go to bed as soon as I've investigated the mail which is on its way. I think it's the dates I've eaten; either that or neuralgia; bloody awful pain anyway. Churchill's in T. tomorrow but we shan't see him; disappointing. Met an off. yesterday who wanted to find some stamps – for his collection!

5 February

1515, in bed: Yesterday I just about passed out after a very bad night sweating like hell and aches and pains all over. I couldn't touch food and was sick and giddy and constipated and had the most frightful headache – whenever I switched my eyes the top of my head did acrobatics. Today I've been in bed so far all day (luckily it's a Regt. holiday) after another similar night but feel better and the various aperients (One No. 9, 2 Cascara, 2 doses of salts) have worked. Also I believe my temperature has gone and my headache has abated. Most of the officers seem to think I have jaundice but I'm not going sick till I have to and I don't think I'll have to now. Letter from Mom (Nov. 22), airgraph from Dad (29 Dec.) and one from Joan Mary written as the new year came in. A lot of my mail must have gone astray as Dad says Mom's recovery will be slow – and I didn't even know she was ill. This sort of thing is very worrying. Mom's health has been rather dubious for the last few years; I often worry about it. Considerable air-raiding of Tripoli during the last hours . . . Mr Churchill's visit apparently went off very well; the Div. General fell over in his Carrier while saluting as the driver accelerated too suddenly.

6 February

2000: Spent all today in bed and am feeling much better; I think all my fever has now gone after another very sweaty night. Also 2 more No. 9s today have produced the desired effects (note the plural). I got up yesterday pm but didn't feel a bit good and felt my temperature coming up again in the evening so rang up the M.D. who suggested a day or two in bed here, as I told him I didn't want to report sick. Tonight a new moon has appeared again; as always I thought of B. immediately I saw it . . . Still no word from her today; I simply can't understand such a long delay – though on looking back I find it's only about 10 days – but as it was such a short letter and the only one I'd had for about 3 weeks perhaps it made the gap seem wider. I see the East Surreys are in Tunisia; I wonder if Roger Andrews is there with the 1st Bn?

The batmen have looked after me well while I've been in bed. I think I've had 'flu not jaundice but I shall soon know – if I start going yellow!

7 February

Woke up feeling bloody but got up in clean clothes after lunch and have felt better since. Saw the M.O. this afternoon. Nice lad who looks about 18. I believe he is somewhat foxed by my disease; has excused me duties for a bit. Rained torrentially from 0700 to 1400. My dwelling surprisingly watertight. No mail. Good flak display about 8 pm. It is now about 2100 and the rain is just starting up once again, tingling on my corrugated iron roof. In these circumstances I can do without rain. Too apathetic to write to anybody.

8 February

Felt much better and spent all day up and about. There are signs of an advance very soon; for example the H.D. games on 10 February are cancelled. Monty is seeing all officers tomorrow, I'm told. Raid as usual tonight; two planes brought down in flames fairly near. Saw the parachute as one baled out from the second.*

Airgraph from J-Mary. Wrote back.

9 February

Lousy day. Cold, with rain at intervals. No mail. Wrote a longish letter to B. Have made quite good friends with D.B. Grant who is now a Lieut. and rather a nice man. One of those rather large lazy, soft-spoken blokes, but with plenty of good sense and some conversation. I rather like him. Kinnaird is also quite a good lad. It's all the people who don't like the unit, that I seem to like, tho' nowadays I get on well enough with them all, but I'd hate to have either Wagstaff or Cameron as my Tp. Comd. – a possibility one of these days. Jack Wilson went to hospital today. Stomach.

10 February

Long letter from George, and one from Moira enclosed, also a receipt from the S.A. Broadcasting Co. who apparently put over (ie. Moira did) my 'Cutey' and it was very well received. All signs of a move very soon now. A Naafi coming in tomorrow which means some smokeable cigarettes – hooray. Have had more laughs than usual today – quite like old times. D.B. said to me 'you know, you're

---

* J.U. 88s it appears later, & found out from Johnny Russ – 18 Feb – that they were all drowned. Also that occupants of first jumped out before Sgt Pilot night-fighter fired at all.

the only sane person here . . .' meaning just what I'm not sure. It was bloody weather with heavy rain this morning, and the men were sent back to bed as most of them are on dock fatigues tonight. Am just going to write back to George. Also by the way a wire from home saying they'd had mine of 26/1.

11 February

Moving tomorrow 0500 to Pisida on the frontier to act as screen for 51 Div. A minor battle may be expected. Filthy weather, rain and gale, and still no letter from B. I am bloody fed up about this. Great flap all day and had to attend a damn fool demonstration 35 miles away thereby wasting most of the day and some precious petrol. We are to do 120 miles tomorrow, which almost certainly will entail arriving after dark. Good canteen and I also scrounged 100 Craven A from the N2 in Tripoli so I am fairly affluent in cigarettes – one good thing among many bad. The gale is rattling my house like a bloody orchestra – but it won't keep me awake tonight!

12 February

1110: That's what I thought. After keeping me awake solidly till 0200 with its devil's tattoo the roof blew off. It rained for the rest of the night and I got up at 0500 in torrents of rain and gale, and every damn thing soaking. Am now broken down 25 km from Zania; big end gone. The M.T. is beginning to crack up now.

1900: Eventually I decided to hitchhike and taking Findlay got via Sabrata to where I am now – the 57 H.A.A. at Zuara. They have been most kind and fed us and tomorrow we'll go on and try and find the Bty. near Pisida. Still very cold with intermittent rain but we are in a house so who cares. Quite decent country up here with roads lined by palm and eucalyptus trees – a lot of craters made by the R.A.F. and quite a few derelict vehicles – also the R.A.F. One minor annoyance; I left my tin hat in the 2nd truck we hitched. I've had it since 1939 so I regarded it as sentimentally valuable. Maybe I can recover it tomorrow. With about 1/2 an hour's sleep last night I am now rather tired and shall be glad to turn in. Also it'll give my clothes a chance to dry being indoors for once.
<u>Note:</u> Got my tin hat next day.

13 February

Jock is dead. It happened soon after I joined the Bty. near Pisida. I am absolutely stunned by the news; he was such a grand chap in all his own way. He stepped on a Teller mine and was killed outright. What makes it worse is that his wife (whom I met in England) has just had a daughter. I simply can't really realise yet that he's dead. I shall miss him like hell. Oh Damn, why is it the best people and the bravest always go. Also, incidentally, the only reason I wanted to stay in this Regt. gone.

1350: They've been bringing in his personal effects, each one a separate reminder of incidents past. I am remembering the little jokes he used to make (how he always pulled my leg about being a reporter) the things he used to say – 'That's just too bad . . .', the way he used to look. It is hard indeed to realise when somebody familiar by daily contact is dead, yet J.O. Cochrane is only a name now and that well known figure with his monocle, duffle coat, and pistol strapped to his thigh, is lying broken and bleeding in the sand near Pisida. And yet a part of me still expects him to turn up any moment and tell me it isn't true. But of course it is and I shall never see him again. To make everything worse I am now with E Tp. – and Wagstaff. I think I shall definitely try and transfer when all this is over.

Letter from Mother (13 December, Air Mail)

2100: 4 miles from the Tunisian frontier. The moon is bright and the stars are out. We have dug our guns in, eaten M & V and now – soon – we shall sleep under those bright stars; somewhere nearby, one leg blown off, the Major is also sleeping. But he will not awaken.

14 February

Sunday, noon: Last night I lay awake for a long time thinking of Jock, remembering him vividly even down to the exact sound of that sort of snorting chuckle he used to make when he was amused at something. I remembered a discussion we had on biscuits and their effect on teeth when he said in his allegedly callous way 'some of the weaker brethren gave up the struggle and had to be removed.' I remembered what he said when I was complaining to him one day about the lack of a proper job – 'Oh well one of these days somebody'll go on a course or to hospital, or get himself killed . . .' And then I realised again that he had cracked his last cynical joke. He was probably the best soldier in the Regt. I didn't realise till he was dead how much I also thought of him as a man and as a friend. So I lay there for hours staring at the Plough in the clear bright sky and feeling an overwhelming loss and sadness. And now I shall have to get used to doing without him. Today we are still in action the same place and unlikely to move till tomorrow as the other 2 batteries have gone forward. It is cold and sunny with a gusty wind blowing up a bit of sand. It is like all days in the desert; I think our next limited objective is Ben Gardane with its aerodrome and several landing grounds.

1530: Have just written to Pam an airmail letter card. Still a desultory day with a gusty wind. I am bored and rather miserable.

1850: This afternoon I had a long chat with Jimmy Gegan, I think the nicest of the officers in this Bty; showing how bad my judgement must be, because I didn't much like him at first. He too is bloody fed up about Jock's death. He told me a good many things about the other officers in the Regiment from the C.O. down, which didn't make me more pleased to belong to it. I think I am going back to B.H.Q. soon as Moncur is returning tonight or tomorrow. Incidentally we move forward into Tunisia at 0845 tomorrow morning. To illustrate a small defeat of Wagstaff by me today. We were discussing rations which came up very short last night. The B.S.M., Forshaw, Sgt. Mackenzie and a L/Bdr. were present. I have studied rations rather carefully during the last 3 weeks as messing officer but Wagstaff evidently did not realise this. There was only one tin of marge. I said 'Oh, only 5 lbs for the Tp.' Wagstaff, with the flat contradiction which is practically the sole form of conversation 'No such thing as a 5 lb tin of marge. Must have been a 6 or 7 lb tin.' I let the subject drop, went to the cookhouse, found as I thought that it <u>was</u> a 5 lb tin, came back and announced the fact as casually as possible. W. was visibly discomforted and sucked hard on his ridiculous little pipe to cover his confusion. How small I am to gloat over such things when Jock is dead; if only I could realise it fully.

15 February

1500: We are about 12 miles from Ben Gardane and thus into Tunisia for the first time. It is hot and the road is broken and dusty and littered with masses of mines. 6 Sappers killed this morning. I couldn't see Jock's grave, tho' I knew where it was just over the frontier. Water is getting scarce again. Again found it hard to sleep last night thinking of Jock. Am in a lousy old 3 tonner which I had to get winched out 3 times this morning going cross country. Driver a regular old woman called Stewart (Favourite response 'Oh Sir, yes indeed Sir . . .') with a long face like a bloodhound, but not a bad chap. Has been driving, in his own words, 'fifteen years'. Passed the Gordons marching up with their pipes playing; as always an inspiring sound even in these surroundings. I wish I felt I had something to look forward to. I find with Jock's death I have nothing; I realise I must have been striving for his approval. I know that when he said 'Stout effort' it used to mean something.

2000, 8 miles E. of BEN GARDANE: We are in action here tho' not firing. Apart from a company of Gordons 4 miles ahead and some tanks S.E. of B.G. we are now the foremost troops of the 8 Army. The B.B.C. seem to think big battles are ahead, and the German attack near FAID pass, where they have advanced 18 miles, seems to presage this too. I have started a one sheet 'newspaper' (written and edited by me) each evening compiled from the news on a No. 11 set at 1900. It is very popular with the Troops. One of them said to me tonight 'It's what we've always wanted Sir'. It's good to feel one is doing something useful. Latest is that 7 Armd. Div. are in contact 5 miles west of B.G. The banging we heard was 'Crumping Charlie', our old pal, and some 88 Mill.

16 February

0910 came orders to move up to B.G. It is now 1030, the recce parties have gone and we are lined up on the desert waiting to go. Very open, desolate country this, with a lot of soft sand and no features. Slept better; bright moonlight and the heaviest dew I've seen this morning. Now sunny.

I find a fact I've never mentioned is that I'm always (in company with all the rest of the H.D.) hungry; army rations, though doubtless technically sufficient, fail to satisfy when in action and are bloody monotonous. Porridge is a great boon for breakfast and helps to fill one up, but a few dry biscuits and ¾ oz of cheese between then and the evening bully or M & V is not exciting. I long for England again nowadays.

17 February

Amazingly back in Tripoli area. Came back to get cigarettes, veg. and wine for the whole Regt. but there are none here, as the Bulk Naafi is moving. I managed to do well for Findlay and the Driver and myself (one whole 1,000!) but nothing on a really large scale. Tonight am with 61 A/T and Peter Lear's Bty. Grand to see him, we are talking over everything. And best of all D. is in the area . . . I may even see him tomorrow. Bty. NW of B.G.

18 February

2130, Pisida (12 miles from the frontier): More amazing coincidences. Having driven about 120 miles here today after collecting wine at Castel Benito we (!) decided in view of sandstorms and general tiredness to leaguer with the R.A.S.C. here. The officer turns out to be none other than Johnny Russ with whom I was at school and who I haven't seen since about 1936. He is a captain. Once again it has been an evening of recollections and reminiscences. It really is amazing. Did not see D. in C.B. as I was in too great a hurry to look for him. The Adjutant told me to be back today but I don't suppose he'll say much – how can he? – and anyway I really don't care. Besides I didn't fancy driving up this very badly surfaced road littered as it is with mines. The sappers have had more casualties here than any time including Alamein. And I myself know too well what they can do. Was in Tripoli for a few minutes; the place is becoming organised again and there are quite a number of different articles for sale now. Bought a lot of sweets for different people having failed to do much else. Perhaps the mail I am taking up tomorrow will help appease them. It is a gusty night with a bright moon and strong, cold wind such as always brings the sand. I am glad to be under cover. Saw the rest of the brigades moving up – in fact the rest of the Div. Obviously something is once again brewing. Peter and Ian and I talked for hours last night; a grand mess; the difference in atmosphere in all these other Regts. is so very noticeable. None of this everlasting shop and back biting and petty jealousy, and you don't have to bolt your food to get your share.

19 February

Reached the Bty. again during the morning and satisfied various people with about 50 cigarettes each. I forgot to say the day I went back we got a new B.C. – Harben, has been with the N.Z.E.F. and is not a regular, but has been with the cavalry. Seems quite a nice man and bodes efficiency thank God. Knew Jock well: 'if he wasn't my best friend he was one of them.' Found to my horror I was posted to E Tp. but the B.C. said was that alright, and I told him straight out I simply couldn't get on with Wagstaff so he said Alright, you shan't go there, and I am hoping to go to F. He said I could anyway.

This would be quite pleasing as Jimmy Gegan is G.P.O. and Cameron the Tp. Comd. is I think quite prepared to be conciliatory, and is anyway intelligent, as is Jimmy who is a schoolmaster. The difficulty is that I am senior to nearly all the subalterns including both G.P.O.s. Quite a good mail: Airgraph from Dad 22/1, Airmail letter from Mom 7/12, letter card from Pam 24/1 and a letter from Val in Durban. Not such good news is that Mom has to have a major operation for removal of the gall bladder. I hope all is O.K. The Regt. is now about 3 miles further north but the fighting has moved to Medenine which, I hear, we have taken. Very sultry evening with a slatey sky. May rain I should think.

21 February

Noon: Waiting to move on towards Medenine. Wrote yesterday to Mrs. Cochrane and home and to Val in S.A. Am much happier in this (F) Tp. and life is taking on a rosier hue. Also Cameron and Gegan both loathe Wagstaff which is a good thing. Donald Grant has gone* to 126 and Boys is of all things Town Major of Ben Gardane! Much speculation over whether Jerry intends to put up a show here on the Mareth Defences or just north of Gabes. I think he will, though he must quite obviously be thrown out of N. Africa eventually. The moon is on the wane again which makes me wonder whether we shall wait another month; this seems to be our usual practice. Airgraph from Dad – 7 Jan.

1810: In action not firing 10 miles short of Medenine. An attack going in tonight but we shan't have to move unless called for. If so a middle of the night flap is indicated.

22 February

Static here all day tho' a possible attack on the Mareth defences is I think an early possibility. I am once again as well as F's Tp. Ldr. Bty. Messing Off., a job I dislike

* Actually he is still waiting to go.

intensely. However I now have a bivouac tent and am thus writing by Darkness (outside) a great luxury for me. Incidentally it rained last night which wasn't too funny sleeping out of doors as I was; however, a scientific arrangement of groundsheets, gas capes etc. kept me fairly dry. Two airgraphs today; one from Joan Mary and another from G. I haven't heard from her since our great quarrel on my embarkation leave. Her airgraph begins typically: 'Thank you for your Xmas feelings – all the more pleasant because in the circumstances of our parting I had not expected to hear from you! Though I have come to the conclusion that you are (a) a great hypocrite and (b) often very annoying – I miss you, and our acquaintanceship has meant a good deal – so here's to your speedy return!' I don't know whether to be annoyed with her or not; generally speaking I think not. The new B.C. has a penchant for prisoner killing or as a milder version taking off their boots and slashing their feet with a razor blade; I am inclined to disagree.

He is fond of telling rather improbable stories specially one which so far he has given us word for word twice and which begins 'Did I ever tell you what the Russians do with <u>their</u> prisoners? . . .' (atrocity story follows!)

Findlay – daily he becomes more indispensable – has just brought me in my nightly cup of tea (better without milk round here as it is curdled by the heavily chlorinated and scarce – $^1/_2$ gallon a day – water). He also brought me in some excellent Xmas cake which he got in a parcel from his sister in Canada today – a generous gesture. I have never regretted having him as a batman and I don't believe he has regretted becoming mine. Jimmy has a real character – McCrindle aged about 42, no teeth, and almost completely unintelligible till you get used to him; but a very excellent batman. I get on really well with Jimmy and also Alistair Cameron who is similar in type to Tony Shaw my Tp. Comd. in 132 with Jock. Can hear an occasional boom of a gun to the North, but things are fairly quiet. I think quite a battle is imminent. Shall be sorry when 'General' Grant goes to 126 as he also is good company – in fact with the exception of Wagstaff and perhaps the dogmatic Forshaw most of the officers are fairly easy to rub along with. Buthy is sure enough a rogue but a likeable rogue and a gent, and usually amusing enough. So now I go on to Diary 3, the book given me by B. in Cairo.

Each mail I wonder when I shall hear from her; nearly a month now, and no word.

23 February

1615: We are leaguered in an orchard near Ben Giarar. Tonight at dusk we are to line up with a view to taking up positions nearer the enemy. In this case I believe it's Italians opposite us. There is a strong rumour of mail which I hope is true. Marched about 30 miles here along a goodish road and through the very pleasant little town of Medenine. Yesterday from Ben Gardane to our last night's position was very bleak country – undulating featureless desert. I started a letter to G. last night but only managed 4 lines as we were called out for orders. (The new Major is partial to mass conferences on the smallest pretexts!) My new driver is 'Davy' Brown aged 42 or 43 and not a very good driver; he drives me nearly mad by stalling at the wrong moments. Certain amount of crumping away to the west of us. Sounds like artillery; may be our own fighter bombers.

24 February

1100: We moved as the moon came up about 2200 but after going a few miles had to cross a salt marsh. This was about midnight. I went up to the head of the column and found a sort of nightmare in progress. A great bog had to be crossed and everything was sinking like a stone. On either side was salt marsh, just passable to light stuff but no good for guns. Eventually after 301 and 304 Batteries had winched every vehicle through with four quads we decided to leaguer for the night, and that is where we now are with the R.E.s making the bog passable. We are supposed to be in view of the enemy but so far there are no tangible results. I got the guns into action at first light today after about an hour curled up on the back of my truck, and got a good hot meal dished out to the Bty. by 0800. The RAF had a full night's bombing. We could see the planes, AA and bomb flashes – Gabes getting the heat put on it perhaps? We now expect to move soon to our 'first base' position facing the Northern Sector of the Mareth Line. It is nice warm weather which is a good thing and something of a change. Away to the west there is much heavy artillery crump crumping away all the time.

25 February

Eventually after four orders and counter orders we moved off by pitch darkness and reached a preliminary position which now (1020) we are waiting to vacate. We are reputed to be going to a very 'hot' position close to the enemy and under frequent shell fire. This, however, is so often the story and proves wrong that we shall see – and anticipate nothing. Certainly there was brisk shelling by him yesterday afternoon, and the R.A.F. has been very active. Today the guns are once again starting up. It sounds as if he has quite a bit of stuff over the other side. Finished my letter to G. yesterday. Slept like a log last night being very tired and woke up in a tremendous dew today and heavy mist. Rather cold, but warming up a little.

Same afternoon: We are moving up to our position at 1800 hours. Artillery on both sides pretty active all day so far and it is now sunny with good visibility which made a move up by broad daylight too hazardous. A great treat today; eggs for breakfast and fresh fish for lunch – both from the local wogs via Buthy – tho' how he got them (ie. money or tea) I don't know – or ask. The men's messing has also greatly improved now; I am really getting things organised – and many bouquets have been coming in; always a pleasing thing. From what I can gather of our forward position they have been shelling behind it as well as in front, so we should not lack interest. Also we are the foremost battery on this Northern Sector being in the F.D.L.s I believe tho' they may of course have shifted a bit forward by now. An attack is forecast for tomorrow night – unofficially of course. I am not as excited as I was at Zem Zem but quite looking forward to it. Cameron suggested yesterday that one's chief reaction is 'scared boredom' which I think is a fairly accurate assessment. Thank God I've got plenty of cigarettes anyway – tho' in fact I sold or gave away about 500 of the ones I collected in Tripoli.

26 February

Duly came into action last night with a mild Divisional concentration at 1945. No shelling as yet tho' we've been having some all round outbursts at 1095 which are fairly active. A good bit of firing from our own guns but Jerry, somewhere behind the grey hills we can see shimmering in the heat haze, is very quiet. Letter card from Pam (2 February) today but also her accomplishments do not include writing a good letter. Still, she writes very regularly dear child. It is now 1130 and we have rather surprisingly received 'Likelihood of a move' orders; if so I am likely to be in the recce party; am correspondingly prepared.

Same afternoon: Interesting developments. Jerry is coming south from the American sector and most of the Div. Arty. is moving south of here. 3 Tps. including 491 Bty are going to dodge about from Tp. posn. to posn. to fox Jerry that everybody is still there. Considerable air and artillery activity all day but we seem to have more planes up now.

27 February

a.m.: Last night we moved and then moved back again and the usual 'order, counter order and confusion' took place. Eventually after working out D.F. tasks I got to bed about 1215. Now the latest is that we are likely to stay after all. Jerry is fairly quiet. A shell has just landed about 300 yards to the left just as I was writing; a little excitement. Two more shells just left of posn. Now being shelled.
Later: Naturally I was interrupted by the activity described above as they started putting down rounds of gunfire almost on our gun position. They were 88 mm. At the same time about five 109s started easing around strafing. The Bofors got one which crashed about half a mile east of us. Just saw the smoke pouring from it before it went down. It is now getting rather hot weather again being nearly March. I am very badly bitten by fleas, I presume, which is bloody annoying as the bites itch like hell in bed. Our own guns have been fairly active this morning. I was woken up by the fierce banging of charge 3 about 6.50 today. We ourselves have had a few shoots. The dew is extremely heavy here in the mornings; I am

damned glad of my tent. I am also quite happy over here in F Tp. as I get on well with Jimmy and I like the rest of the Troop. Findlay and the toothless but extremely efficient McCrindle are adept at conjuring up tea at unlikely times – so generally speaking all is well. I ought to write a few letters but lack the energy. I wish I knew why I am not hearing from B.

28 February

Moved last night after all (I went forward and recced as G.P.O.) and this morning I G.P.O.'d for a 40 Round concentration at 0745. We are likely to move again soon I expect tho – as usual – nobody knows anything. These night moves are bloody tedious and make one short tempered, tired and generally low in morale. We seem to specialise in the bloody things and it is the exception when we get a night's sleep.

Same night in bed: Boys returned today (from being town major – B.G!!!!) but to E Tp. (He was in F) and reclaimed his tent so once again I am without one. However for tonight I have borrowed Alistair's as he's at the O.P., and also his bed which is one of the low, steel variety and very very comfortable. This is the first time I've slept on a bed for a couple of months and it's so nice I am thinking of buying one at the officers' shop which has arrived at Brigade H.Q. I am also toying with the idea of buying a tent, tho' if patient one may turn up in a day or two as I know they've got to division H.Q. My bites are bloody but I have managed to procure some Keatings with which Findlay has liberally annointed my bedding. Perhaps this will help. A quiet day with little firing except by the mediums next door to us, with their long thin barrels and horn like recuperator system. Towards sunset two 109s came over and were fiercely shot at by the Bofors, but sailed most contemptuously off towards the west without even breaking formation. Several long chats with Jimmy today; we get on splendidly as indeed I do with nearly everybody in this Troop. Nobody seems to have any guff about the general situation.

D.B. Grant has also been at the O.P. since yesterday. He hasn't got over to 126 yet and is extremely depressed, mooching around here with no definite job. I have just killed two insects – a woodlouse and a large sort of ant with a knob each end by the sadistic but extraordinarily effective method of dropping hot candle grease over them. It must be an unpleasant death as it solidifies. This place is alive with the foulest insects; tonight in the latrine there were six or seven enormous black beetles which you couldn't have covered with a half crown. Incidentally, talking of money, we have again changed – this time to the Algerian franc. That makes the S.A. pound, the B.M. Currency, the lire, and the franc in about 6 months. Tomorrow I must write home I think or to Pam. Yesterday I sent Anne and the W.A.A.F.s a letter and an A/G to Margaret Pritty. But I am waiting till I hear from B.

As writing to Turkey is such a business now with 2 envelopes etc. I wish she'd write – or rather, as I am sure she has been writing, I wish the letters would reach me. Also the chocolate Anne sent has never turned up. The mediums I mentioned have one of those portable O.P. towers just in front of us; it can be seen for miles and looks most perilous, but I am told the occupant is fairly safe in his sandbags. Jerry seems to have moved back, not having shelled it today.

1 March

Alas for my high hopes. The officers shop had sold out of beds and had no tents anyway. And as Alistair comes in from his O.P. tonight it seems I shall once again sleep in the open. The Keatings offensive has, so to speak, attained only limited objectives. Bites still bad. Jimmy is out on recce for another move. I do not know where to, but I think we are unlikely to have much of a party here in the Northern Sector, unless he discovers how thin we are (One Div. only) and has a crack at us. This might be unhealthy.

Same night: I have scrounged a very wee alleged tent under which I am now writing. It is now divulged that Jerry – with 20,000 tanks, Stukas etc. is planning a general attack, probably on 3 March. Whether or not mainly on this sector is uncertain but not very probable owing to indiscriminate mining in front of his F.D.L.s. Anyway we are to move up slightly tomorrow night (it may yet prove to be tonight!), dig in deep and wait for it. We have 350 fighters, 350 Heavy bombers and 600 tanks so we shall doubtless win the battle, and then, let us hope, finally throw the bugger out of North Africa for good. At sunset Jerry dropped a few shells in front of us, and one airburst. 88 mm I think. Alistair comes in from his O.P. tonight and D.B. is I think staying at Battalion H.Q. Bites still very bad. Not for nothing is my sleeping apparatus called a flea bag . . .

Wrote an airgraph to Pam.

2 March

Early (and unexpectedly of course) this morning, we moved to our battle stations – a little forward of where we were last night. At the moment the sinister silence of those grey-black hills in front of us is being broken by artillery fire. We have had several near us, the last – a few minutes ago – burst just on the position and splattered it with bits of shell casing. I am getting used to it: the dull banging of a door in the far corner of the house – a moment's pause, one's senses tightening up in mixed fear and excitement – and then the whistle growing almost to a shriek – and bang – whee . . . as the shell explodes. We are going down deep here. The guns have only the muzzles pointing over the pits, the Command Post is about 5–6 feet below ground, and I myself have a magnificent dugout whose floor is on a deeper level than the rest, giving my bed the effect of one of those knights you see lying in Exeter Cathedral and other places. A shelf by my head completes the luxurious fittings!

There are 2 rows of sandbags above the walls and corrugated iron over the top. It is easily the best dugout I've had. I'll be sorry to leave it – if I do leave it . . . D.B. has finally gone, to my regret. Alistair has come in from his O.P. and is being very matey. And now we have to sit and wait. If Jerry attacks here we are thin enough for anything to happen – but the outcome cannot be in any doubt. Tomorrow will bring results perhaps.

2130: I was definitely scared tonight. About an hour before sundown (when Jerry is usually most active as the light is favourable to him) I went up to the O.P. – 1,000 yards away – with Alistair.* They were shelling us at the time, or more accurately the flash spotters' tower just in front of us. We were just in the open near this damn thing when they started pumping over rounds of gunfire. The Adj. of the Gordons to whom Alistair was talking went flat at once but A stayed on his feet and – not liking to let the side down! – I also stayed standing. The bursts were horribly near and I had a very great desire to fall flat – particularly when one bit of splinter hummed past my shoulder and another whizzed into the ground not a foot from <u>my</u> foot. What the tin-hatted infantry crouching in slit trenches must have thought of two soft-hatted gunner officers standing (apparently) calmly in the open I can't guess – but I'm sure it was uncomplimentary. I think next time I shall be less nonchalant!

After one lovely day's digging we are – the Troop – on a 'roving commission' from 0730 tomorrow – 1/2 an hour's notice – can you beat it? A. has gone to B.H.Q. for orders now. Other points:

1. Nice letter from Dad (Air Mail 23/12). No new news of Mom's operation. Also from George Long dated 16/2. He is happier but has impetigo!
2. 50 Ardath instead of 'V's this week. A great event.
3. Message from General Wimberley – Div. Comd. – urging us to 'stand firm' as in 1918. Well well.
4. General offensive on my fleas with laconically titled 'AL 63' – Anti Louse! V. strong!

3 March

0810 (N.B. AL 63 very successful so far!): 'Stand to' at 0600 and a conference at B.H.Q. where the usual Last Man Last Round orders were issued. Also a warning that he is expected to use gas – a fact I personally deplore as my respirator is in my truck which has failed to turn up at the post. We are still at 1/2 an hour's

---

*Drew a panorama flat on belly, O.P. being in view.

notice in case needed. It is a clear bright day already getting warm. A Mess. 109 just came over and was shot at by our Bofors, but badly missed – probably because it was in the sun. We are told he may attack as from 0900 so maybe it won't be long now. I confess I feel a little apprehensive. Being on the defensive is not so funny. At 0300 there was considerable gunfire; we were told it was our guns firing on his troops massing.

Noon: Still waiting – also at $^1/_2$ an hour's notice still for some special job – the nature of which is unspecified – after which we shall return here. The day is hot and calm, and an unnatural silence, broken only by an occasional boom to the south, broods over the entire front. The heat haze shimmers over rolling crests and wadis which lie between us and the enemy. His offensive, tho' a dying fling, may test us sternly – and I think about 1600 will be zero hour as it gives him good shooting light and a few hours daylight for the 'thrust point' tactics he so loves.

Earlier, about half a dozen 109s were dive bombing and machine-gun-cum-cannon strafing on our right flank. They set something – a vehicle? – on fire and it burned in black clouds for over an hour, the smoke pillaring up in the still atmosphere. Several others over for a looksee. Have got my respirator back – hope I don't need it.

This morning to mark the occasion I had a complete change of underclothing – feels good. Also smothered B.D. in Keatings. Forgot to mention, one A/T gunner killed by the shelling I described last night – he'd just had his tea. Bob Lambert's (N.C.O. 1/c Sigs.) comment: 'Well at least he died with a full belly Sir.' I'm bound to admit my first thought was similar showing the enormous part the belly plays even in moments of peril! While on the topic let me mention we are eating bread these days – astonishingly more satisfying than biscuits.

1225: 'Prepare to move' and at 1230 up dashes the C.O.2 Bullnecked Oaf ex-B.S.M. 'Bull' (as in Null and Void) Melia. 'You've got to be in action (about $^3/_4$ mile away) in half an hour.' Tremendous activity. I grabbed one gun which we treble-manned out of its pit and dashed after Jimmy. The gun was in action in 22 minutes, the other three in about 35. Eventually we fired at 1315 a round smoke screen the object of which was said to be to try and make Jerry disclose his defences. The wily Hun remained obstinately silent and we came back. I cut my toenails this afternoon. Considerable noise of Light AA from the south and what could be a bomb or two. Balloon going up?

2000: So the day ends without the attack. Two of his companies sallied out about 1700 but 304 or 301, I forget which, shelled them back. The New Zealanders and more tanks – reputed 1 Amd. Div. – have arrived this side of Medenine in a counter attack role. Stand to again at 0600.

4 March

1550: Spent all the morning in the O.P. which is full of sand and midges and drew rather an imposing panorama!

1940: I was interrupted by many events which I shall now proceed to describe. First of all Wily Kaestlin dropped in (I hadn't seen him since Homs) and told me the balloon was going up at 1600 – it was then 1555 and the balloon stayed down. Then at about 1715 Jimmy had gone to the C.P. so I was in charge. Suddenly we all smelled an unmistakeably pungent small – D.M.! The gas gong was beaten and everybody got respirators on quicker than I've ever seen. Gas clear after about 5–10 minutes. Reported immediately to R.H.Q. and I understand it caused a grand flap. About the same time there was a sharp strafe by 109s of which 3* were shot down. One came over here going like hell about 20 feet up. Too low for the Bofors. We had several imposing fighter sweeps today – 26 Hurricanes, 23 Kittyhawks, 16 Hurricanes etc. Other items include an excellent mail: A long A/G from Dad (5 Feb) and an old but long letter from Pam; and from Mom. An A/G from Dennis – now a Captain at 123 O.C.T.U. Also a letter from Tony Shaw who is with 132 in Tunisia (N). He has got an M.C. but poor Owen Morgan is dead and Ronald Norman Walker is probably a P.O.W. I discovered D. is in 73 A/T also round here. A canteen is imminent with – among other delights – 150 cigarettes <u>each</u>. I've started a news bulletin each night when the wireless is free; it is extremely popular; even more so than in E Tp. where I did the same stunt.

2140: Have just written a long A.M.L.C. home and also wrote back to Tony straight away. As he seems to be commanding 496 now, I should like to get back with him. If I meet him in Tunis I shall ask him. This dugout is really palatially comfortable, and every night Findlay brings me a cup of tea and I lie in the flickering candle light and feel a great contentment. Let's hope this next – and presumably last – battle comes soon; it is tedious waiting. The A.A. boys – we have one gun to each troop – expressively told me today that they'd been promised 'Stuka pudding' soon! Forgot to mention also a letter from Dick in Gib. (15/2 – he had just got my Xmas A.M.L.C.)

5 March

2045: Tomorrow, almost for sure. That is the new deadline as computed by no less a person than the (30) Corps commander who, we have been told at an I.O.'s conference at H.Q.R.A. this evening 'has made his appreciation today'. The phrase always amuses me as it seems to indicate a certain measure of gratitude to the enemy. Actually of course the word is correctly used. Today has been quiet. A few

---

* Next day the figure rose to 4.

109s over early this morning and a dogfight in the lunch hour were about the only diversions. Also stray 109s over very high up during the day on T.A.C.R. one assumes.

Did some lengthy letter writing. One to B. – why oh why haven't I heard from her? Also to D. and Douglas Day at B.D.R.A. giving him 132 news and a long one to George. Otherwise I have been lazy until suddenly called out on this bloody L.O. job just before evening meal which I have just consumed. It was rather cold and dank – particularly the rice pudding. The AL 63 has scored a notable success and I don't think I've had a new bite for about 2 nights. Apart from an occasional scratch round the navel I am almost back to normal! Met a bloke from the Sibayak now in 57 Field at the Conference but couldn't remember his name.

2210, in bed: Just back from one of the Major's miniature Nurembergs. It is time and the attack is definitely coming off starting about 0800 with Stuka pudding. He has 3 Infantry and 3 Panzer divisions so it won't be any walkover for us. Occasionally, thinking about it all I feel a thrill of fear but I hope I won't disgrace myself and don't really think so. Saw Bob Root at the L.O. Conference. Had an excellent haircut from one of the Gordons – a Manchester barber in former days. A great quiet lies over the whole front; I wonder what tomorrow night will bring.

6 March

1230: As first light dawned this morning and we stood to our guns in the gloom, the guns on the southern sector began to roar and rumble and are still doing so now. The battle is on. So far intelligence reports show that the main German attack (as expected) went down the Medenine road but has been repulsed by the guards and N.Z. with a loss of 33 enemy tanks. Stukas were over the central sector during the morning. Our own part so far has been small. The attack on this front has been halted. The Regiment successfully engaged an M (Regimental) target during the morning and warmed the tails of 150 infantry with very accurate fire. Our own position has had about 6 shells on it at 9.30 but nobody hurt. During the morning we received another of Monty's laconic but comforting Orders of the Day, ending 'Show them what the famous 8 Army can do; good luck to you all and good hunting.' Much more noise suddenly and planes (I believe ours) above.

2345: I am tired. After tea I went up to the O.P. and the rain, which has been falling intermittently all day, joined me up there. Not much to be seen owing to the bad visibility. Came back at darkness and had to go and man the Battery C.P. phone – a bloody imposition if ever there was one. At 0100 I have to shoot the guns on harassing fire. We have already fired at 2130 and will again at 0330 but

Jimmy will be dealing with that one. The attack is making no headway. Much enemy activity in the late afternoon. Nearly got a Stuka limping for home at about 1200 feet and 50 mph – but our Bofors gun jammed – great disappointment all round. Raining and cold wind now.

7 March

Though doubtless through no pious motives the Boche has observed his Sunday as a day of comparative rest and remained fairly quiet, licking his wounds. We don't know whether he'll have another pop at dawn tomorrow or not. I rather think he will. We have done a bit of firing today ending up with a grand programme shoot in the first darkness. There is a certain excitement in the four blinding flashes and explosions as the guns blast out a salvo by night. At 0100 and 0330 last night we woke everybody in the district; actually I went off duty after taking the former and didn't hear it sound at 0330 but the infantry complained bitterly today that we ruined their night's sleep!

An excellent NAAFI today, whose main feature was 155 cigarettes – a dubious brand – Wills 'Pirate' but incredibly welcome. The men's spirits rose a mile; morale already being higher on account of the failure of the attack. My own spirits were raised by a letter at last from B. dated 26 Feb so it only took a week to get here. She has been writing regularly so God knows where the others have gone. Also a letter from Dad (A.M.L.C.) 22 Feb and one from Roden Parry (26 Feb). So that service is also being speeded up a lot. The air has been monopolised by Jerry today. Interesting appearance of 110s or Heinkel 111s, I wasn't sure which owing to cloud. Doubtless we are waiting for our attack before disclosing our strength.

8 March

Up at 0300 last night for harassing fire by the guns. Very quiet day today; Rommel seems to have retired on the Mareth positions. Somewhere, very faint as yet, I scent a move and a moonlight attack (the moon having started last night).

9 enemy planes knocked down yesterday. We lost one, the pilot being safe. The dubious planes of yesterday were apparently J.U. 88s or F.W. 137. Jerry tank losses 52, ours nil.

9 March

Very quiet day. Rommel has retired so we shall no doubt attack him soon. At long last I have a bivouac of my own instead of having to borrow or wait for somebody to go sick etc. Boys, I forgot to mention, has left the Regt. under a cloud. A/G (15/2) from Dad and a very affectionate Birthday line from Pam to whom I wrote back today. Monty has got us special Airmail priority. 3 days from home. Also wrote again to B. today. Feel dull tonight, so will stop.

10 March

These semi-idle days give one a good opportunity of making up our back mail and today I have written to Joan-Mary, Denny and Roden.

A move is fairly imminent now as we have been shown our new position much further south, and just by the scene of the recent fighting. Jimmy says the new place is lousy with midges and mosquitoes, which will be bloody. It is, then, fairly obvious that the 8th Army will attack during the moon which is not waxing. Tomorrow at first light we have to go off and do this roving troop stunt which is rather irritating and I am sure pretty useless. Just before lunch today, Jerry started throwing a few shells this way, two of which landed rather exceeding near, but the first was a semi-dud which I later dug out and put together and have sent up to R.H.Q., to the great delight of the Command Post. A 'V' ration today tho' everybody is still fairly well stocked with the poisonous little 'Pirate' brand. The possession of many cigarettes seems to drive up the desire to consume them with the greatest possible speed, and thus run out as quickly as possible! The gunners seem to have no notion of conservatism. All they ask, as they say frequently in letters home, is 'a chance to smoke themselves to death'. Nowadays I am really rather happy in this Tp. as I like the other 2 officers, the B.S.M. and N.C.O.s and the gunners themselves who seem, thank God, to have accepted me. One can always feel these things going round the gun pits and talking to them at stand-to and other times.

Am reading J.B. Priestley's *Midnight on the Desert*, a rather well-written – and over-written – account of a stay in the States. The B.C. came over again and gave the troops one of his talks which he seems to relish, and which, one is bound to admit, he does extremely well. The shadow and substance of today's oration was 'Dig Deep or Don't Shit' or 'Flies are Fuckers.' Excuse the coarseness but how I do love alliteration! Alistair, who daily becomes more congenial, likes to talk about the same things as I do which is a great boon, and I never fail to get a laugh with Jimmy. In brief the prevailing mood this evening is 'Life is sweet, brother'.

11 March

Spent all day firing about 200 rounds from a sort of sniping position a mile or so back. Warmish day and plenty of sand flying about up there. Woke up at 0525, the guard having failed to call me, and was therefore slightly pushed to be ready to move by 0530 but managed it rather breathlessly. Life is full of rumours at the moment, many of them centring round what 'Monty Says'. This is a sign of the extreme respect and admiration everybody has for the General and allied to our confidence in him all goes to push up morale and his own popularity. He is always so right about things, times his personal messages so well, and has them written – or writes them – with a kind of impersonal warmth which strikes just the right note. I don't think I have ever seen gunners whose morale and fighting spirit is as good as this troop's. However: Monty says: (1) the battle will take 4 days (2) Cleaning up Tunisia will take 8 weeks (3) The 8 Army is going straight to Tunis (!) and getting there first. We expect to move tomorrow night and zero hour is rumoured for the 17 but not divulged to lesser beings than colonels for the moment.

12 March

1150: We have just witnessed for the second day in succession about this time, the Ferry Service – the name given out here to the 18 Light Bombers who performed 4 times an hour at Alamein and since. Today they swept in from the north east; 18 fierce, blunt Marylands and hightailed Bostons, the hot sunlight glinting on their silver wings and the fighters whirling among them like little grey bats. In three formations of six, they turned west – and over the German lines up came an intense flak barrage, the black puffs breaking, it seemed through my binoculars, right in among them; they flew straight on, occasionally twisting to avoid the flak, and eventually regaining formation zoomed over us without loss, and droned away home again, the fighters still spiralling about their flanks and rear. A quiet morning; only occasionally further south – artillery – with its commotion so reminiscent of workmen banging about a half built warehouse or factory. Very hot.

13 March

1020: Last night in the cold clear light of the half moon we shifted to our new – and preliminary – position. Routine though it is, a night move never fails to give me a kick, with the bulky outlines of the Quads in the moonlight, and the slim menacing shape of the guns. To everything the dim light lends an air of mystery and danger and you really feel you might meet a German hiding in the scrub. Luckily you usually don't. Today we are more or less resting in this deep wadi covered with gorse bushes and scrub and containing, it seems, $2/3$ of all the flies, midges, mosquitoes and other flying horrors of the middle east. The guns are banging away in the mountains on our left and overhead is the occasional heavy drone of a bunch of fighters (incidentally I suggest as a collective noun 'a pugnacity' of fighters). The battle which, it appears, may be rather protracted is expected to last about 8 weeks on and off and to start in about 4 or 5 nights. Accordingly dumping parties for arms are starting tonight and pulling the stuff right forward in the F.D.L.s where our battle positions are to be. We were relieved yesterday by 50 Div. who are also in on the forthcoming party – and the 4 Indian Div. are coming in on it too. The current 'Latrinogram' also insists that after taking Tunis we the 8th Army are to take Crete, Sicily or Greece or maybe all three. 51 Div., it is said, is to be reformed on the higher establishment – i.e. a brigade of tanks and 2 of infantry. Well, we shall see.

An amazing addition to the battery strength is the 5 lambs we bought recently for fattening up. 3 are white with black faces and 2 have brown faces. They wander round the battery area quite happily, and do not seem unduly worried by gunfire. What a tragedy if they got a direct hit before we can consume them!

Same night: Have been surprisingly moved by an A/G I just received from Sheila H. who was my lover for a year. I never think of her without regret and a certain pain, because she was so terribly generous to me, and yet I am sure I was right in giving her up. Surely if you don't intend to marry a mistress who is too nice for anything else, there is nothing but that to do? Anyway I'll write back now as staidly as possible.

14 March

This afternoon the ferry service went over again and came back one light.* Also quite heavy German shelling during the afternoon. Poor weather with showers and this evening a small gale. The sheep were slaughtered today by Gunner Martin, an ex butcher who returned to his old love with much gusto. Weapon used was one knife, but it was not so gruesome to watch as I'd expected. Jimmy and A. are out with the dumping party; I go tomorrow night. Letter from George, which I've not yet read. My birthday tomorrow – 25; my god.

15 March

Devoid of incident. Beware the Ides of March?

17 March

2015 (Received birthday telegram from home 16th): Yesterday the first stages of our attack – nibbling at the outer Mareth positions – went in. I had asked to go forward with Alistair as F.O.O. to gain experience and give a hand and eventually the B.C. said I could go. Now, I lie in bed writing this in the quiet and wondering if the events of last night really occurred or were some awful nightmare – however: We left here at 6.30 pm and by about 9 had reached the infantry debussing point. There was a bright half moon and the night was noisy with our guns whose flashes could be seen round the horizon. Later the Boche air force joined in, bombing back areas by the light of bright yellow flares. All this was the artillery preparation for the Guards and 50 Div. who put in the first attacks. By 2300 we were up at the F.U.P. where the Germans started shelling us fairly violently. Luckily, we were in the middle and most of them fell just right and left of us. At about 0100 our Vickers opened up with a most devilish pandemonium, firing

*Only 17 went out that time.

across the valley we had to cross. Overhead our shells were singing towards the ridge we could just see – our objective — and enemy shells and mortar bombs fell among us. Once I heard a man screaming and sobbing as they scored a hit. I put on my tin hat and lay flat. Eventually the infantry (and my god, what guts these boys have got) went over the ridge and were driven back by m.g. fire but went on again, and we went after them with our cable reeling it out on foot. Then the fun really started. They were shelling that valley quite hard. Once we were lying flat and if you imagine we were the centre dot of a domino 5, we had 4 all round us about 20–25 yards away. They don't whistle when they get close but make a kind of screaming hiss which is very frightening. I found a Gordon with his leg badly smashed by shell splinters. He was lying there in the smoke and cold so I gave him my coat. Later I managed to get a couple of stretcher bearers to him and thus got my coat back. The bearers were as gentle as women with him and I realised the goodness as well as the evil in men afresh. Soon after this our artillery put down an ill-conceived smoke screen, which in the still night failed to rise at all, and soon we were groping and stumbling along in a dense fog which made us cough and stung our throats. I don't know what time it was when we crossed the Wadi Zeuss and got into the gap in the enemy minefield. Time lost its ordinary values, even tho' I did check it frequently on the luminous face of my watch. The minefield gap lay just the other side of a marsh and was a thin lane marked by white tapes and lighted by tiny lights which seemed to shine like beacons. Two Scorpions – the converted Matildas we use for clearing gaps – lay like huge unwieldy beetles, stuck in the bad going. Three machine gun posts stammered in front of us in the fog of smoke and the bullets buzzed and whee-ed over our heads. On the right – a mine went up and I heard for the first time that curious wailing cry 'Stretcher Bearers' and again the groaning of the wounded. Sappers were everywhere, taping and picketing the gap; they are brave and efficient. But bravery in battle is a curious business. It certainly is not accounted brave to be foolhardy, and when shells are flying, you see people lying flat and making no bones about it. I believe that we suffered casualties around this point – I suppose it was about 0330 by then and we were feeling tired, cold, and footsore and craved a cigarette which we couldn't have. To cut a long story short we were on our objective soon after 0400. In the gloom figures poked about with tommy guns and bayonets. The moon was just going down and it was getting dark. Here we left Alistair (who, I discovered, is a good calm leader, tho' he hates every minute of it – and no wonder after going through this sort of thing with every attack) and began to make our two mile journey back. Before we got to the F.U.P. we'd walked about 4 miles and I was beginning to feel tired. Some of the signallers were weary and a bit jumpy so I made them walk slowly in single file which helped. Just before we re-entered the minefield, our lives were probably saved by one of those strange twists of fortune one reads about. Our carrier (the O.P.) had torn a chunk of cable out and we had to mend it. I was impatient at the delay, but a minute later there was a blinding flash and concussion as though somebody had hit one on the chest with a heavy book. In the middle of the 'safe lane' a Sapper had trodden on a B4, largest of all the mines. When we reached the point, he was lying on our cable with one leg blown off. A minute later and we should have been there too, as we were picking our way back by going down the line. Two of his friends were trying to comfort him, tho' he was hardly conscious. 'Never mind' one was saying, 'you'll be alright, you're out of the war now, you'll be going back to Blighty' – all the things men are supposed to say. Now I know that they do. It was getting quiet now, with only the enemy guns shelling the whole area. Our tired little procession stumbled back, every now and again flattening out as shells landed near with that harsh, shattering explosion they make. Bombardier Lambert was a good influence, and stayed very steady. The journey back was, in a way, worse because you knew that once you got back there was a cigarette and a meal waiting and you so desperately <u>had</u> to get back. This feeling easily leads to a mild panic and that's why I made them walk slowly and in formation. We lost the wire this side of the Zeuss crossing but luckily I found my way and about 0520 just as the first signs of light appeared, we got to the F.U.P. where I reported to the colonel, very deep in advanced R.H.Q. At 0700 we were back on the gun position. I went to bed at 1000 and slept until 1700. Several times I was going to get up but was held fast by chains of utter weariness. At tea the B.C., who went up with the right hand column, was back for a spell, and he too – and Wagstaff – had a hot time. All three objectives were reached, tho' the Guards had been pushed off their again. However, the New Zealand force of 27,000 has gone round the rear of Mareth so we shall have the whole lot in the bag with luck. 51 Div. are scheduled for the break-through when it comes though Nobody knows quite when that will be.

Just how bad last night was I can hardly judge, but Lambert says that while it lasted, it was worse than Alamein so I've had a real baptism of fire. Now I know for myself. Next time I shall be scared <u>before</u> it starts, but knowing that everybody else is too makes things curiously easier to bear.

19 March

We moved off last night at 1930 in bad visibility, as the moon was clouded over and rain was falling. Reached our new position and dug in [in the] rain and wind and eventually got to bed about 0115. Up again at 0530 for a stand to in a wet gusty dawn. Our new position is near the F.U.P. of the other night but so far, except for a strafe, last night has been quite quiet. The 1 Gordons are also on the position. I was talking to one of their Corporals, who amazed me by his warm praise of the Gunners. 'They've never let us down yet,' he said. Discovered also that after going through the minefield the other night we laid our cable slap through long grass which was absolutely lousy with S mines and trip wires. Seen by daylight our cable wound through like a snake but by some miracle we were untouched. Since then several people have been killed on the same patch. Also disclosed that the Italian Folgone (parachute) Div. is in front of us which explained the better show they've been putting up. We have 4000 rounds dumped on this position, which should provide a very decent show of fireworks when the time comes – the time I believe being tomorrow night, one night before the full moon.

20 March

I am at 5/7 Gordon Highlands Battalion H.Q. Just the other side of Wadi Zeuss, but not where we crossed the other night; that was at 'Rocky Ford'. This is briefly entitled 'Iti Bridge'. I am I.O. at present, but hardly expect to be here very long as I believe the balloon goes up tonight. The ferry service has just gone over in a cloud of flak but not one of them was hit. The rather odd thing is that nobody heard their bombs dropping. Since they soundly bombed 50 Div. the other day the R.A.F. has been received with just a morsel of apprehension tho' the remarkable thing is that they didn't cause a single casualty. From the quantity of flak just now, I'd say there are quite a number of 88s over there; the ferry service is a sort of aerial Light Brigade 'cannon to right of them, cannon to left of them . . . .' The 5/7 have been showing me some Iti packs they captured last night which contained some of these vicious little hand grenades known as 'Red Devils'.

I find that I forgot to mention a letter from Pam (4 March) and one from Dad (1 March) I received on the 16th. The latter contained the amazing and interesting news that Bé has come back from New York with the kids. Cargo boat, 17 days. I am absolutely delighted about this, and wrote home the same day.

1000: The ferry – 18 strong (Marylands) sailed over. I saw the shining eggs falling and a tremendous screen of grey-blue smoke along the far ridge. All came back.

1200: 17 Bostons. One shot down, went spiralling downward on its back and fell some way away, with a large thump and a pillar of flame. 2 parachutes plainly visible, gleaming in the sunshine, but which side of the line they fell, one couldn't tell.

1230: 18 Baltimores; all back.

1300: And again.

1325: And again etc. during the afternoon.

2040, back at Bty: Zero is at 2245 and at Z-60 we kick off with 7 minutes rapid, from a couple of hundred field guns in the neighbourhood. Already a certain amount of nervous sparring goes on. Jerry with a few planes and guns, and ourselves with A.A. fire. A few flares daub the clear bright sky. We are firing about 420 rounds per gun tonight. Another excellent message from Monty, ending: 'Forward to Tunis! Drive the enemy into the Sea!' No doubt we shall, but he seems to have a lot of Arty. over his side; it may be a toughish job but we shall of course succeed. Monty, by the way, is fast becoming a legend and all sorts of sayings are being attributed to him – most of them doubtless untrue, but it's a case of 'Si non e vero e ben trovato' with most of them. Am now going to snatch half an hour's sleep – a habit one forms by force of circumstances in the army at war (in peace of course it is unnecessary; one snatches an hour's worth instead).

21 March

0945: Punctually at 2145 the barrage roared and crashed out and went on violently until 0245. I have never heard such a noise. All around as far as the eye could see were the flashes and flickers of guns in action and the terrific concussion was such that down in the C.P. the match with which you lighted a cigarette trembled and faltered in the air. The guns fired on average about 430 rounds each. At 2.45 a small pool of quiet formed, broken only by an occasional stutter of machine guns or a droning plane (both sides were busy bombing by flarelight). Then, just as our ammo lorries came back on the position, Jerry started shelling hard, over on our left with some quite heavy calibre guns which we thought may be 5.9s. They explode with a gigantic and raucous sneeze. However, he kept away from us, though during the evening he had shown signs of encroaching on our privacy.

At 0300 we served tea and soup to the weary gunners and by about 0415 dropped into bed, but at five to five our own guns behind us opened up again with a devilish clattering so there wasn't much sleep before stand to at 0530. Most people are now sleeping in the sunlight, including Jimmy whose snores I can hear from here. I did gun numbers on all the guns last night and found the noise and blast makes one almost punch drunk. The desire for a few minutes quiet is very great.

Jerry is still noisy this morning tho' not as noisy as he was. The attack seems to be making reasonable headway. Met Willy again yesterday and had an airgraph from Gerard – still in the Survey Regiment at home, lucky sod (tho' I wouldn't have missed this for the world).

I found the line I re-appreciated last night was Grenfell's: 'The thundering line of battle stands, and in the air death moans and sings . . .' There's a lot in a little there.

1950: A.M.L.C. from Dad (9/3) and Maurice (10/3) now back in England. Also a letter from D., now I believe with the N.Z. force approaching Gabes in our encircling movement. Shelled today by a most godawfully large one. They say there are 'Crumping Charlies' in front of us and that it was one of them (210 mm). If not it was a 5.9. Anyway it was the biggest shell I've had within

75 yards of <u>me</u>. Excellent canteen with 70 cigarettes and a bottle of gin. Expect to fire tonight; also a large battle in Mareth area is said to be imminent. Initial attack has made small bridgehead. Mr. Churchill is speaking at 2100 and we have linked on a tannoy loudspeaker to listen; bound to be good.

2340: I am on duty in the Tp.C.P. Except for the drone of planes the night is very silent. We fired off about 75 rds. at 2200 and are firing again at 0130 when my duty ends and Jimmy takes over. Mr. C. was good – rather more subdued than usual and talking of postwar planning. He warned us the war may go on for at least 2 years longer, which is what I thought anyway. By then, if still alive, I shall have given over 5 years of my life to the army. And 5 of the best. I find this a depressing thought. Typically he ended up 'I have just had a telegram from Gen. Montgomery, telling me the 8th Army is on the move, and that he is satisfied with their progress . . . .' The N.Z. are 18 miles SW of Gabes, and in touch with enemy armour; the timing is beginning to work out. Large bomb dropped near our position soon after dark. Full moon, misty, wild night. Roll on 1.30.

0200: Off to bed. The bellowing fury of our guns has ceased; let me hope for a few quiet hours.

22 March

1220: Jerry counter attack expected 1245. He has been shelling the gun line heavily since 1115. Some casualties tho' none of ours yet. 304 is reputed to have had a direct on one of their guns. Battered cartridge cases all over the end of our area.

1800: These actually came from a 301 ammo. dump. We are being shelled at the moment by heavies and have been intermittently all day by all calibres including these bloody 210s which come at you like an express train. Most of the day, therefore, has been spent in a slit trench with swarms of metal bees buzzing over our heads. Several bivvies have been holed. Ferry Service very active. 15 trips.

24 March

0945: The attack on this front has failed. We have lost our bridgeheads and 30 tanks and 50 Div. and 4(1) Div. have been replaced by 51 Div. However the N.Z. are still doing well, and the 7 Armoured have gone round to give a hand. Naturally this is a disappointment, but such is everybody's confidence in Monty that there is no alarm or despondency. Also we shall probably crack him in our next effort which may be in 3 or 4 days – no less. Nearly had it yesterday from an 88 which burst about 15 yards from the C.P. while I was in the open. I fell flat and felt it breathe hotly over my head. Very hot yesterday and again today; we expect to go into K.D. again soon. Wrote to Pam yesterday.

25 March

1715: I was bloody tired last night and the weather is again getting hotter, and with it everybody's patience and temper is growing shorter. I was on duty first shift last night and after a night of hectic firing got to bed about 0300. Jerry started chucking back some heavy stuff which in the still night blasted and clanged menacingly about the place. This afternoon I was laying No. 2 gun when he sent 6 rounds (88) suddenly, straight on to the gun position. Nobody hurt. Rather a disaster last night when 120 casualties occurred in the Black Watch from our own guns. It was not this Regt. but that hardly matters.

Jerry has a nasty assortment over in the hills, including a bloody great mortar with which he landed 2 on the post the other day. You only hear a crack like one of our guns and a second later a huge explosion with great blast. Another is his heavy which growls away with a hollow boom, but gives plenty of warning; throws a nasty big shell though. Blowing a lot of sand at the moment and my bivvy is plunging. Mediums plonking away south of us. B.B.C. reported last night 'fiercest fighting of the N. African Campaign' on this Mareth front, which does begin to look a tough nut to crack. But crack it we shall.

26 March

2100: Hot, sultry day with sandstorms. 'Busty' the local Bofors officer has gone to Cairo on a course and promised to send me another book like this; which I badly need as I've only about 3 weeks more writing in this – and some milk which is impossible almost to procure. Quiet day much improved by an excellent letter (14/3) from George, long and affectionate. I have written back. Fired at 0350. I am 3rd shift tonight.

27 March

1440: Again very hot with a strongish wind bringing the sand off the desert. Yesterday it was 105 °F in the sun. Today it is undoubtedly hotter. The guns throw out a dusty boomerang each time they fire, and the gunners are serving them clad in pants and a tin hat. Jimmy and I are also stripped to the waist and in shorts again. Wrote to George's cousin Sybil this morning.

28 March

1400: The enemy is reputed, and reported to be leaving the line, and an advance is imminent. Again terribly hot today. Nature notes: I saw a chameleon yesterday for the first time. It changed colour 3 times in 2 minutes; amazing. At night the crickets here are as loud as nightingales.

29 March

0900: Moved at 0300 in the light of a waning moon, and have now crossed the Wadi Zigzaou – where Jerry had the most formidable trench and pillbox system I have ever seen. We expect to move forward soon. Have just breakfasted in an orchard, cool and green and full of palms.

2040: 5 miles South of Gabes which has now fallen to us. The countryside improves and one sees long, green grass laced with poppies, and great patches of sunflowers. However it is still very dusty; the dust is as fine as talcum powder and gets in everything. Atmosphere in the mess tonight very reminiscent of the first Xl at school after an away win. Mareth line extremely deep, formidable and excellently camouflaged. Lucky we turned it as far as 51 Div. is concerned as I am certain a frontal attack – even if successful – would have caused enormous casualties. Not as much mining as I expected tho' what there was, was cunningly placed and rather successful. Jerry is artful in the extreme in this respect. It is said that we have 9000 prisoners now. The end of the campaign is in sight. I expect one more sharp battle on the Tunis perimeter itself, but the 3 airforces should make it a foregone conclusion. Many fighters in the air today including some 109s.

30 March

1415: Sitting in very hot sunshine in the same place. We had orders to move at 12, but they were duly countermanded and now we are not to move till tomorrow – so I expect to hear somebody yell 'Prepare to Advance' any minute now. This place is liberally anointed with fleas (how difficult it is to kill them) and what the B.C. usually describes to the Troops as 'excreta' of all varieties from goat to storm troop. Suspicious phenomenon is increased friendship of Wagstaff who 'Jack Old Boys' me all over the place. It is rather like treading a human minefield . . . he has transferred his dislike to a creature who looks like the invisible man but is visible and is called Houston. With Forshaw this E Tp. trio leave a certain amount to be desired as far as Kultur is concerned. Being very dogmatic Houston returns Wagstaff's fire with vigour, much to my enjoyment on the 'Greek meets Greek' principle. But why is Wagstaff genial? That is the problem I must probe. Letter from Anne.

31 March

Quiet but informative day, the latest form being as follows. We (51 Div.) are now relieving the N.Z. Div. and pushing on to Sfax. From that point we apparently stand aside and let the Americans take Tunis. As they are probably completely incapable of doing any such thing I've no doubt we'll do it in the end, but presumably they have to be allowed the kudos if possible. Strong in our own complacency, the prospect has not unduly depressed us! Our own Brigade (153) has been allotted the task of pursuit force once 154 has broken resistance on the Wadi Akarit 12 miles North of Gabes where the Boche is now fighting a delaying action. The Yanks are closing in Eastwards from El Gettan. The curtain is going up on the last act. April should see the players taking their bows. Another blazing day. Yesterday we were given a malaria lecture by the M.O. It appears the Sfax area and northwards is very malarial and various countermeasures are to be introduced including a pill which makes you feel as bad as malaria. God has nothing on the War office when it comes to moving in a mysterious way . . . I am full of loathsome fleas.

1 April

2000: Information and orders exactly as yesterday. We move tomorrow; myself plus advance party at the objectionable hour of 0530. Wrote two airgraphs to the family in N.Y. today as an A/G service has just been started. Full of strong British understatement . . .

Our Brigade has been given the exciting name of Spearforce. The Corps L.O. comes back from Gabes with tales of lovely women . . . (Sfax for Syph?) One reason I shall be glad to move is to get rid of the fleas which are becoming an absolute pestilence. Am getting fairly sunburnt again. Accent on burnt for knees.

2 April

1430: Up at 0500. As daylight grew stronger we saw Gabes very cool and white in the sunshine. But when you got close you saw the great damage done by shelling and bombing, houses smashed, a great pile of Teller mines on the neat little airfield, and somebody brewing up in what was recently somebody else's drawing room. And even at that early hour terrific traffic both ways as the Army moves forward. Our new position is in a large wadi, very hot just now, and full of flies. A few miles in front great clouds of smoke have risen at intervals as the 18 bombers go over at 1/2 hourly intervals and occasionally guns boom in the still, hot afternoon. 301 and the A.A. took the wrong track, ran into an Italian ambush and lost some men and vehicles. I have a headache, not an unusual event, due to the glare.

2015: 'Confusion now hath made his masterpiece.' As follows:
After sending 2 men per sub. up here to dig gunpits all day (a task which they laboriously and excellently completed) and following them up with all the Nos. 1 during the afternoon (without rations) the Regt. for reasons best known to those above decide (a) not to arrive here tonight, (b) not to occupy these battle positions. So now we are waiting in the cold gusty evening for 4 rations and about 15 sets of blankets. I, it is true, am snug in bed with a phone beside me. This is an excellent dugout, being a converted watercourse with a bivvy over the top. I can even assume the vertical for donning and doffing trousers – the

criterion in dugout design. A good dogfight after tea. 4 Spits v. 3 109s. The latter fled unceremoniously for home, one trailing black smoke. The crackle of cannon was loud in the approaching twilight. I wonder where flies go at night. I had at least 50 in here this afternoon and now, having just killed 4 very dopey ones, I can, I am glad to say, see none. My dwindling diary forbids more garrulousness, but sometime I must digress on the *Herries Chronicle*, a piece of lush turgidity with which I pass quiet hours. For now – enough.

4 April

1115: One of the more interesting features is the increase of enemy air activity. At dusk last night just before we moved forward to this battle position 4 or 5 bombers came over and hit an ammo dump near us; it went on flaming and exploding for an hour with brilliant pink flashes and showers of sparks and flame. One of these raiders was brought down in an enormous sheet of flame. Later, just when we were coming on the position, flares were dropped over us making it as bright as day, and some bombs wump-wumped several hundred yards away. Up here we can see miles back into our own lines and watch Jerry shelling various points. On our right is the Med., very blue and shining in the sunlight, but the wind up here (we are nearly 60 metres high) is cutting.

Today 4 bombers came over, bombed and escaped with great unconcern in an absolute cloud of flak, and later 6 fighters, who started two good brews further back. They flew back about 100 feet up so were not engaged very effectively. From here I can even see 3 large tankers putting into Gabes; the view in fact is like a rather well designed miniature range. Shells are at the moment whistling about, some bursting fairly near; about 30 have gone over so far. I think 301 is getting it. Yes, that was quite vicious while it lasted but we were lucky; most of it fell behind or to our right. Something is burning with a bright red flame 2 or 3 thousand yards back.

He has, it is said, 4 Divs. in front of us, and Alistair said last night that according to Brigade H.Q. this is to be the battle of the campaign. By the way, we have Gren. Guards to our right – somehow they don't look as much at home out here as our own chaps.

5 April

1825: The attack goes in in the early hours of tomorrow morning and we shall be firing for five hours. I don't know much more than this myself but I understand we should have taken our objectives by noon tomorrow.

Fairly quiet day. A cigarette famine is on us. I am smoking my last one at the moment. Actually the B.C. collected 750 from the N.Z. today and is supposed to be letting us have some. In 2 days a Naafi is supposed also to be arriving.

Certain amount of flarelight bombing last night but I was so preoccupied chasing a flea it didn't worry me much. Quietish day with desultory shelling by both sides. Wrote home and to Debroy and Val. (Forgot to mention that I fetched the N.Z. tubes myself.)

6 April

0950: 'And all night long the noise of battle rolled . . .' starting yesterday evening with flarelight bombing and the uneasy stammering of machine guns and continuing now with a tumult of gunfire from Jerry out in front of us. We were working till about 1130 last night and up again at 0330. At 0415 the now familiar crash of the barrage started up, the guns bright in the light of many flares and their black smoke curling and hanging in the yellow flare. We have so far fired 3 barrages and a concentration. It was strange to see the sky lighten as we fired and the guns were starkly outlined against it.

The sun rose red out of the sea on our right and still the endless firing of the guns smote on our ears. Tremendous jubilation everywhere. We are breaking through; thousands of prisoners, and hundreds are coming through here. The Spezia div. crammed hundreds of them into 3 tonners. Dust rising in the wind. I have just been to see the prisoners – there are indeed several thousand, mostly ragged, mostly cheerful, some half naked, some on bare feet. I have never seen such a rabble – these are the boast of the Italian Empire – these 'the 8 million bayonets' – my god, some of them don't look more than 16. Alistair's O.P. party captured some, also a Beretta sub m.g. and a Breda M.G. and quite a lot of horrible cigarettes – if we have indeed broken through we may expect to move today or tomorrow. Jerry is still shelling ferociously the area in front of us. Letter from D. (25/3). Jerry counterattacked till dusk when he sent over 6 J.U. 88s. Three of these were shot down with the utmost promptitude by a mass of flak from us. This about 5.30. They were flying low and presented the perfect target. (5 shot down in all.)

7 April

0930: Early this morning a Jerry bomber dropped a stick of 500 pounders behind us and damaged two of our trucks (very noisy). Enemy said to have gone; we follow today.

8 April

1300: On the road to Sfax. We moved at 0600 after taking up posn. last thing yesterday and have so far moved about 15m.

1700: Moved off as I wrote these words and went into action about 1500, we being foremost troop on this sector. Considerable retaliatory shelling by Jerry.

Much stuff left behind by him, and we have captured 57 guns. Certain amount of mining on the way up. We have now done about 20 miles today. Rationing was a problem as it all had to be dished out from the Bty. cookhouse to vehicles at the first halt. Consequently we've had bloody little to eat all day. Sunny day but much wind and sand. The army is pushing as hard as it can go – an amazing sight with guns, lorries, wireless trucks, tanks, every damn thing lining the road and open country to each side of it for miles and miles. The main battlefield, on the minefield at the Wadi Akarit, was just as one imagines a battlefield. Shell holes everywhere, broken guns, boxes of captured ammo, smashed trucks, equipment, overcoats, and here and there a dead man. We are said to have lost quite a few men there, which doesn't surprise me. The R.A.F. have been giving him hell today – all day long the Ferry Service and hundreds of fighters flying with beautiful, lethal precision. He is now shelling quite near us again, so I'll close down.

9 April

2200 (by torchlight): In a wadi; overhead the sinister whine of a German bomber, followed by a loud crash; he has unloaded perhaps 1/2 a mile away . . . 20 miles to the NE great red flashes spring up as suddenly as a loss of temper as Sfax glows and burns; Jerry demolition no doubt. Up at 4.30 today and hotly in pursuit all day with several actions. It has been rather fun for me as I am doing G.P.O. and go ahead with the Recce Party. The enemy has retreated in a hurry leaving much ammo and materials. Also prisoners. I 'interrogated' 9 Italians near Marhares today. In the town itself, smashed M/T was still leaving. General Wimberly has been much in evidence. It has been a wonderful day for loot! have collected a marquee for the Officers Mess, a pair of Jerry sun goggles (v. good), a Thermos flask, a bayonet dagger, a pair of braces, a wonderful first Aid outfit (Jerry) and sundry other items. And to round off the day, Alistair sent in a half track German vehicle – almost new. All the time I am writing bombers drone overhead dropping amber flares, one hears the whistle of a bomb, nearer, nearer, and then wump! A splintering crash shakes the ground.

It's an evil sound, that growl in the moonlight. Just now one dissolved into flames and came twisting earthwards going up in a great flash and explosion. Can't imagine why. There can't have been any survivors . . . have seen a few dead today, also one of our targets, an Italian artillery mule team scattered by shells with the animals (smelling vilely sweet) lying by the road with all four legs stuck in the air.

I am too tired to describe (4 bombs, 4 more) the chase, with everything pressing on, urgency, speed, more speed – forward always forward, with tempers growing short, no time to eat (this literal), no time to shave for 3 days, the icy dawn wind and the sand, sore face, sore eyes, mouth chapped so that even drinking tea hurts. The tanks churning a great opaque cloud, armoured cars, crews in magenta berets, the guns, always the guns to the fore and overhead the preying wings of our fighter bombers and 18 silver bombers calmly cleaving the clouds. Saw A. in the early hour and had a few amusing minutes; he is in for a medal – deserved. Also worthy of note: between us during the last few days we've collected about 170 gallons of very good Iti wine. Must end now, so tired, one day I hope to write all this so much better.

Sfax tomorrow?

11 April

2100: Yesterday morning we entered Sfax, not very far behind our O.P.s and camels, and the first of the field artillery to go in. We had an amazing reception; cheering and clapping and flowers thrown among us. 'We have waited, it seems, so long' one Frenchman told me, 'and we knew that only the 8th Army could save us.' The populace also regaled us liberally with wines; in consequence there were few sober people last night. I was cheery in the afternoon but unfortunately had to get sober as we were trying to winch the troop out of an enormous bog, in the middle of which was a small concentration (ex German) camp. Up at 0400 this morning and back 5 miles where we (the Div. Arty.) are comfortably leaguered among the endless lines of olive trees. I think we shall only be here a few days however – tho' this is only a guess. A.M.L.C. from Dad (30/3) and also a letter at last from B. whose letters are obviously going astray somewhere tho' she says mine are coming there alright. Jimmy and Alistair are left back on the other position so I have a section and the signals here only.

Sfax is smashed up and almost foodless but has a generous quota of pretty girls. Very chic, very French and quite charming. Monty was on the round yesterday having lunch and the troops are said to have passed him yelling 'good old Monty' while he waved back. The man is becoming as great an inspiration to us as Rommel to the Jerries. Planes overhead; I don't know whose; in any case I am ending now because I am very tired. Up at 0500 yesterday, winching till about midnight and up in the middle of the night again today. And now – blissful thought – reveille 0730 – a real lie-in!! How one's viewpoint changes.

12 April

0940: I was too tired last night to be intelligent. Now let me add a few notes on Sfax etc. As you approach the city down the good main road you see miles and miles of these extremely symmetrical orchards and the barley fields flame with poppies. A few round squat Teller mines line various corners as a reminder that the verges are apt to be dangerous – a fact one frequently has to overlook when in a hurry.

The town itself is reduced in most parts to ruins, specially the centre, the Docks and the railway yard which is a shambles of twisted girders, blackened petrol tanks and smashed engines. There is practically nothing to buy (the inhabitants seem to live on vegetables and have had no meat for ages) but one can get wine and a few eggs and loaves of rather good bread (which is rationed to inhabitants). Almost the first thing to appear on white walls was our ubiquitous HD and everywhere is the tricolour and union jack and stars and stripes. The inhabitants would do anything for us – 'Vive le huit armée' I saw written above one sort of pub. I was talking to a Russian acting War Correspondent (he is a Lieut. Col.) just before entering the city. He was short and genial and very pleased and had a complete front set of gold teeth which gleamed in the sunshine. I asked him what the Russians think of us: 'The 8th Army – very good – the rest; civilians in uniform – but you are learning, you are learning . . .' The entry was like the League of Nations! Americans (a few, a very few) French and us. I saw the de Gaulle column going through yesterday looking very smart in blue sidecaps and flying the tricolour with the cross of Lorraine superimposed. We now possess (F Tp.) a Spandau heavy m.g., a Breda m.g. and Beretta sub m.g. and a few Jerry rifles – useful additions. Sousse has fallen. The 8 Army now linked with the 1st presses North. Wrote home and an A/G to Pam.

13 April

2150: Last night I dreamed of Joan Mary and today I received a lettercard from her.* Such things always start me thinking, was it mere coincidence? Yes, probably; and yet . . . well I can't tell the answer nor anyone else but it teases the brain. The men found a piano in the house at the end of the orchard today, and we have been having a singsong tonight. All very nostalgic with 'Roses that fade in Picardy' and the Desert Song and 'I'll see you again' rising among the olive trees in the moonlight. And our Rubicon still lies 150 miles northwards where the trapped remains of the Afrika Korps are waiting. On to Tunis . . .

    Tea with Nob Sutton at 304.

14 April

1600: Desultory rain and a chilly wind has lowered my morale today. I just want the war to end and to go back home again and write newspaper stories. Instead of which I live here doing a job I did 2 years ago with mentally inferior bumpkins doing the job I should be doing. The man Houston I mentioned some time ago is really almost unbelievably obnoxious. He looks almost the double of Himmler which is (since yesterday, when it occurred to me) now his nickname. The B.C. has turned out to be a crashing bore, a snob, and very selfish. The forthcoming battle begins to take on an unpleasant aspect. It is raining; bah! bah! and again bah!

*Replied today.

16 April

1700: I haven't written for a couple of days, partly because I've been bored and dispirited, and partly because nothing very noteworthy has been happening. One evening we had a 'party' in the mess attended by most of the 304 Subalterns – rather a nice crowd – and a good few senior officers. Actually we get guests most nights now as we have a barrel of vino which we looted en route and which in virgo intacto probably holds about 200 gallons. Probably owing to its presence we have had 2 visits from Col. Perry the C.O. in the last week – the only two I remember. He had an 'inspection' yesterday of clothing (!) and told everybody to stop saying and writing that we were going home because we bloody well weren't so there: net result of such a blank denial nil, as everybody (not me by the way) with a few exceptions thinks we really <u>are</u> now and this is just 'security'. We are L.O.B. for the next show it seems and with the lack of action comes an increase in bullshit; but it isn't too bad as yet. Acute shortage of cigarettes and airmail lettercards and razor blades. A letter last night from Rear Adm. Cochrane, Jock's father, in reply to the one I send the latter's widow. Very restrained, very like Jock. He asks me to send details of Jock's M.C. which I shall try to do.

Speculation rife as to our next campaign. 4 favourites: England for N. France. Sicily or Greece and possibly Crete. Turkey. Burma. I think the second batch is likely, the first is by no means impossible. I wish Jock were still with us; he was so restful in the mess and Harben is forever telling stories of the prominent people he knows or talking shop. Failing these two topics he spends his time complaining about the boils on his bottom or having breakfast in bed on account of a hangover. Not altogether a success, our Eric or Little by Little.

18 April

(Sunday) 1445: The usual desultory feeling aided and abetted by hot sunshine. This morning I was I/C Church Parade, which always infuriates me owing to the complete incompatability of our life and going to church. I know this is a subject meet for many hours' discussion but I have seen men at church and dismiss it in one line. Bulls. increases. Orderly this and Regimental that, and so on. We begin dock fatigues on the 22. Buthy has a rumour that we are moving up to Pont du Falis at that date. The 'going home' controversy still rages. Wrote to Jock's father yesterday. Another horror is P.T. before breakfast. I simply loathe prancing and twisting early in the morning, and anyway nobody has any kit. But things like that are mere details!

20 April

1430: Today quite suddenly at breakfast came the information that the Regt. would move today, and now we are standing ready to do so. We are moving as

Div. Arty., our infantry, are going as far as El Djem tonight where we leaguer. After that nobody knows but I believe we are going into action tomorrow night. I personally am rather glad, as the life of boredom and bullshit entailed in stabilising here rather gets me down, specially with L by L smoking his interminable cigarettes after we have run out. Have been playing a bit of bridge which made a pleasant change. (Lost on nearly every occasion!) Letter from George yesterday and another – rather better than usual – from Pam today. Some grateful Gunner has stolen my German sun goggles – a great blow. P.T. this morning – taken by me!

1830, on the road: Just had an hour's halt for a meal. My 'team' is magnificent. Headed by the villainous Turner (see Diary 2) they whip out an excellent meal in superb time! Situation improved (a) by the fact that most of them went on dock fatigues today and scrounged food, (b) by appearance of wogs from whom 16 eggs were rapidly and expertly extracted for a very small amount of tea. And now, on . . .

21 April

0800: Leaguered last night in an orchard short of El Djem. We are moving on in 15 minutes. Destination unknown but said to be Enfidaville. Rained in the night, but the sun is shining now. Passed 2 dead wogs last night by a smashed jerry truck; must have been booby trapped. I wish my new diary would come up from Cairo as this is almost finished. Memorable event: Issue of an egg per man for breakfast.

22 April

0920: Moved all yesterday up roads crammed with every conceivable form of transport including some American, occupants all busily chewing or spit-ting. After the spick and span aspect of trucks at home, the hairs of C.O.s would turn grey (if not grey already) as nearly all have names of towns, women, or just wisecracks all over the bonnet. One gets to recognise some trucks like 'Busty Nora' or 'Small Fry' from seeing them plying up the L. of C. Talked to a few yank soldiers who, in olive green, look like Italians or, in those helmets they wear, Germans. The last thing you'd expect is to find them on <u>our</u> side. However they are pleasant enough with the goddam and chew-ing gum.

Reached our battle position west of Enfidaville (51 Div. is taking over from 50 Div. who are being removed so it is put about, from the 8 Army) and they dug all night as the ground is like iron. I stayed up till 0300. There was a bright moon from time to time, but chiefly cloudy with rain. Same today. We are in the hills here and it is infernally noisy when the guns fire, 'reverberating round the echoing hills –'. The 1 Army attacked last night, and the order of battle shows that we have 17 Divisions round the perimeter, including 4 Armoured divs., a pretty formidable array. I am most depressed, and in a vile temper and it is raining. There are cacti everywhere and everything is mud, mosquitoes and misery. Jerry has a very strong posn. here; it took the 4 Indian Div. 12 hours to get forward $2^1/2$ miles.

23 April

On the 'Bleeder' which is the 5/7 Battn. H.Q. in the hills round Enfidaville. We – A., Wagstaff, Monty and I – are up here manning in turn a forward O.P. – so exposed that no movement is permissible by day at all. We moved off by first dark and eventually reached an enormous hill which was so steep everything had to be carried up and for this purpose we had a carrying party. The sides (composed of rock and shifting soil) were not quite perpendicular, but the distinction was not apparent when climbed with a heavy load. We were viciously shelled on the way up and crouched low sweating and cursing and the shells whistled and burst round us, throwing up showers of dirt on us. In the darkness, figures of the Ghurkas pottered about. They came out last night. Well, having got here, back we went for another load. A. and I went back to the maintenance point and eventually started climbing back after midnight, heavily laden with bedding. There was sporadic shelling – also 'thunder, lightning and rain!' – and up the cliff went the Gordons with mules carrying ammo – real mountain warfare. Everybody was bloody tired but I though bearing up rather well. I met Peter Forshaw (1st F.D. Regt., a Woolwich and ship acquaintance) also saw the 61 A/t contingent the day before. Example of H.D. humour: Scene dark night (last night) occasional moon, more than occasional rain. Enter nonchalant Gordon with mule.

A.:   Didn't know you people had mules.
N.P.:   Oh the Gordons can handle anything, Sir; by morning he'll have a Gordon cap badge on his belly.

Exit.

This is a hot spot but so far today Jerry has been fairly quiet. The slit trench A. and I dug from c. 0230 till c. 0400 (stand to was at 0500) was useful when a shell landed rather too near after 'breakfast' (a courtesy title as we have hardly any rations and now no water at all). However, all one hears now is the occasional boom of our guns and m.g.s and the clunking of picks on the stony soil. All very peaceful after last night's stumbling and falling, and alternate bath of sweat, and icy cold.

24 April

1020: Sporadic shelling all yesterday with some of it uncomfortably close but no casualties to us, although the Gordons had a couple. A. relieved Wagstaff, and I go up tonight. Monty has gone back to the Bty. It was terribly hot yesterday and the flies were absolutely bloody. Also owing to misunderstandings we had practically no water. They are shelling heavily at the moment just over our heads and bits of splinter are falling about the place. Among other things he used yesterday was his multiple mortar which moans through the air like an air raid siren. Rather a disturbing creature: usually known as 'that moaning bastard' or moaning Minnie. Letter from Dorothy and I wrote home yesterday.

1700: More activity today. He has been extremely spiteful and we are getting a good bit of 105 and 88 fire. A. rang up a quarter of an hour ago and in a rather shaken voice told me his O.P. had been more or less blown in and he himself stunned. Luckily it was no worse. Also the O.P. received bullets in the surrounding sandbags this morning but they didn't penetrate. I view the 24 hours I shall spend there from about 11 tonight with a certain distaste . . .

26 April

1200 – This O.P. was known as Garci Feature (or Djebel Garci): Relieved Alistair about 0100 on the morning of 25 April. Hell of a climb to the O.P. which is perched right on the peak of a well registered (ex Jerry) hilltop. The O.P. being blown in (and it must have been as near a direct as makes no difference) it took Signaller Mealings and myself till first light to mend it. Caution was enforced by Spandau bullets. I don't intend (being tired) to go into details now except to say that we had 80 105mm shells in the area yesterday which was no sort of fun, specially as about 10 were so close they filled the O.P. dugout with splinters and fragments. One large piece hit my tin hat and knocked me a bit silly. I took on an enemy mortar O.P. 400 yards or so across the valley as a close destructive shoot (our own troops being just below it) and got my gunfire on target. Was glad to leave the bloody place, lost our way and got here almost weeping with nervous exhaustion. A few shells down the line then a quiet night. Good chit from 'Good Show' Harben. Sandy Cowie in O.P. now. Terribly hot.

29 April

1540: Came down for a rest last night being the last to come down. A. and the B.C. came the night before. Had no sleep the night before as I was busy establishing communications till about 0400 and after that the fleabites kept me awake. Not much to write up – anyway too tired. Am going up to new O.P. tonight to relieve Alistair. Had a good 2-gallon bath this morning. Washed off the cloying smell of corpses much in evidence up front – some decapitated by the Indians.

1 May

2045: The rain patters on my tent, the crickets cry out into the darkness, and I try to recap a few of the last 48 hours up to last night. On the 29th it turned out I wasn't to relieve A., but establish a second O.P. 500 yards in front of the forward infantry – in fact in no mans land. This rather shook me. It was an inky night when we arrived at Bn. H.Q. and the rain fell, cold and dismal. I had Kelly (a grand signaller whom I am going to recommend for an M.M.) and L/Bdr. Flint with me. Spandau bullets and the occasional harsh crash of a mortar bomb completed the dreary scene. We got to 'bed' about 0215 and left for our post at 0400 accompanied by 2 Infantry Observers. The O.P. was (is) right on a crest and gives a superb view but is hot, mosquito, flea, fly and ant-ridden. An infantry patrol guards it by night. Just before first light an enemy patrol came within 250 yards. I saw and heard them quite clearly. Spent till darkness in that hole, observing and shooting. Next day same again so I was tired by the time I got back last night after A. had relieved me, and slept for 12 hours. Tonight Jimmy has relieved A. and I expect to go up tomorrow night. It is bloody tiring work tho' we weren't much troubled yesterday. A few shells and m.g. bullets, and his mortars were very active. I got some direct hits with salvoes on the house he's using for a sort of H.Q. on both days and saw the entire structure disappear in clouds of smoke for about 50 seconds. Think I killed some inside. Felt nothing but gloating exultation. Nerves a bit strained. Some shells on the gun line today. Am still rather tired. Diary less elaborate for this reason. All our airmail burned on plane yesterday. It'll be too bad if the enemy spots our O.P. – he hasn't so far – as he'll turn all the mortars in the world on to it. This will be to say the least unpleasant. B.C. has coy little trick of finding out all he can about O.P. area from other officers and then relaying same as his own discoveries. Was very interested in my panorama last night, is living comfortably but dangerously oh how dangerously at Bn. H.Q.

4 May

1700: Since I wrote both Gordon Wagstaff and A. have gone ill and been evacuated. Spent all yesterday in the O.P. and got some good shooting. Line got cut so I had to crawl out and mend it. Certain amount of stuff and bullets falling so not too comfortable. I am going to E Tp. in the morning as Tp. Commander tho' whether I get a temp. Captaincy or not is not yet certain. It would appear that R.H.Q. thinks I have 'done well' lately which shows what a little self-advertisement can do. Went to hot mobile shower this afternoon, with B.C. Wonderful luxury.

5 May

1600: No captaincy for at least 29 days owing M.E.G.O. allowing A. and W. to retain rank. Saw Colonel last night. Good chit. 3 109s just over – hell of a din. None down.

9 May

Since I wrote, Tunis and Bizerta have fallen and what remains of the axis is cooped up in the mountains opposite our posn. and in the C. Bon peninsula. We pulled out of the line last night and tomorrow start a 450 miles drive to the Philipville area via Kairouan, Sbeitla, and Tebessa. To do what nobody knows. The entire div. is going. On night 7 May took over O.P. in pouring rain which persisted all night. Yesterday afternoon we were heavily mortared. I fired back but ineffectively. They were very hard to locate. A. has come back. I am still Comd. E. Tp. but don't expect for much longer. The B.C. gets on my nerves. As a matter of fact so does everybody else so I must be tired. Lettercard (23 Ap.) from Dad yesterday. Wrote recently to Pam, B., and Debroy from whom I heard a day or two ago. Very hot. I am sweating profusely. Move at 0615 tomorrow.

Does this move near Algiers presage Com. Op. training and an attack on Sicily I wonder?

Same night in bed: The move is now cancelled. No details given so I can't give any more than that bald statement. We have taken Hammamet and Zaghouan so what is left of the axis this side of C. Bon is doomed; it has no M.T. anyway. I think it will all be over in a week or two. Round Enfidaville and Taklarouma bloody spot of late) the guns of 56 Div. boom out in the gusty wind under a pale young moon. Thank heavens for the prospect of 9 or 10 hours sleep.

Mom's birthday today. I sent her a wire on 2 May amid the turmoil. Pity this diary has been so dull lately but I've been living events not writing them. Richard Sutton is going to R.H.A. which is a pity – I shall miss him.

Masses of fighters going out NE all day.

11 May

Wagstaff returned today so I relinquished command of E Tp. much to the relief of Forshaw who had writhed under it. The Bty. and Bde. move tomorrow towards Algiers, but the B.C. has sent me on a roving commission (ie. booze and cigarettes) with one truck, Driver Mealings and Findlay. We are now leaguered in Kairouan and shall make for Pichon tomorrow morning.

In the last rays of a faint orange sunset the whiteness of the holy city was vaguely ominous; perhaps just a stupid fancy. Nice lettercard from Bé (27 April).

We now have about 30,000 prisoners and the axis is surrounded by land, sea and air on C. Bon. Wild rumours of homegoing. Almost certainly fallacious.

13 May

Nothing new in Pichon except an American Colonel who restored my faith in Hollywood. Thence to Maktar over some high (4000 feet) mountain passes and there I met a Capt. Waters RA, I/C Police in these parts. He invited me to spend the night at Ebba Ksour (where I am now writing) if I completed my mission. This I did very successfully at Le Crib where I got 10 bottles of whisky, 6000 cigarettes, 600 razor blades and 468 bars of chocolate. Lack of money prevented large scale activity! Came back via Le Kef, a pretty town perched right on the top of a hill, and thence to E-K where I ran over a dog and had to shoot it. Today we may visit Souk Aluas or Bone or both. 150,000 prisoners, and Von Armin a prisoner.

Later: Reached S-A via 'perilous' mountain roads extravagantly marked by 1 Army. Town Major has placed me at elaborately named Grand Hotel D'Orient. In honour of my real bed and running water I am about to don my silk pyjamas. I have washed my feet, eaten well and am about to sleep a great sleep. Placed my 2 henchmen with the M.P.s, where they seem quite happy. Good story from man I met in Essex (4 Indian Div.) before dinner. A German doctor prisoner asked him how he felt about his Italian allies! 'Well you have to fight with the Americans don't you?' A more perfect summary would be hard to find.

14 May

Guelmar: Reached here during afternoon. Am billetted with town's leading fascist! A doctor. Also here is a dentist Captain who has looked after me very well. Am going on to Constantine tomorrow.

19 May

Bougie: Went to Constantine only to find the Regiment had moved on quite a way towards Algiers. So I drove on to Setif where I spent the night at the Hotel de France, a rather comfortable hotel. I got rather pleasantly drunk with an American flier Lieut. who has bombed Naples. Next day I drove on to Bougie, 2 kilometres from which the Regiment is stationed. Magnificent scenery specially in the Keratia Gorge, the road through which took 7 years to build. The Bougie coast is full of huge mountains with a very blue Mediterranean and trees and greenery everywhere. Enormous numbers of cigarettes, chocolate, whisky etc. I have been drunk about 3 times so far. Am going on leave to Algiers (we get 3 clear days each) which promises to be a real blind. Notable event was when the Colonel called me Jack today not once but several times.

Bad blow is the departure of Buthy. Everyone of course wonders who is due for the next Captaincy. Incidentally I have forgotten to mention I am now G.P.O. of 'E' Troop, thus replacing Harry Forshaw who took it rather hard. However, there may be more changes again now.

From here we are to do an invasion. Nobody knows where to etc. and the whole thing is shrouded in tremendous secrecy. So I shall say no more of it now. Letters yesterday from Dad, Pam, Joan Mary, G., Maurice Porter, 2 from George, Anne the W.A.A.F., Dorothy. Wrote back today to Bé, Dad, J.-M. and Ann and shall write to the others later. Am now closing this, Diary 3.

 PART TWO

5 July – 26 November 1943

In the words of Alexander's message to Churchill, we were now 'the masters of the African shore'. What next? Sicily. In the fearsome heat (118 °F in the non-existent shade) plagued by enormous malarial mosquitoes, it was still such luxury to guzzle bunches of grapes and have water to spare. After a month, we had ground our way from Cape Passero to Messina, defeated the enemy and were facing the toe (or was it the heel? Who cared?) of Italy. Beyond our small island, the larger war was starting to go our way. The Russians had inflicted a massive defeat on the Germans at Stalingrad; the Americans had already fought alongside us in North Africa and Sicily and were arriving in large numbers in Britain ready to invade Europe.

Joyful news: we were to be home by Christmas. A bit less joyful: Second Front next. Yet as we sailed homewards we felt a hard-earned pride in Winston's slightly old-fashioned but honourable claim: 'In days to come, when people ask you what you did in the Second World War, it will be enough to say: I marched with the Eighth Army.'

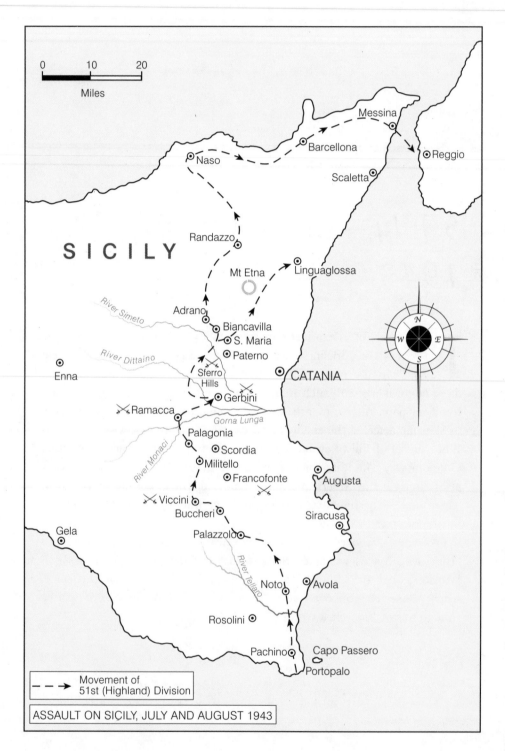

0　　10　　20
Miles

Messina

Barcellona

Naso

Reggio

Scaletta

S I C I L Y

Randazzo

Linguaglossa

Mt Etna

River Simeto

Adrano

Biancavilla

S. Maria

Paterno

River Dittaino

Enna

Sferro
Hills

CATANIA

Gerbini

Ramacca

Gorna Lunga

Palagonia

Scordia

River Monaci

Militello

Francofonte

Augusta

Viccini

Buccheri

Siracusa

Palazzolo

River Tellaro

Gela

Noto

Avola

Rosolini

Pachino

Capo Passero

Portopalo

- - - →　Movement of
　　　　51st (Highland) Division

ASSAULT ON SICILY, JULY AND AUGUST 1943

5 July 1943

The sun is setting over Sfax harbour in a dim orange ball. Silent and bulky under the grey and copper sky the L.S.T.s are lying at anchor. They look like small streets on the water, lined as they are with 3-ton trucks and Jeeps etc. The L.S.T. on which I, the Major, Captain Frankie Philip – acting B.C. of 301 – and his C.P.O. Jimmie Lowe are quartered is filled with curious things like 'Ducks' – the $2^1/2$ ton amphibians – the Beach Group with its various technical appliances – the A/T, the 'Diehard' machine gunners and others. It would appear that we are the first L.S.T. to hit the other side, hot on the heels of the assault infantry. At present all the ships are lying outside. We do not yet know officially where we are going. Our coded maps make it look rather like Sicily but there is a strong school of thought which favours the mainland as our destination. As soon as we sail we shall find this out and be given 'real' maps. Our party – which lands at least 24 hours before the guns and the rest of the battery – consists of the B.C., myself, and Signaller Kelly, so admirable on Djebel Garci. Our transport, a Jeep (driven by me) whose engine, smothered in waterproofing materials, looks quite revolting. On it is enough food and water to keep us going for 4 days. As always my feelings are mingled excitement and apprehension; with this difference: that this time I know too damn well what action is like and I rather dread it. This feeling will pass like all introspection with the first action. The Middlesex have a pet on board. A baby baboon which is absolutely entrancing to watch. I sat absolutely enraptured tonight watching its small wizened jaws champing on a piece of chewing gum; every so often it pulled out a long strand. Shortly after this it started scratching its testicles with intense concentration, which was rather funny.

6 July

I had to stop writing last night as the Major pulled me into a bridge game with 2 other friends of his, also Majors, one with a D.S.O. I was tired and played badly. In bed it was terribly stuffy even lying naked on top and tho' I slept very soundly I didn't waken till 0855 this morning and then with a headache. Last night before going to bed I went on deck. The night was as calm and cool as a nurse's hand. After the stifling sweaty nights at Sousse it was grand. It was completely dark with only a faint pattern of stars and an almost imperceptible new moon. Somewhere at the back of the ship the soldiers – or maybe the sailors – were singing sentimental songs to the strains of a concertina.

I am not feeling very fit. I almost wish I <u>had</u> gone into hospital after all. This devotion to duty stuff is all very well but one is not 100% efficient if not absolutely fit. Still, perhaps things will improve. Also, had I not stayed up I shouldn't have met D. which was rather a grand thing after such a long separation. Incidentally as I ended my last diary as far as I recall with a query as to when I was going to hear from B. again, it is worth recording that I had a letter from her a few days ago.

She has had her baby (a girl) and wrote of her newly-found feeling of calm etc. I wrote back a long, cynical and unworthy letter in a fit of envious pique. I remember now, before I'd seen action, I used to say I wouldn't mind dying etc. Since then I have realised how callow and essentially unsound were my words. Life has become (even in its worst moments) very sweet, and I certainly do mind dying now. This makes me fear that I shall; it seems to be so often the case. Yesterday afternoon we swam from the open doors of the L.S.T.; up at the front where the ramp will in a matter of hours unleash a cargo of destruction. The water was warm and buoyant.

Later: More bridge today and also a swim after tea. I don't think our departure will be long delayed now.

This evening several more small naval units have joined us and a miniature armada lies turning on the fairly heavy swell. This afternoon also, we had an aircraft alert with agitated Klaxon horns but no further developments. Most people are rather optimistic, and quite convinced Italy is going to pack in. I am not quite so sure. The R.E.M.E. captain on board (there are 16 army officers) said after supper: 'It'll be like landing at Bournemouth Pier.' 'That's what you think,' said the ship's Chief Engineer. And there the matter rests.

8 July

We are almost ready to sail, I think. The ship's captain had a conference on shore this morning and the O.C. Troops has broken open his sealed orders. Yesterday it was much cooler with quite a choppy sea making it impossible to bathe from the ship. Up on the upper deck (the quarter-deck is it, where the bridge is situated?) I noticed one of the Oerlikon guns with an American tin hat propped on the magazine. On the tin hat (all the equipment, like the ship, is U.S. built) was painted a cross and the words 'in God we Trust'. I was sorely tempted to chalk on it 'But we keep our powder dry too' but refrained. Another useful find yesterday was in the tiny canteen where I purchased a tin of vaseline and 2 sorely needed tins of talcum powder.

Played bridge again yesterday and won. I am now 47 hundred up, easily the most. I wonder whether our crossing will be eventful – I think almost certainly we shall find the Luftwaffe out against us, and among these bulky ships they are certain to find a few unmissable targets. One of the forms of action I have not yet seen is attack by sea. I am mildly interested. The food is rather good. We eat our own rations supplemented by the ship's larder and are apparently to pay a mess bill at the end of the trip. Thus we get small individual packets of cereal at breakfast, and similar delicacies which make quite a difference to the unrelieved boredom of hard tack. The ships officers are quite a pleasant bunch who have provided reading matter and are generally obliging. The ship's Captain, a Lieut/Comd. is a small dark man who is rather like an Illingworth drawing but quite conversational. Another looks like a sheep, with mild blue eyes and a faraway expression as he chews rhythmically at his food. In contrast is another small sharp featured little man who sort of snaps his food like a repeating mousetrap. The army officers are all quite tolerable and contain no bones of contention like our own Battery Mess. The night before we left, Monty – whose life is made a small military hell by Wagstaff – eventually turned like the proverbial worm. We were all sleeping in a small marquee and Monty was doing his comic-snore act which is quite amusing. Waggy told him to shut up – or else, but Monty, being rather pissed, continued as if he hadn't heard. W. then sneaked round the back of the tent and destroyed his bedding. M. sallied forth and attacked Wagstaff who, evidently unprepared for this, protested with uneasy jocularity in his awful twang 'O come on Monty a joke's a joke' etc. They fought for 20 minutes or so, Monty in grim silence, Waggy continuing to make feeble cracks as they rolled about in the dirt outside the tent. I positively hugged myself with delight and I could feel thrills of pleasure coming across the tent from Sandy and Jimmy. Only 'Jim' Forshaw hoped to see Waggy obtain a clearcut victory. In all honesty the physical victory appeared to be non-existent on either side, but the moral effect of an attack on the loud-mouthed dogmatic Wagstaff was tremendous. It was one of the most enjoyable incidents since I joined the Regt. I see endless chances for spiteful cracks at Wagstaff – such as 'Have you been fighting again' if he appears untidy etc. Even the limited possibility of suggested blackmail – as one who fancies himself as a prospective Major (my God!) his reputation would suffer. O joy, a lever at last.

9 July

The armada is at sea. We sailed at about 1700 yesterday and our destination is Sicily and our task to put Italy out of the war. As Monty's message said, 'The Italian empire has been exterminated and now we shall deal with the home country.'

We are the second L.S.T. ashore at first light tomorrow – i.e. about 4 hours or less after the assault infantry go in. The Canadians are now officially 8 Army. I knew this some time ago but it has been a very closely guarded secret. A slight breeze this morning and the ship is rocking a little. One has no feeling of history-making except from time to time; but the general reaction is just that it's another job to be done; in fact of course it's the greatest combined op. that has ever been undertaken.

12 July

Last night when I lay down under the stars, it was exactly 39 hours since I had slept at all. But I should begin at the beginning. Firstly there was an abrupt break in this narrative because we ran on July 10 into a rolling sea, and our flat bottomed L.S.T. rolled so badly that by 1030 I was heartily and decisively sick. This process repeated itself at fairly regular intervals until 1700 when, fully dressed, I fell into an exhausted sleep until 6 the next morning. At about midday, unmolested by aircraft or submarines, we sighted the sandy beach which we knew to be our destination. On the right was a rocky promontory and a lighthouse and the sea was filled, it seemed, with ships. Ships of all shapes and sizes, almost colours. L.S.T.s lurching and swaying, slim M.L.s almost invisible among the white capped waves, destroyers, the odd cruiser and over on our left, bringing the Canadians from home, several large liners. We beached about 1300 about 30 yards out and our Jeep (myself at the helm) ploughed gallantly ashore in nearly 3 feet of water. The performance was somewhat dimmed by its giving up the ghost about 500 yards inland; but we got it going again (and it only conked out twice more that day!). We then pushed on inland and met the Colonel near an enemy R.D.F. Station which contained one stiff. We had a quick cup of tea (eternal solace) and a couple of bits of bacon and then back to the beaches to wait for the batteries. Frank Philip sent a mine up under his Jeep which shattered the Jeep and sent Frank off to hospital with bad shock and a lacerated bottom.

At about 2100 the enemy came over and did quite a bit of bombing by flares. In the moonlight and the yellowish glare you could see columns of smoke rising and hear the vicious 'sneezing' of the bombs.

In the harbour, the L.S.T.s lay bulky and silent waiting to beach. The flak was terrific; absolute streams of red Bofors shells and occasionally an Oerlikon gun from one of the ships squirted a necklace of white cannon bullets. The battery came off into the rocky shallows about 2200, formed up a couple of miles inland for de-waterproofing and at 0245 recce parties moved off in the dark in a cold mist. We went through Pachino – white and silent and giving the impression of being quite a pleasant town by day and then on to our first position about first light, and heralded by several bombs over the other side of the road, dropped by a roving enemy bomber. We did not fire from there nor have we in fact fired though we moved forward a long way – about 12 miles – yesterday. No opposition on our sector at all and only saw a few Iti prisoners coming back down the dusty roads. We ended up south of Noto last night and the rest of the Regt. (we are in reserve) has gone up to Syracuse today. Very slight enemy air activity – the R.A.F. are giving us wonderful cover. I slept like the dead for 9 hours last night. Everybody rather cheerful and optimistic; certainly less opposition than expected has been met. We are 8th army again thank the Lord, and under Monty who was seen yesterday in a Duck on our front.

Saturday 17 July

Saturday 17 July it says. For all I knew or cared it could have been 18 August or any other date. Such things are really very unimportant. There is a full moon and from our position either side of the mountain road to Paterno one can see the peaks and valley luminous as a giant Christmas tree. Or perhaps I could give the other side; myself writing on an artillery board by the light of various small bulbs etc. filched in various places; all the men dead beat, getting a few hours sleep between actions and damn moves, and nights interrupted at twelve o'clock in that first numbing sleep to get orders or movement at first light.

After the last position from which I wrote, in the initial bridgehead area, the invasion progressed with such rapidity that today – D + 7 I believe it is – finds us at the gates of Catania in the East, advancing on Enna in the West, and ourselves in the Centre pushing on to Paterno with the situation extremely obscure, over 20,000 prisoners in the bag and the sun as hot as ever. At Vizzini there was a fierce fight with the Germans before we took the town. I was in there soon after dawn and saw the Canadians thunder through looking grim, and extremely comic as they poked their tommy guns etc. at the disinterested population. In fact the population is either quite passive or amazingly friendly. We went through Militello last night to positive roars of applause! On these moves along the glaring white roads, the dust is like a peasouper fog and everybody gives the effect of having been working in a flour factory. One gets thirsty too, and in these parts there are fewer tomatoes, melons, grapes and peaches which were it seemed ad lib lower on the island. The Regiment has been having casualties. Alistair Gill of 301 is dead, killed when his truck turned over. Frank Philip up on a mine. Neil Gillanders wounded by mortar splinters near Vizzini. Patterson, the sigs. officer, strafed and wounded. In our own battery we got it the other night when 6 Messerschmitts roared out of the sunset onto us, the Recce group, and almost as we dived for cover opened up with a hideous snarl of machine guns and a hail of lead. McCleod got about 9 wounds and Flint one, and the major's armoured car was holed. It was a near squeak and most frightening. I shouldn't like to look like 3 of the corpses I saw a day or two ago; one completely decapitated and the jagged stump where the head had been black with flies and dust as 'it' lay rotting and smelling on the dusty road. Incidentally I had another near one in Vizzini when I was clearing civilian looters from the house. As I was entering a room one of them went up on a booby trap and splashed blood all over my shorts and legs. Another moment and I might have gone up too. It was near this house that I 'captured' about 14 Italians and, steeling myself to the deed, searched them and produced about 9 watches all of which I've given away, nice one to Alistair and one to Jimmy. All night nowadays one hears the drone and moan of the bombers; occasionally one is shot down and erupts in a burst of fire, silhouetting the unchanging hills for a moment in pink fire. Am not working over well with H.F. who is touchy, lacks sense of humour and has an overdeveloped inferiority complex. This makes things rather difficult. I had about 3 hours sleep last night and so far, at 2310, there is little hope of sleep, every possibility of a night move, and an almost virtual certainty of recce parties at first light. When I first came to war, these things nearly killed me with fatigue, now I just feel very tired. One becomes acclimatised. But it is impossible to describe these feelings adequately to outsiders; the hot sandy feel of the eyes, sore feet, a tired, oh so tired, body and the having to overcome that drugging inertia and whip the uncomplying brain into activity. I was astonished the other day when I asked the time; I had that 'middle of the afternoon' feeling and it was only 1030. This is a disjointed narrative but we lead a disjointed life nowadays.

19 July

I fully intended to make some entry yesterday evening when it seemed we might get a night's sleep after a move at 0200 the night before and a day's firing. But just as I was sitting down to it, orders came through once again, with the result that at 0100 last night we once again pushed on towards the Paterno–Catania sector, where the Germans seem to be concentrating for a last stand. We are beginning to get rather tired; two snatched hours sleep each night, or less, becomes a bit of a strain. Last night I led the recce parties up the wrong road, and was only halted when the still night was broken by the sinister crump of mortar bombs. On the correct track the moon was dimmed by an enormous fire, one of many which half hide this barren landscape in smoke by day and illuminate it by night. Our position – a saddle between what has been described as the 'twin titties' – had only been taken a few hours before, and was virtually in the F.D.L.S. At first light the enemy started lobbing what the C.O. 2 so expressively calls ''ot shit' into our gunline, more particularly Peter Dawson's troop – E – on the right. Monty was wounded and one man – Barries – killed outright. We were lucky not to have more casualties. Pity about Barries – he was one of those gunners who always worked willingly and cheerfully; a real loss. From the farm in which I made my command post came good loot – soap, matches, plates, laundry and a few eggs – much appreciated when breakfast was taken at midday in an alternative position to which I had to shift the battery. Here we are all digging hard; a few casualties reduce the amount of goading necessary in a remarkable fashion . . . What are I believe called artillery duels are lethargically taking place in the blazing sunshine among the cornfields. Our bombers drone overhead. One thinks of iced lager and green Sussex and sighs.

To give you some idea of fatigue. During a two-hour spell a couple of nights ago I was woken up to take a call from the adjutant. In the middle of the call the signaller had to wake me up with the phone in my hand! Talk about the retreat from Mons . . . All this countryside is dominated by the enormous yet graceful peak of Mount Etna – a useful landmark and a stiff obstacle. It is from there that their O.P.s are warming up this left flank of the Plana di Catania where the guns lie thumping lazy death to the blue Mediterranean sky. I forgot to mention that the B.C. has a small splinter in his eye; he goes round with a black patch – and makes reference, semi-jocular, to his 'wound' at least 2 times an hour. Trying.

20 July

We fired a programme starting at 2330 last night; I regret to report that owing to technicalities I don't propose to go into, we were a bit late starting but otherwise all was O.K. I fell into bed about 0230 and slept till 0600 when we fired again. Have been very busy all day, specially during the morning. which was nearly 100 °F in the shade.

Just after firing last night Jerry lobbed a few shells back fairly close, but left it at that. A coolish breeze is blowing now, thank god, and people are crawling from under trucks where they have been panting like puppies in the midday heat. Am bloody tired; about 12 hours sleep would improve the situation. Also we are heavily flea-bound.

21 July

Monty has been in the area today leaving in his wake the usual spate of 'Monty Says-s'. However, the general impression is that the Div. has done well and that the whole do is getting on fine. It is getting on for midnight and I am still at work on a new flood of D.F. tasks which have just come in. Some Jerry guns must have lobbed a few shells into a night whose quietness is otherwise almost undisturbed. Heavy day's firing today; we must have cleared about 800 rounds, cracking away there at 105 °F in the non-existent shade, with Etna peering at us, frowning mistily in the heathaze like a disapproving maiden aunt.

Yesterday I had quite a good mail including an L.C. from Pam, Gerard, Winsome (terrible name), his wife, and, of all people, Buthy, now languishing fatly in Cairo. Apparently there is a pretty large size flap on at the moment owing to an expected counter-attack.

23 July

It is afternoon. Between targets I am lying flat on my valise in the Command Post, trying not to sweat. It is about 110 °F in the shade. I play idly with the small locket on a chain around my neck, together with my two identity discs.

'To JS from BB, Dec 42' it says; and on the front 'Regarde St. Christophe. Puis v'a t'en rassuré.' Somehow one can and one is, which is curious. A hot wind is blowing; it always gets up about midday. I must go again – Target calling.

24 July

Tremendous flap last night when the enemy counterattacked about 10 o'clock. Not very usual for the Boche, who doesn't seem to go in for night attacks in a very large way as a rule. However, after a burst of firing and a slight local withdrawal, things became quiet again around midnight. I quite like the Command Post in the middle of the night. It is quiet, and only the hushed middle-of-the-night voices of the signallers, the occasional buzz or ring of a phone, and the sounds of instruments and pencils clinking round the artillery boards break the silence. Somewhere behind Etna's formidable grace a German gun bangs flatly in the night. The moon shines on the yellow cornfields and shows the mountains shadowy and vast in front of us. Everybody is rather tired; the small electric bulbs and hurricane lamps glow harshly on strained eyes. We seem alone in the world, marooned, a small technical island in the infinite complication of the night.

Somebody brews up. We sip the stuff loudly and with satisfaction making the invariable remarks about the incomparable qualities of tea, which always accompany a brew – particularly at night.

When morning comes and the daylight shows up the untidiness, the tired unshaven faces, one wonders that midnight could have touched the scene with mystery and almost romance. During the afternoon Jerry opened up a short but violent bombardment on 301 about 400 yards to our left. I understand they killed 4* and wounded 7 in a few minutes. R.H.Q. who were by their standards rather near (about as near as us) have of course moved hastily southwards. I find myself almost impossibly exasperated by the Major, who is unbelievably dense at times and a terrible credit stealer (other people's ideas and shoots . . .) and also I am so allergic to Jam that I let him off duty frequently to give myself more peace.

26 July

Night again in the C.P. Away on our left flank is the continuous thud and rumble of the guns. I think it is the Canadian artillery. Our own sector is quiet. I suppose the real 'news' (an excited voice called me to the phone at 0500 today to give me it) is Musso's resignation – cause of much delight all round, though I personally fear a revival of Italian morale, under the efficient Bagdolio and that popular squirt Victor Emmanuel. Anyway that's the first of the dictators gone, and they can't hang or shoot the fat sod quick enough for me.

*It turned out to be 5.

Today I went up the the farm area we occupied near hill 199 the other morning when Barries was killed. I was with Alistair and the Padre who gabbled an extremely perfunctory 'few words' over the small grave with its rough wooden cross. The hot sun (it was 120 °F in the shade yesterday) beat down, a breeze from the sea carried the thump of guns and shells to our ears, and the droning of the lord's prayer mingled with the stern voice of Spitfires overhead as gunner Barries' earthly remains were entrusted to his alleged maker. I'm afraid I didn't find the scene as touching as I should have found it. Rather pointless. I'm sorry I did but there you are. Passing 301's old position four more crosses mark the place – and a fifth is since dead – and all around is the desolation of empty gun pits, burned trucks, paper flapping in the wind, and the black scars of the hillside where the shells have fallen.

Letters from Jock's wife; painfully brave. Dad. And one from Sheila who is engaged to somebody in the R.A.M.C. and going to be married early next year. Well well.

29 July

Things have been quiet for the last few days. This is of course a relative term as the guns bang and thump most of the time day and night and the usual flaps and irritations never fail to occur. We are losing men rather unduly rapidly with malaria and various other types of lesser fevers. Today Sandy Cowie left for A.D.S. and all points south so heaven knows when we shall see him again. Meanwhile Jimmy Gegan has taken over and 'Jam' has gone as G.P.O. to F Troop. I can't say this is in any way displeasing to me, as he was beginning to get on my nerves more than somewhat. There is a large paratroop flap on tonight. I'm bound to confess that one of the prospects which chills my blood is that of being garrotted by night by some brawny aryan paratroop. However the guard has been doubled which is supposed to give a measure of assurance against the loud and sinister roar of non-identified planes now passing overhead. The night is very dark but starry after the thunderstorm and rain of this afternoon. Fairly soon now there is another 'show' due but I'll not write details in case of capture before it occurs. I think we are all getting a little tired and stale. The Canadians, clean and fresh, are doing very well and somehow the eighth army, tired and desert-stained, seem to be rather stagnant here on a defensive base. Letter from Dad yesterday and today; some books coming out soon thank the lord. B.C. is holding forth about everything to a group of much-impressed signallers. General theme being 'we musn't see what we can get out of this war or after it, we must see what we can put into it' etc. etc. (we have been here before!). Effect somewhat spoiled by his gloating confession this morning that he had benefited more than somewhat over De Beers already. (Much talk of hooked noses and the 'real old families of England' – meaning our Eric of course.) We are now onto the current J.V. Rank scandals.

31 July

It is 2250. In just an hour we open up with over 150 guns to blast the way onto two high features – points 224 and 193 across the railway from Sferro bridge. Actually all has been ready for some time, and everything is hot and quiet under the naked glare of the small electric light bulbs in the Command Post.

North of us we can hear rapid bursts of spandau fire; does the Boche know there is going to be an attack? This attack, rather like the one of 16 March at Mareth where I had my first real baptism of fire, is on the suspected outpost line and after the larger events we have experienced is using a mere 220 rounds per gun on the programme. How one's ideas change. On my first programme I thought 110 r.p.g. was big stuff.

Goodish mail last two days. From Pam, and Dorothy and Dad, and today from Mom, Bé, and Griselda whose letter annoyed me as it always does nowadays; but I like hearing from her.

The days are still hot and humid. We are losing quite a number of men through malaria. Did I ever mention that the C.O. left about a week ago for M.D.S. and all points south . . . 'Bull' Melia the Lancashire oaf has been commanding since, but (presumably) will be replaced soon. He sent round 'Hints to G.P.O.s' this morning ending up 'Saying of the last war: "The guns, thank god for the guns . . ."'. This has been repeated by all and sundry in more and more hollow tones throughout the day. A bandaged head would complete the picture! Anyway, time marches on so I must end for tonight. A few shells in the gun area today added to the illusion of war in this land of corn and sunshine and homesickness.

1 August

At 2350 the guns duly crashed out and the night was loud and hideous until nearly half past two. During the barrage I went outside to have a look at things. The night was dark save for the continuous flashing of the guns. The reports hit you in the face like a blow. It is almost impossible to think, let alone speak. Later the Boche started shelling back; though we had no casualties there were some rounds in the Battery area. Two of the crew of the Bofors protecting our position were hit, one dying on his way to hospital. On 304's position, a gun pit which had caught on fire flamed and exploded for hours, lighting the bare hillsides. A few flares hung in the sky, and occasionally a bomb or two thumped in ahead of us. At 0300 I fell into bed but was up before 0500 since when we've fired nearly 800 rounds. It is now 2215.

The attack has been successful and penetrated further than expected. The 2 hills were taken and high ground beyond, and the div. is now well on the way to Aderno. A move is in the air for tomorrow as we are nearly out of range. I am very tired and hope to get a few hours sleep shortly. This is the 22nd day of the Sicilian Campaign but it feels as though it had been going on for ever. The days, with their stifling heat, sameness, dull food (though 'Compo' rations are a great improvement with their daily cigarettes, chocolate and sweets) and tired people; pass slowly, yet many have gone when one starts to count. Today we have become C.M.F. – 'Central Mediterranean Force'.

3 August

We moved – ie. I moved in a Jeep – at 11 o'clock yesterday morning when the army began once more to advance through the hills towards Aderno and all points north. It took a long time along dusty, perilous tracks and steep wadis, and eventually we reached the position here – just south of Muglia – in the late afternoon. The guns were up and in action by about midnight. As the recce parties went forward at one stage, the front vehicle hit a mine. We stopped and a passing Sapper officer – a Lieut. with a double M.C. – lifted nearly 20 Tellers from our path. I stood on 2 which fortunately were set for heavy vehicles. A soldier in the Black Watch carrier (the vehicle blown up) had his left arm blown away above the elbow and was in great pain so I gave him 1/2 a grain of morphia. He kept pleading 'Dinna write hame' to his friends. His arm was quite unrecognisable as such; it looked like a skinned and twisted rabbit, and a piece of shattered bone stuck nakedly out like a reddened thing. As always on these occasions I was moved by the compassion of the soldiers who were looking after him. They are as gentle as women. Today the bombers flying north, have been passing over in an almost continuous stream, sounding even by daylight, full of menace. I think we may spend a night here which will be a good thing as I had nothing to eat or drink between 08 and 19 hours yesterday and bed at 0200. The Major grows daily more maddening sitting eternally round the C.P. always in a mild panic, always boring with his improbable 2nd hand stories, his pink and somehow debauched body naked to the waist (he never wears shorts) and his feet encased in nasty blue socks which make them look smelly even when they're not!

5 August

We are now in position some miles east of our last position, right in the heart of the hills. This is real mountain country; the kind of thing you find Hollywood portraying as the N.W. Frontier, and the kind of pictures people painted of the last war in the alps with the Italians invariably spiking their guns. It is a little trying at the moment. The Major – recounting his well-tried and extremely boring stories of life in the New Zealanders – glorification by insinuation – and Wagstaff is being aggressive about his wonderful signallers who are certainly the world's worst in everybody's eyes except N.B.'s (as they call him, the men I mean, ie. Napoleon Bonaparte).

On this position we have dumped 500 Rounds p.g. which seems to indicate a bit of shooting tonight. It is terribly hot – at 0900 it was already 105 °F in the shade. Water – heavily chlorinated and in short supply – is a worry round here. Worse than the desert where the heat was pleasantly dry.

Paterno is ours – taken by the division yesterday, and the present objectives are apparently Adrano and Brancanila. After that we, it is said, are to become another spearforce which should be tremendous fun in this hot weather. Letters since I wrote this up from the Kaplans in Durban, New York, and Debroy who must soon be on the island I imagine.

Same day: It is the cool of the evening. The only bearable time after the fierce heat of the day. Now a cool breeze is blowing. Probably at home it would be a hot evening – it is certainly so in the shade, but to our thinned blood, the light wind blowing against our sweat soaked shirts and hair matted after the day is like a healing hand. The day's irritations and flaps fade behind me and I sit calm and quiet listening to voices dwarfed and strange in the hollows, and the chinking of spades on the rocky ground. Occasionally somebody fires, and the valley dances with light, and the tremendous voices of the guns boom and beat against the mountainsides.

There is a young moon above, a few stars have already come out, the coppery west fighting a losing battle against their brightness as night comes steadily on. On my truck, the long thin whip mast of the 19 set is sharp against the sky, its two little red pennants fluttering. A canteen came in today; the B.C. distinguished himself by decreeing that non-drinkers (I am one, temporarily by M.O.'s orders) should not have whisky. Sandy Kinnaird was equally penalised. This ensured more for himself. I had the hell of a row, having bartered my whisky with the adjutant. Result, B.C. kept the whisky. No tiger in defence of its young fights harder than Hotstuff Harben for whisky, cigarettes, razor blades or in fact anything we can get more of than other people. Selfish is a tailor-made word for him.

7 August

Last night at 11.15 a programme shoot came in involving 250 rounds a gun. Zero hour midnight. So at just that time about 200 guns crashed into the night until after 0330 when a blissful quiet descended and I went to bed. Apparently the guns fired in such a way as to cause a German officer captured last night to ask for a view of our 'automatic 25 pounder'. The noise in these confined hills was tremendous. Like a series of smacks in the face. It blew out lanterns, made lighting a cigarette difficult. Hot (120 °F in the shade) trying day with Hotstuff and N.B. at their worst. I nearly had a stroke out of sheer impotent fury. The rear party has joined us, bringing a trail of useless people like our temperamental and very bad cooks. Most of us are fed up with the Major, the Regt. and the war. It must be the weather. The safely ferocious papers from home are also maddening. Feel too tired to write well tonight so I'll stop. Letter from Mom today. Incidentally I got a good mark for our work last night; the specialists take most of the credit and did very well.

9 August

Two more quiet days, bringing such items as another 120 °F in the shade, 500 more Churchman No. 1 from Dad, a couple of Naafis – Sandy K. and I got our whisky this time by being quite firm about it from the outset. I am now almost a cigarette millionaire – a delicious state of affairs to have more – many more – cigarettes than one needs for once. Another pleasant luxury was a batch of parcels for A. One contained some crushed pineapple which went down well with a drop of whisky, and another a rich and encouraging fruit cake. A hunk of this plus the usual afternoon torpor sent me soundly to sleep today, waking to find some hideous bully and dough (pronounced 'duff') for my evening meal. Things like setting up a mess are beginning to occupy the major's mind, meaning the usual run of cooks asking to go back to duty, the argumentative presence of N.B. and 'Jam' (now mercifully out of sight – and mind – most of the day) and disgruntled batmen. It seems probable that as the enemy shows signs of defeat on the island, the Div. may not be required for further action. This means a 'rest' of a month, according to current rumour. All said and done I – and I think the men – prefer action. 'A rest' as one of them said tonight 'means they (the usual, mysterious omnipotent THEY) start buggering us about again.' Yesterday received a parcel of books from Dick in Gib. which was rather thoughtful of him. The comforts Radio which (theoretically) circulates between the Batteries and R.H.Q., arrived again tonight, lending the usual spectacle of 20 or 30 homesick gunners sitting listening to such nostalgic treacle as 'Yours' and 'Begin the Beguine' – tunes which I enjoy as much as any of them when I am not feeling bad-tempered and superior. The moon is gaining in brightness, and tonight the sky has again been loud with the sinister drone of bombers. Chances of promotion, at one time I thought, fairly bright, are beginning to recede, largely owing to my frequent clashes with 'Little Red' Harben. Jimmy for example is commanding F Troop in Sandy's absence, and looks like being recommended before me. As I like Jimmy this doesn't really worry me, but it shows which way the wind is blowing. Bivouacs and bushnets are the order of the day again, which eliminates one of my greatest pleasures: lying gazing up at the sky with its enormous host of stars.

True it is a hackneyed emotion but particularly back in the desert, the clear softness of the blue night skies and the impersonal compassion of the stars produced a feeling of sadness and futility that came near to tears. Why? one asks. I don't know the answer. The thought that always crosses my mind when I regard the distant, disinterested universe, is the lines of scraggy wooden crosses which blaze the trail from Alamein to Etna. Here we still are and always shall be, the stars seem to say, and there are you – finished, burned, forgotten in less than seconds of time's scale, already perhaps the earth and the ants are part of the bodies that yesterday laughed and grumbled. In each little cross is a story. Each of these left the womb with its pain and patience, lived a childhood happy or unhappy and continued his life till that one moment when something stopped it. Why? That is the great query. Why? What is the answer? But only the tantalising twinkle of the night sky is one's answer. I sometimes wonder if I shall try and publish these pages, then I wonder if anybody wants to read them. Many of the observations are trite, the incidents commonplace and the expression undistinguished. The trouble is that in action one is frequently too tired to 'do justice' to the events of the day; and leaving them makes the image grow faint. The cup of tea snatched in the dusty afternoon is so often more important to the individual than the thunder of a barrage. But can anybody who has not travelled these roads be expected to understand that? My letters home are often tinged with bitterness because of just these things.

I always think after the war its events and emotions will fade or become trivial. But some events will linger like a pencil pressed too hard on thin paper, and leaving an unintelligible but distinct enough imprint on the pages to come. And how many pages are there before somebody, something, writes The End to most of our novelettes? Too full of queries tonight and it is stuffy in the Command Post (rather an elaborate C.P. this one with rocky walls and sandbags) so I shall go to bed.

12 August

On the evening of 11 Aug, just after I'd gone to bed, word came through that Recce parties were at one hour's notice from 0800 the next morning. With almost uncanny adherence to form, an agitated voice down the R.H.Q. line called us at 1500 and told us to R.V. there at 1530. Just before leaving I intercepted the Q. who most dramatically handed me a letter containing Pam's photo which was very pleasing. There was also a letter from her. We moved off in clouds of this fine foul dust down an astonishingly sheer and dangerous track, till eventually we reached the river round the southern foot of Etna. Thence NE through Paterno – very thoroughly bombed but by no means deserted (large notices 'This town is out of bounds to all Troops . . .') into Belpasso where I bought some pears, through Pedara, and Trecastagni – neat little towns – and into the vineyard country, now in full greenery. Guzzled several bunches of grapes. Eventually into action in a most impossibly restricted position north of Fleri. A tumultuous night occupation. No sleep. Hotstuff <u>quite</u> impossible.

13 August

Bad tempered sort of day so far. Everybody is sandyeyed and short of temper. I'm not sure why. It may be lack of satisfying sleep, the flies or the dirt, and perhaps it's the general tired and browned off feeling which usually comes at the end of a campaign. The Germans are reported to be evacuating, but are fighting pretty stubbornly, and the demolition and destruction along this road is pretty extensive.

A great boon is the ample water and fruit. Bunches of grapes, oranges, pomegranates, and prickly pear – a queer-tasting fruit rather reminiscent of apples or watermelons. At last we are making up our Vitamin C deficiencies in full measure.

News has just come of another possible move forward. I hope to God it's incorrect.

Same night, by torchlight: . . . But it wasn't. We moved off in a hell of a hurry just before lunch and are now in action about 2 miles N of Zafferama, among the terraces and vineyards which slope down to the Mediterranean. Pursuit is likely tomorrow. Again we have occupied 'impossible' gun positions, where almost every gun has to be winched or manhandled in. I believe our speed in getting guns up is a factor in the withdrawal and evacuation the Boche is reported to be doing. Fruit is still abundant, with apples and plums now in evidence. Wonderful moonlight night, nice and cool here about 2000 feet above the level of a sea we can see gleaming in the moonlight. We are almost clear of Etna whose peak, patched with snow, smoked as we pushed up the much demolished roads toward Messina. Our destroyers clearly visible by daylight.

14 August

Still in position. My C.P. is just off the main road, and the war moves past us – Medium guns with their enormous horn-like gadgets, a long mule train led by Algerian arabs in K.D. and British tin-hats, and the pathetic though sometimes cheerful stream of civilians, old and young, going back to their homes. Most of them are rather dirty, rather ugly, and very ready to please. It is said that the Germans are nearly out of Sicily and that we are unlikely to go into action again.

15 August

Still in the same place. The battle has moved right forward of us now and it is said that Jerry has evacuated Sicily. The Army continues to roll past us on its assorted vehicles. Almost everything, it seems, has gone past; just now – it is 1700 – the Bofors guns are grinding slowly Northwards. The number of bridges blown ahead is apparently large and thorough. But just here all is peaceful; the green sloping vineyards; and the flat blue-grey sea with an occasional warship looking tinny and metallic below.

The coast of Italy was clearly visible last night, somewhat ominous and hazy across the water.*

A mail is reported to have come in and is at present being sorted at R.H.Q. which lends the atmosphere a certain expectancy. Sudden tremendous excitement occasioned by the appearance of two British nurses in a truck which has stopped so they can scrounge a cup of tea. They have very successfully. They are neither of them young but have had a great success. Half naked men materialising from every corner of the wood to examine these rarities. Certainly a contrast to the Sicilian women we have seen, who are dirty, ill-clad, and prematurely aged. Word comes at 1745: no move tonight.

18 August

In bed: We are still in the same place, and it seems we may be here for a day or two more. Hotstuff's latest rumour about our next move is to predict coast defence near Messina. The mail I mentioned was a very good one. One from Debroy – now on the Island and not far away. One from Bé and also a long letter from B., more or less repudiating what she said in her last one; strange. Otherwise the days have passed quietly and relatively uneventfully with an occasional querulous outburst from Hotstuff and the capture of Messina by the 7th (U.S.) and 8th armies. Today after lunch, a small girl of I think about 13 came up to my bivvy and started talking. I gave her a basin of water, some soap and a towel and she washed herself using her large brown eyes (aged about 25) on me all the time. Eventually she asked for some 'Comayo' which is Italian for bully. I gave her a tin and was astonished when I discovered that in return for it I was expected to lead her into the wood and do whatever I like. It was a revelation of what hungry people will do. She was an attractive little thing. Eventually I put her in a Jeep going to Zafferana and the last I saw she was clutching the bully in one hand and blowing me kisses with the other, her white teeth gleaming in a brown face, and her black hair streaming in the wind. I had just written to George Long today and posted it when one from him arrived. Also wrote B. a huge one two nights ago and sent Pam some silk stockings yesterday.

20 August

Still in the same place. One or two more developments. Chiefly that an attack is being done by another Corps and supported by us in the Messina peninsula. The locals are doing tremendous and thriving trade in silk, bedspreads and almost

*Discovered later not Italy.

anything. Yesterday I swelled the ranks of the stooges by buying two yards of the most exquisite white silk which I've sent to Pam to make panties or a slip or a nightie or what have you. Actually all the shops from Zafferana to the sea are just about empty now. We are handing over M.T. as fast as we can, and tonight our last radio truck – ie. H., which is mine, was scheduled to go. Its fate was averted by my proving that it is mechanically unfit to go anywhere at the moment, though I've no doubt it could stagger off to war if it had to, just as it has done before. I am quite unable to concentrate as Hotstuff is pouring out some of his usual fantastic anecdotes. As follows:

1. His father translated the whole of Dante at the age of 7.
2. His sister, aged 17, was chief harpist to Sir Henry Wood.
3. He bought a South African gold mine which quadrupled in value in 10 years.
4. I am his son – he is to die in one year.
5. His grandmother produced 17 children and lived to 89.

These five stories are a very typical Hotstuff cross section.

21 August

Strange today. I was going in a Jeep towards a little village called Via Grande to get some stationery at a magnificent stationery shop when on the road I saw my little 'bully beef girl'. She asked with flashing smiles etc. to be given a lift to Catania. I took her part of the way and she chattered gaily. She was made up today and looked quite enchanting with a blue and white (very thin) silk dress and those very expressive eyes. She remembered me ('Ingelese Tenente Buono . . .)' and issued a similar invitation for tomorrow. It's a pity if what I hear is true – ie. that she is anybody's and has been nearly everybody's. For all that there is a certain piquancy and allure about her which is very attractive. Incidentally I asked her how old she was today and she said – 19! I can't believe that but I suppose it could be true. Anyway, it's rather ridiculous to think about her at all.

23 August

Desultory days waiting for our new move to battlestations. The subject of our move (the day after tomorrow) was the cause of a 2 hour 11 minute conference this morning by Hotstuff. It could have been done in 20 minutes. Rather impossible to write with any clarity as an argument is raging about indents. It makes it rather difficult to concentrate. So I'll stop now. Sent Pam two more pairs of stockings.

26 August

A Square in Messina Town: We moved off yesterday morning 0800 in the hot sunshine and the first place we reached was Linguaglossa. After that we had the enormous and difficult mountains to go through, past Francavilla with its poverty-stricken streets, crowds of small boys and girls calling 'Biscotto, Cigarette' and giving V signs, and its sallow but sometimes amazingly attractive women unconcernedly suckling babies in public, its mules, flies, dirt and disease and withal its attractiveness.

At the top of the long climb up from Francavilla where you cross the river we felt the air grow cold and fresh; and the smell of the pines was as refreshing as a hot bath after those long cricket matches back at school. The demolition and mining all the way up – and as far as here – was fiendishly thorough, and there were some damnable diversions and water crossings though these were minimised by the dryness of the rivers at this time of year. I did nearly the entire trip on a motor bike and was smothered in dust and nearly blinded. Eventually we reached Novara with its spirited war memorial and thence onto the coast road near Milazzo.

We had a meal and a wash and started the last stage of our journey (which was nearly 100 miles) at 1845. The tortuous road to Messina (littered with a good bit of Jerry equipment) was crammed; vehicles were nose to tail including the enormous 5.5s of the Scottish Horse. We pushed slowly on down the precipitous track; once a 3 tonner went over and lay there with the front wheel in the air, blocking the track to everybody but we unloaded it and towed it out with 2 Jeeps and 20 men pushing.

And so we reached Messina, and crawled in the darkness to our present position. On the other side of the straits one could see an occasional gunflash, and hear the exaggerated crash of shells in the houses. (I remember thinking the drivers managed to run their engines a good bit less noisily than usual!) We got to this square and at about 0100 dossed down in the open, a thing I regretted at 0500 when I awoke to the angry whine of many mosquitoes who have bitten my forehead very thoroughly. 0630 a recce with the C.O.2 and G.P.O.s. Hotstuff also dancing attendance and being a nuisance. This is a dirty slummy area which badly needed the turn-out and sweep up we gave it this morning. The guns are one Troop – Jimmy Gegan in the square here ('The village Square Troop') and the other – Pete Dawson – slightly right rear in among houses and shacks. The C.P. is in the school building in the square, requisitioned by me in faulty – but improving – Italian. It is large and clean and even has running water. The large grass courtyard at the back is surrounded by a high wall, but we have taken a section down and so the Troop and H Truck are now bivvied there. There is also rather a pleasant room serving as officers mess. Unfortunately there is a possibility that we may leave here and go onto the beach to fire tracers or something of the sort. Failing that on 3 September – 4 years after the war began – this small square should shake to the roar of guns (will the remaining glass go?) as the assault goes in on Italy. The locals – numerous and unbelievably friendly – are mostly intrigued by our preparations; gun pits, ammo pits, flags, directors etc.

Just before we left, Sandy Cowie returned from Tripoli, but A. went sick with a raging fever (104.6) after spending days trying to shake it off. I hope he'll be back soon. Not a snippet of mail since 17 August for anyone. Why?

Night falls, thick since the moon waned, and in the village streets the dogs are barking and the people singing – probably many Deserters among them (I know at least two, and one asked me if it was O.K. to stay home now!) as the tune is 'Lilli Marlene', the song of the desert. Went into Messina today and saw Italy across the water, close enough to touch, it seemed. Messina is utterly destroyed; scarcely a building stands untouched and there are craters everywhere. People sleep in the tunnels at night. Our first load of ammunition comes in tonight. The mediums are still sending a few rounds to Italy, banging and echoing immensely in the confined town. I believe there is bathing tomorrow.

27 August

Ammo dumping went on all night – or more accurately, should have gone on all night but nearly all the lorries broke down and so it started about 0400. Another convoy tonight and so on until we have 50 r.p.g.s dumped here, all dug in and hidden from Recce planes. Mail today from Mom, Dorothy and Bé, and a nice book from Gerard by T.S. Eliot called *Old Possum's Book of Practical Cats*. One of them is called Bustopher Jones! It is terribly hot here at night, specially indoors, but better sweat than mosquito bites any day of the week. Wrote as above and also to Pam.

Curious, but lately I have been missing Pam more than ever before. I can't think why this is.

29 August

I am doing a spell of O.P. duty in the citadel, perched high above Messina. Across the straits, almost part of us, is Italy. Now and again the mediums crash out and echo across through the tremendous mountains of Calabria. I have been watching the brown-grey-black smoke of their bursts on various targets. Sometimes at night the enemy does a little harassing fire and one hears the familiar whine of ironmongery floating about. But he is very quiet. I shall be very surprised if our assault troops meet more than an Italian rearguard. I never mentioned that we have a new C.O., George Baker, M.C. Regular beefy and healthy but seems O.K. Bathed with Jimmy today.

30 August

Yesterday afternoon soon after I finished writing great thunderclouds rolled over, and with much preliminary lightning it began to thunder sonorously round the hills behind Messina. I have heard clouds described as angry, but I never realised how accurate this was till yesterday afternoon; these were positively ferocious. Anyway the rain held off till I got back when it began raining hard – a most refreshing experience after so long. There were two letters last night, one from Bé and one from Dick in Gibraltar. I wrote back to the former at length last night. Bé has asked to try and publish some of my letters ('Letters from Sicily' or something like that . . .). I should be rather pleased if this were to happen. My Italian is really getting along rather well now. With the assistance of the local barber I can just about carry on a conversation and certainly can understand quite a lot. The women round here are some of them damned attractive, particularly their white teeth which flash in brown faces. Their figures are good and particularly what somebody called their 'superstructure', which has a universal uplift quite amazing to see.

Apparently the Boche (or the Eyeties) shelled us quite heavily last night, but they didn't wake me up. I did wake to the crack of our own mediums.

2 September

In 7 hours and 5 minutes, 4 years after the war began, we assault the mainland of Italy, and begin to carry back into Europe the war started by the axis. One cannot, however soured or cynical, fail to feel in the bones, the atmosphere of an historic occasion. Dug deep into sandbagged gunpits our guns lie in the village square, and tucked in among the houses and vineyards, and rubbish heaps and back yards, all waiting to raise their now familiar voices in a chorus of welcome to 'Der Tag'. How many more 'D' Days and 'H' hours before the last round has been fired and peace comes again?

More localised news is also by way of a bombshell – though much more welcome. Hotstuff left us today after an immediate summons yesterday morning, to become 2 i/c of 165(A) Field Regt. This morning we had the customary farewell address to the battery ('Not a dry eye in the house . . .') and last night the officers suffered a torrent of theoretical communism till 0200. He was by no means sober. Incidentally the other day he had a magnificent workout on 'Morale' for $49^1/2$ minutes. The troops sat bored and uncomprehending till exasperation caused footshuffling; and eventually Eric ended on about his third 'Finally and in conclusion'. The Messina Bye-election was over.

Letter from Pam yesterday. My Algiers present to her must have been sunk. A pity because it was for her birthday. I am immensely jealous of the sleek stay-at-homes who can take her out while I sweat here. Sweat literally too as I've got the most bloody cold of all things, with a painful cough and a bit of fever. Very tiresome.

My old H Truck, veteran of Africa, has gone at last, which was a shame. An old soap-box type, it had great personality. Last night we had a torrential rainstorm which made the air deliciously fresh, though this morning it was hot again. Had a fairish day's work getting the gun programmes out but all was finished by about 1500. Incidentally one of our guns (E Tp.) fired a test round at 1920 and thus became the first field gun to drop a round on Italy this war. And now for a few hours' sleep.

3 September

Never in my now reasonable experience of gunfire have I heard anything to equal the monstrous blast of our guns last night. The doors strained and blew open, windows smashed, ceilings fell in and the command post wall disintegrated by slow stages. First the veinous crack, then the chip falling out and finally great chunks of plaster cascading on the floor in clouds of dust. By the dismal grey light of dawn our village square was a sad spot, all the houses stripped of plaster and cement, every window smashed and roofs where no tile was left intact. Dazed and deafened we sipped a cup of tea afterwards. The landing is a success and already the airfield south of Reggio is in our hands. This morning the sky is full of our bombers – Bostons and Mitchells, 24 at a time sailing in tight formation with the bright sunshine on their wings. Over the straits the first barrage balloons are beginning to blossom exactly like early snowdrops.

5 September

We are now in a new location near Francavilla, right on the coast. As I mentioned, Hotstuff having gone, now we are waiting for a new one. Apparently he is to be an outsider. It was very nearly – of all people – Wagstaff, as he complacently informed us today, but thank heavens that at least was averted, as he would have been unbelievably objectionable. However, my own star has also set I fear. At one time I had big hopes of a captaincy but now, when there is a vacancy in the Battery, I think Jimmy or Bill Carney from 304 will get it. Hotstuff was all for me after Enfidaville but I got so fed up with his nattering selfishness that I fell right out of fashion. Also the C.O.2 doesn't love me. It's the old old story – you must get 'in' to get on. Oh well, what the hell, still I must confess it's a disappointment to have juniors promoted over your head when you've done your job satisfactorily. However cosa sara, sara.

Went bathing in an enormous sea with Sandy K., Sandy C., Jimmy, and John. 10 foot waves smashed one onto the beach knocking the breath out and leaving one bruised and sore – but glowing with health. It was grand. Helped to save

B.S.M. Hamilton from a watery grave; he told me he couldn't have kept going for another two minutes. Towed him in under water bounced along by an enormous wave. We are in a lovely spot here. Terraced vineyards and orchards and plenty of large trees. From my tent I see as I lie down, the green waving fig trees and pomegranate bushes, the vines with bunches of dusty blue grapes already beginning to shrivel, and beyond, the yellow beach with the never silent sea pounding away at the shingle. Why do I think suddenly of the long lonely desert near Agheila? Maybe because there too under the solitary sky, bright with stars, I used to lie in my tent and hear the endless shishing of the shingle under the moon and be sad, with that same sadness I always feel in the presence of death and quietness and crowds. I wish the war would end.

Later: The blow – if so it can be called – duly fell this evening. Jimmy is the new Captain. I find it hard not to be jealous. Jimmy was still a civilian a year after I'd been in the army but still – fortune is a fickle jade. Anyway Jimmy is my friend and I like him. One must try to rise above pettiness. But the stage has been reached when I cease to strive, seeing as I do, that efficiency and endeavour are not enough if unbacked by favouritism. Or maybe it is something in me which is wrong. Perhaps I prefer friendliness and all round 'getting a laugh' to that ruthlessness and disregard of others which is essential to get on in our army. And maybe it should be. Maybe I am wrong in thinking I – and my methods – combine the maximum efficiency with the maximum regard of my men. I only know I have been good enough to do a captain's work under the most protracted fire and worst conditions the Battery has had, and satisfied. And I am good enough to run my own Troop of nearly 70 unassisted, as are the other two captains, by 4 full Sergeants and a B.S.M. But not, apparently, 'the type' for promotion.

And so with the wind gusty outside and the sea booming beyond I go to bed tired and dispirited.

When will this bloody war end . . .

7 September

Yesterday was full of good incidents. After a grand bathe in the afternoon in another crashing sea, afterwards went in the Jeep actually to find Harcourt. However, to my joy I found 132 of my old home Regt. and part of 1 Army in N. Africa, now part of 8 Army. Tony Shaw my old Troop Comd. now an M.C. and a major was there, also John Bevan who came over from 146 after Mareth, and Jim Gilbertson who was adjutant in my day. Another officer was Jim Burgess who was B.S.M. then but gained an immediate commission by knocking out 4 Tigers at 75 yards range with an A/T Rifle! Eventually I came back here, went to a pissy party at 304 where a lot of officers from the Regt. were gathered, drinking and gossiping. Staggered rather tipsily to bed at about 0700. Received three books from home, among which was *San Michele*.

8 September

This is, I suppose, an historic day. Italy has capitulated on terms of unconditional surrender and is co-operating in throwing the Jerry out of Italy itself. I couldn't – don't ask me why – pluck up the correct mood to join in the jubilation which is rampant tonight. For one thing I don't believe the war is over by any means. I think the Germans will go on fighting for at least a year more. And secondly I am feeling very strange and distant with the large doses of Quinine we are taking for 3 days against Malaria. My ears are ringing and my head feels strangely detached. Instead of the cheering and the victory I find myself thinking of those rows of wooden crosses that line the pleasant orchards before Tripoli, and in particular of Jock's lonely grave, out on the windswept marshes of Pisida. It is so vivid I can see it now as if it were only yesterday I was there . . . the red house, battered by shellfire on the left of the road, the wire and the concrete, and the built-up narrow road with its craters and scars and burnt out skeletons of lorries and tanks. Mines, mines, and more mines. A grave – 'Capt. Evans D.E.' – who was he? – I shall never know. The great crater where six engineers died suddenly in the flailing lead of an S mine. And Jock's grave under the white moon. Jock, gone for always, and yet always present in the memory. Other crosses, and other hideous corpses. And those who fought in the desert, and died there in the hot sun, before we ever came. All these are the price of victory and the reminder in the hour of triumph.

Speculation is rife. Shall we at long last – go home? Shall we garrison Italy? Shall we go into Turkey, Greece, Yugoslavia, South France? What shall we do? These are the topics of the hour. No doubt of every unit of 8 Army. We should know before long.

Letter from home yesterday. Dad is very ill, which is a bad thing. Discovered yesterday that Dick was the fag of Major Charles Napier (M.C.) of the 5/7 Gordons, who came in for a drink last night. I had met him frequently before without the possibility occurring to me. Coincidences of that sort are fairly common in wartime.

9 September

We are moving on 12 September to a new area about 6 miles east of here. Went and recced it today and to my joy find that Debroy is only a mile or rather less away so we ought to be able to see a lot of each other for a week or two. I do hope so. My god it makes a difference having a real friend about the place. Had a wonderful afternoon on the beach, full of 'sunburnt mirth' and childhood in the water.

The Germans have 21 Divisions in Italy, 3 armoured; so maybe my pessimism of last night – regarded by the other officers as a piece of typical eccentricity – may be justified. Maybe these peaceful 'green days in forests and blue days at sea' are numbered.

10 September

Still the days pass, peacefully, sunnily and in general, rather happily. Wagstaff is being very tolerable as a B.C., and everybody else rather cheerful and amusing, and full of practical jokes. The latest is that Peter Dawson, who looks rather like Stalin and is nicknamed 'The Marshall' or 'Joe', is going to have a large and impressive hammer and sickle painted on his bivvy.

Good news; Alistair should be back very soon. Only – a slight crisis is indicated for obvious reasons. Can't write any more tonight – too much noise going on.

11 September

Bathing today, I stubbed my second toe of my left foot viciously on either Sandy Cowie or a large stone. I sprained two muscles and tonight I can hardly stand on it and my whole left foot throbs most painfully. Otherwise the bathe was simply idyllic with marvellously warm sea and scorching sunshine. My tan is deepening and improving daily. It's better now than it has been for a very long time. In Italy most interesting events are taking place, with the Germans and Italians fighting each other. Several heavy units of the Italian navy have reached Malta – air-covered by the R.A.F! Rommel is in charge of operations and our '5th Army' landing near Naples is pushing ahead. We have occupied Taranto. These are very tranquil nights with a ripening moon, and cicadas singing among the lemon trees. In the distance, the calm and shining sea.

I discovered today that Hotstuff definitely reported against me when he left, which shows the degree of the man's fickleness and general undependability. How much weight he carried I don't know but the C.O.2 has not been particularly affable of late. From other sources come reports of a favourable impression made by my C.P. in action, and Wagstaff seems well disposed. I am manning H.Q. at the moment most scrupulously – and I hope, and believe – efficiently. I have revised and reorganised quite a few things and all seems to be smooth. But you can't go on that. If a frame is in progress you can be super-efficient and it counts for nothing. I fear Jimmy may become C.P.O. if he has to revert, and I'm bound to say this would be bitterly disappointing to me, and, I think, very unfair.

But what of that?

13 September

We moved on 12 September, across the hills and back onto the plain and coastal road where we now are. The only difference being that we are now high on top of the cliffs. Our new location is also rather lovely in among olive trees and lemon groves.

Last night Debroy came up to see me and gave the welcome news that my Algiers parcel for Pam had arrived. Apparently she was delighted with the slippers, and rang up Joan, who wrote to D. I have had no mail from Pam for rather a time now. The whole delivery is bad at the moment, which always causes discontent. Also Alistair arrived back last night and we talked until 0100 over the evil times we have fallen on lately. Naturally the ascendancy of Wagstaff is as irksome to him as the elevation of 'Jam' was at one time to me. However, a sort of hopeless resignation is as far as I can see, the only attitude to adopt. Today has been very hot and I have been orderly officer and been wearing the desert boots Hotstuff 'sold' me. I put sold in quotes because I never paid the little cad for them, a source of some pleasure to me. (I bet he writes to ask for the money.) Incidentally they are rather tight, which has made my temper rather short.

Tonight a mass indent of hat sizes was called for, as a preliminary to the expected arrival of berets shortly. I am annoyed to record that I wrote recently to Herbert Johnson for a new cheesecutter. However, what the hell little Archie as they say. Letter card from Gerard yesterday and I replied today. A full moon has slid over the hill tonight. Last night the whole place was bathed in the most glorious silver light. Curious the controversy which rages over the age of the moon. Is she a young lustful maiden whose ghostly white arms encircle the watcher in his madness? Or an aged cynic watching almost sadly and disbelieving? I only know the moonlight never fails to fill me with melancholy and nostalgia. It is just 7 months since Jock was killed and I remember so well the reddish moon that rose that night as I lay outside E Tp. command post under the desert stars. The guns stood out stark against the bright sand and the plough was clear and gleaming. And how I remember the inconsolable sense of loss which swept over me that long, lonely, sleepless night of 13 February with Jock lying in the bleak marshes where the single cratered road drove into Tunisia.

They are fighting hard in the Naples area, with the 5th Army having a poor time, and the eighth pushing slowly up from the heel. I haven't heard tonight's news so there may be something new.

The new general is arriving on the 16th and I believe some sort of ceremonial parade is indicated, though it is possible such a thing may for once be skipped.

Bought two pairs of splendidly sheer silk stockings today and sent them off to Pam. Do hope I hear from her soon.

14 September

Went out with D. today and had a furious bathe and orgy of reminiscence. Slept badly; it was so hot and humid. No mail today. I think the planes are in use on the battlefront where our troops – 46 and 56 Div. – are having a pretty tough time with an aggressive and air-supported Boche. Met a Padre at Corps who said the war would be over by November. I said 'Yes, November 1944.' We shall see. News of leave to Palermo. I am unenthusiastic, though shared with D. and Peter

Dawson, it might be a good laugh. I dislike this 'rest' and would rather be in action and help to get the bloody thing finished. I think most of the soldiers feel the same. Ink has run out.

15 September

Gloriously sunny day after another bad night's sleep in the hot damp weather we seem to get these nights. At about 0300 I was wakened by the high miniature violin of a mosquito humming around the tent. There are few more maddening things than this. Quite apart from the probability of a bite, the hideous emasculated twang, suddenly low in the ear, or the small wings tickling the nostril, make sleep impossible. I got out my torch and silhouetted the pest in its beam like a bomber at night with the searchlight showing tiny silver wings. I slew it against the wall of my tent with great satisfaction and the map reference code. (Rather a good zeugma.)

Bathed today with D. at his unit and met Col. Perry, now at the 73 (D.'s unit). He was extremely affable and muddle-headed as ever. D. came back here for supper. There was a small mail today but nothing for me which is maddening. G.O.C. making an inspection tomorrow with appropriate pomp and circumstance. Sandy Kinnaird went sick, leaving only 6 officers in the Battery and me with no A.C.P.O. I hope he won't be away too long. He had a very badly poisoned finger. Today in the sea I swam out further than on any occasion since I left home. It is simply grand right out there beyond almost anybody (not D. who, a strong swimmer, was about 50 yards beyond me) floating in the blue transparent water. Down below you could see little shoals of small silver fish darting about, or just pushing ahead in formations, as unruffled as the bombers we see flying towards Italy. You feel a thousand miles from the earth. On the beach and among the rocks in the near-shallows you can see brown bodies lying on the yellow sand or sporting and leaping like some miniature painting. They are out of earshot, and might be figures on the stage of some impossibly far-removed theatre.

Cool and curving were the right words to describe the Kingdom of a fish.

17 September

Yesterday the G.O.C. arrived. After the usual cursory inspection of the area (cleaned and 'bullshed' for days by all) he had the Regt. out in the blazing sunshine, and delivered an address. It was too long and not particularly interesting. Here is the passage which struck me as most significant. He was discussing the hero type of German sneak-raider which shoots down Brighton High St., 'Kills off a few dozen people and drops two 500 Kilo bombs which knock down a couple of shops – WHICH PROBABLY BELONG TO JEWS ANYWAY . . .'

This sally failed to rouse the applause which apparently was expected for it. I was amazed and disgusted at the bad taste it showed. True or false, for a

General to make such a remark in a Regiment which includes Jews and part Jews in its number seems to me to nullify most of those things which we have tried for so long to instil into our soldiers. Another lecture also too long and full of platitudes was delivered to officers of the Div. by him at Barcellona this morning. In appearance he is unprepossessing. Slight, with rather protruding teeth, a somewhat rattish face, which somehow reminded me of one of those little grooms who have worked in stables all their life, and quite penetrating blue eyes. He is a heavy smoker, wheezes a bit, and aged about 45. In general the Div. officers are not very impressed, tho' he must be fairly good to have been chosen by Monty.

Letters from George and Debroy's fiancée Joan, yesterday. Replied to both. Today met Peter Lear ('King') for the first time in months, also 'Big' Arthur, all companions of the long trip out from England last year.

I am not sleeping well these days. The nights are hot and humid with pallid moonlight (now beginning to wane) and the cicadas whining in the orchards. In the distance the bagpipes of the 1st Gordons wail. I read *San Michele* in bed last night. It is full of beauty and profound thought, and rather sad.

In Italy the initial crisis round the Salerno bridgeheads has passed, the 8th and the 5th Armies have joined and the Germans are retiring northwards. We must have lost quite some material.

18 September

Went over to have dinner with D. today and also bathed in the afternoon. Very pleasant and very amusing. Got a 'good chit' from Wagstaff today over the H.Q. lines which were the best in the battery. Case of bread cast on Monday's waters.

19 September

Tonight as we were sitting in the Mess the news came through that our Gordon has got his Majority. I find myself uncertain to determine in my own mind just how good or bad the news is. He's been quite friendly to me recently but you can't tell just how he'll react to a crown on his shoulder.

It gets dark very early nowadays and the men have little to do and nowhere to go. However, leave to Catania starts for the O.R.s tomorrow which should cheer them all up. Under Wagstaff there is no doubt a new regime of terror and efficiency will come into force. It will be quite good for the Battery but rather wearing. He is so opinionated and dogmatic though he doesn't _mean_ badly! Alistair will be quite shattered by the news. It will be better for all concerned really if he doesn't come back here, though I shall certainly miss him. Another Captaincy is now going but I shan't get it – I think Bill Carney probably will. I can't say I care very much now. The route to success is not one I seem to be much good at travelling – in the Army.

23 September

Not much has been going on; that's why I've made no entry for 4 days. Partly that and partly because I've not been feeling too good; a sort of attack of 'Sicilian Doldrums', bringing sleepless nights and sweaty days full of lethargy and heaviness. Wagstaff, one must admit, is making a good job of running his battery, and general efficiency is greatly improving all round. In my own troop, the lines are worthy of Aldershot each day, whereas at Bougie they looked more like a leper colony. Also I don't think the soldiers resent this discipline – once they have realised that (a) it is necessary and (b) that it will be enforced.

We visit each other quite often. I frequently go to 304 who are a grand crowd, particularly their cynical and intelligent Major, Ken Pooley, who is as far as Subaltern and Major can be, a very good friend of mine. Also Bill Carney and Stewart Watts are grand chaps. My mail has been poor lately, which always has a depressing effect, but yesterday at last came a letter from Pam, full of Holiday Conquests and my present from Algiers. I could wish that Pam was a little more profound but she is young and enjoying life. I often doubt if I shall marry her, and was rather surprised when D. told me on the beach one day that he had a similar feeling in his case. D. is still leading a confined life due to the impetigo and purple dye all over his face. Peter and I go on leave to Palermo on 3 Oct. and we are hoping he'll be able to fit his in at the same time. The war, in general, goes well, both in Russia and Italy and New Guinea, but I still think we have at least a year's fighting in Europe. The Division is still being rested – probably for some time. At the moment we seem to be supplying all the fatigues in Sicily and nearly all our transport has been taken away too. But the guns, polished and painted, are dazzlingly smart. Sandy K. came back 2 days ago, but is going on leave for a week tomorrow.

24 September

Rumours are in the air. The chief of these is the evergreen 'we are going home' supported by a series of semi-circumstantial pieces of evidence. On Sunday Monty is coming, it is said, to address the Div. Arty. I am looking forward to this considerably. Went to Spadafora with Jimmy this afternoon for watch-straps. A very excellent brand, hand made by a local cobbler I discovered a week or two ago. We also bathed, and had an excellent 75 yard race in which I was beaten by about 3 yards. We have frequent races and the improvement in my swimming is considerable. I now cover distances with ease, which at Bougie were quite impossible.

Anyway it all goes to improve the stamina a bit, which is a good thing. Actually Jimmy is something of an expert and used to compete in tournaments so I find it rather encouraging to extend him. Yesterday we had a race with Gordon and John and Sandy, whom I beat fairly comfortably. Wrote home and to Pam yesterday night, also an A/G to New York.

The latest 'stunt' of the General's is an 'Assault at arms' which is a tedious business involving an impossible amount of training with the few men we have left. Included – hold your breath – is an <u>essay</u> for all Subalterns with the delicious and original subject matter of either 'Post War Reconstruction' or 'The effect of Air Power on our sea power'. Subjects which have provided every journalist with a few make-weight columns for the past 4 years. Still, we're getting round to it. We'll be up to 1942 soon! Am reading *Anna Karenina*.

26 September

So it is true. Rumour, for once, has not been the lying jade. Monty in his speech today said we are going home. Actually, amid roars of laughter, he said we weren't to take it that we were definitely going home, but that he was doing his best to arrange it – and 'pretty soon'. So we all know what that means. An atmosphere of unrestrained delight reigns everywhere tonight. The officers Mess is running a sweep on the day the first man in the Battery touches Great Britain. I've nominated 24 November. Also great news is that it would appear that Monty will come home too and re-form the 8th Army on English soil, as several units of the 'real' 8th are on their way home, or already there. So it looks as though we may be among the first to land in Europe from the other end. What an army! The afternoon we spent on the beach swimming in a tumultuous sea, and gloatingly reviewing scenes and welcomes we shall receive. Monty was tremendous today. He's a grand little man with enormous personality. The troops cheered him furiously at intervals. A gem: 'We have chased the Germans into the sea at Cape Bon. We've chased them into the sea across the Straits of Messina.' Pause. 'And if there's any more sea . . .' roars of laughter 'we are quite prepared to do some more pushing!' More roars of laughter. The great affection felt for Monty by everybody is a wonderful thing.

28 September

Tremendous battle in progress between our skill at censorship and the deep cunning of the men in dropping the un-noticeable hint. 50 Div. said to be already on the way, and already our own Recce Parties are warmed for a move towards Taormina, and there are mysterious comings and goings among the great.

Went to see D. yesterday. He has had a bad dose of impetigo lately and alas he has had to go into Hospital yesterday. However he should be out in about 10 days, but alas he'll miss our leave together in Palermo. But – great news again – he is also coming home so we ought to have a grand time with our girls once we do get home. Last night a tremendous gusty wind fell upon us, flattening R.H.Q., throwing our Mess Tent all over Sicily, and raising clouds of reddish dust. I lay in bed fully expecting my tent to disappear any moment. I remember waking up at about 3 and thinking my god it's gone and stretching out my hand into the dark, but it touched the bounding canvas and I knew all was still well. Gordon has gone off with the C.O. on a few days course or something so things are rather more restful than usual. I killed 8 flies with one blow of the flyswat yesterday which is a Battery record. No mail today, but a letter from Bette in S. Africa yesterday. Foul gale still raging. Feeling a bit frowsty not having bathed today – an unusual omission these days but it was too rough and the sea was a mass of white horses. I've finished my essay – a most uninspired piece of tepidity.

29 September

Last night at five and twenty to nine the wind died as suddenly as the hum of conversation when the theatre curtain goes up. Later in the night the rain came in full force and today was calmer and fairly sunny with a magnificent decrease of flies owing to the furious gale. Bathed today with Sandy and Jimmy in a rough sea but it was extremely invigorating. My pen nib seems to be giving up the ghost. It's certainly had a long trek and written a good many thousand words.

The war is continuing to go well on all fronts. We are closing on Naples. All Battery conversation still hinges on the burning topic . . . shall we or shan't we, and if so when? Certain it is that we are moving to a new area soon, and that the C.O. has gone by plane to Cairo. Letter from George Long again today. He is still very despondent in Iraq. Otherwise no mail today. My mail from England has been damned bad of late. I can't think why.

30 September

A day full of sunshine and more, interesting rumours. Our move from here will not be more early than 4 Oct. – the implication being that it won't be long after that date. We shall move to an area – either the one at present occupied by 50 Div. or if they have at last gone – and surely they will go soon – to another area just north of Catania. And – and this is the interesting bit – 'and if we only stay about a fortnight' we shall stay there till we go.

Had another wonderful bathe with Jimmy and Peter this afternoon. Jimmy and I raced 100 yards – he won by about 5 (but ended up in much better condition). The last 20 yards full out were quite a strain. However we were feeling full of beans and came back up the 400 foot of cliff in about 5 minutes. How good it is to feel healthy. It was grand on the beach. One lay in the warm sand, dreaming – chiefly of going home – and hearing the repetitive surge and crash of the waves on the shingles. One stood knee-high in the warm foam with the sun warm on a tanned back – how Jock would have loved it all. Today came a short but pleasant letter from Bé, also a note from niece Monica aged about 10 all about how she lost her bag on the moving staircase, and how she's going to get a new kitten because Twinkle is lost. How old it made me feel. And yet this afternoon I too might have been 10 again, laughing and leaping in the surf.

Conflicting reports on Palermo, where Peter and I are going on leave on Sunday. Bill Ovenstone the Adjutant says it's lousy, Debroy's friends say it's good. Obviously a case for personal investigation.

Wrote several letters today. To B., to Pam, to Bette, to Bé, and to George Long. Pleasantly complacent feeling which comes of correspondence successfully caught up with.

Remarkable recovery of my new nib which I thought had definitely had it. Also by the way sent an A.G. to N.Y. asking for a year's sub to *Esquire* and ditto for *Life* for Ken Pooley.

2 October

Sullen afternoon with a chilly little wind and occasional showers. Somewhat depressing 'nothing to do' feeling as sometimes on Sunday afternoons back in England, while waiting to go on leave tomorrow.

Yesterday afternoon rather an amusing incident. Sandy Cowie and I have been having stone battles in the water for the last fortnight. The stones, at first fairly modest pebbles, have grown larger and larger, till yesterday a young grapefruit coming out of the sun, landed slap on the back of my head laying me low in the surf, nearly knocked out, with blood reddening the water. Remarkably the damage was only superficial, though I had to go up to the doctor and have a stitch put in after tea. I had no idea my cranium was so powerfully armoured! Jimmy, who was watching, tells me the projectile bounced off with a hollow, gong-like sound! Have finished and banged out on a typewriter, my essay on Problems in Post-war Britain. About 3000 words and not as dull to read over as I had expected. Letters from home and Dorothy yesterday. The former contained good news of various parcels and a regular cigarette supply which are on the way, and the latter was interesting because Dorothy has met Pam in town and gave me a series of impressions which I value highly, she being a person of unusual discernment where I am concerned. She thought Pam 'the goods', so to speak, but may be too young for me. Maybe she is right. I look forward to seeing Pam again to find out if she has altered much or grown up mentally to any extent. Replied to both those letters last night. News yesterday of the fall of Naples, so all is going well. 170 miles to Palermo so Peter and I are making a fairly early start, accompanied by the faithful Findlay. Saw Ken Pooley today and he gave a most dismal account of the billets and just about everything else, so we are going to try and get into a hotel recommended by Debroy's people. At least that will mean a (clean) bed and maybe even some hot water.

And on this note I will end this 4th section of my diary. No. 5 is an altogether more luxurious effort, with a stiff cover. Army Book No. something or other, but I don't remember just which.

5 October

But I must begin at the beginning. On 3 October quite early in the morning, Peter and I, with Findlay in the back, set out on a cool, sunny drive to Palermo, 160 miles away. We drove hard, two hours at a time, with the steering so stiff it gave you blisters, and reached there in 6^1/$_2$ hours, about the best time yet. The country along the coast road past Barcellona (irritatingly and invariably pronounced as in the Spanish city) and Cefalu is very lovely with its unchanging fringe of very blue sea. After Ken Pooley's gloomy reports we faced Palermo with very mixed feelings which were destined to change rapidly to great pleasure. Coming through Cefalu one came into the American Army Zone. Enormous tented camps, the odd sentry lounging against a gate, and huge trucks and Jeeps whizzing everywhere. The area almost as liberally signposted as the H.D. When we reached Palermo we went to the Billeting officer and found a most obliging captain who told us that though accommodation was down to 'rock bottom' he'd give us a room in the Hotel Sole. This was Triumph No. 1 as one of the lousy things about this Palermo leave is living in the official officers billet where you sleep on the floor; it is lousy with mosquitoes and full of rather dim types; altogether in fact like an officers mess, one of the things one goes on leave to escape. So this was fine – here we were in the Sole – two real <u>beds</u>, and running water. What more could one ask? We fixed Findlay up at the billet, because we couldn't get him in here. There wasn't much to do that day, as it was already getting late and we were rather tired after a long drive in hot sunshine. We found a good place to eat – the Ristorante Napoli where we had Minestrone, Spaghetti and steak for exactly 3/6 and then came back to the Sole Bar to talk to the Americans. 'The Yanks', a much debated topic of conversation, are extraordinary creatures. Some are straight off the films, and they are very unsophisticated. But I rather like them; the ones we've become friendly with here have been damned kind to us. The first of these is the gum-chewing, bespectacled Mortimer Katz (loot) of the 507 Paratroops, who went right through the Yanks Officers Shop for us and bought me two shirts, a tie, a belt, a pair of slacks, and Peter slacks and shoes. These clothes are superb quality, and one of our leave 'aims', so that's another satisfied. Another, as we left to go to bed the first night, turned to us and said, 'Gee, I get a great kick out of hearing you guys talk'. Next day we got up late and pottered about town in the morning. I fished out a bottle of gin and Katz, Peter and I slew it. Peter and I then went to the Excelsior for lunch and drank more wine, came back to the hotel, and discovered we'd been very drunk for some time, and fell onto bed and slept till 6. I was then sick as hell and retired feeling very miserable for the night. Katz and our Australian flyer whose name I never discovered, but who, apropos of nothing, said 'Shit' every few minutes, came up and drank more whisky and then Peter and I, with all the Bicarbonate of Soda tablets I could find inside us, went into uneasy slumber. We remembered today that we went to a hospital after lunch to have my stitch removed, but I had violent hiccoughs and the doctor told me to go away for a few days. At the time we couldn't think why. . . . About Palermo: it's a 'spaciously' built city with long straight streets in blocks, and some fine modern buildings. The Post Office is a pillared monstrosity which simply cannot be described more adequately than that. A good many shops are open, though not very well stocked. A certain amount of bomb damage. Everything very efficient and swarming with Yanks – including coloured troops, though I've also seen R.N., R.A.F., 8th Army, and a good few kilts and H.D. in general. Also some marines.

Today we got up earlier and have spent most of our time eating. Breakfast at the billet, which made us glad we hadn't stayed there, tho' the food was O.K. Then a shopping tour. I had a manicure and we bought: lingerie and a nightie for Peter's dame, also 3 pairs of stockings. A damn fine navy blue silk scarf with red flowers for Pam, a primus stove each – god knows where they came from but they're genuine and new. Toothbrush and soap holders, and various other items – all the sort of things we've been wanting for ages. After lunch (spaghetti and more wine) we motored out to Modello, the lovely lido of Palermo. We found a grand restaurant, where under a bower of grapes, we ate immense lobsters, fresh as daisies. A grand smell of fresh fish permeated the place, and our tomato and onion salad was crisp. Then back, and more town crawling. The women are not so hot here in Palermo though their figures, particularly their breasts, are very good, also their carriage. Complexion generally speaking poor. We met 'Wily' Kaestlin also just arrived on leave, but all ignorant of this splendid hotel. In fact I believe we're about the only ones who have found it, apart from the Yanks and some of the Gordon Highlanders. Supper tonight: Minestrone, lovely fish in sauce, and a damn great steak. We haven't eaten like this for years; it's a wonderful feeling to be full of good food. I am growing a moustache, which is actually beginning to darken the lip a little. I feel a bit dubious about it, but Peter, who sports a fine bushy model, assures me it's doing well. It gives one a new interest in life, and is tenderly vaselined each night! Tomorrow another Yank officer is going to get me some shoes if possible so all is well. This has been a grand leave so far; I've really enjoyed it and it hasn't been the alcoholic riot Algiers turned out to be.

9 October

Two more delightful days of leave. We managed to get some American ration cards which entitled us to cigarettes (Camel – ugh!), shaving soap and other useful oddments. And another American officer bought me some good shoes at the same place. This was a good thing as the one I mentioned in my last entry was unable to do so because they hadn't my size at the time. Came the 8th and we set off back, but after about 10 miles the prop shaft sheared and with horrible grindings and groans the car skidded to a halt. We had been expecting something of the sort. Followed a rather irritating day. On examination we found both petrol tanks holed, the H.T. lead cut off and various smaller items, so first we sent a message by one of the homeward-bound 126 trucks, and then started stripping the shaft. This took till 1730 during which time I'd touched a nearby Yank unit for plenty rations! All day we had expected to see Sandy Cowie coming up the road in his Jeep, but no sign, so we assumed leave to be held up. Also, six appeals to the nearest Depot with a wrecker produced no luck. Eventually we stopped the night – having been towed there – with the local A.M.G.O.T. officials. That is where I am now, still waiting for a truck to tow me back, for Peter has left in a Fiat 500 to render explanations etc. The A.M.G.O.T. H.Q. is a pleasant villa by the side of the road, containing:

Lt. Ted Marshall: An ex R.A.S.C. Lieut. who looks rather like Goering and has no teeth; they are being repaired. Quite affable. It was he who first extended the invitation.

Capt. Bill Hare: An ex-Detective Inspector who talks a lot but quite interestingly. A baldish rather sinister man. Very friendly.

Major Sir Charles Buchanan: An amazingly pukkah relic from the H.L.I. at some time in his life. A regular. Very much so. Service in the East y'know and last war ribbons. Changes for dinner – of course. Is rather horrified and puzzled by the other two. Don't know if he's a Bart or not.

The place is lousy with mosquitoes – I hope it's not malarious as I've been much bitten. Can't think why no relief waggon has arrived; it's all most peculiar. The moustache is genuinely visible and coming along O.K. Very dull entry, but I don't feel too good.

11 October

Spent the 10th waiting for the relief waggon, and as it hadn't turned up by lunchtime, Peter decided to leave in a Fiat 500. A.M.G.O.T. raked up for us. By 7 nothing had arrived, so I went out to dinner with a local princess who spoke

English well. Dinner served amid tinkling glass and silver. Dinner was soup, fish, joint and sweet, preceded by vermouth, accompanied by wine, red and white, and followed by champagne, coffee and liqueurs. So much for poverty stricken Sicily. After dinner, two gloriously lovely girls came in and spent the rest of the evening. When I got back, the waggon had arrived, and next day we went back. Started 0900 and 90 miles from home the Morris brakes went, and it finally became untowable. We unhooked and went on, leaving an N.C.O. with the truck. Reached home about 1815. Bad gippie tummy and I went to bed early. Letters: one from home, a letter from New York, one from George and one from Pam. Quote: 'Jack, dearest when you went abroad, you knew, because I told you at the time, that as I hadn't been about very much or met many people I didn't know whether my feelings deep as they were for you were the marrying kind or not; your being away hasn't made me any the wiser naturally, and I shan't know until you come back and I see you again. Damn it, it's obvious I'm very fond of you or did you think I'd bother to write to you so often or for so long?'

This has given me much food for thought. Today it rained furiously and I've had frightful colic so I'm off colour – wrote Pam, Home and N.Y. Everybody a bit short-tempered and touchy. We are moving to Syracuse in two days with an 0615 start and similar trials. Very dull, I'm a bit fed up with the diary at the moment tho' I don't know why.

14 October

Syracuse: As far as I remember nothing much occurred between my last entry and our move, except a very rapid deterioration of my stomach condition. Also, it rained and thundered with great enthusiasm and violence for two or three days during which time we crept about, miserably inadequately clothed in our summer clothing, and tried – frequently – to use the cavorting lavatory in gusty rain. On the very early morning of the 13th – 6 o'clock to be exact – we moved off and a long the coast road toward Faro and Messina, and through that familiar town – now much placarded and signposted and with its quota of Yanks – towards Taormina and Catania. We halted short of the latter about midday. I had eaten nothing till then owing to my tum, and I had a stiff neck, so I wasn't feeling particularly exuberant. Anyway we went on past Catania whose airfield and southern approaches bore witness to the struggle for the city. Burnt out tanks, broken guns, charred indeterminate ruins, and wooden crosses everywhere. We reached Syracuse towards evening and scrambled into billets in the rainy darkness. (It has been raining on and off ever since and is now.) Syracuse is a rambling city with a good harbour and winding narrow streets. Rather like the screen set for *The Testament of Dr. Mabuse*. Our billets are in bombed hotels and old houses and flats. Not very comfortable but at least a roof over one's head.

The mess is well furnished and very comfortable. The food, alas, cannot be eaten by me as my guts are still very queasy though improving. All speculation leads to the question 'Are we – and when'. All reliable information points to a short stay here and then homeward bound from Agusta. Certainly we are losing the rest of our transport tomorrow, and the guns are said to be going soon afterwards. Anyway we shall see. It is delightful to be in a real room again, and I have scrounged a small spring mattress. So it is comfort positively unknown. Letter from Gerard today also a statement from Barclays in London informing me that I have in my a/c on September 30, £216.18.9. This is rather a goodish sum and will be rather more by now, as it should include some more (not much) army pay, the remainder of my Cairo credits, and a £25 cheque which falls due this month.

15 October

Last night just after I finished writing, a grand flap set in and Waggy was sent for by R.H.Q. – everybody bursting with secret information etc.

Anyway this morning a conference – the upshot of which was the information that we are going home on or about 6 November! So today a frantic packing up etc. of stuff started with all the usual checks and sort outs.

Nearly all our equipment is going away immediately. All the guns, trailers and quads leave at 0600 tomorrow. Of course everybody is frantically excited and morale soars high. Incidentally the Regtl. Advance party leaves in about a week. Sometimes I find myself daydreaming of scenes when I get back – what I shall say, the questions they will ask . . . it's strange that I don't feel more excited than I do, but I expect I shall, as the time draws nearer. And Pam: will she love me less, or more; and shall I love her less, or more. This is one of the more difficult of my problems.

My moustache is now beginning to assume the resemblance of a real one. It is very dark, but a little thin on the ground. I have daily battles with myself whether or not to remove it, but the mess is solidly in favour of giving it a chance, so thus far it remains . . . anyway it's 3 weeks till we sail, so there's plenty of time to reconsider such things. Till we sail . . . how casually I write the words, and yet how much they mean after our long trip across desert, mountains, and sea to this moment in time. Yet here we sit, writing, playing draughts and reading, in complete silence and we seem almost to look on it as 'just another move'. But we don't.

Incidentally I don't think I ever mentioned that Alistair is now town major of Milazzo, and Monty, wounded at Hill 199, returned the night before I went to Palermo. A great raconteur, he keeps the mess very much amused. We are a happy enough mess these days; Waggy is doing well as B.C. and most of the old jealousies have gone. I won't pretend I don't get an occasional pang looking at Jimmy's third pip but what the hell little Archie, what the hell.

17 October

Still the days, occasionally sunny, occasionally filled by gusty showers, pass by amid the usual flutter of handing in stores and heightened anticipation all round. On the morning of the 16th in a fit of discouragement, I shaved off my none too profuse moustache. Now that it's done, I can't say I regret it as I think it wouldn't have suited me so very well, even had it attained notable proportions. I am orderly officer tonight, but as I'm not feeling too well, Gordon has rather considerately allowed me to turn out the guard at 2130, whereas I was going to do so (out of some latent sense of duty) at 0300.

On the debit side comes news that my kit, together with that of all the other officers who joined the Regiment after it landed, has not yet been located by B.D.R.A. Agitation will suitably be made to the C.O. tomorrow.

19 October

The advance party has left. Already there is talk of their arranging leave trains in England (in England . . .) and today has been warm and full of sunshine. So I feel unusually contented tonight. Today I had my photograph taken for some Regimental History or other. Several small but pleasing things have been happening lately. I scrounged a nice little black box for my kit, a few days ago; and L/Bdr. Dougan gave me a small and very neat basin for which I got the local cobbler to make a strap on leather and canvas lid. The entire issue is the envy of the mess, and cost me precisely 3/6. The equivalent article cost Peter 26/- in a shop.

Then again, there was an excellent Naafi today from which I got 160 cigarettes, two boxes of fat English matches, 3 bars of chocolate, a tin of fruit drops, a tin of Kiwi dark tan, 2 razor blades, and a bar of Lux Toilet Soap. Excellent. Another Naafi tomorrow morning it is said, and Sandy K. goes to fetch yet another tomorrow.

Again I had an excellent haircut and shampoo yesterday. Again, my troop is smart, contented and behaving itself. Again, I am in good odour with Gordon, which makes everything pleasanter and prospects a little brighter. Again, the new shoes I bought in Palermo are damn comfortable. And finally – we are going home. England, at Xmas, and the war being won. No need to think of next Spring, when we shall almost certainly lead the attack onto France. I wonder how many of us will come out of that alive. I, personally, have very little personal emotion left for that consideration. At one time I had a strong premonition that I should die in action. Now I have been under rather harrowing fire several times I have escaped, and face the future speculatively but without anxiety. Cosa sara, sara, as they say in these parts. If I am to die, then die I shall, maybe swiftly with a merciful bullet, maybe slowly in great agony. I should consider the latter just in some ways, as a sort of retribution for the wrongs I have done, believing that that would be my atonement, not one in a future life in which I still – rather regretfully at times – find it impossible to believe. Death is so swift and final. I am always preyed upon by this swift finality, seeing it as something by which I don't wish to be convinced, realising its material truth, yet longing to be led to some kind of faith more or less impossible to my type of reasoning. Maybe some day it will come to me. And if I should die on some undistinguished battlefield (. . . the scarred slopes of Hill 199 with shellfire murmuring in the sunshine, and the mumbled words . . .) it would be wrong to grieve for me, for the thousands that are 'we', for in dying we live – not in a 'life everlasting' but in the very moment of our death – the completed picture, the lovely poem, with no time to spoil them. But I don't want to die, I want to feel the sunshine on my face, and the salty sunburn on my arm after bathing – 'Life to be sure is nothing much to lose, but young men think it is and we were young.'

To descend to more mundane matters. I have to go to Messina on Saturday to give evidence at the court martial of an R.A.S.C. driver I put under arrest the morning we left Messina. He hadn't a hope, the bloody fool, and having been ingrained with a certain amount of military discipline by now, I hope they give it him hot. We play draughts often in the mess. Sandy Cowie is the champion; unbeaten except by me, and I've only scored 2 wins against about 50 by him.

Bought some little boxes of lemons and oranges for Carole and Nicholas – Dorothy and Denny's kids, and Bé's children. Also wrote to Pam and Gerard and Debroy the other evening.

23 October

And now it's Saturday – but I'm not in Messina. I'm in bed, feeling not very good. The sequence of events is as follows. On Thursday evening I began to feel very hot with an eye-closing headache and icy hands and feet. So I went to bed with 3 aspro and a hot drink, and sweated like hell all night. Next day, Peter, who's also been feeling lousy, but with different symptoms, went off to hospital with jaundice. In the afternoon the fever came up again and the iron band of headache, and the doc came along. My temperature was 102 °F. Dover and Aspirin and another hot bath in my sleeping bag. Today I'm feeling a bit better but have pains in my glands down the inside of the thigh and the M.O. said my temp. was still up this morning. It certainly is this afternoon. Same treatment tonight. Sandfly? Jaundice? Hospital? Home?

24 October

I lie in bed. Inside the room the late afternoon sunshine is mellow on the white walls. My mosquito net not being in use in day-time, I am pestered by furiously inquisitive flies. Outside across the street a gramophone is playing; an Italian soprano is shrieking the sort of operatic song that sopranos on Iti gramophones always do shriek. Hooves and roller skates clatter and grind along the street. Occasionally the upward whine of a petrol engine or the hoot of a car. Children's inconsequential voices and sometimes an outburst of rapid Italian. On the ceiling the tap of our neighbour's shoes. It is all very solitary and depressing marooned here in bed. Doc. couldn't come this morning but may do so tonight. My fever has decreased, perhaps vanished, for I feel much better and can stand up without wanting to vomit. Glands still a bit tender but Leech says only due to poisoned foot. Curious. Read a very good book, *A Narrow Street* which showed me how small is my own talent for description and understanding of life. I often think I shall never become a really successful writer though at times my emotions and inspirations are quite considerable. Letter from Dennis Carter yesterday which I answered today.

Last night I had to do another bloody great sweat and woke up in the middle feeling like hell. Only relief being that my usually burning forehead was icy cold with beads of sweat. They trickled all over my body feeling like insects, and lodged in my ear where they tickled me into wakefulness.

About midnight, a crowd of drunken Jocks (yesterday was Alamein anniversary and everybody was tolerant) came hooting and lurching down the street. One in particular serenaded our window with a volley of Fooks doing service for any adjective adverb noun pronoun required. Monty boomed 'shut up' and the Jock yelled loudly back 'Fook you, you bastard!' with complete aplomb. I laughed so much I nearly threw up. Findlay buys me oranges daily which I suck by quarters but they are as tart as lemons and my gums are sore! In fact, in the words of the famous narrative poem, 'Life presents a Dismal Picture'.

Battledress has been issued. We shall embark in it. At least I hope I shall.

26 October

Got up yesterday for the first time; the Leech having departed for Malta to see his brother, he sent round his thermometer and I was sub normal so as I say I got up. My foot and gland were hurting like hell. Later I went to see the M.O.'s stooge – an uncommunicative but quite pleasant Bombardier, known by all and sundry as Dr. Death. I limped round for the rest of the day feeling like the proverbial two cents worth of god help us, and eventually after a very pleasant dinner attended by Bill Carney and Stewart Watts where we all laughed a lot, eased off to bed and didn't sleep very well.

Today it is raining and thundering vigorously as in fact it did yesterday, though I forgot to mention it. I am feeling old and seedy and my gland still hurts. I'm in a most hypochondriac mood and every little squeak of pain that runs through me makes me wonder if I'll get home or not etc. The streets are awash with flood water and people are pottering miserably from place to place. Frequent lightning and an erratic electric light system make one feel slightly bilious and the thunder booms and crackles hilariously in the pallid sky. Sunny Sicily my bottom.

Later: Nothing further has occurred by which the day has been rendered in any particular way noteworthy. Letter from Mom tonight. Groin much better as poison continues to ooze from the offending foot. It looks as though I shall be going home after all which becomes rather an exciting thought as the days pass slowly by.

28 October

Last night saw one of those mercifully rare occurrences, a Regtl. Guest Night. We shambled along at about 1930 and absorbed a few rather desultory whisky-and-grapefruits and glasses of Marsala. Most people were feeling pretty low in health; I am, for example, the only member of this mess without a violent head-cold at the moment. Eventually we filed into dinner, which actually was rather good. Hors d'oevres, soup, fish (swordfish!), turkey and pork, ice cream. War is hell. The guests were various members of the 1st Gordons. Kilted and quite pleasant. I had Ken Pooley on one side and Denis Pullin on the other which was good company. After dinner we had the pipers, very noisy in such a confined space, but impressive. A breath of moor and mountain crept into the smoky room as the melancholy music skirled out. I like the Pipes. They are haunting and sad and individualistic. After dinner – in fact, at 2330 – we were permitted to leave the table, and most of us left the place, a fact which called forth a rocket, patiently borne by senior subalterns today. I forgot to mention one or two recent decorations. Ken Pooley has an M.C. and so has Gordon. The C.O. an O.B.E. and – and what a magnificently accurate assessment of his value – 'Bull' Melia an M.B.E!

Latest innovation into the mess – a naming of members after Eliot's delightful *Book of Practical Cats* (mine). Jimmy Gegan is 'Growltiger', Gordon 'The Great Rumpusscat', Sandy Cowie a humdrum 'Gumbie Cat', Monty – perfectly – 'Bustopher Moncur, the Cat About Town' and myself 'Rum Tum Tugger' – a 'curious' cat. Latest in the home stakes. Embarkation 6–10 December, voyage to take about 3 weeks, which is longer than most of us expected. It looks as though Peter (expected back shortly) with 30 Nov. or Jimmy with 2 Dec. will win the sweepstake. There is daily less for the men to do, but they are simmering quietly enough in the fat of anticipation. I have acquired a Beretta .32 and some ammo. A wicked little black-blue automatic. Managed to get a new Battle Dress which is being altered by Andrew, the F Troop tailor, and an old friend of mine. Poisoned foot and gland much less painful.

The author, 1946.

there eventually wriggling ahead of my
carrier and spent the night in
heavy shelling. We had about 100 in
the first hour most of them very close
one, seven yards from the carrier which
cut the wireless lead. Trees were sawn
in half by the vicious, slashing
splinters and the pieces of warm steel
tinkled down unnerving, with the rain we
were cold, tired, and hungry. When we
advanced to the canal bank my
carrier got bogged, so did the tank I
got hold of to find it out. Eventually
a half track did the job, but as we
did the last open stretch to the canal
(I was still on foot) we got caught
in a rain of about 50 shells which
were so close one had to lie down &
wait & hope for the best as they
screamed towards you and crashed
— some about 10 yards away — hitting
the eardrums painfully and sending
the lethal fragments whizzing only
inches overhead as you pressed close to
the soft earth, then hat close to the
floor, body straining to press lower
nerves shrinking, hope fading... Several
times in those few minutes I thought
"this one is it, this time it'll hit
me." But we crossed in our own assault
boat. We had to leave the carrier
& carry our wireless & necessaries (no
food) in helped by a party of Jocks

Part of the author's diary entry for 18 November 1943.

Left: Jock Cochrane
(Photo: Jane Cochrane).
Right: Bobby Burton.
(Photo: Bill French)

Left: Bill French *(Photo:*
Author's collection).
Right: Gordon Wagstaff
(Photo: Bill French).

Left: Bill Carney *(Photo:*
Bill French).
Right: Steve (John
Stevenson) *(Photo:*
Moira Stevenson).

EIGHTH ARMY

Personal Message from the Army Commander

TO BE READ OUT TO ALL TROOPS.

1. Now that the campaign in Africa is finished I want to tell you all, my soldiers, how intensely proud I am of what you have done.

2. Before we began the Battle of Egypt last October I said that together, you and I, we would hit Rommel and his Army "for six" right out of North Africa.

And it has now been done. All those well known enemy Divisions that we have fought, and driven before us over hundreds of miles of African soil from Alamein to Tunis, have now surrendered.

There was no Dunkirk on the beaches of Tunisia; the Royal Navy and the R.A.F. saw to it that the enemy should not get away, and so they were all forced to surrender.

The campaign has ended in a major disaster for the enemy.

3. Your contribution to the complete and final removal of the enemy from Africa has been beyond all praise.

As our Prime Minister said at Tripoli in February last, it will be a great honour to be able to say in years to come:—

"I MARCHED AND FOUGHT WITH THE EIGHTH ARMY."

4. And what of the future? Many of us are probably thinking of our families in the home country, and wondering when we shall be able to see them.

But I would say to you that we can have to-day only one thought, and that is to see this thing through to the end; and then we will be able to return to our families, honourable men.

5. Therefore let us think of the future in this way.

And what ever it may bring to us, I wish each one of you the very best of luck, and good hunting in the battles that are yet to come and which we will fight together.

6. TOGETHER, YOU AND I, WE WILL SEE THIS THING THROUGH TO THE END.

B. L. Montgomery,

TUNISIA, 14th May, 1943.   General, Eighth Army.

Monty quickly became renowned for issuing communications like this to the troops under his command. *(Author's Collection)*

The victory parade in Tunis on 20 May 1943, led by pipers of 51st (Highland) Division. *(IWM NA3011)*

Monty offering cigarettes to the troops – a characteristic gesture. *(IWM NA4933)*

Advancing on Catania a 5-ton lorry comes to grief on one of the bridges. *(IWM NA5544)*

Sicily, July 1943: 25-pounders in action. Good terrain for gun positions was scarce. *(IWM NA5910)*

Sicily, 1943. On the author's right is Jimmy Gegan. Bottom right is Tom Findlay, the author's batman for over two and a half years. (*Author's Collection*)

The author (with binoculars) and men of his troop in Messina, August 1943. (*Author's Collection*)

51st (Highland) Division loading at East India Docks, 3 June 1944. *(IWM B5215)*

51st (Highland)
Division in the
English Channel,
6 June 1944.
(IWM B5208)

Opposite: Troops of
51st Highland
Division marching
towards La Roche-en-
Ardennes, finally
liberated on 11
January 1945.
(British Official)

Troops of 5/7 Gordons cross the German border from Holland, February 1945. *(IWM B14411)*

The Reichswald Forest
– a strongly contested
natural obstacle.
(IWM B14412)

Sticky going for a
bren-gun carrier in
Germany, February
1945. *(IWM B14420)*

C Company, 5 Black Watch (and the author) enter Gennep, where the author was wounded on 13 February 1945. *(IWM B14629)*

I would like to pay a compliment to the gunners, and I would like this to be passed on to every gunner.

The gunners have risen to great heights in this war; they have been well commanded and well handled. In my experience the artillery has never been so efficient as it is today; it is at the top of its form. For all this I offer you my warmest congratulations.

The contribution of the artillery to final victory in the German war has been immense. This will always be so; the harder the fighting and the longer the war, the more the infantry, and in fact all the arms, lean on the gunners. The proper use of the artillery is a great battle-winning factor.

I think all the other arms have done very well too. But the artillery has been terrific and I want to give due weight to its contribution to the victory in this campaign.

B. L. Montgomery
Field-Marshal
C-in-C
21 Army Group.

Germany
27-6-45

Once victory in Europe had been achieved, Monty was unstinting in his praise for the Royal Artillery. *(Author's Collection)*

127 (H) Field Regiment headquarters, Verden, 1946. *(Author's Collection)*

The author riding his horse Kondor, in Germany, 1946. *(Author's Collection)*

30 October

Yesterday we all sallied forth in the evening to see 'Sicilian Follies', a display at the State Theatre by some local ex-lovelies. The theatre was crammed full of sweating gunners chewing nuts and clamouring for sex. From every box they overflowed, and the high balconies were a sea of faces. Eventually amid roars of applause the curtain rose and four or five rather faded trollops started waving their fannies at a highly appreciative audience. The show followed fairly orthodox lines. There were the 3 youngish dames who weren't too bad to look at. One aroused considerable speculation by wearing a brassiere throughout the evening. Bill Carney thought she had false breasts, but popular opinion decided that, on account of the generosity of her bosom, it was a measure to prevent it popping out. (This, incidentally, was a turn in itself and evoked about 4 encores.) There was an apoplectic soprano who sang Madame Butterfly and Ave Maria with every vein bursting out. There was the local tenor who looked like rather a seedy edition of George Raft and sang with throbbing emotion and scant regard for the time. Later he reappeared in a pair of black trousers about 25 round the bottom and hitched up under his arms, and a pink shirt, and beat on a tambourine and cavorted round the stage. The audience was puzzled but polite. The comedian relied almost entirely on sex and scored something of a hit. The show wound up by a two woman scene, one being dressed as a male, and singing lustily they performed antics of an extremely sexual nature, with much indecent caressing and undoing of fly buttons. What they were singing I am unable to say – as it was drowned in the roars of applause.

Altogether a most enjoyable and amusing evening.

Today it has been raining and thundering and we have all got colds and coughs. I had a good mail from Pam, B., and Bette in South Africa, who enclosed a couple of snaps. Yesterday there was one from Bé to which I replied with 3 L.C.s at once while on orderly officer the other night. Pam's L.C. included the fact that two more pairs of stockings had got home and that her Xmas present to me is on the way. Also the usual round of parties . . . 'I grow old, I grow old, I shall wear the bottoms of my trousers rolled . . .'. We are all getting an Africa Star soon, with 8th Army clasp in the case of those who fought between Alamein and Tunis. Most of the Battery qualifies for this clasp.

2 November

My worldly troubles continue. Now I have very bad pains round the kidneys, which may perhaps be rheumatism; whatever it is, the pain is most trying, particularly at night. I do hope the bloody thing clears up soon. We are embarking on the 9th at Augusta and I am full of apprehension in case something lugs me off to hospital before the long-awaited day. The C.O. is there with a fractured skull, acquired driving a Jeep into a 3 ton lorry at speed. Mail has been good for the last day or two. I've had L.C.s from Pam, Bé, Mom, Dad, and today another from Mom, and one from Dorothy. I have replied to nearly all of these. Yesterday Monty and I went by truck to Catania to try and get some things from the Officers Shop. Almost needless to say we failed to do so; officers shops are like that, and in any case plundered by base wallahs long before we ever get anywhere near them. So we mooched about Catania – it was pelting with rain most of the time – and did at least acquire some undies and stockings. I then drove back in pouring rain most of the way in darkness, and ended up here waterlogged up to the waist which probably hasn't improved my kidney pains to any extent. I am feeling depressed and ill. I hate being ill, and I hate it most when one cannot do so in comfort. Matt Simm is posted to us from 301 and goes to F Tp. as G.P.O. thus dashing 'Jam's' hopes. He is rapidly returning to his former aggressiveness after a spell of comparative normalcy. I forgot to mention I also had an A/G from G. Tonight just to add general joy to the situation in general, I am orderly officer and have to turn out the guard at 0315 hours! I curse and rage with inward rebellion at the system and the people and the bloodiness of the war, which can ruin my sleep, my life, and generally contribute to the mental inertia and physical woes which seem to beset me on all sides these days. It rains frequently nowadays and is chilly.

3 November

Too depressed to write much. Pains diagnosed by M.O. as rheumatic. Very bad tonight and have extended round to stomach. Wrote long L.C. to Dorothy. Recd. letters from Debroy and George. Former in N.A. but hoping to be back soon.

5 November

It is afternoon. This evening I am going with Gordon and Jimmy to have drinks and possibly dinner, with the 5/7 Gordons over at Augusta. If only the trip doesn't prove too murderous to 'me rheumatics' (which are at last showing signs of big improvement owing to massage with Italian liniment) it should be quite pleasant. We have to take down our 'H-D' before embarkation, and probably will be unable to resume wearing them till after disembarkation, which is rather a blow to morale, and in any case rather pointless, as everybody will know we're coming before we get there owing to the departure of 152 Brigade weeks ago. Wrote yesterday to George, Debroy and G. The C.R.A. who is flying home has agreed to inform the next of kin of 3 officers in the Bty., of impending events. Names out of the hat: Gordon, Peter Dawson, Matt Simm. These in turn are writing to their relative giving them name and address for <u>us</u> so they'll know at long last, though probably not very long before our arrival. Just read *Nelson* by C.S. Forester. Very interesting. I didn't realise Nelson spent so long in Palermo and Siracuse and was indeed made Duke of Bronte – valueless though it proved to be. We are embarking on 9 November, leaving here in the morning. 'Evening meal will be served on board ship' says the movement order. A rather thrilling sentence. To think, we shall be home at Xmas; and yet the whole business to me still lacks reality.

6 November

The party turned out to be quite good after all. When we arrived (after a foully bumpy journey in the back of the truck) it seemed a little staid and formal. Service dress, kilts and what have you in evidence and the be-medalled great here and there. But after general absorption of alcohol (which was plentiful and quite good) the thing warmed up to the degree that the Naval Officers started firing rockets into the garden, and finally letting off smoke canisters in the house, which though objectively childish caused much amusement. We got a little tipsy and arrived home about midnight.

Rather a cagey mouth this morning, which was heralded by a violent thunderstorm and a terrific downpour of rain. It is still questionable whether we shall actually be on leave at Xmas itself as rumour now says the voyage home may only take 10–12 days. This puts me well in running for winning the sweep. I forget if I ever mentioned it, but after Monty's speech all the officers at 5/- a time named the date when the first member of the Bty set foot on shore. As far as I remember it was something like this: 'Jam' 12 Nov., Gordon 14 Nov., Sandy C., 15 Nov., myself 24 Nov., Peter 30 Nov., Jimmy 2 Dec. So Peter and I seem to be prospective winners. But you never can tell. Rheumatics much improved.

8 November

Well, tomorrow we go. Everything packed up in crates, parades laid on, luggage packed, H-Ds taken down and everything and everybody prepared. And yet I still feel this overwhelming lassitude. I wish to God I could get rid of it, yet it persists, sticking to me everywhere and infecting all I do. Perhaps it is the mere effects of physical sickness, for I still feel pretty lousy, with the remains of a cold and twinges and aches in the belly and kidneys. When I think how I had hoped to go home - sunburned, fit and happy – and then view myself now – pale, thin and generally disgruntled – I could weep with vexation. Perhaps a sea trip will blow a little good health into me. How I hope so. As a matter of fact most people feel the same. Among the officers I mean. Latest Guff: the liner, a yank – God help us – is said to be the *Argentina* of about 30,000 tons and used on the S. America service. I suppose it will be crammed to hell. Wrote final letters home and to Pam. Have given them absolutely no hint of our homecoming. Only hope I feel more cheerful about it when I get to the other end. How unpredictable life can be. Message from the General including the ominous reminder that the Division will 'take a part, possibly a leading part' in operations launched from the U.K. So that before another year has passed, a good many of us will no longer be here or anywhere else. Of course the penalty – and the reward – for being in a crack Division like the 51st – is the certainty that you'll not spend the war stagnating in some backwater. All said and done I think I prefer it that way.

10 November

S.S. Argentina: The *Argentina* (American Republic Lines) is a high, modern-looking ship with one large very streamlined funnel and a rakish cruiser stem. Tonnage 23,000. Considering the stage of the war, and the number of troops on board, we are all very comfortable. Even the men, who usually lie on dirty floors or swing miserably in backbending hammocks, have bunks of a sort. Meals are only two daily – for us 0830 and 1800, but are so enormous that they keep one pretty well stoked up for the intervening hours. They are also pretty well guaranteed to produce indigestion of the acutest variety. For example supper last night consisted of hors d'oevres, soup, fish, an enormous dish of pork with etc.s, pudding, ice-cream (that is as well as pudding), cheese, fruit and tea. Breakfast today was in proportion. It is 1400 and I am not hungry yet. We had the usual day getting here, from 0430 till about 1730 when we got on board from an L.C.I. We expect to sail tomorrow. Coming out, the convoy in which this ship was included was bombed this side of Gib. and lost 2, 3 or 4 ships according how far below decks the witness happened to be.

Before leaving, I had 3 letters (all very out of date) from Debroy and also a curiously nostalgic letter from G. This is about the oddest passage: 'It may surprise you, but I rather loved you in the old days. Even long after I first broke off any physical relationship – in all the days up to the annulment of my marriage – now there is neither amity nor hostility, but I sense something like a complete lack of interest on your side, now reflected (because I'm sensitive to reciprocate) on mine! How <u>do</u> you feel these days about <u>me</u>? I'm right, aren't I? Or do you prefer not to discuss it?'

Well, is she right? – I don't really know. I think G. made me so happy and unhappy, so contented and so exasperated all in turns – and several times hurt me so bitterly and made me so furiously angry – in fact so upset my emotional equilibrium – that I eventually decided to wash my hands of her completely. It wouldn't be true to say I feel a complete lack of interest in her as to say that I just don't feel I can cope with her any longer. She and Sheila are apparently irrevocably parted mentally now – as the latter is convinced that G. came between us. Only partially true.

I am feeling pretty seedy still. My belly aches in the pelvic area and I still have rheumatic twinges all over the back. God I feel really sick of myself. I simply <u>must</u> cheer up a bit before we get to England again. Otherwise heaven knows what they'll think. Probably that I'm shellshocked or something!

11 November

We sailed at 1100 on a calm sea with sunshine. Now, at night, we are sailing along in the moonlight – the other 5 or 6 liners of the convoy being quite visible. I am feeling much better today thank the lord and only hope it persists.

Shipboard life continues much as usual with our 2 enormous daily meals and not much to do. Our steward is one Hardy Whitaker from Oklahoma way in Texas, and says 'Jesus' quite a lot. We are well in with him, and he gave us cigars for supper tonight. That is for after supper. Played bridge with Pooley, Kirk and Brockie today and lost 9/-. Am in cabin with Sandy C., Jimmy, Peter, Monty and Jimmy Kirkwood. Good company and very amusing. Armistice day 1918. When again?

12 November

Night. We are cruising gently in the moonlight opposite Bougie, where we spent such lovely months during the summer. This morning we awoke to the sight of Cap. Bon – a sight not many of us had seen from this side. It looks rugged, bare, and lonely. Some more ships have joined the convoy. I am feeling a damn sight better, pains nearly gone. Played Bridge with Pooley, Gordon and Jimmy and won 6/6.

13 November

This morning broke, full of rain and with a heavy swell. The ship sidled along, creaking a little and shuddering every now and then. A few people were seasick. I did not feel very good myself. Later in the day the sun broke through, and about 1600 we sailed past Algiers, gleaming in the sunny haze. A large portion of the convoy broke off and put into Algiers, but we sailed on into the sunset. Tonight it is calm again. Going down to dinner I was seized by a tremendous wave of nostalgia. Suddenly, seeing the men sitting on the stair, I remembered how I used to walk downstairs on the *Niew Amsterdam* with B., and how her appearance was always greeted with vocal appreciation by them. Once I drew her attention to this, and she replied with that vulgarity which was so pleasant in her, 'Yes I suppose they look like that because they're trying to penetrate my blouse . . .' (not surprising for her breasts were very shapely and stuck out almost like a caricature in *Esquire*). Hard to realise, thinking of the full moon last night, that it must be almost to the day, a year ago since those strange spells the red sea wove about us. And now we are nearing home every hour. I am beginning to want to get there very very badly. Particularly to see Pam on whom so much of the future may depend. I only wish my mind were clearer on the subject, but perhaps seeing her will make things easier. We are said to be passing Gib. tomorrow night, and docking on the 22 or 23. Bridge today with Pooley, Brockie and Ian Kidd, cost me 14/-. Had poor cards and played several hands badly.

14 November

During the afternoon, the sea got up and in a headwind with the tremendous seas rolling against us, the convoy battled through the misty afternoon. Occasionally the sun broke through, and I saw the silver grey gleam of the escorts – fragile ships leaping effortlessly along. The spray exploded against the sunshine and shrouded the ships in cobwebs of colour. It was a magnificent and significant spectacle. As always, I realised afresh the far reaching power of a maritime nation, and was struck by the beauty of the ships thrusting their bows against the living ocean. After tea we had some excitement, in the form of a depth charge attack from an escort, but against what we haven't yet found out. The sunset, baleful and yellow, sprawled against the western sky as the convoy reformed and drove towards Gibraltar, the Atlantic and England . . . tonight the wind howls in the riggings, the deck is a fury of wind, the spray blasts over the decks, into nooks and crannies, and outside, like the smack of distant gunfire, the sea knocks endlessly at our unresponsive walls.

On a more prosaic note – earlier in the evening Sandy Cowie, venturing onto the forward well deck, returned to the cabin drenched. The spray on the deck had been a little too quick for him. We've been playing Monopoly today as a change from Bridge. Several people feeling not so hot today owing to the movement of the ship – which actually is very steady – so far – but luckily I seem to be alright to date. Tomorrow will almost certainly bring heavy seas and – ?

15 November

We passed Gib. somewhere about 0530 but although the Rock was visible in the moonlight, I didn't get up to see it. The sea had calmed down by this morning so a few pale faces were the sole tangible evidence of last night's gale. Did P.T. this morning. Bridge in the afternoon with Dennis, Alistair and Charles J. and won 4/-; also two exceedingly acrimonious and amusing games of Monopoly. Clocks back an hour tonight. Am beginning to get excited more and more at the prospect of home – and leave, real leave. Feeling very much better, though my stomach still feels lined with E.P.N.S. most of the time, particularly after the roast pork tonight, when a giant hand tied reef knots in my lower bowel.

18 November

Swung north during the night and woke this morning with the sun on our right and, far away, the Azores on our left. Rumour now gives us 4, 5 and 7 more days at sea. I should think we'll be about 6. Being in southern latitudes, it is still surprisingly warm – almost too warm for battledress. Curious contrast: when you're inside a liner, say in the dining saloon, with silver, glass, and bright lights, you'd never guess the sea was only a few feet away, yet looking out of your porthole you see these tiny ships pushing along in the apparently infinite sea and wonder at their fragility, and more still at sailors of 400 years ago who crossed the enormous Atlantic in such small wooden ships.

Not much doing on board. The sea is comparatively smooth most of the time and we play bridge, Monopoly or chess, or read books. The ship being so full, there are no concerts, all entertainment is done over the ship's broadcast system, and rather well done at that. Am writing a few letters to post as soon as we arrive back. Feeling daily more excited at the prospect of homecoming. Clocks back another hour last night. Lost 10/- at Bridge.

19 November

Big event in my Bridge history last night when for the first time I called and made a grand Slam vulnerable. Dennis Pullin did likewise a few rubbers later and we took 12/6 from Alistair and Charles after being 23 points down in the first two rubbers. Lovely grub as Charles puts it. Just re-read *The Harsh Voice* by Rebecca West, a masterpiece of understanding morbidness. I'd give a lot to be able to write as well as that. The sea is still calm – or rather we have got used to the swell which is nearly always present causing the cabin to creak day and night – and the convoy is sailing slowly northwestwards. Our E.T.A. is now 25 November. Another canteen – our third on board – yesterday, containing the usual American candy atrocities such as 'Sky Bars' and 'Bolsters', also cigars, Coca-Cola, and American cigarettes, the last being a bit of a blow to me as I don't like them at all. I managed to swop my previous 200 Chesterfields for 150 Gold Flake, but yesterday's Camels look like having to be somebody's Xmas present!

Later: Depth charges this afternoon and hooting throughout the convoy. They make a hell of a noise in the quiet of the sea, and even at a distance the ship trembles. It makes one realise how bloody it must be in a submarine with somebody throwing the things at you. My camels finally realised 100 Gold Flake with Gordon. Bridge as usual. Lost 4/-.

20 November

Uneventful day. Opinion divided between Liverpool and Greenock as our eventual landfall. We are going very distinctly North now, and it's getting much cooler, but it's rather pleasant to feel genuine cold on the bones again. Haven't been beaten at chess yet. Laid off Bridge today; one can become almost trump-drunk at the game.

22 November

Yesterday, for almost the first time, it was bitterly cold. Nearly all portholes were kept closed all day against the icy wind, and the meagre electric heaters switched on. Even so we shivered all day. Today it is not quite so cold, though to us it feels like midwinter (which, after all, it is!). Did P.T. on deck this morning in half darkness, but got up a good sweat. Played quite a lot of bridge yesterday and won 7/6 in the afternoon, losing 11/6* at night when Dennis and I didn't sniff a decent card for 3 rubbers running.

Most people feeling rather seedy today. Dawson in bed, and Jimmy Gegan apparently bronchial. Myself O.K. but twinges of rheumatics, blast it. In moments of gloom I frequently think I shall never feel really well again! Voyage nears its ending: collection of B.M.A., kit in the holds and so forth; clocks advanced an hour last night. East Anglia or Essex still warm favourites in the destination stakes.

Later: Rough day with a following wind and grey sea flecked with white caps. All the ships in the convoy rolling and pitching. Our own fairly steady but sufficiently lively to have made most of us sick a week ago. Very cold. We should be landing on Wednesday – or Thursday early – at Liverpool probably. What a thought. Jimmy Kirkwood gone to hospital with a bad knee. I am writing a serial letter to Pam on this trip as I did going out. I only started a week or so ago and it's quite long already.

23 November

Away on the starboard side is the misty Irish coast. Part of our convoy – a few ships have headed north, probably towards Glasgow – plunges steadily on through a fairly high grey sea, always getting nearer home.

We should reach Liverpool tomorrow. It seems almost yesterday we left it, so clearly I can remember the scene as the *Sibajak* nosed out into the Mersey; but much has happened since then. Too much. We are not a very fit little collection of heroes. Jimmy has been in bed with a feverish chill all day, Sandy C. has a rash on his forehead and Monty has a cold. And I have rheumatism, almost as badly as at Siracuse; no perhaps that is a slight exaggeration, but it is certainly pretty achy. Excitement still holds us.

24 November

There's many a slip – in fact we are not likely to land until Saturday now. So we have several days to wait. Everybody somewhat downcast. Reason varies between bad weather and arrangements – not expecting us at the other end. Anyway we're all unpacked again. Rheumatics much better today.

*Won 12/- on 21 November.

25 November

Good news. Destination Beaconsfield, 14 days leave, H-D's up again and probably our Africa Star too. We are lying in the Mersey by Liverpool, almost where we were in July '42. It seems almost yesterday looking at it in the mist and the rain. Only a day or two now. Last night I found it hard to go to sleep, thinking of home and leave.

26 November

Today Jimmy G. and the M.O. went to hospital with diphtheria. Naturally a wave of rumours concerning quarantine, postponement of leave etc. have burst out, but so far we disembark at about 1500 tomorrow (thus losing me the sweep by exactly 3 hours!) and arrive at Amersham at the congenial little hour of 0137. Fog this morning with a clean November smell – lovely. But I do wish we'd hurry up and get home as I am anxious to see a specialist about my rheumatics – or whatever it is.

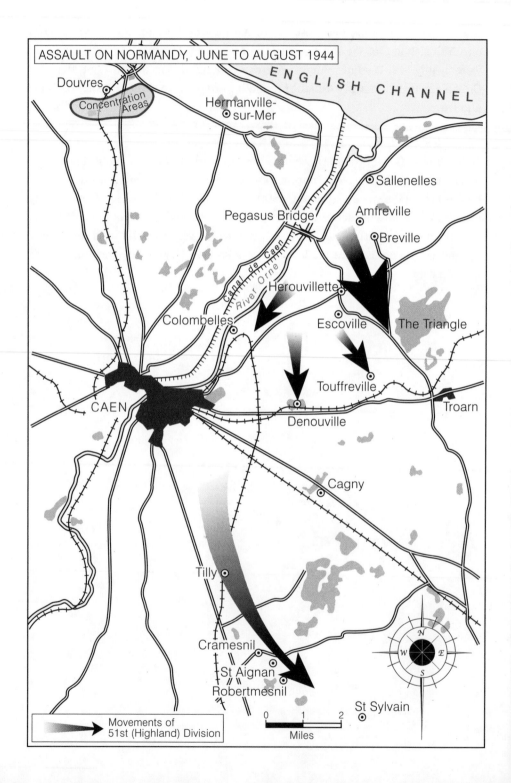

ASSAULT ON NORMANDY, JUNE TO AUGUST 1944

ENGLISH CHANNEL

Douvres

Concentration Areas

Hermanville-sur-Mer

Sallenelles

Amfreville

Breville

Pegasus Bridge

Canal de Caen

River Orne

Herouvillette

Colombelles

Escoville

The Triangle

Touffreville

Troarn

Denouville

CAEN

Cagny

Tilly

Cramesnil

St Aignan

Robertmesnil

St Sylvain

N
W   E
S

Movements of
51st (Highland) Division

0   1   2
Miles

 PART THREE

26 May 1944 –
14 February 1945

etween the end of November and the following May, the Regiment
trained and prepared to invade Europe. We lived in Nissan huts near
attractive places like Beaconsfield and Long Melford. Described by our
desert opponents (in captured documents) as 'elite troops', we proudly
displayed our Africa Star ribbon with its '8' clasp, and the days passed
pleasantly enough; though it was difficult to escape a certain uneasiness
which was never completely absent.

The home counties were inundated with troops and weaponry – Guns,
Tanks, Trucks: everywhere sundry bangs, the rumble of engines and the
clatter of tracks. We encountered many unfamiliar Divisional signs. Their
number was a pointer to the scale of the operation we were to share.
My own life had been changed by someone I met. I motorcycled (an art
acquired as a bombardier in 1940) at high speed through the countryside –
so beautiful that spring – to hasty meetings and unwelcome partings. There
were parades. There were inspections even by Monty and the King.

We didn't know our precise destination; and thanks to an ingenious
deception plan, neither did the enemy. The Intelligence people initiated
fictitious radio traffic indicating the presence of an (imaginary) army in
South-East England, complete with inflatable dummy tanks, trucks, guns
etc. readily available for aerial photography. A manmade harbour had been
constructed, to be served by Pluto – pipeline under the ocean.

All this was unknown to us ordinary soldiers as we waited to open the
Second Front. It was to be very unlike our recent battles.

And many desert veterans would not see their homeland again.

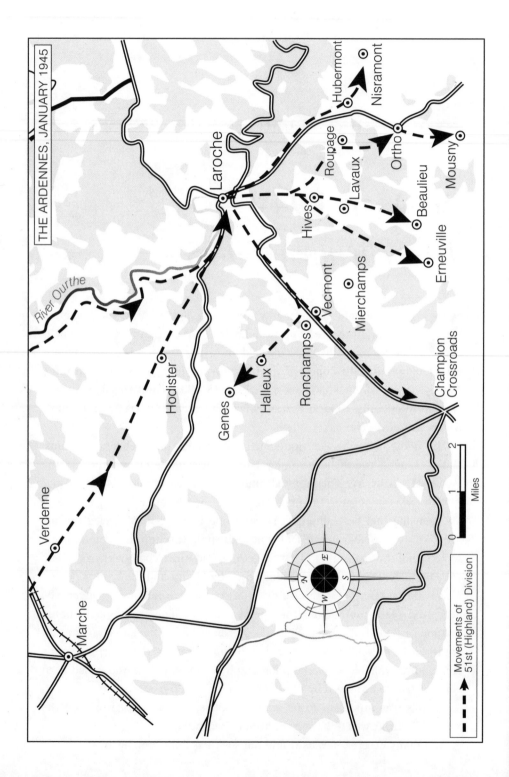

THE ARDENNES, JANUARY 1945

River Ourthe

Hubermont
Nisramont
Roupage
Lavaux
Ortho
Mousny
Beaulieu
Laroche
Hives
Erneuville
Mierchamps
Vecmont
Genes
Halleux
Ronchamps
Hodister
Champion
Crossroads
Verdenne
Marche

N E S W

0   1   2
Miles

Movements of
51st (Highland) Division

Friday 26 May 1944

Now, finally we are shut in. It is rather like those advertised P.O.W. drawings. The dusty camp, and the triple dennert wire around it, and the rather miserable faces of everybody inside it. We have been paid in francs today, which removes any lingering doubts about our destination. In more detail, my own guess is that we shall try and bite off the Cherbourg peninsula. The last few days have been noticeable for one thing which at first is almost imperceptible – very few of our own aircraft in the sky. At Melford the sky was almost always full of them and I remember that my nightly letter to C. always referred to their drone overhead. I am finding it hard to get into the diary habit again; it is a long time since I was writing it last. Now that we are shut in and there is no chance of seeing or phoning C. I hope they get on with the job quickly and get it over.

I remember starting Diary 4 just before we invaded Sicily. I started 'The sun is setting over Sfax harbour in a dim orange ball . . .' And now tonight as I start this 6th book, the sun is setting again over Wanstead flats this time and where there were palm trees and square white buildings, there are chestnuts and many trees and trolley buses and shabby houses.

Yesterday in London – did I imagine it or did I with the acuteness of imminent departure seem to notice everything more clearly than usual? The sentry at Buckingham Palace just turning, he had a red shoulder flash – some infantry regiment. And the shadowy glades in Green Park. Tired faces in the tube, and the smoky friendliness of Liverpool St. Station – 'our station'. And C. – if you read this many months afterwards, when I may even be dead – I remember so clearly just as we were near the Bank of England your turning to me and saying: 'Yes you <u>do</u>, really, don't you?'

And now you know I do – really.

The wireless – Sandy's portable – is playing some awful tosh by the Andrews Sisters – typical of the dope they serve out nowadays to people who hear but do not listen. I'll end on this bad-tempered note.

27 May

Hot today; makes this place a vague reminder of the marshalling area at Sousse; particularly the way the dust spurts up from the paths as thin as talcum powder. We do P.T. stripped to the waist and sweating like pigs. Another letter from C. today – I had one yesterday too. Another influx into the camp – some Canadians and some British Pioneers. More of our planes audible and visible today. It is about 1600 now so I'll head off and go to tea. I suppose it's over 80 °F in the shade today – and we had some sort of steak pudding for lunch – god!

In bed at night: We are marshalling tomorrow morning which is, I suppose, an indication of sorts. A chap has broken out of camp tonight which caused a bit of a flap. They have been community singing in the big marquee just near this tent – the strains of Suvla Bay and Tipperary mingling with the setting sun and voices about the camp. I wonder how many of them will come back. I try not to dwell on the thought too much but it's difficult at times to keep away from it. Dougan (Bdr.) has had malaria during the last few days, and reached 106 °F, but is coming as a passenger, and tonight Sandy Cowie has got it too but is also coming as a passenger. Matt is having to do the O.P. job for them. B.C. said to me: 'It's either him or you, and I'll leave you where you are for the time.' But I shouldn't really be surprised if Matt beats me to a troop. Still, he's a good chap, and anyway promotion is another of the things I try to avoid thinking about. It's too disappointing.

I feel I am well prepared for <u>this</u> invasion with over 800 cigarettes, 3 lb of slab chocolate, tea, milk and various other amenities of life which were almost unknown on other parties; curious to think this is the third similar occasion. I never can think of myself as a veteran. Chief speculation over the 'Second' front centres in the quality and quantity of air opposition we can expect. My own guess is as follows: considerable bombing of the beachhead at dusk and by night, and a good few strafing fighters. ME 109s nearly put paid to my career once before so I shall keep a very weather eye peeled. Trying to analyse the prevalent feeling, one can certainly detect no enthusiasms. There is resignation about the whole business. Men are ready for the worst but not altogether without hope for the best. After all, they say, look at Sicily.

To end on a more prosaic note: I am taking 1200 francs and <u>lots</u> of soap to France. I've just finished my nightly letter to C. Oh to see her again . . .

28 May

Sunday: A hot, busy day with a continual flap over the marshalling which is being (it is 1740 now) mismanaged by the camp movement control. They are starting again at 1800 and I suppose may be finished by dark with any luck. The hot camp – more like a Stalag – daily presents a veritable picture of resigned boredom. Men are lying about nearly naked, sunbathing, or gambling either at solo or throwing pennies. The glare here gives me a headache. It's an odd feeling to be shut away like this with 'civilisation' (meaning hot baths and phones) so near the perimeter.

Idle thoughts pass through my brain as I lie on my bed. I flick my cigarette ash off and it explodes like a little silver bomb in the sunshine . . . this time last week C. and I were in a number 22 bus on the way to Piccadilly Circus – 'Look, Snowdrops,' she said pointing to two white-helmeted American M.P.s. This week's *Lilliput* has a picture of two of them – I thought of her and wondered if she – having also a copy of the paper – thought of it too, as it's one of our small jokes.

We are being briefed on the 30th. I wonder if they will tell us anything worth hearing; probably not. Good few rumours about the camp; chief form of humour – fictitious 'news bulletins' such as 'Rome burning camp unsealed' or 'Anybody who wants a 24 hour pass stand to his bed now.'

29 May

Amid considerable flap it has now been discovered that all the vehicles are leaving here for the docks starting at dawn tomorrow. We do not join our trucks until later; no time specified. It has been very hot again today and one cannot find any relief in the camp. Letter from Admiral Cochrane, posted at Liverpool from which I gather he has already started on the trip to America.

The barbed wire is lined with half naked men commenting vociferously on the passers by. Girls on bicycles get rousing cheers, anything representing authority, from our armed guards of the Queens Regt. to motor cycle cops, a volley of boos and catcalls. Outside the camp there is a pond in which we wistfully watch brightly-clad civilians having a bathe. A pity they could not have extended the perimeter a little, then we could have used it. Meanwhile our interests centre almost entirely on such animal comforts as are available such as cool showers, packets of (very good) fruit drops made by Needlers, and much hot tea; also the newspapers. Following dialogue I heard not long ago is rather self explanatory:

> Charles Jones: 'What's she doing today?'
> Leslie Wager: 'Oh, she's dressed.'
> She, being of course, Jane.

Good article by Alan Moorehead in today's *Express*, analysing the feelings of troops who have been brought home and have to go off again on this next do. He puts his finger on the 'restlessness' most of us have felt; the inability to sit contentedly through a film or stay in one place for long. My own sole exception to this rule has been time spent with C., when I felt completely contented.

Otherwise the old 'What you can while you can' feeling has been the order of the day. It is evening and growing colder.

2215: I am lying on my bed. I've had a lovely tepid shower an hour and a half ago and am feeling good. About 2100 we had a short thunderstorm and violent rain in big drops. The camp now is sodden and grey. Little wisps of blue smoke mingle with the grey after-rain and the gathering dusk. I've just finished my letter to C. When the rain came down there was a rush for shelter growing more furious as the rain did the same. And now, officers in pyjamas and mackintoshes are pottering dismally round the puddles smoking cigarettes. Harry says to me (as we are sending all our kit except one blanket away in the morning) 'To think we should look on a camp bed as a luxury . . .' It certainly is a strange way of thinking one has got into after all these years. I can hardly remember peace as a coherent entity now. I hope very deeply that the war will end this year. I am genuinely tired of the army, weary of the war. And though like all of us I am ready to fight it till either it or I shall end, I feel no ardour or enthusiasm for the future. I can hear the train from nearby Snaresbrook Station chuffing away to Liverpool Street . . . it is getting too dark to write any more, and my hurricane lamp is packed away in my trunk.

30 May

It is hot summer and about 1430. I am lying on the floor of my tent (only Harry and I left in here now) with everything undone and my shoes and socks off. Yesterday was the hottest day of the year, which doesn't surprise me. 83 in the shade. In Sicily it was 120 °F. Lovely letter from Clare which I shall start answering during the afternoon. We only have one blanket left now. I have kept my sleeping bag instead. Let's hope the nights stay warm.

Briefing, as we'd expected, a farce. A few code names and a coded wall map (quite incomprehensible) and we now wait for the when and where on the craft. Only it is confirmed we land on D + 1.

31 May

Almost nothing has happened today. A piece broke off one of my teeth today and I have to go to the dentist tomorrow morning. It always reminds me of that chap Watson who was killed on a bike recently. When I saw him all dead and bloody I noticed a lot of his teeth were stopped and thought of all the pain it must have caused him and what a waste it had been. At a further briefing today by the C.O. we were given some good titbits: Monty thinks it can be over by November if we do our stuff. We have 4,500 fighters and fighter bombers, and 6,000 bombers in the Tactical Airforce alone. We are the first brigade (and therefore Field Regiment) to land from the Div. Sandy K. is back with his wireless. We all slept a bit uneasily, with hip bones unaccustomed to the hard floor. Sandy tells me the ship's crews are having all shore leave cancelled from midnight tonight. I don't think it will be long now. The half moon is about 3 June, and it looks like being about then. It is Clare's birthday today. I have wondered frequently what sort of time she has had, what she has done.

1 June

Morning: Nothing very glorious about this first of June. The weather has broken up the wind, veering round to where it was when we first came here – i.e. just behind my head – is gusty and full of showers. There is a rush on the Q.M.'s for blankets. I have got two more which will be a pleasant addition to my sleeping bag – which is, however, extremely good value. This morning I went to the dentist. My nerves were delicately sharpened by watching the tribulations of 3 O.R.s who had mass anaesthetics, extractions etc, but my own tooth merely needed 'toning down'. I suspect uneasily that the real job was not done to it. The dentist told me that this camp brings him so much work that he's praying for the 2nd front to open. 'One man's meat . . .'

Almost a week since we were incarcerated here. And a week today since I saw C. It feels like a year.

One of the diverse characters in here is the P.R. Officer, a captain from the K.R.R. He wears the 8th army clasp and looks rather like Anthony Eden. As he has somehow got a pass out of camp today he's going to buy me a new pair of braces. My present pair – purchased, incredible as it seems, for 3/6 in 1933 – are just on disintegration point.

Evening: This afternoon an enormous thunderstorm and heavy rain fell upon us. The frail tents seemed to cringe in the fury of the storm which has stopped now, but the evening is grey and chilly. The walking party of the battery is off to join its ship tomorrow morning, so I suppose we'll go the day after. Early reports say the ships are Liberty ships and the living conditions admirable for a crew of 30 but somewhat inadequate for a crew of about 500 soldiers. However, we shouldn't be there long. Am about to eat supper and may continue later.

Soon after ten: I am lying on the duckboard floor of my tent. Night is falling fast. The door of the tent, not the usual open one but the one opposite and facing NE, is open. In the near distance the trees have lost their full summer green in the evening mist. The tents are drab and brown. Slit trenches with their mounds of gravel, scar the ground. The concert party nearby warbles 'Tea for Two'. When the comedian is on, laughter surges across the camp with the rhythmic regularity of surf rasping on a shingle beach. It is hard to realise, lying here in these last few hours of peace, that soon I may be hearing the waves on a real beach, and the sound of gunfire, flares by night, the crunching crash of bombs and the moan of the dying. Equally hard to realise that a week ago almost to the minute I was saying goodbye to C. in a compartment of a train in Liverpool St. Station. Though I can remember it with absolute clarity, it seems a year ago. With these hours of strained waiting we are paying for those wonderful hours of anticipation when the *Argentina* lay safe in the Mersey and the gulls wheeled about us and it was misty and cold and raining – and home.

Last June 1st I was eating cherries in Bougie. And next year . . . ?

2 June

About noon: Hard to realise today that a few days back we were sweating in a heatwave; today there is a boisterous, cold wind, bursts of sunshine and a good bit of cloud. The sea must be rather choppy. I woke up with a fierce headache but removed it with a couple of Veganin at breakfast. I don't think I mentioned that we have a new C.O.2 called Lambert. Sharp featured and monocled and a scarred right cheek. I was prepared to like him because of his monocle alone (Jock had one) but I think I am going to anyway. He is not ex-8th Army but has the Palestine G.S. ribbon. Calls me by my christian name which surprised and pleased me, and seems the type who won't flap – which also pleases me. There's supposed to be a Deanna Durbin film in the camp today which I shall try and see, being a D.D. fan.

Later: I went – quite good.

Dusk: Overhead the deep note of the bombers and inside the tent the strains of 'Wanting You', one of 1929's sentimental efforts. And this is our last night on English soil . . . We have been issued with everything: waders for going ashore, emergency rations, morphia and two simply excellent 24 hour packs containing among other things 4 bars of chocolate, boiled sweets, biscuits, dehydrated porridge and meat and tea, a Tommy Cooker with 6 refills, a tin of bully, salt, cigarettes, OXO cubes, chewing gum (2 packets) and a few other oddments – and all this in one pack. Rather amazing. We also have 3 Vomit Bags and a blow-up type of lifebelt. We really are rather well catered for this time for we really have things like water sterilising outfits, hitherto inclined to be theoretical. Today I was so pleased; a letter from C. arrived. I had already managed to get a letter off to her and added the fact on the flap on the envelope. Tonight in the shower I dropped my mirror – but it didn't break. I'm not superstitious but I'm still glad it didn't break! It is a baleful night with an overcast sky and the multiple balloons of the London barrage are low down and floating about like silver sausages. Another thing that happened tonight was that just as I got into my sleeping bag I put out my knee. It was bent double and I simply couldn't get it back by kicking which is the only way. I nearly passed out much to Sandy K's amazement as he couldn't make out what was wrong. Eventually I managed to force it back with a nasty hollow click which Sandy heard the other end of the tent. Some drunken Sergeants are singing 'When they sound the last all clear . . .' not far away, and all the time it grows darker and darker as our last midnight on England approaches. I've got to draw and carry the deadly secret maps tomorrow, which will not be opened till we are at sea. I am quite sure that it will be France. I wish it could all be over – general opinion among the officers places the assault at the small hours of Sunday morning. That will be the anniversary of Dunkirk Sunday 4 years ago and therefore an appropriate (and Churchillian) moment at which to strike.

I am writing by torchlight. I'd like to send C. another letter but our mail closed at 1700 today.

3 June

1400: We are sailing down the Thames on our Liberty Ship from East India Dock. This evening we shall be, it is said, in the anchorage off Southend somewhere. We left camp in lorryloads of 26, and passed for the last time through Leytonstone, Bow (where I used to take the tube for Sloane Square) and Stratford and thence to the East Indian Dock. We sailed less than an hour after embarkation was completed and somewhere about noon. The ship is unbelievably loaded with trucks, stores, rations – and men. Everybody is stowed in a hold aft with no room to swing a cat, but some of the ship's officers have been very good to a few of us, and I've been superbly lucky enough to get the couch in the Chief Steward's room. This will make the trip instead of a sort of floating Black Hole quite enjoyable. There are no washing arrangements except for a few buckets, and sanitation is almost non-existent. Meals, composed of compo rations, have to be eaten where a bit of space can be found to do so. In this cabin, however, I've no complaints. There is a radio which can be played till we leave anchorage and a desk at which to write this, and running water. What more could one ask? If these are to be my last few hours they will at least be comfortable ones. Amazing as we swung down the grey Thames this afternoon to think that two years ago I was <u>at</u> Woolwich also waiting to go overseas. How life passes . . .

I was talking to L/Bdr. Kelly in the Naafi last night. He said when we mentioned Jock's name, 'Christ I wish that man were back with us now,' little knowing how closely he echoes my own thoughts – two fifteen on a Saturday afternoon – in happier days there are so many things which one might be doing. The men generally are in very good heart but I don't mean it in the newspapers' way. I just mean they are putting up with the bloodiness of everything with proportionately little grumbling.

1730: We are lying at anchor in the Estuary. As we sailed down river towards the boom and the flak towers beyond it, we passed an enormous gathering of all the different kinds of vessel required for the invasion of an enemy coastline. I saw L.S.I.s – the ex passenger ships whose lifeboats are now assault boats, and from whom the Commandos steal forth in the darkness; and troopships; and then like one of those oldtime ballroom dances a huge line of L.S.T.s, each with its barrage balloon floating above it. And in between the grey 'little ships' slid about the grey river – M.T.B.s, corvettes, destroyers and gunboats. And others – more sinister like the rocket boats – which I didn't recognise. This evening an enormous Compo meal was served. Vegetables and bully and sort of Xmas pudding and for supper a tin of soup which heats itself. I can't sleep in this cabin now as Chas Jones the O.C. Troops feels it would outrage some of the Captains who are still in the Black Hole. However, I <u>can</u> sleep in the corridor outside and use it for all purposes.

The cabin doesn't belong to the Chief Steward but the Chief Officer (or Mate) an altogether more important type! He is being quite charming to me. Cigarettes and matches ad lib and any meals he is sending for he has duplicated – not that I feel I could possibly eat any more but I had a cup of tea in here. (A Lieut. Col. (R.A.S.C.) is sitting in here with me now. Quite a pleasant man.)

2230: I'm about to doss down in the corridor. We are still in the estuary at anchor with a great fleet around us. According to popular calculation the party should start tomorrow morning – but so far there is no sort of official word.

Tonight the ship's radio played Warsaw Concerto, which reminded me strongly of my last visit to Layer where C. played it for me and we stood in the sunny drawing room and drank cocoa and were very happy. Funnily enough they played it last night too.

4 June

Chilly wind whipping about the deck today and choppy waves outside. I slept pretty well in the corridor where it was warm and quiet. This morning I washed and shaved in lovely hot water. The breakfast was singularly unappetising; a cold sausage and cold bacon and a piece of bread and butter and jam. The tea was cold. However I suppose it could have been worse. No news of any attack yet. No news in fact about anything. Interesting talk on politics in here last night.

1930: Nothing has happened all day. There is something approaching a gale blowing tonight and the sea is whipped white from here to Southend Sands.

Played bridge again today. Surely it can't be long now? It seems such ages since I talked to Clare and now one can't even concentrate enough to start on a letter – though I think I'll have a try tomorrow. A Sapper Officer told me he thinks D will be Tuesday, but nobody has any real idea, all guesswork.

2300: A most convivial evening swopping stories and gadgets with the mate. He's given me a lovely torch and is sending C. one when he gets back from this trip. He is also sending her a letter from me. Small gale blowing tonight and outside the bombers have been flying in, releasing clusters of red flares as they cross the coast. Somebody drew attention tonight to the fact that as we are going through the Straits of Dover we shall probably be shelled by the Jerry shore batteries. That will be a new experience. I am going to sleep in my corridor now.

5 June

Life is as stagnant as a tin of syrup. Had I not known yesterday from my diary to be 4 June I should have had no idea of the date. The wind was still strong this morning but now (1600) it is dying down; so if the delay is due to the weather, we may start soon. The Captain and Mate (my pal) still have to be briefed however before we start. This morning the L.S.T.s sailed past us, out of the boom, and towards the open sea, so evidently something under way. I had only bread, butter and jam for breakfast as the sight of cold bacon nestling in a sea of congealed fat was not conducive. Lunch turned into a scramble from which I emerged with a tin of 'Brunch' (Spam) and my breakfast menu repeated. 'Compo' tea has never been its strong point – it always tastes vaguely of dishwater. With real tea added it is much improved, but this must wait till we land. I've been writing to C., which wasn't as difficult as I'd expected and I've covered a dozen pages already. Everybody listens anxiously for IT on the ship's radio but so far nothing more exciting than the capture of Rome (with St. Peter's and Vatican City intact) has come to us. The 5th Army went in last night.

Strange to think that in the outside world it is Monday today. Here it makes absolutely no difference. My pen shows signs of running dry. Blast.

2015: The Captain went away in a little boat to a conference at 1650. He is still away.

2115: He is back. We sail at 0400 tomorrow.

6 June

It is eight forty five and we are sailing for France. No details except that we were supposed to leave at 04 and actually didn't until about 3 hours after that. It is a crisp clean morning with sunshine and on our starboard side we can see Kent. The corvette next to us sent a message that we were bombarding Le Havre and in his opinion the party had started – midday – and we are just about at Dover harbour. The chalk cliffs dazzle in the sunshine but a strong wind is blowing, and it is cold. Eastwards down the channel stretches the long line of grey ships, with little escorts bobbing among them. Across the water I can see Calais shrouded in mist or smoke. A few Spitfires fly above us, their lines as slim and beautiful as the gulls around the vessel. But so far no breath of action, not a sound from the enemy 20 miles away. Can this really be the invasion? It is so far like Sicily all over again. The wireless is silent so we know nothing at all. We are passing Dover now, and I can see the barracks beyond the castle where I was stationed 4 years ago. The mate has just told me the radio has announced that landings have been made – shells and explosions outside – I shall go and have a look see.

1215: Shells from France. One Liberty ship behind us on fire. Escort laying screen. Everybody to wear tin hats.

1315: Later this ship which we thought at first to be the one with the rest of the bty. on it, blew up with an enormous pillar of flame that plunged over 200 feet into the sky. It wasn't the ship we thought, though. The damage was caused by German shore batteries in France. It was the very thing needed to add a touch of reality to the situation. Realising that the ship was only two behind ourselves shows how very close is the margin between safety and danger on these occasions. We have just passed Folkestone where Clare's father is Naval O.i/c. I wonder if he saw the incident.

2330: Full moon outside and we steam towards France. Breakfast 0500 so I shall lie down for a few hours soon. We are landing near Caen, which has already fallen. Sky full of planes before darkness. Rumour says Channel Isles also taken. It has taken me 4 hours to sort out my maps, messages and a mass of documents. Too many and too much!

7 June

0720: Up early this morning (0430) but as dawn broke, everything was apparently quiet. Only a heavy swell and overcast sky, and everywhere ships making for France. Personal messages from Eisenhower and Monty. I didn't think the latter's touched his old ones. It completely lacked any personal note.

Current latrinograms insist there was some sort of battle in the channel last night but I didn't hear anything. Still it's a good thing to be landing by daylight as they'll almost certainly bomb the beaches at night. Saw a small tug this morning towing back 3 captured E boats. Included in our kit now is a small book on France for each man. It is quite well and understandingly written and has a useful list of words and phrases in the back. Owing to wireless silence there is still absolutely no authentic news. When I join Sandy K. he will have his (I hope) which will be a very good thing. Breakfast in the cold light of dawn was particularly repulsive, consisting of a cold tinned sausage, bread and butter and jam and a mug of lukewarm tea.

0830: Dropped anchor.

1330: This is an amazing sight. The morning was cold, with rain, but this afternoon the sun has come out, turning the water green and blue. Everywhere as far as the eye can see, are ships stretching to the horizon. The bay is absolutely full of them of all types. Cruisers have been shelling from here, and away on our starboard side, the horizon is ringed with battleships each occasionally spurting flame and brown smoke and booming. There have been sporadic air-raid alarms but no enemy a/c yet; I expect they'll come by darkness. The radio ban is off and we heard the one o'clock news from London which included No. 3 bulletin from Supreme H.Q. but not much information. I can imagine how they must all be listening intently at home (I wonder if Clare heard that bulletin). Everybody bored and waiting to land. So far very little sign of our doing so. Hope we don't wait till dark! You can't see much of the shore except the yellow beach and a water tower and a little church with a spire; we are still at anchor but just going to move in a bit. I suppose we must be nearly a mile off shore at present. There is our 'Air Raid Red' on again but one can only see and hear our own planes in the sky.

2040: I expect to go ashore within an hour. The interminable unloading into L.C.T.s proceeds and it rather looks as though I may be the first officer ashore except the C.O. who landed on D. The enemy shelled the beach to the right of where we land intermittently during the afternoon, but no enemy planes have been visible by daylight. The battleships *Nelson*, *Warspite* and *Ramilles* boom on the horizon. The fleet has been shelling inland sporadically. BBC news adds nothing to what we already knew.

2120: Navy firing hard onto the beaches. The ships suddenly rippling flame and blast. I go ashore soon. Situation obscure but enemy reacting.

8 June

1330, near Bayville: Eventually our L.C.T. cast off at about 2300 just as it was getting dark. We spent the night on her in the harbour. The Skipper, a very decent Sub. Lt. R.N.V.R. gave us stew, pudding and coffee and we spent the night on deck with one blanket. Noisy night with the intermittent air raids. The harbour a mass of coloured flak. One or two bombs too close for comfort. 2 ships set on fire and a huge green fire on the beach.

Up early today and bleary eyed. We had to go about 120 yards in 3 foot 6 of water, but made it O.K. and soon after 9 set foot on the sands of France. (I did remember my promise to C.) The beach was covered (it was low tide) with broken obstacles and 'drowned' vehicles. All over the upper beach where they had landed at night tide lay the L.S.T.s, L.C.T.s and multiple other craft looking like the skeletons of prehistoric animals. Then on inland, where all the houses are smashed, tanks lie broken everywhere and all the usual relics (human and otherwise) of war were on view. The few remaining locals were friendly enough and waved a greeting. Signposting and general organisation first class, and the long line of trucks, halftracks etc. rolled inland on the dusty road almost without pause. Mines were numerous beyond belief.

1740: I had to dash off on Recce as I wrote the above. We are now in action near Revier. Bayeux has fallen to us. Have a bloody headache. Yesterday too. Am taking too many Veganin.

Midnight: Only now am I able to return to this as we've been in action since my last bit. Now, at midnight, I am getting tired. Outside comes desultory shellfire, or a shower of flak as a raider comes over and unloads. I can hear the heavy beat of bombs at the moment. Also one can hear m.g. fire and occasionally a nearby rifle or Sten shot as nervous sentries shoot at shadows – or each other – for snipers are still in evidence. The Middlesex on our position have already had casualties this way. Jerry resistance seems to be stiffening according to local reports and he is said to have 2 Armoured Divs. in Caen. I saw about 200 prisoners being marched back today. Some were very young (16 or so), others fairly old. They did not look cowed, but rather defiant, and were being firmly handled by their Canadian guards. Among things I noted coming ashore were the lovely fields of wild flowers enclosed by barbed wire and the grim skull and crossbones sign of the word 'MINEN' – MINES . . . a wonderful bunch of huge red poppies growing alongside some white peonies . . . the dusty roads which made one's jeep throw up a dust wake like a destroyer. This is a good position overlooking a bakery and in some trees. My Command Post is in an orchard. Stand to at 0545 tomorrow so I'll turn in soon for some needed sleep as I had only 3 uneasy hours last night and no shave till 1100. To hear the radio reports of flowers and joy you'd think this was a carnival. Still it's good to hear the news bulletins if only through knowing one makes them!

9 June

0020: Stick of 3, whistling loudly, just landed about 200 yards off. Extraordinary noise they make – heard it last night too. Boche fairly active in a minor sort of way. But enough –

1055: It rained steadily during the night and on past breakfast so I've moved the C.P. into a nearby farm, a thing I was loath to do before on account of the lack of protection. It is now clearing up a bit, and there isn't much firing on our sector. There is talk of another move later in the day. We have just fired our first rounds of the Campaign at 1115 on an enemy Radar Station and strong point.

2315: It is stand to. A nuisance in a way because it means it is almost impossible to sleep longer than 5½ hours, and with the nightly raids, rather less.

Just as I write a raid develops. About a dozen large ones are dropped fairly near. Everything shakes and trembles. Not much ack ack as there is patchy cloud and they come diving through it. It is now 2320 and they are still at it with a lot more flak this time. Wrote short letters today to C. and to home. But we still aren't allowed to say we're in France; stupid as our letters wear 'O.A.S.' and are addressed England. But you can't expect the staff to think of that.

10 June

1000: Snipers in the area last night. There are a lot knocking about the place. Harry Forshaw was wounded – shot through the hand at short range, but it's not serious.

Some lovely wild flowers here – everything seems twice the size it is at home. In the orchard here there is orange blossom, apple blossom, huge wild roses and peonies. Warning order for Recce parties to be ready for movement by 1400 hours. Dull, miserable weather with a hint of rain.

Frank has found a local farmer who purveys some rather excellent cider but eggs are not easy to come by. Chocolate and sugar seem to have the best barter value.

11 June

0125: In the Command Post the small light falls on this paper. I am weary. We dashed off at about 1300. Up through Hermanville and St. Aubin eventually into recce 7 miles or so west of our last post near Blainville on the Caen canal. We were shelled and sniped there and I had to pull the Recce party out. Eventually the whole Regt. had to withdraw. We were furthest forward and had about 150 shells in the area. It rained heavily and consistently during the afternoon and was bloody. I'd had no meal since breakfast (having been called on Recce on the point of lunch) when we came into action here at Benouville at 1900. I got a plate of soup at 2115. This is 6th Airborne area and full of gliders – hundreds of them lying about. Before dark four Stirlings dropped a cloud of parachute borne supplies; the chutes were all different colours and very pretty. A few bombs only near us today but snipers everywhere very active. These are only notes; I'll add more details tomorrow. Night noisy with desultory shells, mortars and m.g.s.

0915: This morning is muggy and rather cold again. I eventually fell into bed at 2 o'clock and was asleep within two or three minutes. The B.B.C. is still meticulously cheerful about everything, including the weather. I noticed one thing particularly yesterday on the move up, and that was the cheerful and prompt way all the ordinary soldiers in the sappers, pioneers etc. all the way up, were getting on with the job. I suppose most of them are still getting a kick out of being in action but all the same it is good to see them working well.

The roads are not in a good state, being broken and torn by shells, guns and tank tracks. Mud and pools of water lie everywhere. Also the constant threat of snipers keeps everybody very alert. I've never seen so many people carrying their personal arms! An attack goes in tonight by one of our Brigades with the armour passing through it. We are likely to be here in support for two or three days – so they say!

2330, in the C.P.: At 1500 I was sent for at Bn. over the canal and some miles up. I went off in a Jeep and passed through some country over which, obviously, some very heavy fighting has been done. Here and there lay the unburied dead of each side, and the villages were battered, deserted and sinister. Snipers prevalent and at each corner you wondered which side you'd meet. Broken vehicles, smashed weapons and houses, everything in ruins and hardly a person in sight. Draped among the fields and houses were gaily coloured parachutes, this being the 6th Airborne Div.'s area though the 51 has come through them now.

Eventually we reached Battalion H.Q. just in time to be informed that the last village (Escoville) we'd come through was big with German patrol and snipers, and the party before us had been shot up! Anyway I collected the dope and went back on the alternative route only to be informed once again on the blower by Sandy Cowie that he was pinned down by snipers on it. However we proceeded and got back home safely. I remember some women in Escoville who were the wildest looking creatures I've seen for a long time. Half crazy I suppose. We captured Touffreville, the cause of my trip, during the evening, but have been firing heavily since 2250 as they are counterattacking. Our gunfire has broken them up. Still working here on a fire plan of 210 Rounds per gun originally scheduled for 0400 tomorrow, but now postponed indefinitely. I believe they are worried about German armour beginning to congregate somewhere on our flank. Monty is on the mainland. Hope we get sight of him sometime. Enemy now shelling on our right; it sounds very large and lethal in the stillness of the night. The B.B.C. on the news tonight provoked derisive laughter by informing us that troops moving through London 'to join their comrades in France' were mobbed and given tea and cigarettes by enthusiastic crowds! Bit of a contrast to our own departure in the misty East End streets. B.B.C. has given 50 Div., 1 American Div., 6 Airborne and 3 Canadian as being here, but no mention of us yet which is a poor do. We are allowed to say we are in France now. Am just going to write to C. Probably a dull letter as I'm tired, very tired.

Following snatch of conversation shows we are getting war-minded again! L/Bdr. Langlands, after hearing somebody say something was as easy as falling off the Eiffel Tower: 'That'll make a marvellous O.P. won't it.'

12 June

1930: Not a very good day. Things are sticky in front. Dennis Pullin's wounded, Ken Aitken (so far) missing. In our battery Dougan is badly wounded and Brown killed. Wootton (L/Bdr.) wounded. Worked till 0320 and slept till 0420 then fired solidly till 1045. The enemy have been counterattacking like hell and Jimmy Gegan's just come back from a bloody 36 hours pretty shaken. The situation is completely obscure. Mail today – 2 letters from Clare and one from Judy, also newspapers. (Very sensational and D-Dayish.) I think I may have to do some O.P. work soon – a prospect which doesn't appeal awfully much.

Sunshine today. I've been getting eggs and milk from a nearby farm by barter. We give salmon, sardines, soap, bully and candles, also chocolate.

They listen avidly to the news in French, twice daily. I am losing McLeary to go and drive the B.C. The gliders on the position have yielded much booty. Cushions, lamps etc. and in one I found a first aid kit containing 2 more tubes of morphine, which I hope I shan't need. Casualties bring the war home. I am disliking the war at the moment. It is beginning to make me feel doubtful of seeing C. again.

0130: I am in the C.P. At 0400 a programme starts so I'll be up again (I am hoping to lie down soon). Around midnight the shelling and heavy small arms fire which had been making the mist on the left flank hideous, developed into a pretty heavy air raid with bombs in this area. They dropped ordinary H.E. and also A.P. which go off with a simply fiendish clatter. They flew in very low over here – one was only about 500–1000 feet up and clearly identifiable as a JU 88. Even the Bren guns fired at it! Red and white tracers everywhere.

The battery has used about 1500 shells today. Bad news; Dennis Pullin whom I like very much has been very badly wounded today.* Two children to whom he's devoted. Only about a week ago I was playing bridge with him on the ship coming over. Heavy air raid and shelling by sea due on Caen tonight. God I <u>am</u> tired. About 4 hours sleep in 3 days. 3 British Div. announced by B.B.C. No mention of 51 or 7 Armoured. Keeping it as a nice surprise for Jerry! Churchill, Eisenhower and everybody over here today. Not here of course (and nobody would wish it).

More heavy shelling on our left flank near 301 bty. Great splintering crashes, much louder by night. You can hear them whistling quite clearly.

14 June

0205: I am in the new C.P. – the one I had dug by bulldozer (for an emergency) the other morning. The reason is as follows. At about 2300 the usual nightly raid started; heavier than usual tonight. Eventually it culminated in a stick of bombs right across us, the last precisely <u>5 yards</u> from the dutch barn under which we were located. It blew a good hole in the road and the barn roof collapsed in a shower of tiles. Splinters flew in and punctured one of the trucks, some petrol tins, water tins, and brew cans. Two hurricane lamps smashed. Miraculously we had no casualties. At least, I say miraculously but some intuition (or was it?) had made me uneasy this evening and much to everybody's irritation I insisted on moving tonight and digging out and finishing off the hole. So nearly everybody was (as we were in the middle of moving) able to get to the ground. We are actually just behind the barn and showers of everything fell on us. Otherwise I don't like to think what might have happened. During the day the enemy have shelled the area quite heavily, particularly towards evening. The Div. is carrying out a slight (mile or two) withdrawal tonight and the counter attack is likely to be heaviest in this area. Typhoons fired rockets at Sandy Cowie and the B.C. today. Anyway we are now adequately fixed for further enemy interest in us. Bed 0220–0320 last night, but got a little sleep later. Fired heavily up till noon then slackened off a bit. Hell of a lot of guns concentrated in this area, particularly mediums.

* Died in Normandy.

Saw gliders going over high tonight in complete silence each with a tiny light – a very eerie thing. Now bed till 0530 . . .

I believe the Div. has had fairly heavy casualties already, specially among the poor old infantry. 5 B.W. have lost 50%.

2330: A fairly quiet day until this evening when 4 Stirlings came over at 600 feet and unloaded a great cloud of coloured parachutes (containing stores) on (or more accurately, just behind) our position. Everybody – including a lot of civilians – rushed towards them, and I went off on a bike to stop any looting. Jerry then sent over about 50 air burst 88 just overhead. A lot of stuff flew about the place. Some came through the cover into the C.P., hit my bed and made a hole in an artillery board.

Jimmy Lowe wounded today – that's another captain gone – also the R.Q.M.S. (generally regarded as a bit of a joke this) wounded on this post tonight. The bombers are over again but not as active as last night. Sandy Cowie came in today after an unusually bloody session up forward. Shelling over on the right.

15 June

Uneventful day; hardly an enemy shell. Good mail; letters from C., Bé and Judy. Wrote a lot of letters today. Had a half chicken for tea, and looked just like Henry VIII! And now for bed, only just midnight, hooray.

16 June

1045: At dawn today the enemy put in a heavy counter attack, assisted by fairly general shelling of the gun line, and waggon lines. We fired 27 D.F. tasks and nearly 700 rounds (from the Bty) and are still firing (a counter-battery task) at the moment. More casualties today. We've had 2 killed, 2 wounded, and 301 had a direct hit on one of their guns with at least 2 killed and quite a few wounded. (Actually I find now, it's 3 killed.) We fired solidly from 0445–0900 and the air was loud with the crash of guns, whining of shells, and thump of enemy shells around the place. It is now 1130 and quiet again. During the chaos this morning it started raining again, quite hard, and the general scene was pretty desolate with heaps of rubble outside here, various things like motorcycles torn by shrapnel, and the grey, shell-noisy dawn with no sun to warm and cheer. Haven't shaved or washed yet today and feel pretty lousy and scruffy.

2000: I've just had my wash and shave and feel rather better. Also, Sandy K's wireless has been repaired after being damaged by the bomb the other night, which is a good thing. It is generally expected that he'll counter attack again tomorrow morning, and prisoners say he's going to use 120 aircraft to assist. It should not take long to liquidate those. This is becoming almost a static war, and we are well dug in for such an event as the main counter attack falling on us – which people seem to think is likely. Managed to get a rather inadequate letter off to C. today; there seems so little to write just now. Another casualty today when a bloke shot himself cleaning his Sten gun. I also carry one of these admirable little weapons now, as they are ideal for dealing with snipers. I am damned tired. Jake Mason the Parafoo from 127 came in yesterday after dropping on the night before D. He'd been hunted for over a week, and had some astonishing adventures.

2100: David Kirk (B.C. 301) and his driver, have been killed. 2 Signallers wounded. Our casualties are mounting daily now, and Sandy Cowie, back from battalion tonight, seems to have had another 25 hours of pretty average hell. The prospect grows daily more depressing. I must say quite frankly I don't want to be killed. I want to live and have fun and see Clare again. Might be lucky and get a wound; no use worrying about it anyway. The fighting is very bitter – no prisoners –

17 June

2315: It is just getting dark. The twilight tonight is very lovely. The sky above is a profound blue shading down in degrees of pearl to the horizon, where a sort of blood-orange effect shows up the hedges and trees and walls. Away towards the harbour the barrage balloons show up like black beetles in the air. Overhead planes drone to and fro. There is nothing to indicate whose – yet. They sound rather unlike ours. A quiet day today. I worked till 0300 last night and so stayed in bed till nearly midday. Breakfast in bed – most luxurious (including an egg!). Today I got some butter – real yellow, farm butter, from across the road; it's quite delicious. I give them all manner of things now, including razor blades, toothpaste and biscuits and sweets as well as other things already mentioned. Things are beginning to assume that monotonously hazardous aspect of action with its various contrasts: deep in this hole in the ground Peter, Matt, the C.O. (who'd just dropped in) and I knocked off the most delicious bottle of champagne today. Sweet and cool. This is a peculiar position we hold here, with Jerry extending from our left flank to our right rear. Could be awkward, but probably won't. Getting some good food with stuff picked in the fields such as new potatoes, onions, carrots, and peas. Certainly varies the diet a bit. I had a grand 'salad' for lunch the other day. Compo, of course, varies with the type of box you get. 'A' is generally the best. I am now going to bed; it might be worth putting on pyjamas tonight – a good measure of one's gauge of the odds on a bit of sleep! Actually last time I did, I was up again quite soon. Bombers now active and some beginning to drop near. First the growl and zoom, then the earthshaking crump. And above it the Bofors pumping up their little red shells.

18 June

2040: Wonderful mail today. Letters from Bé and Dorothy and 3 from Clare which was marvellous. Also another food parcel from N.Y. I had tinned pate de foie gras from the parcel on my biscuits for lunch. Strange fare for the trenches! I've written to C. but shall write again tonight. Many newspapers have also come in today. The heavies are dropping more parachute supplies at 2130, and everybody is wondering if they'll shell the area again. It's rather cold tonight.

19 June

1945: God what a bloody miserable day. A night of nuisance planes dropping bombs in the area (Stewart Watts had his C.P. door blown in) and then as dawn broke, rain, which has persisted all day varying in ferocity. The C.P. has done its best, but shell splinters have punctured our covers, and we are not revetted, so it's been pretty wet at times. Now, as night falls (or seems to fall) we have baled out water from the roof and sides, and seem temporarily on top. Vicious enemy shelling in the next door orchards after lunch, but nothing near enough to worry one unduly.

Wrote again to C. and Bé but the incoming mail continued no letters though there was an *Esquire* for me. The Americans have cut the Cherbourg peninsula; they are doing well. Everything seems to be going O.K. though obviously we didn't capture Caen on the first day, which I think must have been the intention. The Regt. today gave the M.O. an entire day's chocolate and sweet ration for his children's orphanage nearby. I've never seen so many bars at once, and the sweets looked like hundreds and thousands. I think it's good of the chaps to do it.

Still raining miserably. It patters unevenly on the covers, and flips about the grass behind us. Men stand about singly or in twos and threes, smoking dejectedly. They wear strange makeshift unmilitary garb and headgear. They curse everything impartially and without enthusiasm. Here and there they huddle over smoky little fires, brewing the extremely unattractive 'Compo' tea, a cup of which I am now sipping. Some use the chocolate ration to make cocoa, a rather better idea. If you walk 5 yards here, you pick up about 5 pounds of mud and straw. In two days it will be the longest day of the year. Today I could believe it.

20 June

2330, Command Post: Tonight I paid (or this evening) my second visit to the real front across the canal. It is a sinister little world across there, of deserted villages – or what remains of them – and the broken relics of war machines and men. The O.P. was in a barn roof and I spent some time there. The farm was almost deserted, only a few very neutral-looking civvies are left in it, with slatternly hungry looking children. And the grounds are thick with mines. There were some gardens there, all overgrown, with weeds encroaching on the onions, and geese and hares moving about quite unmolested. Over a concealed slit trench sprang a great bush of huge red wild roses and some other flowers the colour of bluebells, which I did not recognise. And over everything hangs the quietude of death and danger, broken only by the sound of shellbursts or machine guns rattling.

In front of the O.P. cultivated fields and tidy hedges. Farm houses, and on the horizon (which is a near one) a thick wood where the Germans are lying. In front of the wood are a couple of knocked out tanks, but I don't know whose. I think his. In front of the O.P. are two dead cows, already swollen and with legs stiff in the air like upturned rocking horses. All the nearby villages are smashed and the desolation fills one with amazement and sorrow. This is Herouvillette, which both sides wanted. Over by the bridge (Benouville bridge) going back, a Jeep (I was also in one) had been hit. By the roadside lay those bundles one begins to recognize so quickly, covered with blankets, and still for ever. Driving back in the twilight I shivered . . .

Lovely letter from C. today. She's a grand correspondent. I've written back tonight. Sun and wind (and repairs!) today.

21 June

2330: I went to Battn. again at approach of dusk. Quite quiet East of the River Orne. Indeed today has been generally a pretty quiet day along this front. We get planes over most nights, the other night's entertainment included one of the new pilotless variety, but the Americans now on the outskirts of Cherbourg have captured some of their landing platforms so maybe we shan't be troubled by them for a while. Very cold today and tonight. For 6 tins of sardines I acquired each of the truck crew a steak for supper. Tomorrow I've been promised some more butter. A good dish; biscuits butter and ground chocolate. Considerable labour but worth it. No mail today but I wrote a long letter to C. and one home. Maybe the Channel gales are holding up the mail. Big attack due on Sunday and a diversion by our 154 Brigade on Friday. Latest 'Monty Says' rumour: we shall be in Paris 19 days after we break the Caen defence line. I doubt it, though I suppose there isn't much to stop us after we punch through there. Work still going on in the C.P. It rarely does cease till midnight. Split another bottle of champagne today with Sandy K., Peter, Matt and Frank. Hope there's a letter from Clare tomorrow . . .

22 June

2330: All set for tomorrow's party for which H hour is 0300. Today we received a programme of a dozen D.F.s and 30 Concentrations on call. These all went to the guns by 1700. A day of great air activity. Through a Jerry telescope – binoculars appropriated by me (they are A.A. gun equipment with 4 polarised filters) I watched 48 Mitchells and 24 Bostons unload on the factory towers (now famous) near Caen. They flew through pretty heavy flak unmoved. A huge column of smoke took half an hour to clear – but the chimneys were still there; they had unloaded NW of the target. Late in the afternoon about 500 Forts went over in an unending procession shining in the sunlight. Towards dusk we saw others flying homewards. No mail today blast it. Maybe tomorrow.

More butter today; lovely stuff – actually I seem to remember that this butter from the 'granary of Paris' is famous. If not, it should be! Enemy planes overhead and quite a bit of our own flak. The planes sound damn sinister at night as they zoom – now a fairly distant bomb shakes the ground. A series of them in fact. We are investing Cherbourg. It should fall soon.

24 June

0915: (Sgt. Knight and 2 men wounded in the gun line.)

I am in the O.P. at Herouvillette. I came up here yesterday afternoon and relieved Jimmy Gegan. Actually the snag is I've been feeling like death as I've eaten something which disagreed with me and yesterday evening I could hardly see for headache. It's been fairly quiet so far except the first thing this morning when the enemy put down a smoke screen and an armoured car came right up to the O.P. here firing a bren or something. A six pounder next to us shot at it but missed and everybody blazed away with rifles and brens but the thing got away. A lot of mortaring last night, some fell very close to Bn. where we went in for the night but I felt too bloody to care. I have Sandy Cowie's party (a good bunch) with me. Tonight we are having chicken and vegetables so I hope my appetite comes back. I've not eaten anything yet since tea yesterday. That is except 2 Veganin for breakfast today! Awful smell of dead in Herouvillette and here where the cows in front of the O.P. are getting pretty high. One or two enemy planes over here this morning.

2 July

Queen Elizabeth Hospital, Birmingham: So much has happened since my last entry. I'll try and recall some of it. The night I last wrote this I felt very ill and had to go back. Doc. Dewar found my temperature was about 104 °F and made me go back to the M.D.S. I remember lying there feeling lousy and full of quinine, and outside the guns were crashing and so, occasionally, were the bombs. They took a blood slide and decided I had malaria. At dawn I was evacuated still on my stretcher to the C.C.S. near the beach. More bombs. Then to another place and finally to an air evacuation centre. They took me from there about 1500 and we bumped and jolted about 16 miles to an air strip.

Loaded into a Douglas Dakota and we made a very smooth crossing. Got to a place near Swindon about 2100. After a night in the C.C.S. where I literally steamed with fever they brought me here. This is a superb hospital and everybody in it is very nice, nurses and patients alike.

Life since I've been here has resolved itself into personal problems such as collecting clothing coupons, deciding how to get back etc. I've been through to Clare on the phone. Hell it was good to hear her. I hope I shall see her soon as my course finishes in about 8 days and I'm supposed to get a week's leave. I shall try and take 10 days and then avoid the depot completely and hitchhike back by plane. Bé has had another baby girl,* and Laurie has been injured by one of these damned P. planes as they call them now. I've heard disquieting rumours about these. It seems London is getting another pasting. I've been amazed from the first moment I was put on a stretcher, how good everybody is to sick and wounded. They do absolutely anything for them. It was a good moment to arrive back and be washed for the first time for days. Also I ate nothing for 3 days. One of the less pleasant features of malaria is the shivering fits you get. Also the blazing head and eye ache. In fact you ache all over. But I'm much better now. The treatment is 3 days quinine, 5 days Mepacrine and 5 days Pernacine when you have to go back to bed. My clothes have been washed and pressed by some A.T.S. gun girls who really are quite sweet. They go miles to do it for us. I feel so restless it annoys me. Here I am in Blighty and I'm anxious only to get back and give a hand. But that will undoubtedly come soon enough. My M.O. is a woman and very pleasant.

9 August

1430, on board L.S.I. Empire Crossbow: 6 weeks or so since I wrote in here and now, within minutes, we shall sever our last connections with Southampton – and England. The gangways have just come in, and I suppose we shall lie in S'ton water tonight, as we are said to be landing tomorrow morning. This ship – a fairly small one – usually caters for about 600. Today we have 1400 of all sorts and shapes and sizes. Our own draft which on leaving Oxford spent last night in a comfortable camp in the New Forest, is the only one which is returning to Normandy – the others are first time out – and look it; that peculiar expression, a mixture of exasperation at being bitched about, excitement at the future, refusal to admit any sort of excitement over anything – all generally to be summed up as a 'I-have-done-all-this-sort-of-thing-before-but-actually-I-haven't-the-vaguest-idea-what-happens-next' expression!

Anyway I had done it before – quite a few times now, and finding we are mostly sleeping on deck (and having no blankets) I swiftly sought out the 3rd Officer and got permission to sleep on his couch, which will be better than the deck. There are 19 officers and a couple of hundred men in any draft. The men

*The baby died after 5 days.

have all behaved admirably – though the arrangements for transit have been so smooth, there's no reason why they should have done anything else. Coming through Southampton in our troop carriers, the populace indulged in a good bit of waving, 'V' signing, and cries of 'good luck boys' which was the first demonstration of its kind I myself had seen. Showers of pennies – even an occasional sixpence – came from the vehicles, thrown by the troops to the grubby children by the wayside. Interest in money began to fade . . . I noticed our draft were quite a lot quieter than the first-timers, which wasn't really surprising.

When we got on board we were given a good meal which did surprise me after our Liberty Ship – but there was white bread and butter and coffee with as much sugar as you wanted. This has eased the strain on the 24 hour pack we were given this morning together with the usual stuff as detailed for my last trip this way. We were up at 0600 today but didn't leave till 1100, which actually <u>was</u> rather necessary I suppose, because there were so many different drafts to be sped on their way – with encouraging cries from the base wallahs who stayed behind! Large numbers going back to H.D. though nobody from 127 except a new gunner who says he's going to replace Jimmy Mailer the survey officer – killed while I've been in England. There are some very pleasant officers in my draft, in particular two from D.L.I. in 49 Div. and a 3 Div. South Lancs. Subaltern who caused laughter by telling us how he recently went into hospital to be circumcised. 'I was O.K.,' he said 'except for bursting a stitch while reading *For Whom the Bell Tolls*'. I told him I'd have to make a note of that for this diary, so I'm glad I've remembered.

As to going back, I have no feelings at all so far this time. I might be going to post a letter, so completely devoid of any emotion am I. But it gives a sudden start of misery to remember that exactly a week ago I was in Selfridges with C., buying corduroy trousers.

1545: Break for the usual burst of instructions about what to do if and when we get sunk. By now a week ago we were either in or near Knightsbridge, probably in Harvey Nicholls.

We are moving down Southampton Water. England looks very green and pleasant from this hot and welded box. Green fields, and great trees under whose shade one lies in imagination, while here is only the steel deck and there is no shade, no cover from the shimmering grey metal. Everybody is somewhat browned off, but only in that mirthless army way of those expecting bloody treatment and usually getting it. Breakfast tomorrow is at the rather appalling hour of 0600, and we are meant to land about noon. So if we are on shore and in the transit camp near Bayeux by evening, I shall feel faintly surprised. It seems only fitting that in the midst of everything, a nearby officer should enquire whether anybody has seen Jane today. It restores normality to the situation. So far I have got the typewriter with me. Sweating and cursing, it has been dragged and bounced about the place, and now lies in an after part of the ship with some baggage. To say I shall be glad to get rid of the damn thing, is rather as if Guy Fawkes had said he would be glad when his barrel of powder was safely lighted. However, these things are usually worse in theory than in fact. Funny to think C. and I nearly had our first quarrel over the stupid machine. When I reach 127 there should be at least one letter from her, which will be such a good thing; it gives me, absurd as it may seem, a feeling almost as if I were going to see her again instead of a letter. Every moment, England, and everything associated with it, seems increasingly remote. Can it only be a week ago that C. and I were going into Nell Gwynn's house for tea? Yet I can see it as clearly as if it had been yesterday; but the scene somehow lacks meaning, it's as though I saw somebody else doing it. In fact to prove how a week can wreck one's memory I have suddenly remembered that the things I mentioned happened tomorrow. Today was Wednesday and we were having tea in Ariston's in Argyll Street, and talking about a lot of things which matter. Curious, I thought it was Thursday. Probably because such a lot happens in a morning in transit. I am sitting in their operations room (this being designed as a ship to carry an assault battalion). Officers are sleeping, reading, writing, or just sitting. I can see 6 different Div. signs as I look round the room. Amazing how the same people have done the fighting in this war. Still, they must have thought that in the last war, too. No more for now.

1940: Evening begins to fall round the Isle of Wight where we are lying at anchor, bringing a chilly wind and cloud. We sail at 0400 tomorrow. Awfully good dinner tonight. We had soup and then fish, and I thought dinner was over, but a joint and 2 veg followed, and then jelly. And coffee.

A week ago – and this time my memory is not playing tricks – we were having dinner at Coq d'or and not enjoying it much because we were both feeling sick. I had jelly then, too. The ship's broadcaster system is blaring out Dancing Cheek to Cheek . . . No blankets or pillow tonight, but I hope to sleep O.K. on the couch. Really all one needs is the horizontal attitude and a bit of fatigue – both of which I can now supply.

10 August

1040: Actually I didn't sleep very soundly. Though it was fairly warm in the cabin, I kept waking up shivering. Lying in my trousers with no boots or socks, I had fitful nightmares. But I had a wonderful wash and shave in here, and didn't go into breakfast till 0800. As expected, there was porridge and eggs and bacon.

It is overcast today and rather cold, but the sea is very smooth and our convoy, which is small, but strongly escorted, is making a good speed. There is an officer of the Royal Sussex also in this cabin who went to school with its owner (who, by the way is the 4th officer, not the 3rd). The former rather amuses me by calling me 'guns' as I believe they do in the Navy. I'm told we are going to a Reinforcement Gp. near Bayeux, which is rather a pity because the one near Caen has Alistair Cameron as Commandant and that would have put me quids in.

However, there shouldn't be any great difficulty getting back to 127 and if there is, I shall just go, and leave the questions to be asked afterwards, as the C.O. has asked for me by name. Let's hope there will be no difficulty – and it doesn't really look as though there will be.

2230. 36 Reinforcement Unit near Bayeux: Went ashore at about 1600 after having to change course because of mines. It was blazingly hot and the first halt was about 4 miles inland, when hundreds of men lay about on open hill country. This was the camp! It consisted of notice boards and one mobile canteen. The dust ashore was appalling and covered the marching columns. From there we went another 1½ miles to this place which is like all these places; actually could be a lot worse from the comfort point of view. We are supposed to go on again tomorrow another 3½ miles to another place where we go to our units. France looks exactly the same – no battle here of course. There is a Norwegian officer in the Green Howards in my tent – he's had some amazing adventures and is, among other things, a parachutist. We came ashore in Assault craft but quite dry as they've now built a wonderful pier and a complete harbour made of portable concrete slabs and sunken ships.

Enemy planes – quite a few – about the place – loud cries of 'put that light out' but all the bombs are very distant. Am sleeping on the floor but have collected 4 blankets and made a very comfortable bed. And now for some sleep.

But just before sleeping I must remember to add that my typewriter is beside me. What a weight it seems to have become! Never again, but never! Oh and one other point. Supper tonight was cold bully and prunes and custard. The things we do for England!

11 August

2145: With dusk comes a ground mist rather like the kind you find in the Welsh Mountains. Overhead, as all day, are Spits, Typhoons and Mustangs, and voices come from all the corners of the camp together with all the other mingled sounds of singing, laughter, music, enquiries, rifle bolts clicking and in the distance the rumble of artillery. We haven't moved today, after all. 'Perhaps tomorrow' is the official dictum. Spent a very lazy day doing nothing. In the afternoon, Hammer (the Norwegian) regales the tent with a detailed account of some of his sexual adventures in England. 'His hobby,' another officer told me. We have located a base wallah I knew in England – at Woolwich in 1942. He is Mayor Alcock, once Uncle Arthur in the B.B.C. – a simian poseur. More bully for supper tonight with

M & V for lunch though the permanent staff had roast meat and potatoes. I was moved to declaim Sassoon's 'Base Details' in its entirety. I've put on pyjamas tonight and with my 4 blankets have constructed a very comfortable bed. Let's hope tomorrow will see a move, if only to another of these places. It is getting dark and I want to write to P. so I'll leave this. I've taken to pencil because my pen is nearly dry and my only bottle of Quink is at the battery. Still hard fighting on the British–Canadian sector. Americans have taken Nantes.

12 August

2120: Same place; hot lazy day but two things have happened at least. One is that we move to 101 at Bayeux tomorrow, and the other that Jim Cowper, an officer from 301 turned up here, and I've sent him back to the Adjutant with urgent cries for rescue. Also I have fleas, contracted from the blankets issued here. Still, we've had some good laughs here, about nothing in particular. 'Graham' Moffat, our draft conducting officer, left for England today so I gave him 2 Mars bars and a milk chocolate bar to post for C. Bully again for supper. Messing here is a racket. Sunset tonight is a wonderful red-pink glow in the West. According to Jim the Regt. is right up forward with this latest push and plenty of stuff flying about. Leslie Wager is missing and Chas Johnstone was wounded yesterday or today.

13 August

31 Reinforcement Unit: Today after lunch we moved off, three gunner officers, Cookson, 'Gillie', Potter and me. Together in a lorry we went, with 14 Gunner reinforcements. Awful ride through the back areas amid clouds of dust to this place, which is exactly like the last one, differing perhaps in that it is a damn sight less comfortable and its inhabitants are correspondingly more objectionable. We have parted from our infantry friends which deprives life of many laughs. So that by the time we had been shifted from here to there within this tented tomb, there were three exceedingly browned off officers. Even the typewriter was no longer funny. In this place we've all the reinforcement officers who were discarded as unfit for the original landing. Looking at them, and listening to them, the reasons soon became apparent. There is also a department for ex-Normandy officers, but as the base has made a balls up of the reposting orders, this has overflowed, so we find ourselves (plus the usual 4 blankets, very motheaten and grudgingly given by the Q.) in the reinforcement lines. I hope none of them ever reinforces us.

Cookie and I went to see the Colonel who is a very good type and going to speed things up. C. will probably leave tomorrow as his Regt. is coming into the area we have just left, to refit, but as 127 is up front I can't go off till 'official' word comes through. I hope to god that won't be long. A spell in this place would just about finish me off. I feel like the man in *Decline and Fall*, who, on seeing the Welsh band, exclaimed 'I do not believe it; such creatures simply do not exist . . .'

Let me give two excellent examples of the base-mentality. The sergeant who showed us to our part of the camp, said complacently: 'Actually this is my day off but I'm doing this all the same' and the batman who had to get some blankets for us grumbled that he 'was working till half past ten last night fetching and carrying . . .' To the Sergeant I said nothing. Such a man who had reached 3 stripes and could yet speak thus, was obviously beyond recall. To the batman I pointed out that half past ten was not usually considered a late hour in a front line unit. This naturally is a resumé of my actual speech, which included a few well chosen if not uncommon words. However, my temper was frayed by then. We have 4 pints of washing water per day – quite like the desert except that there nobody grumbled about it. Daily, I loathe the back areas and the small things which crawl about them, more.

I am lying in an orchard under a canvas cover, not a tent. It is 9.30 and dusk is coming on, giving the trees that usual hazy appearance caused by slight ground mist. Cows, fixed by chain to a picket, graze about the place, and overhead in the light blue sky, the square shape of a Mustang pirouettes like a noisy bat. I am most depressed by this shuttling about and would willingly exchange this relative quiet for the noise and dust of real people at the front. I am too depressed even to write to C. All this doesn't make a good letter. I must tell her about it one day. Trees <u>are</u> beautiful with the last of the sunset behind them. There they stand, quite still, dark and green. They form no sort of background for the passing affairs of men, which they ridicule by their serenity and permanence. They always make me rather sad at dusk. Somewhere in Layer, also I expect touched by gloom, stands the tree in which we heard the nightingale one night, singing and singing, so near, a few yards away.

14 August

2105: Today has been spent quite fruitlessly – bothering people to try and get something done. By comparison, the job Moses did on the rock was merely a matter of deciding which tap to turn. However, hope springs and all that, and we hope – Gillie and I – to go tomorrow. Cookie goes anyway, but he has advantages. Oh the horrors of this place! Sleep last night was broken frequently by the intractability of the ground to the hip bone, the furious barking of most of the dogs in France, and anti-aircraft guns not far off, which make life hazardous for the permanent staff by depositing large pieces of shell about the place. We have moved into a dug in tent now. The floor is an inch or two deep in dust and animal life. Asked why they persisted in this habit, a battery clerk told us: 'Well Sir, a land mine fell over there' – waving his arms in the rough direction of the sea – 'and the order came – DIG IN!' He later admitted the missile was out of earshot. By the same token, Uncle Arthur, on cookhouse inspection recently, heard a bomb about two miles away, and seizing the nearest dixie, clamped it over his head and dived into the greasetrap. The authority of this story is vouched for by his sergeant-major who was with him. War is indeed hell. A dog is again yapping outside, and from a nearby tent comes an irate yell of 'Take that bloody dog away Bill.' The owner of the yell must have been annoyed or he would have said 'Fucking dog.' I only pray to leave here tomorrow and get back to the Battery. There, I hope will be a letter from C. and it will give me work to do and stop my thinking all the time of these last few weeks. The war is going very well. I'll miss it all if I don't get back soon. The weather is breaking up; gusty wind and a hint of rain.

15 August

1100: Morning has brought nothing – more or less as I expected. Cookie has gone so Gillie and I went to see the Colonel again. He is trying to get something done on the phone and promises to try and get us out by 1500. If he doesn't succeed I shall go crazy in this place. Very bad night – the hard ground gave me cramp and large pieces of A.A. shell kept falling around the tent. Very hot today.

2330, in the Command Post: I am back with the bty. somewhere in the spearhead near Falaise. Soon after lunch I got permission from the C.O. to go, posting order or not, so I hitch-hiked rather successfully to just beyond Caen, finishing with a 1 Corps Major who gave me tea, and after tea a Jeep in which to finish my journey. The roads and tracks were crowded and dust swirled worse than the desert. One was choked with it. Caen is unbelievably smashed. I don't see how ever it can be rebuilt. Eventually I got back here on the dusty plain. I passed most of the Canadian Army on the way. Good welcome back, but Sandy K. is wounded and lots of the chaps, including Sgt. Lambert, killed. The R.A.F. bombed the Regt. heavily yesterday and destroyed 15 of R.H.Q.'s vehicles. There are only 7 officers functioning in the Battery as the B.C. has gone back with a bad leg or something. I am taking CP back from Matt.

A lot of my kit seems to be missing, including – so far – my best battledress, which is rather a disaster. But it may be about the place somewhere. I am now in the C.P., dug in as usual and it is raining! Here, there are millions of wasps by day, and millions of huge, ravenous mosquitoes by night. Worse than Sicily by far. Huge mail including lots from C. – 4 written since I left – we are now being fairly heavily bombed by the Jerry – H.E. bombs and A.P. as well. I shall be here till about 0200 I should think as there's plenty of work to do – a stick fell damn close then – the whole place shook violently. Still going on – about 30 planes I should think.

I must read some more of my mail and write home and to C. Bombs still falling pretty close.

16 August

1545, nearing St Pierre: Off to an early flap-start after 3 hours sleep. Situation much improved by a nice letter from C. which I read at the first halt. It made the enemy dead lying in the field seem very strange, reading of the dress Hylda had given her, and other things of home.

1710: (I was interrupted by a long spell of firing and other usual activities.) We moved up past the scene of recent battle. Here, a knocked out 'Tiger' – scorched and seared in the green woods – the first smelt wonderful in the early morning. Then on to the dusty plains, moving along tracks so thick in dust that a truck thirty yards ahead is invisible in its wake. Past the broken Shermans, and the shattered German guns which stopped them. Past the huge shell holes, and bomb holes left by the R.A.F. Past the discarded equipment and wooden crosses of a retreat. We are now in action in some dusty fields with stagnant water in an orchard below it, giving the usual quota of wasps, mosquitoes etc. We are expecting to move any time towards or past St Pierre which we have taken. I found the C.P. in nothing like as good a state as I left it and I've been busy reorganising things. Bill Masson is doing A.C.P.O. I've seen Jimmy and Sandy, but Frank is still away at battalion. Guns have been passing through us all the afternoon, which has gone incredibly quickly – rather unusual.

I have changed my shirt and gone into shirtsleeve order. One of my Signallers, Taylor, has gone bomb happy and been sent back. I have a very good new man called Diver – a L/Bdr. We are on an old Jerry position, which must have been rapidly evacuated by the amount of stuff they've left behind. The war continues to go well, including the new landing in the South. Found my b–d, but all the tea, milk etc. I left behind – finito. With everything, it's good to be back. Very good. Refilled my pen today, so I must give up these pencil entries – but the lead makes it possible.

Very hot and sunny today; I am already getting tanned. Also noteworthy – there is an issue of mosquito cream.

1750: Alan Brockie (301) killed, and his O.P. Ack wounded.

1945: Hundreds of tanks moving up. Orders to go on recce now. Have actually eaten!

17 August

1215, Bas d'Esemes: Went forward on Recce last night and after digging till darkness was ordered back! Got back about midnight and fired at 0100. Burning haystacks made us nervous but the Luftwaffe bothered somebody else last night. Up again at 0530 and moved up to position of last night. Three things have occurred.

1. We have been firing hard.
2. We were strafed by 9 F.W. 190s – one man wounded.
3. It has rained.

We have now had Prepare to Advance again. About 50 Cromwells went past sometime back. We should cross the river near St Pierre this move. It is starting to rain again and we look like missing our lunch – as usual. Hell of a lot of flak but no F.W.s shot down; one came over at treetop level.

1700, Bretteville sur Dives: Just after getting well dug at Bas we moved well and rapidly over the river above St Pierre to here where we've been digging for about 3 hours now and I have almost finished a new sandbagged C.P. We are on the river bank by 2 very completely blown bridges, and a waterfall, where most of us hope to get a bath. We've been firing quite a bit. The boche seems to be holding the high ground about 6 thousand yards ahead. Forgot even to mention that my mail included an excellent food parcel. It had cake, sweets and chocolate. I'll send the sweets to Bé if I get a chance. Had a wonderful hot water wash and shave before breakfast today – and boy, did I need it! It's not often my stomach turns over, but a dead German I saw today was most unpleasant. He'd been hit in the head by a piece of shell, and was covered with flies and wasps. (The same wasps who share our meals . . .) A German horse-drawn battery had also been destroyed. The animals looked awful. Hope to get a chance to write to C. this evening, unless (horror) we move again.

18 August

Heavy work-session last night but got into my bedding roll about 0200 and fell asleep like a leaf of paper falling from unimaginable heights. Slept till 0700. Today is warm and sunny and the little waterfall looks lovely. Everybody has washed, shaved and slept and we are ready for further advances if necessary. Not yet certain whether they will take place today. I'm wondering if I'll get Alan's troop – don't really want to shift to 301, 3rd pip or not. I missed Leslie Wager's troop (ex Dennis Pullin's) when home. I'd have liked 304. R.S.M. is wounded, also B.S.M. Spalding who used to be E Tp. B.S.M. when I was G.P.O. Frank came back from 5/7 Gordons in great form; good to see him.

1605: Wonderful bath in the rushing water of the waterfall after lunch. Water cool in the sunshine but so fast that one came out tingling and invigorated. At 1530 strafed by some F.W. 190s and a (captured?) Typhoon. Two ammo vehicles on the road outside set on fire and still burning. A few wounded, none in the bty. Wrote to C. last night and am writing again today. Also home and to Sister Spencer at the hospital. Findlay has done some washing for me this afternoon. Sounds of more strafing . . .

2230: Firing a programme of 60 R.P.G. The blast is considerable in this position. It's my early night tonight so I'll be going to bed inside half an hour unless anything drastic crops up. Been working hard all day as we changed onto a new grid Zone this morning, which involved plenty of work. The thing was only satisfactorily concluded about 2115. Lots more tanks moved through us this evening. General information nil – it is hard to find out exactly what is going on. Jerry bombers growling about, flak going up – one very low. One Jerry down.

19 August

1750, near St Julien de Faucon: The day started (after harassing fire during the night) with a sudden advance about 0800, and news that Ken Aitken (B.C. of 304) had been killed. That means that out of 30 officers in the Regt., we've had 2 Majors, 3 Captains and 1 Subaltern killed, and 1 Captain and 3 Lieuts. wounded – 33% casualties among the officers. On this position we found in the C.P. – a barn – a cask of cider and a number of brand new Jerry containers made in Milan. I filled 3 of these (6 gallons) – one for each Tp. It is overcast and raining a short time ago and very thundery weather.

2300: After my last entry it rained hard for some time, and we all got rather wet and browned off. We have moved into a dug in Command Post banked by large wooden crates filled with earth – good protection. Usual strafe and bombing at dusk, but not at all heavy. And as a good surprise after the mail came in bringing nothing for me – a second mail with a very nice letter from C. Our bombers droning overhead. We are supposed to take Lisieux tonight, but in fact information is most scanty and the most I've got has come from the *Daily Express*, which came in with tonight's mail. On the roads today were many horse and carts loaded with household goods (the French rather wisely seem to preserve the pram at all costs!) and flying white flags. The people in these parts, not having been hit as hard as, say Caen, are very friendly. I had 2 eggs today and milk for the Troop in exchange for biscuits and raisins. Am told my truck used to say when I was in blighty that while I was there they got an egg a day but now never a one.

20 August

1030, same position: Almost midnight, over came the Luftwaffe – about 50 bombers, quite a lot for them – and gave us a good pounding for about half an hour with assorted unpleasantness, ranging from H.E. to the crackling fusillade of A.P. bombs. Also some shells on our left flank, and some strafing.

At 0300 we were shelled by a heavy gun or two, which woke me up. This morning started dull and overcast, but it is now patchy with occasional bursts of very light sunshine. No news of a move yet.

2300, Command Post: This evening the C.O. came over in a Jeep and told Frank and me he'd put Frank in for a majority to command 304 and I would get F Tp. 'You'd rather have a tp. in your own battery I suppose?' he said. So that's that and now we just have to wait and see if Frank's promotion comes through. I'd quite like a third pip, but it does potentially shorten one's lease of life pretty considerably.

21 August

0010: Some very large bombs being dropped in the vicinity by quite a large number of Jerry planes. I forgot to mention 301 and 304 had 7 casualties last night. I had to break off above because of pressure of work on D.F.s and similar horrors. Today Frank and I bought 10 lbs of lovely fresh butter which we shared among the troop. I think it must be association of ideas – but I had butter the day I had malaria, and even a little of it made me feel quite sick. The raid is continuing and is joined by rain which patters on the canvas-and-planking roof. But all the boys have made excellent little dugouts, so they should keep pretty dry. I also got 6 eggs today. Am giving Frank, Bill, B.S.M., Findlay and Jordan the Cook one each for breakfast. (The earth trembles to the thud of bombs, and the flurry of bofors fire mingles with the pattering rain.) Sporadic shell fire by the odd Jerry gun ahead of us all during the day.

No mail today.

1530, north of St Julien de Faucon: The armour roars down the road to our right. The Divisional arty. crashes all around us as the advance on Lisieux continues. We have been promised 4 days rest when it is taken. North of us is the 49th Division, south the desert rats, the 7th Armoured. And it is raining. It rained all through the night and the C.P. leaked horribly all over my bed. The floor was approximately 3 inches deep in muddy water. Furious firing early in the morning, and then, just as everybody was eating a disconsolate breakfast in the rain, the order Prepare to Advance came over the phone. Immediate and awful flap. Everybody soaking wet and the rain pouring down, but soon after 9 away went the recce party, followed soon afterwards by the guns. St Julien is badly smashed, and both bridges blown but replaced now by the Sappers. The 'main' road is developing into a muddy, shell-pitted track, churned deep by the armour. We are in a barn at the moment, but outside the C.P. is dug deep and nearly ready to have the 'permanent' roof which we carry on Y truck, put on it. This C.P. is a very excellent one, blasted as well as dug, by some dynamite (or amatol or something) and gun cotton, collected in various places. It is dug to about 4 feet and 2 rows of sandbags around the rim. I may, however, put Bill in there tonight and sleep in a deep and massive Jerry 'doovah' just nearby. Everybody is wet and tired but remarkably cheerful. Advancing in the HD is always the same – the same signs out at every field and turning, the same faces. But I never remember quicker movement than this.

2230: Still in the same place – and within 3 or 4 miles of Lisieux. Mail tonight – one from Sandy K. at 108 general in Bayeux and one from home. Nothing from C. Am very tired tonight and still rather damp and am going to bed soon. Bill is taking the night shift tonight. Today's bright remark (from Signaller Schofield) was when somebody suggested a local farm lass would make a good pin-up girl – 'a good pin-DOWN girl is all she's good for,' says Schofield. It has started to rain again hard, oh hell. I hope my doovah remains dry. Got four eggs from the local farm and gave them 2 tins of sardines and two packets of biscuits in exchange. Yesterday by the way, sent my nieces some boiled sweets from my American scoff parcel.

22 August

1600, St Pierre des Ifs – 5 miles from Lisieux: Moved off at 0830 in better weather, which has now turned into good weather; sunny and breezy. I am in the C.P. now – a rather cunning one built against a bank and with huge logs rolled as sides, and sandbags. Much safer than houses. We were shelled during the night but I slept through it. A new B.C. has arrived for 304, which means Frank doesn't get it, and I don't get F Tp. In many ways I am disappointed, not so much because I want the job, but because it is not easy for people at home to realise that my lack of a third pip is not due to inefficiency but sheer bad luck. Because oddly enough, the job I do is a damn sight more complicated than a Captain's, though much safer. But for the bloody parsimoniousness of the Treasury, the C.P.O. would be a Captain. However, there are more important things than a third pip to worry about. But I suppose I must be more militarily ambitious than I think, because undoubtedly I am disappointed, no two ways about it. I've earned that bloody pip.

23 August

1100: In the afternoon it was more or less officially announced that this was to be our rest area, and in the evening the O.P.s and Frank were called in, flushed with loot, booze and sex from liberated Lisieux, which fell to the 5/7 Gordons. At about 11 I settled down for a good sleep in the large and comfortable C.P. only to be rudely awakened about 0400 with details of a fire plan at 0700. I also had to rouse Frank and Jimmy to go as F.O.O.s to the Gordons. Back to bed for a catnap by 0630. It rained all night but is now hot and gloriously sunny. Our rest is cut down to 48 hours. The war goes on well.

1930: Raining again and only a parcel mail, in any case nothing for me. Most depressing. Paris has fallen – to the F.F.I. as they now call the Maquis – stands for French Forces of the Interior. Nothing doing here; the odd Frenchman driving cows about, otherwise we are all lying about taking it easy – we can't find out if our official rest has started yet. Anyway when we do get going it seems we are going to the Seine and all points east. An incident caught my notice tonight. Outside here is a narrow lane. Coming one way clanking and snorting was a Sherman tank, the other way a farmer driving his cart with one horse. The tank on seeing the cart slowed to about 5 miles an hour as it passed and then roared off down the lane again. Smiles and thanks from the farmer. Have started a long letter to C. and found a tin in which to send her her sweets. Early bed if possible, tonight.

24 August

2200: Pretty miserable day really because it's been raining all day until towards evening, when a rather feeble sun pushed through. It rained all night too, and I started the night well by getting soaked by a frightful cascade of water which suddenly poured through two places in the roof. At 2315 I was woken up, and had to send out yet another O.P. party – poor sods – in the pouring rain. Today I have been organising the new map issue, burning the old, getting trucks maintained, wireless sets overhauled etc. in preparation for our next advance, which is on 'not before 1200' tomorrow. This afternoon I went by Jeep to a farm and got 5 lbs more of butter, 6 cheeses (2 of which I've sent Norman Carter) and some cream and 3 eggs, which I shared with Bill and Frank. Wonderful stuff the cream, and I feel slightly but pleasantly sick. Tonight we are non operational, which means everybody should get a good sleep. Letter from C. in tonight's mail which was what I'd been waiting for a very long time it seemed. Wrote to her and Hylda and Dorothy tonight. Enclosed in her letter an excellent sketch by Sig. Schofield of this Command Post. He is a really good artist.

25 August

1115: Wonderful, hot sunshine today, and an atmosphere of good cheer and drying blankets. Everybody looking at sexy copies of *Life, Bystander* etc. and even some extremely revolting and unlikely postcards (date about 1896) which one of the gunners rooted out somewhere or other. A feature peculiar to this campaign is that everybody has more cigarettes than he needs. This is a factor promoting good morale. So far no further intelligence regarding the move – still 'not before 12' but no state of readiness given. Sandy K. is in England – he rang up C. to ask for Mom's address as his service dress is at her flat.

2230: A thoroughly excellent day. The sun has shone, and it has been very hot. Also the mail brought a lovely 18 page letter from C. to which I have replied tonight. A move seems imminent tomorrow. Bridge tonight with Fran, Bill and Chas Jones. More rumours that Norman Dixon the 301 B.C. is about to be sacked, and Frank to get the Bty. but so far none confirmed. News tremendous with Rumania reversing role (the rats) and us probing deep into France. General opinion that he cannot fight again before the Somme, if then, and everybody talking about 'when the war ends'. Hope we're not all being too optimistic.

Tremendous force of heavies out tonight under the young moon. There must be about 500 or maybe more. One cannot tell.

26 August

2130: Tomorrow at 0830 we move. We are going first to a harbour near St George, about 30–40 miles on from here. The first move time was 0630 so we've been packing up tonight – almost everything and I am now writing by candle light – all very *Journey's End.* As darkness fell I had a really good surprise – 3 letters – 2 from C. and one from Dorothy. I haven't even read them yet. Today's good points: a lovely haircut from McLeary and a shampoo and wash. And an officers' shop to which Peter and I jeeped to get there 1½ hours early, and I bought a trenchcoat, 3 pairs of socks and a toothbrush. Also a kit sort out with Findlay. Bulgaria has packed in. We are advancing everywhere. This is very like August 18 all over again. L/Bdr. Rees has returned (one of my Acks) after being hurt in the R.A.F. bombing. I am now going to read my mail and go to bed. Not yet known if Frank is getting 301 – odds are on a chap from 128 – the C.R.A. being ex-128 C.O.

27 August

1030, near the Seine: Flap orders to move came suddenly at 0545 and the Recce parties tore away at 0715, which doesn't sound very quick but is! Up through Lisieux and eastwards down the long straight road at 45 double banking all the way.

Lisieux well nigh destroyed completely by bombs. We are making for St Valery – doubtless as a gesture because it was at St Valery in 1940 that the remnants of the Highland Division surrendered. We crossed the Risle about 0945 – the bridges are surrounded by <u>enormous</u> craters and the scene (as they are filled with evil water) looks like Paschendale. But the only bridge actually destroyed seems to be by Jerry Sappers! We are now in the flat country between Risle and the Seine waiting for somebody to give some orders. None yet today as far as I know anyway. People are busy digging potatoes. We have no food with us so the sandbag-ful we have is a good thing. Wrote 7 pages to C. last night, which I have with me to continue at an opportune moment.

2300, Tonville: Night finds us about 6 miles from the Seine. It is quiet – so far – with a rising moon and occasional gun flashes from the river. After my last entry, we dashed on two or three miles, and went into action, though we didn't actually fire from there. The gun group didn't arrive for another couple of hours so the potatoes we'd picked, made a good meal, with a brew of tea which used up the last dregs of my condensed milk. At about 6 just in the middle of the meal, came the order Prepare to Advance, and we went on another 3 miles or so, where we are now in action. The guns are in the field to my right and the Command Post in a small field surrounded by trees. No time to dig a full scale model, so we've rigged one up, incorporating the side of a three tonner (Y), the two roof sections used as sides and myself under the extended tail board – the issue covered with canvas, giving quite a good effect. Inside there are two slit trenches – a three man – L shaped and a small one for me. The brigadier is advancing to the Seine tomorrow and we may have to move up in support, but it is said not before 10. Frank, by the way has not got 301 so that's that. The 128 man got it. We have advanced 40–50 miles today, which is more tiring than you'd think on these dusty roads in this heat and glare. Lots of people have headaches, so night has come as a relief. I had one this afternoon, but it went at sundown. I'll just add a few lines to P's letter and then go to sleep. Sounds of possible Luftwaffe activity further back but a good way away, but it may be guns as there is still some sort of a pocket I believe. Nobody seems to think the Germans can make another stand in France except possibly on the Somme line, and then, it is said, he has only the mangled remains of about 20 Divs. – we have 50 – some, such as ours, also rather mangled. Heavy gunfire from the South. Most intriguing. Hell I'm tired.

28 August

1800, Bourg-Achard: We advanced again at 1000 going north to where the Seine does a big loop. We are only 2 or 3 miles from the river. We are in a big farmyard area, and the first troops to have come here. We got a wonderful welcome with flowers and kisses, Calvados, cider, butter, eggs and Bordeaux white wine. I was amazed when I turned up on a motorcycle to be kissed and hugged by all sexes and ages. Tonight they are cooking Bill and me a chicken, and won't accept a bean for it. We, in return, have given cigarettes, matches, chocolate, sweets, soap and various other oddments. They are a very pleasant family with the usual sort of Starkadder impossibility of telling who belongs to whom, etc. We've been doing well for eggs and butter yesterday as Bill Masson did a good kill yesterday and I've succeeded again today. Good weather. Everything resolves on whether or not we once again move tonight. Slept for 7 blissful hours last night; finished and posted a letter to C. this morning. Bill has just come along describing the chicken in terms which make my mouth water. They had laid out all the best china etc., but unfortunately we can't leave the C.P. which is in a barn. We've fired heavily here – on Germans trying to escape across the river.

29 August

0900: The day finished magnificently with half the best roast chicken I've eaten in years, then red and white wine and coffee, followed by Calvados which was so strong it nearly lifted the hair from my head. Bill was on duty so I turned in into a doovah about 2300 and slept well till about 0400 when the incessant gunfire combined with a ferocious nightmare woke me up. We had orders last night for the Recce party to stand by from 0730, but this morning they say no move before 1000. My chicken was brought down here by Hélène, the first girl who welcomed us here, and served on the best china, with two different wine glasses, tray-cloth, napkin etc. They simply cannot do enough for us here and are really nice people. If enough of the French are like these, they deserve a good place in world councils. The husband of the house is away serving 2 years in gaol near Coblenz for helping to hide allied airmen, and Hélène's fiancé has been a prisoner for 4 years.

2045, near Yville-sur-Seine: I doubt if any regiment since the S.P.s on D-Day have given closer support than this – targets at 1500 yards, charge 1. We dashed off (in the rain) at about 1100 hours and went into action at Barneville; but before the guns even got up to us, we were off again in the steaming rain, till finally we rendezvoused with the C.O.2 at a corner where an infantry jeep had just been shot to ribbons by a Spandau. You couldn't go much further than that – the tanks were only a quarter of a mile ahead, and Battalion H.Q. was in the area. The mortars were behind us. They were still bringing in dead, and wounded about the place, their poor wounds ineffectually covered by stained blankets. Anyway we set in firing vigorously – we've used 1000 rounds today in the battery – disturbed only by an occasional mortaring on our right. 100 tanks have passed through there on their way north to clean up the peninsula tonight, which is formed by the Seine bend at Duclair. At 2030 the area was fairly heavily shelled by 4 or 6 seventy fives. No casualties.

The digging is good here, and the C.P. is about 3½–4 feet deep – just as well. I shouldn't be surprised if we have a little more activity tonight. Jake Mason (D/304) is missing – believed captured, as they've found his carrier but not the crew. It is still raining and very overcast.

2110: More shells. Vehicles in Waggon Lines hit; no casualties.

2120: More shells, no casualties.

2230: Intermittent shelling.

30 August

0030: At midnight a fire plan started, and until quarter past one the thunderous tattoo of about one hundred guns echoed round the battery and woods. I've been working solidly since about 2100, and I'm pretty tired now; it's amazing really what long stretches one does at a time. Now, it is nearly 17 hours, yet there's no prospect of sleep for quite a time. Mail came in tonight, but R.H.Q. having been terror-stricken by the shelling and retired to unheard of depths below the earth's surface, we have to wait till tomorrow morning before collecting it. Every time the Battery fires, the C.P., deep though it is, trembles and the signallers' hurricane flickers with the shock. The gun blast is like a sharp blow, or a box on the ears.

In a letter to Frank, Waggy indicates arrival soon. Faces fell all round on receipt of the news. Nothing coming back at us now, though I suppose I shouldn't speak too soon.

2200, La Grève: Moved suddenly and with terrific speed after lunch and are now in the finger caused by the Seine bend below Duclair. As we moved into Yville, we turned the corner, and there was the Seine, broad and calm – a wonderful view. Theoretically we are overlooked for about 180 degrees here from the high ground the other side of the river, but it is doubtful if there are any enemy there save the odd straggler – which is just as well. This is very thickly wooded country with much heather, and was only cleared this morning so there may even be stragglers here. It rained last night and till about 1100. Set in again about noon, and after a short pause started again furiously. Luckily the digging is good here, and we went down 4 feet in about an hour. The rain is pattering on the C.P. roof now. Conversation is flowing round politics – laconically described by Schofield as 'all balls'. Langland says 'If I had a button and could blow the whole of Germany to pieces I would.' Hughes says: 'Did you see those bloody Mongolians today?' referring to some Asiatic types raked in as prisoners by the Gordons. There was even a negro in German uniform – the Herrenvolk 1944 model. Rheims and Rouen have fallen. Up at the end of the peninsula the Germans have left many trucks and other booty as they swam the Seine. Some hold brandy. A stream of units have been going to the tip, but I am too tired. I told the fitters to go and have a shufti.

Rain, rain, rain; how damn sick of it I am. It is beating down on the corrugated roof as I write, but so far – thank god – we haven't started leaking. Started a letter to C. today which I'll finish now. Can't go to bed yet because I'm trying to establish wireless contact with Bill at Battalion. The bloody fool didn't net before he went out, and now we can't get him. Mail today a letter from Joan B. and 200 duty free cigarettes (sent by myself while at Oxford!). Horribly tired and damp and longing for sleep.

31 August

1250: Up until 0230 trying to get the sets netted but woke today and had breakfast about 0930. Sunshine at intervals today. Probable move across the Seine tomorrow either at Duclair or Elbeuf. Had all my laundry done at the last position; it is now hanging up to dry having been dragged here by the faithful Findlay in a ground sheet.

1700: It's extraordinary how sentences juxtapose ironically. I wrote 'the faithful Findlay' and yet the following occurs. This afternoon I've been told I'm to go to 304 to command D troop as soon as Wagstaff returns (a Jeep is going back for him today) and Findlay refuses to come with me. He's an obstinate fellow when he makes up his mind so God knows what I'll do if he really means it. The rival merits of Findlay and a third pip are pretty equal, specially as the latter (pleasing to my self respect though it be) is no sort of pleasure trip nowadays. This diary may also suffer as I shan't have much time to write it up, I imagine – and anyway it is a dangerous thing to have about the place. Jake's entire crew being missing, I shall have no driver, Signaller or Op Ack – what a prospect! We start the day after tomorrow, for St Valery – Amiens and Calais. I hope they don't hang on to those bloody bomb sites too doggedly! Furious rain this afternoon.

1 September

1715: I am now over in 304 and by tonight I shall officially be captain. I've been working like a nigger today trying to get things organised, meeting the Nos. 1, saying how do you do to the Tp. etc. It is a good troop I think – bolshy but good in action. A good bit of work remains to be put in on it. The Battery C.P. is inefficient. Findlay decided to come with me after all, and has met a lot of his friends so <u>he's</u> quite happy. We move off very early tomorrow.

2130: Nearly dark. I am writing by the rising moon. We move at 0545, and I am still waiting for my Jeep which has gone back for a new carrier.

2 September

1930, near St Valery en Caux: It's hard to do justice to today because I'm tired, and it began so early. We finally got the carrier and jeep fitted up about 0115 and I fell into bed for a few hours. Got up at 0400 and sure enough it was raining and I gulped down my Soya link sausage without much enthusiasm, in the rainy darkness, loud with engines revving, cookers roaring and the blasphemous shouts of hurried gunners. However, the Troop was ready on time which rather pleased me, and we began the long march here, which was to have terminated at Pavilly, but as St Valery has fallen without much fight, we find ourselves here instead. The march here was quite memorable. We had a tremendous welcome in Rouen (whose cathedral is <u>lovely</u>) and the column showered cigarettes, biscuits etc. all along the route. Coming up towards the coast, people were weeping and laughing with joy. Looking at them, it was impossible to believe our coming here has brought them anything but happiness. The Bty. is now leaguered among some farms etc. and I've got the whole troop quartered under cover after a certain amount of wangling and door opening. However I finally presented the farmer with 20 Players, which nearly felled him with joy. I've never seen people so short of tobacco as those round here and in Rouen. Every prospect of a good night's sleep here; when we leave, and where we go, I don't know at all, but I suspect Germany via the Pas de Calais and Luxembourg. Lousy weather today; very cold and lots of rain on and off. My vehicles, now a carrier and a Jeep, are both very open, but I've taken steps, and the Carrier will have an excellent home made hood on it by tomorrow midday. The jeep is also undergoing modification. Have collected quite a good crew. The driver is first class but I may lose him through nose trouble. The Ack* is quite new to the job, but intelligent, speaks French, sketches etc. and for want of a better expression, is a gentleman. Shows signs of becoming a first class scrounger. This is his first campaign, but John Clark, my G.P.O. (same applies) says he's good under fire. The two signallers – Allen and Horton. Allen is goodish, Horton fair. I could do worse, also much better. In the Tp. the B.S.M. is a weak link, the Nos. 1 are, I think, patchy, but I like the troop. I may add more later if I get the chance. Lovely long letter from C. brought me by Howell, my ex-orderly, in the column today. I'll add a bit to the letter I started last night. I wish this Diary were a little more interesting but it's likely to get briefer and briefer I think!

3 September

2210: Having been promised two days here we received orders to move tomorrow – not before ten (so far) – to go and clean up Le Havre which is still resisting. The Radio gave a big write up to the S. Valery business, so C. will know where I am tonight anyway. I had another letter from her tonight, also one from Dad. Massed pipes etc. in St V. today but I had no time to go as we had a lot of work to do. Had a good bath however, in a 3 foot diameter bucket. I could just sit down and there was plenty of hot water. Went over to 491 and drank Benedictine at the local estaminet. Very good. Wrote to C. yesterday, also a long letter by candle-light last night (as this is) which I finished and posted this evening. I found the cook (who is a champion heavy-weight boxer) an oven and he presented me with a HUGE piece of plum tart he'd baked – covered with <u>awful</u> custard made by Findlay. I gave it to Stewart (who has an insatiable appetite) at tea and he munched it down with delight. I don't relish my first job as street fighting – very dangerous – but I shall get the next attack job in the battery. We work with the Black Watch – it was the Gordons before.

Mess conversation is along the 'it's been nice knowing you' lines so I am (in spite of myself) somewhat depressed. I wish I could see C. again, which is silly because it would only make things harder. Damn the Germans and roll on peace! . . .

4 September

1845, near Bordeaux St Clair: We are leaguered about 25 miles North of Le Havre. The two contrasting sounds which occur to me are the sentimental music coming from the 'comforts radio' standing in the orchard in which the troop is leaguered, and the roll of gunfire from the South. Apparently the Boche is numerous and well

*Name – Butcher.

dug in both in Havre and Montvilliers to the north of it, with plenty of ammo, food, and will to resist. Too bad. Today's march was much the same as our last, to St Valery. Cheering crowds, flowers, apples, outstretched hands to touch, and cries of 'ceegarette, shockolar, beesquee'. The defences on the coast we passed were very deep and formidable and bore evidence of tremendous pounding by the R.A.F. An old woman and her daughter are picking apples in this orchard, the latter coming in for many a lascivious look or shouted suggestion from the gunners detailing a useful and busy programme for the hours of darkness. She grins cheerfully at it all and her large bust shakes with laughter.

5 September

2030, Marnevillette, 10 miles N of Le Havre: After a night and morning of heavy rain we left during the afternoon and are now in action heavily dug in, as the rumours of Jerry strength in guns increase hourly. The defence overprint map is also a horrible mass of blue legend. Bill Carney is out at the moment and I shall probably go out tomorrow to a new O.P. The R.A.F. (Lancasters and Halifaxes) did a tremendous bombardment this evening. There must have been 3–400 planes and I only saw one knocked down.

6 September

Went and saw Alistair C. at 126 last night. (Benedictine, champagne and brandy . . .)

8 September

I want to write up yesterday fully, so that in days to come if I am ever tempted to say of all this 'It wasn't so bad', I have at least one reminder of an occasion when it bloody well was so bad!

The day really started on the evening of the 6th, when after hanging about for hours waiting for instructions, I was told that owing to an R.A.F. programme, I should not man the O.P. at first light, but no sooner had I returned to the carrier than I was told we had to be ready at 0630. OK. I warned the crew and the guard and went to bed. It was raining and some was dripping in so I turned my bed around. At 0240 hours there was a sudden awful gush of water and about 3 gallons of it poured into my trench. The cover had collapsed. The trench was quite soon 9 inches deep in water. The next half hour was true nightmare. Somehow I got dressed into wet clothes, got my bedding into the soaking Jeep (it was still raining hard) and huddled into the front of a 15 cwt wrapped into wet blankets till 0600. At 0630 we set off for the O.P. still in the pelting rain, and eventually after scrounging a little breakfast from the infantry manned it about 0830 with an infantry platoon as local protection. Prior to this I went up with the B.C. before daylight proper. By then I was of course quite drenched. We had to leave the carrier about 1/2 a mile back and carry phones, remote control etc. up to the O.P. ourselves. The O.P. was in an orchard and gave a good view of the Boche defences round Octerike which are very numerous and formidable. I need hardly say that to crown everything the local weather and one thing and another made communications almost impossible, as the phones kept breaking down and something was wrong with the wireless. At 1500 we retired for an R.A.F. bombing which never took place (still raining furiously) and after a cup of tea went out with the relief platoon about 1730. We also had a tin of M & V which tasted unusually good. Well, it went on raining till near darkness (Alistair C. came up to the same place to man the 126 O.P.) so we went in. We were mortared twice by our own mortars and shelled once by our own guns but otherwise it was a quiet enough day. We knocked off 3 chickens and 2 lbs of sugar from a deserted farm. When I got back Findlay had dried my blankets and sleeping bag, put me out a clean pillow case and made up my bed in a loft (my new safari camp bed arrived from the Hornsfield people of Croydon on the 6th) and at 2300 after a wonderful cup of tea, and issue of rum, I took off all my wet things and fell straight asleep – god how good it was – and the last sound I heard was the rain beating on the roof.

Today it is changeable but we have had one terrific downpour already. I'll be going out tomorrow. R.A.F. bombed Octerike area heavily at 0730–0900. Still no mail from Clare though last night's lot included a food parcel from New York.

2200: Went up during the evening to see Bill at the O.P., with the B.C. and C.O. The O.P. is <u>miles</u> forward at a place called Emfrayette, sole protection – five infantry men. If tomorrow's bombing (which is just in front of the C.P.) takes place, I shan't be going out until 0845. If it's cancelled, about first light. I hope it takes place. The big attack takes place on Sunday night – Monday morning – and I'm trying to keep down the awful lather at the prospect of F.O.O. with the Black Watch. F.O.O. is a job all gunner officers dread with good reason, and in my opinion this attack may be damned sticky. However, we are at least second brigade not first which is something. That is, you have time to gauge your chances of survival. Lovely long letter from Clare today and I wrote back at some length myself. It's getting damn cold with a north-ish wind and cold showers. I am beginning quite to like the B.C. – and ex B.M.R.A. from 3 Div. who now he is beginning to forget the text book and get into our cynical ways is really quite nice. Also I think he'll be rather good in battle. Too good, maybe! Quarter past ten, and my candle flickers so I'm going to sleep.

10 September

Sunday, 1420: At 1745 today the attack begins with 49 Div. breaking through to Harfleur. The Brigade's role starts at 0500 tomorrow morning when we attempt to penetrate the enormous Foret de Montgeon and debouch upon the rear of the enemy. The plan is a very clever one as it intends to cross almost 'impossible' country including the Forest and come up behind the enemy. It is not without hazards, not the least of which may be the weather – and the almost trackless forest may be a death trap of mines, boobytraps and mortars etc. Bill, the Major and I join the Black Watch this evening and go in with them tomorrow morning. Rations, water etc. for 4 days. The attack is a very full scale one and we have with us tanks, flails, flame throwers and all manner of other devices. Also there is to be a terrific air bombardment, and an ammo. allotment of about 500 rounds per gun. My stomach flutters a little but I shall be almost glad in a way when it starts and we can get it over.

Fairly good day at Emfrayette. It rained like hell till midday-ish and then the sun shone for the rest of the day. Had some good shooting and observing particularly on two 88mm batteries quite near us, and the strong point at Bléville which is our objective for tomorrow's attack. (That is, our battalion objective.) Got some useful loot, including crockery for the mess, poultry, Calvados, brandy, rum and wine and two small bottles of perfume, besides odds and ends. The carrier simply bulges with food and drink, chocolate (as we live on Compo) and cigarettes. That's the great advantage of O.P. parties – you can forage and (while you live!) live well. When I got back last night, there were 3 letters – one from C., one from her mother and one from Hylda; a good mail. I would write back to C. now, but I feel too taut – I think I'll leave it till after the attack. I am just going to give the Troop a talk on the attack and what it hopes to do ('1 Corps will capture Le Havre,' starts the Operation Order . . .) and how it hopes to do it.

1545: The afternoon wears on, and here, or no doubt all over the front, last minute checks are taking place. Have we enough water? Are the Sten guns oiled and the ammo clean and dry? Has the carrier sufficient oil? Are my binoculars clean? Have we enough shell dressings? And a thousand other queries. Forgot to mention we were shelled by 49 Div. Arty. yesterday. V. close.

13 September

1330: Le Havre has fallen and tomorrow we set off for Boulogne and, it is said, after that Calais and Dunkirk. The battle finally was something of a walkover as the Hun showed no readiness for combat, and save for a few occasions we had an easy run. The night of the 10th was made more hideous by the crashing of many guns, and we had hardly any sleep in the battalion area, which for gunners is unusual, but a battery just behind us blasted us each time they fired. In the morning I was sent out to a flank O.P. where I watched and reported on the battle till it overran Bléville, and I then moved up through the 3 minefield gaps which were full of blown up tanks etc. and into and through Fontaine la Mallet, which was almost totally destroyed. It was a very hot day and the air was thick with dust. Here we were shelled but not heavily. The defences were very strong and magnificently camouflaged – it is lucky the Boche had no stomach for real resistance here. The R.A.F. bombing had apparently demoralised him completely – as well as killing either 2 or 3 thousand civilians in Le Havre. The defences were given a tremendous pounding on the afternoon of the 10th, and at dawn on the 11th a great fleet of heavies flew in the sunlight almost unopposed to drop another load. As we moved up during the dusty afternoon, the columns of prisoners, in evidence since the day began, started to grow longer and contain more officers, and in the Foret de Montgeon which was full of ammunition etc., a long column passed us headed by a Colonel. A woman jumped out and spat in his face. Towards evening we got into the outskirts of Le Havre and I was ordered to establish an O.P. in or near the convent or church of the Sacre Coeur. This proved impossible for some time owing to the presence of snipers and the odd Spandau. So the Company Commander blew the ornamental tower off the church with a six pounder firing H.E., and then sent in a flame throwing carrier (known as a 'wasp') which burned trees etc. all over the place. A most horrifying weapon. We had a Sherman with us, pumping away at a pillbox nearby, and suddenly as darkness began to fall, the rumble of treads was heard ahead of us. 'Christ,' said the Tank Commander and began to back away. 'It's the Tigers.' I was in the middle of the road when the first stream of tracer bullets shot past. I flattened out and managed to crawl into the nearby orchard and put through a call to the B.C. on the blower for a couple of tanks. The bullets flew for about 20 minutes before somebody discovered it was one of our own Shermans shooting us up! Mopping up then continued, and I got some wonderful personal loot from the casements of the strong points about the place – including: A dagger, a camera, binoculars, a waterproof watch, a typewriter (made in Milan for the Germans) and a couple of small bottles of perfume. Got to bed that night about 2 am after nearly being shot up by the Maquis who were numerous, bloodthirsty and helpful. It's wonderful how they've organised the resistance movement. Up next morning at daylight and established a wonderful O.P. in the ruined tower, where we watched the final mopping up and extracted a useful pair of 'donkey's ears', the name given to the German periscopes used in their O.P.s. They'd had an O.P. in the tower too. Soon after midday we were ordered to return to the gun line. I slept like a log last night, but woke about 7 to find the Recce party about to leave for Boulogne, and we follow tomorrow morning. There was a lovely long letter from C., the first I've had addressed to Capt. J.S.S. I also had one during the battle and a grand parcel from her, and two from home containing tea, coffee, milk, Ronsonol etc. Wrote back last night. The Colonel got a case of champagne last night and has invited Majors and Captains over at 6.30 tonight to dispose of it, so that's another good thing. The Black Watch are grand boys to work with, particularly the officers, and we did this whole party with very light casualties. I find the B.C. excellent to work with and get on with him pretty well, in fact very well. This afternoon I am taking my numbers one over the battlefield to show them what's what. Meanwhile Findlay has repacked all my kit and I'm all set for the next do. I gave him a watch and a lovely cut throat razor. He's quite happy over here now. Went over to 491 this morning. Waggy was very genial but almost terrifyingly dogmatic and I noticed the two troop Comds. writhing under it. All his officers simply hate his guts.

2105: Two reinforcements have arrived tonight – one subaltern – and one . . . Captain —— Can you beat it? As long as I remember this is the first Captain ever imported to this Regt. and it has to be now. It is not yet certain that I have to revert. The verdicts are as follows:

1. The C.O: 'Jack, what are we going to do with this bloody captain?'
2. The B.C: 'I shouldn't fuss unduly about this captain if I were you. I intend to have him running the mess.'
3. The Adjutant (in a drunkenly expansive moment at the champagne booze-up): 'I shouldn't worry. As a matter of fact the B.C. gave a very good report of you yesterday, and if anybody reverts it won't be you.'

I don't know how reliable this is. Actually the whole business is pretty browning off but I can only wait and see. We move to Boulogne tomorrow. Reveille 0530 so I am going to bed soon.

14 September

1000, road to Boulogne: Heavy mist and rather cold. 3 letters last night, Mom, Daddy & C. Dad very pleased about 3rd pip; hope I don't have to disillusion him!

15 September

1000, Frencq near Boulogne: After a run of 166 miles we pulled in here about an hour before darkness, which was pretty good going. We passed through the famous Picardy country and over the Somme at St Valery. All round those parts the land is flat with gentle undulations, and large woods and forests. The roads for the most part were long and straight and well surfaced and there was hardly a sign of the great advance when our armour swept through a week or two ago. It must have been a cake walk. It seems Boulogne is surrounded but defiant, and certainly the defences etc. are pretty thorough. Good reception from the locals; funny to see small children about James' age giving the V sign and shrieking in their tiny voices 'Vive de Gaulle'. The new Capt. is attached to C Tp., and as yet no sign of what is going to happen except that the C.O. apparently told him he may go to 301. This is a harbour area and we shall probably move into action later today.

Moved at 1515 hours.

2230, by candlelight. La Capelle, 5 m from Boulogne: I am in my doovah with a Jerry tent in all its multi-coloured camouflage above my head, getting gently soaked and starting to drip as the rain patters down upon it. So long as the rain only patters it may hold out; if it pelts I seem to be in for another delightful night. Boulogne it would seem is to be defended by about 6000 fanatics with 200 guns – the largest of these being about 300MM, which is a lot of gun. One has been banging away tonight, a fairly small one I think, and the shells bang viciously on our left, just about R.H.Q. area probably. Weather permitting the attack goes in tomorrow morning after a two hour 'demoralisation attack' by R.A.F. heavies. The digging is bad here – clay with streaks of rock. Also mail will be slow or non-existent as we are detached from the div. and attached to the 3rd Canadian Div.

16 September

2130, by candlelight: Although today dawned bright and clear the attack did not come off – probably it seems, owing to an adverse weather forecast! However the enemy strong points on the hills surrounding Boulogne were intermittently submerged in smoke, dust, and flame, as our Typhoons dived on them with a howl of rockets and cannon. Towards evening some light bombers completed the job, and a pall of smoke hung against the sunset. On the floor, the mediums and heavies (I estimate we have 250–300 guns round the port) have been booming away on registration. Tonight, infantry lorries are moving up and the attack should go in tomorrow. I am at ¼ of an hours notice as O.P. should an O.P. be required. I suspect one will be. Mail came in tonight, bringing me one from Bé and two (10th and 11th) from C. Wrote home and to Bé today and am in the middle of one to C. Swarms of mosquitoes and Daddy long legs in my tent tonight, though I have already slain a good few. Also a fat spider (which I spared – C. would be horrified!) and the usual band of fleas etc. Clocks back an hour at 0300. In England the blackout is being modified or abolished; makes one wish the war would end. No developments over the new Captain; I gave all my N.C.O.s a pep talk tonight which shook them a bit.

17 September

1130: Punctually at 0825 the first Pathfinders arrived in the misty sunshine and dropped their clusters of red markers. Then came two or three hundred heavies, and for the next hour the landscape disappeared in clouds of flame and smoke. The noise from the gunfire was tremendous, as the heavies belted away all round us. One bomber flew low over us with an enormous piece shot out of one wing.

One wondered how it flew at all. Two of the crew baled out not far away. the attack seems to be going fairly well as far as one can tell from here. I believe Calais will be <u>our</u> job, and after that, presumably Dunkirk.

2145: The attack has gone on all day and seems to have done fairly well. Now the night is pretty quiet. An occasional burst of gun fire booms and echoes round the countryside whose darkness is broken by Very lights from the hilly front line. Mail tonight. One from Dorothy (Norman's cheeses arrived) and one from C. which I shall read in a few minutes before sleeping. It is very cold with frosty dew night and morning, reminding one that Winter is not far away. I hope we can finish before then. Large airborne landing in Holland today. In two days I become a paid T/Capt. as opposed to an A/Capt. – still no developments, though Charles Jones told me secretly today that the new chap is probably going to one of the other regiments. We shall see . . .

18 September

2130, just East of Mont Lambert: We moved in the early evening in quite a normal sort of way and are now dug in a mile or two nearer Boulogne and from a position in which we can shoot onto ground the far side of the river Liane. Am in my doovah which is dug in one side of the carrier with a waterproof sheet over the top. Very comfortable. I understand Boulogne has nearly fallen, should do so tomorrow. Then, they say, we go on to Calais. A rest would help.

19 September

2040: Already – in fact since 2000 – it is quite dark outside, and the rain falls slowly (it seems) and hopelessly on tents, guns, trees, corrugated iron and people. My bedding is all damp owing to a leakage in the doovah this evening, it makes me remember how everything in C.'s house is washed and ironed and then put in that lovely hot cupboard before anybody wears it. Long letter from her tonight – that's every day for 3 days and what a difference it makes. I've heard such letters described as '5 minutes leave' – rather well, I think. I wrote 7 today including a long one in bed last night to C., also her mother and sundry others I should have written ages ago. But for the news: we cease firing at midnight and move to a rest area at 1000 tomorrow. Also we do NOT now take Calais or Dunkirk – this after all maps of those areas had been issued; so it looks like Holland and Germany for us. Second item: Captain Preece left us today for 126 so I keep D Troop which pleases me very much. Raining weather all day – overcast and depressing, and I fell asleep for an hour before tea, and woke up cold and with a stiff neck to eat bully and spuds and dehydrated cabbage and 'duff' – as depressing as the weather – though I should add that Gavigan my Irish R.C. cook (and ex-boxer) is a marvel and I'd hate to lose him. Found him a much needed table in this area to his joy.

20 September

2040, by candle: Moved at 1000 into this area, 2 or 3 miles back from where we were. It is not, as areas go, particularly good as there are no houses or barns, but all the chaps have nowadays got canvas or corrugated so we're all pretty comfortable. I have a small, but excellent doovah with my Jerry tent over the top. I am getting daily happier in my troop; where at first I could only watch and form opinions, I have now reached the stage of making alterations and putting over my own ideas. For example, before we moved off today I inspected the whole troop at 'detachments front' and where this (for this troop highly unusual) measure would have been resented 3 weeks ago, today I could tell by their expressions that the men didn't mind it. The rest of today has been spent in maintenance on guns and trucks, and they've made a good job of them. I got them some beer (a quart each) and all round the leaguer I can hear them getting cheerful and garrulous. Some are singing, some are talking but the general sound is contented. Mail today included letters from Dorothy and Norman Carter and a lovely parcel from Bé including a pound of tea, a pound of coffee, cocoa, chocolate puddings, Ovaltine tablets, and the various other things she can be relied upon to think of. Our future may now include Calais after all.

My Jeep driver is another character. He is called Smith – 'Long Smith' – and has exactly that lugubrious way of talking associated with the chap on the Radio who says 'I don't know mind – but it makes yer fink.' Another worthy body is Bdr. Brown the M.T. Bdr. I don't think there's another Troop in the Reg. whose M.T. is better maintained or kept than mine. And with an egg for breakfast tomorrow I close on a note of good cheer.

21 September

2145 (Had a wonderful bath): So it's to be Calais after all – and probably moving tomorrow – depending on the final cleaning up of Boulogne. Hard day's work and now nearly everything is done. But hell what a lousy rest! We have the comforts radio outside and all the chaps are singing 'Chatternooga choo choo'.

22 September

2140, Sombre, near Calais: Moved off at 1100 up to our position here which is in open, hilly country. We, actually, are in an old Jerry position, which has been dug with his customary thoroughness, thus providing us with a command post, cookhouse etc. I myself always fancy a million fleas in these places, and am sleeping in my tent. Hot, sultry weather, rather unpleasant. One of my gunners – Campbell – was trying to burn earwigs out of his doovah tonight and blew up some petrol all over himself. He was screaming with pain and smelt of burnt flesh and his arms and face were in a pretty bad way. We got him away to the M.O.

within two minutes of the accident, and I'm afraid he'll be on his way to hospital by now. Militarily speaking no news about Calais, but rumours that the Div. is coming up about the 29th – Dunkirk? No mail tonight. Much discussion of government proposals for demobilisation. I think the scheme is excellent – quite correctly places emphasis on length of service as opposed to age, marriage etc. Surely overseas service should count for a bit extra though, apart from more leave on a one month–one day basis? How C. would hate my tent area – it's full of little cold-bodied frogs!

23 September

2030: Rather a cold, dull day and this evening I fell into a fit of depression from which two letters from C. only raised me a little. This morning I went with the B.C. to Marquise, a neighbouring townlet and got some face cream for C. called Crème Simon, which – according to Stewart – is about the best you can get, though frankly I'd never heard of it. I also got some for Dorothy. Had fresh meat today, and Gavigan served up 2 large steaks and roast potatoes which made something of a red letter meal. R.A.F. light bombers came over in strength towards sundown – one dropped a stick about two hundred yards away in error which made a lot of noise but didn't hurt anybody. Today from some high ground not far from here, I saw the white cliffs of Dover – a long stretch of coastline clear in the sunlight which came out at intervals. Maybe it was seeing England so near, and yet so impossibly far, which has made me depressed. Shall write to C. now, before going to sleep. Last night, I was called out of a deep sleep at 2330 to go and speak to the C.O. on the phone about Campbell. The M.O. told me today that he's pretty serious; may even die – of shock. Diary very dull lately, but not much is happening – to us, that is, and with the war so possibly nearing its end it's curiously difficult to concentrate and makes danger even less welcome than usual.

Got C. a good bottle of perfume called 'Sans Atout' from Marquise.

24 September

2030: A chill and miserable night and day (a Sunday incidentally) with fierce gusty wind bringing bouts of heavy rain across the clouds and moorland of this dreary channel coast. The attack which, one gathers, was due to start today was postponed 24 hours as the bombers couldn't operate – and on the same score is, I should think unlikely to start tomorrow either. My tent stood up fairly well to the onslaught of the weather, though here and there the outer defences were breached by water.

After tea tonight went with the B.C. pottering around the utterly deserted coast defences near here. Everywhere is sown with mines and barbed wire, and obstacles, and out of a sea slashed white by the wind rose line upon line of 'Element C', the standard beach obstacle. The Germans have mined the invasion coast and filled it with the most amazing and I suppose Teutonic, thoroughness. Every field for miles inland is filled with anti air-borne poles on a scale not dreamed of in England (what a hopeless chance we should have stood . . .) and four long years of preparation are evident. Yet what use are these things without the troops – and the morale – to use them? Looking from one of his beach O.P.s across the beach and hostile channel this evening, I wondered how often some homesick Nazi has looked uneasily out at dusk in case the Commandos came. And now they are all gone, all this plague of grey locusts. I do not think another German führer will look from here across to the chalk cliffs of England, ever again. This time they have left too much hatred, broken too many hearts, spoiled too many lives. The papers came tonight (and a letter from home dated 20) full of the demob. scheme and also a large increase of pay scheme by which I benefit to the tune of 26/3 a week . . . but lying here in the candlelight listening to the roaring wind, and the rain beating down it is hard to realise that in all this loneliness are the seeds of future security, and out of our dying will come real living. Hard to realise also this evening, that so few miles away across the wind-roused channel, were the orchards and hills of Kent – the magic familiar names – Maidstone and Canterbury, Ashford and Sevenoaks . . . The more often I have the time to sit and reflect, the longer and more hazardous seem the five years, the long five years through which we've just passed. Even more wonderful that out of our peril has come this moment when we are into Germany itself – that the agony for Europe has almost ended – and that we have won through again. And paid again with our fine dead. What a world it is; I am sad and homesick tonight on the shores of Calais.

25 September

1845: Various items of news today. Firstly Jake Mason has died of wounds; what rotten luck – and the more so as the three members of his crew who were captured at the same time have been recaptured and are O.K. Also it is reported, but not as a confirmed fact, that Leslie Wager, Jake's predecessor also missing since the battles on the Orne, is alive and wounded in a Belgian hospital. Whether or not this is accurate I don't know. Thirdly the B.C. told me that we, with 153 Brigade as the spearhead of the Div., move up to Antwerp on the 29th. Thence not yet announced, but presumably the front line. Went forward today to watch the battle which started this morning and has gone very well. I saw the Canadians capture all their objectives on the high ground ahead of us, almost unopposed, after a tremendous artillery bombardment which was accurate and impressive. There was also an R.A.F. bombardment which left the ground pockmarked like smallpox with huge craters. Cold and chill today with bursts of sunshine. Letter from Dad this morning and a parcel of writing paper and envelopes from C. tonight. Am writing to her tonight. The Gris Nez gun is still active – or guns. It shelled the place the B.C. and I were in this morning, late in the day, killing a chap; and after we left Marquise, bombarded the square, killing about 100. It also fires on Dover and did this morning.

26 September

2320, Audembert: I returned from pottering round the beach defences this afternoon with the Nos. 1, to find we were ceasing firing at quarter to six and moving out of action at half past. This we have done and I am writing in the attic of a large house we use for an officers mess. The troop are all quartered in a nearby school and all under cover. Immediate future not certain but we move into Belgium anyway by the start of October. Tomorrow there is calibration. Watched today the bombing of Cap. Gris Nez (where several guns are still active) by the R.A.F. heavies. It really was terrifying – wave after wave of Lancasters, seeming almost immobile against the blue sky – and then the great black gouts and powerful flash as the bombs fell in stick after stick till the target was obscured by rolling clouds of smoke and debris; and still on they came inexorably – first the sparklike shower of red markers into the inferno and then the tremendous clusters of bombs and the steady bang and thump as they fell.

But the worst thing I saw was when a Lancaster, flying very slowly and low down, must have had its pilot hit for quite suddenly it turned over and plummeted nose down into the earth, bursting into violent red flame as it struck. Nobody in it could have had a chance, and yet they must have had eight or nine seconds in the certainty of death. And as they burned with their plane, still more of those bombs struck all around where they lay, till their flaming pyre was hidden too. I felt rather sick. And yet – one could hardly believe it – by afternoon those damned guns were firing again. Letter from C. this morning. I sent two off to her. Meant to write tonight, but we moved and now I have a big headache so I'm going to sleep.

27 September

2120: Pretty miserable day with no mail and culminating with the information that the Regt. moves to Antwerp on the 29th. Other two regiments follow on the 1st October. Everybody rather gloomy with a feeling of impending doom – possibly exacerbated by the apparent failure and decimation of the 1st Airborne Army near Arnhem. Calibration today, and everybody working out results tonight. A good mess this – we have even got a fire going which is very cosy. Lots of people have got colds – Jimmy Gegan is supposed to have gone to hospital with a chill or something. One of my signallers – Saunders – cut my hair very short today, and I also washed it so I feel much cleaner as it was getting rather to the shaggy and matted stage. A winter campaign – the bogey we used to discuss in those lovely Spring days at Melford – seems to be looming unpleasantly close on the horizon – it seems hardly possible that already it is nearly October – and one's sixth Xmas in the army is drawing on – sixth – what an amazing length of time.

I seem to have used up rather more than half this book; I'll have to think about ordering another one. Damn nuisance moving again so soon, involving all sorts of things like unfinished work here, changing French to Belgian francs, detailing advance parties etc.

28 September

1930: We move to Belgium starting at 0630 tomorrow (reveille 0500) and the distance is about 175 miles. Today has been spent getting ready in the multitude of different ways one does get ready. Letters from Judy and Joan B. but nothing from C. – not very surprising really as the mail was all 21 September vintage and I've had hers of that date already. Good weather with sunshine.

30 September

1240, near Noordervijk – 25 miles from Antwerp: Yesterday was a long and tiring day and as I couldn't get to bed till midnight I couldn't write this up. We did 189 miles, starting at 0630 and arriving at 2100. We seemed to pass through history yesterday; right through the Ypres – all the old historical names – Sanctuary Wood, Paschendale, Mount Kemmel. We went through the huge Menin gate carved with its thousands of names. The graves are in many small, beautifully kept cemeteries; each tombstone beside the name etc. had the man's regimental badge carved. Belgium made a good impression – clean and friendly. Brussels is – from the little we saw – well laid out – and designed with several large parks. We got in cold and miserable to find there had been a shambles and it was raining. I find my Dutch is very useful here, as the Flemish is very similar as spoken hereabouts.

Shops seem well stocked with everything but nobody has been able to do anything about it as we had no money – it all being in for changing.

2100: We move tomorrow 'not before 0915' so far – though we know what that can mean – and I am waiting for the B.C. to come back with orders so that I can go to the huge double bed I've got for tonight. Today went shopping in Mechlin with Stewart and did some wonderful purchases – perfume – a bottle of Goya by Paquin (315 frs), a bottle of Coty 'Vertige' (245), Schiaparelli (135) and two bottles of 4711. The first is for Clare, second for Dorothy and the others for Mum if I ever manage to send it all away.

Supposed move is NE and it seems we may go to Holland after that. Am getting damn sick of these 1–2 day halts when we are promised a rest. The men are utterly tired and we need a week out of the line – we won't get it of course, not a hope in hell. No mail today.

1 October

Towards dusk – on the road N. of Eindhoven: We moved off this morning and crossed into Holland at Lomund on the Meuse Canal, during the afternoon. So far we've had nothing to eat or drink since breakfast, as everybody expected this to be a short move. The usual balls up. It seems the enemy is resisting quite fiercely in this salient and I can hear stuff coming back from here. The Dutch gave us a good welcome, though not as good as the Belgians, who were very popular with everybody. Am moving up now prior to going into action. Am i/c the column at the moment. It has been raining intermittently and is bitterly cold.

2 October

1530, Mjnsel: Finally went into action after dark, not far from where I made the above entry. It was cold and rained fiercely for a short spell about 2200, making everybody very wet and browned off. About 2130 had a meal of stew and potatoes and tea – very welcome. This morning I went up to the O.P. to see the form as I'm taking over this evening as soon as it's dark. It's an O.P. in very close country, and has to be manned by night as well as by day which is a bit wearying. Fairly quiet up there except for a few mortars and one large gun which pounds the area intermittently. I am leaving this diary behind for this time because I feel it contains too much useful information to be taken into a forward area. Sent off letters, home, to C. and to Joan B. Today for the first time we've been on A.F.V. rations – a tiny packet made up for 3 men for one day. Quite good if a little scanty. Sunshine today with the odd shower.

3 October

2000, at the O.P.: Didn't go up last night as orders were changed at the last minute but went instead first thing this morning to a smashed up windmill, where every movement inside brought clouds of dust, and the wind and rain howled through the ruined brickwork. Got breakfast – stone cold – at 1000 when we were more than ready for it, and when eating it the order came over the blower to move into B Company (Black Watch) area. This took quite a bit of time, but by about 1300 I'd established an O.P. of sorts right among the forward platoon. The Germans, when they took it into their heads, were in a house about 100–150 yards away, and an afternoon patrol brought one in crying and swearing he wasn't a Nazi, he didn't want to fight, he only wanted to go home – 'Germany, lose, lose, lose, Germany Kaput –'. It is hard to hate even Germans, in practice. It's easy if you have some deep personal reason and it's easy to say, but even these Germans – except for Waffen S.S. – command a measure of pity when they come miserably and beaten in – because these rather elderly garrison troops are not the same men who've over-run Europe. However I've no doubt they applauded in their day and

I've no softness for them – only a general pity for humanity which suffers so. Quietish day with a few shells and about 30 heavy mortar bombs in the area. I shelled the latter and they shut up. You can hardly see any distance; an O.P. is – as such – almost useless. A Sten gun is a valuable possession up here. We are sleeping – fully clothed – in a farm very near the O.P. and coy. H.Q. and manning again at first light. Should be relieved tomorrow evening I expect. Very cold first thing today. Apparently mail up tonight and for us tomorrow. Hooray.

4 October

a.m. O.P.: It is difficult to convey a good picture of night in the front line. It grows – it seems – suddenly quite dark – and every bush – so innocent by day – seems to hold an enemy sniper – every shell which lands seems to be the enemy. Last night the Gordons started firing everything off on our left, by way of a demonstration and it brought back a decent measure of retaliation by way of mortar and shellfire from the Boche. However, I see that sentence means nothing unless you were here. It doesn't begin to give you that feeling in the stomach as you hear the fantastically loud rattle of machine guns, and the splintering crash of mortars, or the sudden approaching scream of a shell — and you know it's close and you say as nonchalantly as you can, 'Down boys' and down you all go and the damn thing crashes just in front of you and the splinters come hurtling through the trees like steel rain. And you pick yourself up and say to the Company Commander as casually as you can, 'Hm, fairly close . . .' and hope he won't notice the slight unsteadiness of your voice, but when he answers, his voice is unsteady too so you feel better about it all. It is never silent for long up here in the woods at night. Nervous triggers make every short silence end suddenly – and indeed the sound of bullets is almost less worrying than silence. I am with the same Coy. here as at Havre and a damn nice lot they are. There were two casualties – neither fatal – last night. Up at dawn today and by now – it is nearly 0900 – have washed, shaved and eaten. The brew of tea first thing was heaven-sent. Had in it a rum issue which came up last night. Quite decent weather so far today and also so far – quiet.

Night, same place: Am very tired and going to sleep soon still with boots on but tonight in a Doovah vacated by some unfortunate Jock on patrol. Some quite vicious mortaring and shelling during the afternoon. Also sniping. In fact, Jerry, stiffened by a paratroop brigade, seems rather more aggressive than yesterday! Quite a lot near the O.P. Mail this evening – 2 from Clare and one from Dorothy. Some more mail coming in. We are being relieved at dusk tomorrow which is a long spell – 60 hours – at an O.P. More rain this evening and my feet are sore. Killed a young pig to take back to the bty. Foster, whom I took in for Horton, is a big improvement and the others are all doing quite well.

6 October

2145, gunline: Got back at 2330 eventually after a piece of bloody luck when a track came off the carrier just past A Cap. Took us four hours and some cut hands to get the thing repaired. However we did eventually manage to grind home in the moonlight, where Findlay was waiting and put my bed down etc. and I had a wonderful night's sleep. 2 letters – long ones – from C., one from Bé and one from Debroy. Have spent today having a general rest. Also have now got rid of B.S.M. Heath and got a new chap in today called Keating. Hear tonight that they've shifted the O.P. 100 yards west to a house which while I was up was hit 11 times out of 12 by a Jerry gun and 100% by some mortars. Not a pleasant place to occupy. Very cold and sunny today and we all have bloody awful colds too. Have replied to all my mail and sent off parcels to C. and home, of my Mechlin purchases.

7 October

1845: For nearly a week the main road outside our position has never been silent. Convoy after convoy – tanks, guns, petrol, ammo., men carriers, R.A.F. trucks, bulldozers – every gadget of modern warfare has streamed past – the big push is obviously being made up here, for once we cross the two rivers, the plains of NW Germany lie nearly open, and it will be just about over.

Up the road today went Monty in a staff car, but I didn't see him. Mail is in but won't be up for a while. I am in the middle of a letter to Clare so I hope this mail will give me something to answer – ah here is the mail and so far one from C. (4 October). I am about to read it. Going to O.P. at 1700 tomorrow.

11 October

Night, in bed: I don't seem to have written this up for a very long time, but in fact I simply had no chance during this spell at the O.P. The O.P. when I went up there on the evening of the 8th – Sunday – had been moved to a house 100 yards or so forward of the Company area. The O.P. itself was in a haystack in a Dutch barn and just in front of a collection of houses etc. known as Pig Farm. Masses of dead livestock everywhere; pigs which had exploded on booby traps, cows frozen into grotesque angles by shell splinters, even an occasional horse. We sleep in Btn. H.Q. for this O.P. as we have to go out each day with a Standing Patrol. Both days were much the same – out in the gloomy dawn, back in the sinister dusk, and hushed voices all the day as German patrols come as far as and beyond the O.P. One was caught 150 yards in our rear the first afternoon. Two of our own snipers who had gone out a bit early on the second day, were caught by a Jerry patrol in the O.P. area. We found their rifles complete with telescopic sights as we got there. All this called for rather unusual vigilance, and as tiring, but daylight only lasts for 12 hours now. One of the main attractions was 'Otto', a Spandau nest 400 yards in front of the O.P. whom we watched minutely for two days. I wasn't allowed to shell it as they want our snipers to get it, but so far they haven't succeeded. There are 3 Germans in the post, and 'Otto' as they call him has become quite famous.* Not much stuff came back at us, and most of it was 3 inch mortar. I don't <u>think</u> Jerry knows we're in the place by day. I hope not as we only have about a dozen Black Watch there for our own protection. Second day it rained solidly and turned all the tracks into a quagmire and I was glad to get back last night. Spent today having a bath and writing letters to C., home, G., and Dorothy from all of whom I got letters while at the O.P. Also from Gerard Tallack.

One of my trucks was stolen in Eindhoven containing my grip inside which were among other things a brand new trenchcoat (26 August), a bottle of Benedictine, gumboots, shoes and my beloved hot water bottle. What is so infuriating is that there is simply <u>nothing</u> one can do about it except hope against hope that it will turn up – and I don't expect for a moment it will.** When I think how long I'd waited for that trenchcoat . . . I have a tiny pup from Pig Farm called Happy. His mother was Snow White and he was one of seven and he seemed a bit bomb happy but isn't. He is very wee, about 3 weeks old, and brown and white. Mixed spaniel and setter with floppy ears and he 'points'. He's most amusing and very pretty and full of life. Findlay who knows a good bit about dogs, is more or less looking after him for me. I'll add some more to this tomorrow before going up for another two days. Have had an awful head cold for about 5 days, also my foot – bad since April, and infected in the desert – has been troublesome and I'm getting it dressed at a nearby Field Ambulance. All very muddled this. Final note: The B.C. doesn't want officers to wear corduroys and shoes on the position which is a bloody nerve and has caused much dissatisfaction as we almost all do as it happens.

12 October

Afternoon: Up to the O.P. again this evening. We have been told today that we're likely to be here another fortnight, so I'll know this damned O.P. well by the time we leave. A Jerry patrol cut the line from Battalion to the O.P. last night, so it seems he must know we occupy it – not altogether a good thing. Bill Carney shelled Otto and reports he isn't in residence today which will rob life of some of its interest. Went into Eindhoven this morning and made some useful purchases – chinagraph pencils, a sketch block and two rubbers – all things I needed quite badly. No news of the missing truck – I guess I've lost that kit now all right.

*Later my carrier had the name 'OTTO's DOOM' painted on it but it was the doom of the carrier because it burned out on the Belgo-Dutch border at the end of Jan '45.
** It never did.

Bloody annoying. Dim weather with a hint of rain, though this morning was bright. I've noticed how the Dutch have thawed since we came here. At first they were very reserved but now they're as friendly as the Belgians, and the usual scenes take place – the soldiers get on wonderfully well with children everywhere – language seems no barrier at all. They do our washing, we give them chocolate etc., and life goes on well. The road outside – the main Second Army axis is still crammed each and every day as the Salient fills up for the big push – which may be the last push we all hope. All the old signs appear – the white boar – HD – TT – the Desert Rat – and new ones like the rampant lion of the 15th Div., the 49th's Polar Bear – and the 3 feathers of the 53rd, and many others – and tanks and more tanks, and the overloaded ammo 3 tonners. Almost, it seems, endlessly.

15 October

Sunday morning: Spent a fairly uneventful Friday the 13th in the O.P. and took Stewart up at first light the next day and then came back to the gunline. A very hush hush visit to Eindhoven by the King took place on Thursday to decorate Gen. Graham, 50 Div. Comd. who commanded our brigade all through the desert campaign. First light on Friday was ushered in by a volley of 68 mortar bombs from Jerry, but we had no casualties. Yesterday went into Eindhoven with Bill, and pottered round doing a bit of shopping. I got Clare some sewing silks – not real silk but they seem fairly good, and the colours are good. Cold weather and no mail for 3 or 4 days complete the picture. Wrote to Sandy K. yesterday and have had my Jeep water – and weather – proofed, by the addition of plywood doors. Under the surface of apparent quiet (though Aachen is being counter attacked by the Boche) big events are beginning to stir, but I give no date in case this diary falls into enemy hands. A B.W. fighting patrol which went in dead of night to try and get Otto, had one wounded and one wounded and missing. Damage to Otto – one probably killed.

18 October

1830, near St Odenrode: Today – it must be, let's see, Wednesday – we moved, starting at about 0900 this morning to a position not so very far from our old one and from which we shall fight the impending battle for Schijndel and Hertogenbosch. I came down from the O.P. yesterday night in pouring rain down the quagmire which is now the track from the main road to Btn. H.Q. It was the darkest night I remember in years, and the Jeep lurched and dived along in the thick mud and huge expanses of water which started as puddles. Anyway I got back eventually. During the day we spotted a German H.Q. which provided some interesting observation. We were heavily mortared twice during the afternoon – about 50 bombs each time all round the O.P. which cut our lines to hell. No casualties.

The new area is wet but reasonably comfortable and we have most people under cover in barns, pigsties, henhouses etc., also some sort of mess in a farmhouse. Two letters from C. last night – I've posted several to her recently – and sent another and parcels to Jane and Monica tonight. Will try and add more tomorrow. I may be going up to the O.P. again tomorrow night but B.W. are being relieved the day after so it may not be necessary to go. Let's hope not.

Happy fell out of a barn tonight and I'm afraid he's hurt his inside. He's certainly hurt one shoulder, poor little hound. I hope I shan't have to shoot him.

19 October

1830: Quiet day; I've got to go to the O.P. tomorrow as B.W. pull out tonight which means a night's sleep tonight which is an excellent thing. It's rained all day and been cold and miserable and I've been violently depressed. Last night in bed I was thinking about life and death and it suddenly occurred to me that though people talk a lot about it, when you actually think to yourself: 'in this next attack I may actually die – and find out about heaven and hell, and completely and suddenly <u>end</u> as far as this life's concerned –' Well it's a different matter. It's as well one doesn't think that way too often because it's rather frightening in a deep, disturbing way. So it's better just to look on the forthcoming battle as just another battle and not go too far into details. Dumping 300 rounds per gun tomorrow morning. Wrote home.

20 October

Pelting with rain outside. No wonder it's so hard to get on with the war, for communications become almost impossible on these bogged tracks. Dope for the attack this morning. Seems it is now part of the main attack to clear Holland south of the Waal, the idea of driving SW to join the Americans having been temporarily dropped. Our objective is Schijndel and I am with A Company – the forward company – commanded by a Major Smith-Cunningham, whom I already know fairly well and like a lot. He's (unfortunately!) as brave as a lion and doesn't give a damn for enemy action. Nobody knows how sticky or easy it's going to be. It starts with a midnight attack by the Gordons and we go in at dawn. Not a cheering prospect. F.O.O. is a lousy job. Had a wonderful B.&A. in a wooden tub this morning and the chiropodist hacked my foot around this afternoon. There are now 3 warts instead of 2. Two lovely letters this evening – a long one from D. and one from C. which made me very happy as she's having a good time at Bé's. Am going to sleep now, after adding a bit to a letter to C. Sent her one this afternoon and also wrote to Dorothy as I want to get such letters as possible written while I can.

Cold today.

21 October

a.m.: Today we are getting things what in the army is known as 'Teed up' or 'laid on' or simply organised. Wireless sets checked, batteries filled, maps marked, chinagraphs sharpened, bootlaces tested, stens and revolvers cleaned, rations, petrol and water loaded, binoculars cleaned, compasses tested, vehicles checked, cable checked – these are only a few of the larger and more important things one has to do before going forward with an attack. I alone have 3 wireless sets – a No. 22 to communicate with B.C. and guns, a No. 18 to talk to the infantry, and a No. 38 if my remote control cable from me to my wireless in the carrier, is destroyed. That is, if my O.P. is away from the carrier which it nearly always is; you then have what is called a Remote Control Unit by which you work the No. 22 as much as 1/2 a mile away. We are attending a conference at the Black Watch this afternoon, when our 18 sets are being netted. About 300 guns are supporting this attack, including about 80 mediums and some heavies. There is also to be some extensive Typhooning starting tomorrow. The enemy has about 5 depleted battalions round Shijndel and a number of 88s at Hertogenbosch which is also to be taken. It looks like being quite a severe battle and my stomach flutters gently from time to time. However, it's no use worrying – but it's difficult not to!

22 October

1830: Joined the B.W. in their assembly area near the gun position. The atmosphere in a battalion the night before an attack is tense but usually quite confident. Anyway the Jocks are reasonably unruffled tonight. I go in just behind A Company – the leading company – as previously arranged. Zero hour for us is 0645 but we started moving up at 0430. The operation starts at midnight when the 5/7 Gordons go in to attack and take Weibosch. It's amazing how many things the average Battalion Commander has to take into consideration – ours (Col. Bradford, a grand person) showed a remarkable grasp at his orders group which we attended yesterday afternoon. One really good thing; a lovely letter from Clare tonight. She seems to be having an awfully good time at Bé's, which is exactly as I hoped it would be. Well – that's all for now. Next time I write, our attack will be over – and the pursuit will probably be on, but it may be a day or two before I <u>can</u> write again.

23 October

1740, Schutoboom: Up at 0300, breakfast at 0345 and at 0430 the advance began under the brilliant artificial moonlight. We knew the 5/7 had taken all their objectives, and morale was good. On we pushed towards the start line on muddy tracks and through ghostly battered villages, little roads blocked only a few minutes before by huge felled trees. The sky flickered with gun flashes and the explosion of mortar bombs or Very lights. Machine guns crackled. All sound was very loud in the quiet of the night. Figures moved quietly forward, tin hats silhouetted. An occasional stream of tracer from a Spandau hung a necklace of bullets on the darkness. Soon it got light and as dawn broke, the great thunder of the guns broke loose and the attack went forward. Occasionally shells fell near us with a menacing whistle and a great crump. There was also a little mortaring and m.g. but generally not much opposition. Got onto the objective with only a few casualties. Established an O.P. in the windmill – the smokescreen was heavy around us. Then another in the factory but later moved on with A Company mounted on tanks, till we got here, getting a grand reception en route. Not much to add – now anyway – and I'm going to bed soon – very tired. A pretty full and successful day. Destruction in Schijndel appalling. No rain.

25 October

0940, near Esch: Moved on yesterday moving towards Esch again mounted on tanks and the remainder of the battalion in kangaroos – Shermans without turrets and full of infantry – rather like an armoured Trojan Horse. The sun was out and opposition was light and we moved on in clouds of dust – great ovation in St Michiels Geste and then onto these woods where some dead boche are still lying around. Prisoners have been coming back in better quantities now. They found one about 10 yards from my carrier. Where we are used to be a German Div. H.Q. till about 2 days ago and I got some interesting information from a priest who speaks perfect English. The Sappers have had rather bad casualties trying to build a bridge here, and may have to give up the attempt, but an early bridge is essential to get the 7th Armoured across. Our immediate future uncertain but we may go north and cross at another bridge the R.E.s are making and then attack the boche who are attacking the 5/7 bridgehead the other side of the river. Heavy mist and cold this morning. Odd notes: Bill Carney has the M.C. for Colombelles. Also Alistair Cameron who of course is in 126 these days. Letter from C. (20 Oct.) last night; still enjoying it at Bé's and makes no mention of leaving. Excellent.

26 October

1330, O.P. in Heesakker: Half an hour's sleep sitting up and a dawn attack on foot are the headlines of the last 24 hours – however to go into a little more detail: I didn't get to the crossing with A Co. and the tanks because my right track broke – 11 links gone, and it took a very long time to get new sections put in and then the sprocket didn't fit etc. . . . Meanwhile the tanks came back as they couldn't get across owing to stiff opposition. Eventually after a welcome meal of pork and veg – just ready before darkness fell – we pushed on. All the usual details of an impending attack – tanks crashing about and tin-hatted infantry silhouetted in the artificial moonlight. Figures doing things everywhere and dim signs with CCP 75,

HD and the like. Got up to Esch church about 9 o'clock and then walked up to Btn. H.Q. about a mile on. Very footsore on arrival, but after attending an O. Gp. by the C.O. had to go back to fetch up the carrier and the B.C.'s and Bill's Scout cars. They had to come up with the tanks when the class 40 bridge was completed. This was first scheduled for 2200 then midnight, then 0200, 0300 and finally we crossed about 0700 after a very cold night broken by considerable sniping and mortaring and a thunderous arty. programme supporting 1 Gordons on a night attack. Arrived just in time to go forward into the misty morning with A & B coys and the tanks. My carrier crossing a bit of open ground was greeted with a burst of spandau tracer, but I got up O.K. and really rather enjoyed the attack during which we took a lot of prisoners and had only a few casualties. I went with the leading platoon – strictly against orders! I really don't know why except that something gets me on these occasions and I like to be well up. More curiosity than bravery, I hastily add. Certain amount of sniping, m.g., mortar and shell fire on route to the objectives which we took O.K., but were shelled fairly heartily when on them. I had some bloody near squeaks from the odd bullet, and one shell splinter – a big one – missed my ankle by less than 6 inches. However, six inches is a long way on occasions.

The tanks started numerous fires with their big guns, and a sight which sickened me was some cows screaming and trying to escape from a flaming barn as they burnt to death alive – flames from nose to tail. Awful, and one could do nothing. Mercifully the barn fell quickly in and ended it. (We had an excellent breakfast cooked on one of these flaming barns.) I am now with Charles Munro and Sandy Leslie — ie. B. Coy. I quite miss A Coy. but these are also a grand lot. I've appreciated lately what completely splendid chaps these infantry officers of ours are. There can be none finer anywhere. They go on through anything. They are the real heroes of the army. After we secured our objectives, the 7th Armd. went through and the battle has passed on rather, and seems to be going awfully well, as has this entire offensive. Have washed and shaved and feel almost human again – but my feet hurt, oh boy they <u>do</u> hurt.

27 October

2000, at the gunline: Too tired to do more than jot down a few oddments. Slept with B. Coy. who did me awfully well with rum and coffee and we finished some whisky I had. Just as we were going to doss down, orders came for a move at 0800 so I didn't doss till about 10 but strangely enough woke bang on the dot of 0600 and got up. Then I went back to the gunline as the carrier tracks broke again and the thing wasn't safe to use. Drove back myself. Upshot – new tracks and sprockets tomorrow morning. Letter from C. and 200 cigarettes from home.

They have a room for me in a house on the posn. and I'm more than ready for some sleep. Just starting to rain outside, but every day it grows colder and new rawness is apparent at night. Read Maugham's *Moon and Sixpence* – a wonderful piece of writing – he gets his emphasis and cynical touches at just the right moments and never overdone. Shot a wounded horse with my Sten. Both front legs broken and it wouldn't stay still, but my first shot right in its forehead put it out of pain for ever. Matt Simm's been made up to Capt. to replace Jimmy Gegan who's gone back with bad malaria, so I'm no longer the Junior Troop Commander. The Bn. moved unopposed to Haren today and are there most comfortably leaguered. Went up to see them tonight. Got Findlay a wrist watch on this party thereby gaining further devotion in great measure. Happy is in great form but has something like a cyst on his tummy; must get the M.O. to look at it. Bill Carney's also got a most amusing pup called 'Maxie'. Sort of Alsatian and lots bigger than Happy (who's beginning to know his name by the way).

29 October

1110, Loon-op-Zand: Too much activity altogether. Had a night's sleep on the 27 and on the 28 the Regt. moved in the morning. Long drive up to a place near Winkel – only good thing about drive (we went independently) was I got a good sheepskin for 4 tins of bully and ditto sardines, and had it made into a grand jacket. In new position we were shelled during the afternoon and had 4 killed and 2 wounded included Sgt. Kell and L/Bdr Holt – i.e. the entire Bty. office staff. In the late afternoon came a cryptic message 'Rejoin friends before dark! Same location . . .' This meant a hasty switch of carriers as mine wasn't yet repaired, and then towards dusk, off we went; the brigade was to do another attack. Joined them, and moved up in column to this place last night. Reception committee included mortars, spandaus and even bazookas. Also a few shells. An unhealthy spot. Bill was picked for F.O.O. this time; I am in reserve. Four and a half hours sleep – not bad in the circumstances – in a barn. Early this morning we had two bouts of shelling, some of which was uncomfortably close. Quite a few casualties including several very nasty Germans with brains all over their faces etc. Prisoners and snipers coming in, and a lot of noise. The enemy is still resisting as we cut west and north from freed Tilburg. Very cold and a little rain last night.

Good remark from a Jock this morning as we trudged forward: 'I hear they're giving us a rest' – pause – 'when we get to Berlin.' The troops have a wonderful sense of humour at the worst moments. Machine gun last night greeted with 'Tell him to put it away – somebody will get hurt if he isn't careful.' 'Somebody ought to tell that bloke there's a war on.' Trouble is I can't remember a quarter of the bon mots people drop during the day.

1930, gunline near Loon: Guns came up during afternoon. Enemy shelling continues at intervals under a cold white moon. Bitter tonight and we haven't so much as a barn on the position. I am in my Jerry tent in a slit trench. Very damp, sandy soil, but not as bad as it will be in the flooded areas, where, as far as one can see, it won't be possible to dig at all. Letter from C. I should write back but I'm really too tired tonight. Maybe I'll get a chance tomorrow. Flying bomb going north early this morning has caused much speculation. We are approaching the Maas, which may be something of an obstacle.

30 October

2045, same place: Day un-noteworthy except for talk of the German counter attack on the East of the Salient and a sudden move which was cancelled. We expect to move tomorrow into a defensive position along the Maas. I am now in a leaky doovah with corrugated over the top and it is raining hard. A few bombers over tonight. Excellent mail – 2 more from C., one from Bé, one from Dorothy, Pam (full of what she wore at Una's wedding!) and one from Joan Mary. Also small parcel from home with scarf, mittens, toothpaste, razor blades. Have written to C., home and Dorothy but am too tired to write more now. Have Happy in my doovah – did I mention he has a small hernia? But the M.O. says he can operate easily on it. My own carrier is back. I am getting rid of the driver – windy. (Who isn't – but he doesn't hide it!)

1 November

2000, nearer the Maas: It appears yesterday was the 31 so I've made a date error somewhere, though it's of no great importance. Lousy wet night last night and a move today in mist and cold into the polder land near the Maas which we're reported to have crossed. Apparently further attacks towards the Waal are in the air with the Div. as usual in a prominent role. Very depressed tonight; no end to the war in sight, lousy weather etc. Did I mention that John Ingle 301 B.C. was wounded the other night? Frank Philip has got the bty. not yet known who's got F Tp. Am up in a dirty old attic but at least it's dry.

2 November

2020, near Helvoit – gunline: Last entry should have been dated 31 Oct but such things are apt to be confusing nowadays. Anyway the Bty. moved next morning – I to an O.P. with A Coy. in 's Hertogenbosch. The town, which is surrounded by a canal, and seems to have almost as many bridges as Venice, is badly smashed and shows many scars. The main road approaching it through the infamous Vucht, is one of the finest I've ever been on. I was in the O.P. all day today and handed over to Jimmy Hogg of 126. We attack on the 5th – an assault crossing of the canal south of the Maas – in assault boats. This is a new one on me but should be fairly interesting. 2 letters from C. last night and one from Sandy K. Also an *Esquire*. Cold but not unpleasant weather, and I have a room in a house tonight.

3 November

2125: Main activities today: a magnificent B. & A., a recce of the battle O.P. on the banks of the Maas Canal which I cross as soon as the first bridge is up, a new trenchcoat (wrong size so I'll try to change it tomorrow), 2 vests and 3 hankies from an officers shop and Findlay losing my brown boots. Also had my foot hacked again at 5 F.D.S. Wrote 8 letters: C., Bé, Home, Joan, Sandy, Judy and Gerard and Debroy. Very cold and raining hard tonight. Hope it doesn't rain for the party, which is first light on Sunday. Letters today from Gerard and Debroy. Clean clothes today and pyjamas and pillowslip tonight. Findlay really is an excellent Batman even though he is apt to lose things; eg. I've only 16 out of 30 or so hankies left – tho' heaven knows where they all get to. Incidentally, re the sheepskin jacket I got on the 29th, another is now on the way from C. whom I'd written asking for one a week ago. It costs £5.5 but if it isn't as good as my own, Gordon S.-Cunningham will buy it from me. Actually, knowing C., I am pretty sure it <u>will</u> be what I want.

5 November

Sunday, 1645, Haarsteeg church belfry: Early in the morning – about 0300 – on the 4th the gunline received about 150 shells but no casualties. At 0900 attended an O Gp. at 5 B.W. and discovered the attack was due at 1715. This meant a day of exceedingly hurried preparation but by 1530 I was in my O.P. on the canal bank. It was all very impressive and film-like. The enormous smokescreen in front – the tanks lining the bank and shooting – tracer bullets everywhere – both ways – and the sudden crash of nearby mortar bombs. At 1715 over went the assault boats amid the tremendous tattoo of the guns. Everything went O.K. and we crossed at 0330 on the class 9 bridge and pushed right on to the final objective here. Tremendous welcome – the town was deserted when we arrived but within a quarter of an hour everybody was up. The boche had left 2 hours before. Huge fires burning along the front but not here. Am sleeping in the vicarage and have made great friends with the local priest whose brother-in-law owns the shoe factory at Loon op Zand. He says he is giving me a pair of shoes for C. tonight! Very young, curly haired and jovial and full of gusto. Hates the boche. Letter from C. yesterday. Howling gale with a hint of snow, up in the belfry – very cold day. Everybody else has been sleeping but I got 3 hours last night which they didn't get. Should sleep well tonight. It is said 152 are pushing on to Nijmegen – God where next – will they never rest us? Two wounded Germans surrendered to me today – both crying. I left them as they were by then harmless and not very badly hit anyway and I had to push on.

7 November

Afternoon: We came back on the morning of the 6th after sleeping the clock around. Had a wonderful feed of young roast duckling for supper the night before. The shoes the priest gave me for C. were damn nice black suede court shoes and I've already sent them off. Two parcels from C. containing mainly Happy items – collar and lead, powders etc., also some writing paper and a tin of Nescafé. Just the job. We have salvaged a German 30 cwt which is being made into a cook's wagon – which in fact it already is. We move tomorrow – it seems to the Venlo sector which is reputed to be an unhealthy spot. Have changed my carrier driver again – I had already replaced Dotchin, but the new bloke lacked experience and now I've got a really good fellow who was the B.C.'s D.R. but being a Driver/Mech. has been posted to me. Called Shepherd and I think he's going to be exactly what I need. Bloody awful cold weather with rain and hailstorms. Also forgot to mention I lost B.S.M. Keating who went to be R.S.M. but I have a new chap who shows signs of becoming very good – though being ex-coast arty. he lacks experience in field. I wish we could go out of the line for a bit of a rest. Instead of which, we seem to be going into rather an unpleasant bit of it.

9 November

a.m., near Leende – Venlo front: Outside, the snow is falling heavily – the first this year. It won't settle as it's driven by a high wind. The weather is very cold. Moved yesterday morning to this concentration area which as far as the troop is concerned, is an excellent one as we have a large farm all to ourselves. Steve and I share a room in the farm which is a sort of Super Starkadder-hood, there being father and 6 sons and 6 daughters – ages ranging from 25 to 9. All 6 daughters are really rather attractive and lively and it's a very pleasant household. We expect to leave on the 11th to go into action, but nobody knows any more than that. The family sat in here complete till late last night, drinking coffee and talking in general – how my dutch improves! And gave us an egg each for breakfast today. This is a main road and much traffic passes up it throughout the 24 hours. Just now some enormous American guns (240?) just rumbled past – everybody very impressed. Somebody has stolen Happy's lead which is infuriating.

10 November

We expect to move into action tomorrow, otherwise there is no news except that it is bloodily cold and rainy. C.'s sheepskin arrived yesterday, together with two letters from her. Went to see B.W. today and sold skin to Gordon. It was a jolly good one though not quite as thick as my own, so there was no point in keeping both. Wrote to C. and her mother. No mail.

11 November

1910, Nederweert: Moved about midday in cold, sunny weather and got in to an uneventful occupation. Quite a decent area with a tiny farmhouse. Went up to Bn. H.Q. and the O.P. and have to go up tomorrow morning with a view to recce-ing and occupying another O.P. The ground up there forms a sort of cross-canals and is apparently strongly held with the boche making sorties across the water at night with bazookas. A big attack is imminent including assault crossings – not by the battalion thank god. 600 guns are in support, and I suspect Roermond and Venlo are the ultimate objectives. No mail.

17 November

0930, near Heithuizen: So much has happened since my last entry that I find it almost impossible to remember it all. Anyway it must have been the night of the 12th that I went up to man an O.P. not 50 yards from the canal bank. We spent nearly all night recce-ing and sandbagging the semi shattered house we were to man all the next day. In the night an enemy fighting patrol crossed the canal and slung a few grenades about the place. We had a corporal wounded, and killed one German. Spent all next day so close you could see the expression on the enemy's face. No sleep that night – no, one hour. Next night none at all except at 0500 by which time we had pulled back ready for the attack. We spotted 7 machine gun posts during our stay at the O.P. The attack started on the afternoon of the 14th being much the same as the last canal assault but on a much larger scale. I was F.O.O. and got to the objective about midnight where a large fire was burning – a result of our 6 pds. fire while repelling a small counter attack. We had more resistance for this crossing including quite a lot of shelling, but casualties were light. One of the B.C.'s signallers is missing believed killed. Next morning early – it had frozen during the night which was again sleepless – the 154 came through us and advanced. The day was uneventful but cold, and that night (15/16) I had nearly 12 hours sleep. On again yesterday morning (heavy frost) to the next canal, and back into the gunline last night – another 12 hours sleep. A parcel with a warm scarf and pullover. Signaller McPherson killed by a shell which came into the C.P. but didn't explode – it cut him in half. B.S.M. also lightly wounded. This morning's news shows that 6 allied armies are on the move – it seems the attack on Germany is on, but there are hopes that we may be rested for a while, having had 6 weeks in the line without pause. Heavy frost again today and some mail – not yet examined. Had Chester Willmot of the B.B.C. in my O.P. for the first stage of the canal attack and I also broadcast but didn't hear the result personally. I've seldom been so dead beat as during the last do, and my crew stood up to everything very well – I was very pleased with them.

18 November

Night: Called out yesterday in the pouring rain just before evening meal, and arrived soaked at Bn. H.Q. to find I was F.O.O. for yet another canal assault that night. Hell, how it rained and how cold it was in the artificial moonlight waiting for the flails to finish beating the track forward to B. Coy. I got there eventually, walking ahead of my carrier and spent the night in heavy shelling. We had about 100 in the first hour, most of them very close – one seven yards from the carrier, which cut the wireless lead. Trees were sawn in half by the vicious, slashing splinters and the pieces of warm steel tinkled down, mingling with the rain. We were cold, tired and hungry. When we advanced to the canal bank my carrier got bogged, so did the tank I got hold of to fish it out. Eventually a half track did the job, but as we did the last open stretch to the canal (I was still on foot) we got caught in a rain of about 50 shells which were so close one <u>had</u> to lie down and wait and hope for the best as they screamed towards you and crashed – some about 10 yards away – hitting the eardrums painfully and sending the actual fragments whizzing only inches overhead as you pressed close to the soft earth, tin hat close to the floor, body straining to press lower, nerves shrinking, hope fading . . . Several times in those few minutes I thought 'this one is it, this time it'll hit me.' But we crossed in our assault boat. We had to leave the carrier and carry our wireless and necessaries (no food) on helped by a party of Jocks. Got to Bn. H.Q. in time for another plastering and found the B.C. half dead with fatigue, on the wireless. Then marched on to B. Coy. and established an O.P. about dawn. Cold but no rain. During the morning word came that the Bn. was pulling out in the afternoon, and our party returned in the sunshine. Coming back over the sunny, green pinewoods and grass near the canal, it was hard to re-visualise the hours of fear in the darkness, when each hundred yards seemed a mile, and the newly dead turned their waxen faces to the unreal moon, and the wounded sobbed as the stretcher bearers plodded back with them through the mud. War is not pretty, and though I am used enough to dead men by now, it always seems such a waste to see them lying there cold and white and gone so far away. Can't we find a better answer to life than this? I hope my son, if ever I have one, won't have to do the things I've done; before I knew I used to think it was 'exciting' this thing they call battle, but it isn't, it's achingly tiring, and heartbreaking. No sleep of course last night and I'm going to sleep the clock round now. Letters from George Long and Clare. Must try to write to her tomorrow. Spent all last night drenched to the skin, what a luxury to take off wet socks today and bathe one's tired feet and have a wash.

20 November

1815, same place: The battery moved up over the canal into the wide open spaces today, but Bill the B.C. and I have stayed here as it was originally thought the 5 B.W. were doing an attack tomorrow. However it now seems they are only taking over a bit of the line right on the bank of the Maas. Have had a couple of lazy days – yesterday a wonderful bath. Letters from Dad and C. today – the good perfume I sent her from Mechelin seems to have gone astray. Damned annoying. Some shelling in this area. Went up a track with the B.C. today and got hopelessly bogged in knee deep slime. It is raining furiously today, and I was once more soaked and mud-drenched. How sick of mud I am. Wrote off the other day for another of these diaries – since when I've hardly made an entry!

21 November

1800, gunline over the canal: Moved up today over a series of vehicle-made tracks which were nothing more or less than a sea of mud. Bogged trucks everywhere and the bulldozers doing yeoman work. To give you an idea of the conditions. Last night there were about 100 guns stuck fast trying to get up here, and our Quartermaster, endeavouring to deliver rations (he arrived at 1600 today!) was the 192nd vehicle in the queue waiting to be towed out of the bog. The Sappers have been feverishly building a log road for the last two days – a wonderful job – as there isn't a single road from the road to the canal except via Heijel and that is being used by another formation. Papers in tonight make it clear that the six armies at present on the offensive are pressing forward into Germany damned well. Out here we are in the open – I am in a very comfortable doovah with Steve, which we constructed with our batmen today. It is deep, dry (so far) and has bags of straw on the floor. Size about 9 feet by 7 or 8 and plenty of room. Certain amount of enemy shelling, but not very close. Cold tonight; I think a frost will follow the day's rain. I expect to go to the O.P. tomorrow. Heavy and persistent rumours of a rest for the Div., but how true I don't know. A few days real rest would be heaven. Morale is fairly high but everybody is very tired and ready for a rest. We've been on the go for a long spell now.

22 November

Next morning: Rain–rain–mud–cold; that is today on the Maas battlefront. It set in early this morning and has been beating down steadily ever since. The doovah lets in a stealthy stream just near my bed, and as the guns crash out, little clusters of wet sand fall from the roof down one's neck. However, at least I am still fairly dry so no grumbles. But on a day like this it is quite impossible to visualise surviving this bloody war. Perhaps the very will to live is sapped by the endless rain and the soul destroying mud. Put forward the idea a day or two ago that a kangaroo would be a good O.P. vehicle and went with the B.C. to the C.R.A. to suggest it. This morning the latter had sent one up to H.Q.R.A. and a series of R.A. officers passed opinions – one and all were in favour, and it seems I may get one for a week on trial. (Even so it would probably take 10 months to get the thing generally adopted by which time I hope the war will be over.) The advances seem to be going well, but this appalling weather must slow us up. Not even a plane in the sky. You can't even go to the lavatory in this weather. Yet the official issue of tents (bivouac) to the troop is so far precisely 3 for 55 men. I suppose 'they' are waiting for it to become winter or something – probably the offices in Whitehall are not much colder than they were 6 months ago! Up to the O.P. this afternoon. Right on the Maas bank I'm told, and plenty of Boche in view. Might get some shooting. This time last year we were 5 days out of Liverpool and getting all set for home . . . Wrote C.

23 November

2045: Back after a night and a day on the banks of the Maas. Boots etc. on since I left here. Two days of pouring rain. Mortared heavily last night and shelled too damned accurately today – two in the garden of the house, smashed all the windows and – incongruously – set the cuckoo clock going. Brigade relieved tomorrow and we go out of the line but only – it is said – for 24 hours and then to join 1st Canadians. It's about time we had a rest; everybody really is jumpy and tired. You only realise it when you come away from the front line and the relief surges over you, what a strain it is to be there. Steve and I have a stove in our doovah now which makes it marvellously warm and cosy. Too tired to add more now. The Bty. moves tomorrow morning.

24 November

1430, harbour near Roggel: We are only spending one night here and supposed to be moving on to Nijmegen of all places, tomorrow morning. However no details yet. Meanwhile there is a canteen in and a bottle of whisky and other equally important items to take one's attention. We are in a farm by the main road, everybody under cover, and Steve and I in a room with a warm stove. Just the job. Raining all day so far, every track a swamp; every road a track. Situation normal, in fact.

25 November

Between Nijmegen and the Rhine: Hell of a journey here. I was woken at 0100 to say one O.P. was to go with the Recce party. This required some walking about in the middle of the night which was rather annoying. Set off at 0700 and arrived about 1230 after bumping over some of the worst roads I've ever seen. Awful country here, flat and flooded and bleak. I'm establishing an O.P. tomorrow morning. Rained like hell during the day. We relieve the U.S. Paratroops here – a good though scruffy bunch. Scrounged much excellent food, torch batteries etc. including marmalade and a 3 lb tin of coffee which I propose to retain as possible barter when I go – if I go – on leave. Some shells coming back but not many.

A quiet sector, but the larger picture is vague and nobody seems to know what's in the wind. Wonderful mail last night – one from New York, one from Mom, one from Mrs K. for a friend in Nijmegen and best of all a 16 page one from C. telling me among other things that the Goya perfume did arrive after all. Wrote back home and a 20 page one to C. Long political discussion with Steve in bed lasting till about midnight. Happy – who grows daily more dog and less puppy like – ate a whole tin of Irish stew in about 40 seconds tonight.

27 November

O.P. Doodewaard: Yesterday was cold and clear, today is only cold, and the bleak semi-flooded landscape is a depressing sight. Nothing doing here – the enemy is the other side of the Rhine. I went up through the totally ruined and deserted village of Opheusden, along the bank of the river but not a soul is in sight. Only a profusion of dead cows, pigs etc. with an occasional Jerry or British soldier – one already turning black having been left unburied for 3 weeks by the Americans whose ideas of sanitation are nil. Their living quarters are absolute pigsties.

The O.P. is a smashed up house with a moat around it. We look out of the 2/3 or so roof still remaining. Good view but no detail. The sparrows hop about in here, and every room is deep in bricks, mortar, smashed furniture etc. Jimmy Herbertson the I.O. and Sgt. Taylor of 5 B.W. each had a foot removed by these bloody schumines in Opheusden yesterday. The place is stinking with mines and booby traps. At night I go into Bn. H.Q. to act as Rep. there, but I am relieved tomorrow morning – and I <u>must</u> go into Nijmegen and find the F.D.S. as my foot is giving me 7 kinds of hell these days. Did I mention Chas Jones is doing B.C. while R/T acts as 2 i/c? Sandy Leslie gave me 4 smashing pork chops yesterday.

29 November

Nothing to report except mud and yesterday another day of torrential rain. I was caught the other side of Nijmegen and had 3 successive punctures in the Jeep so I had to return in a borrowed open one quite late. Found some relatives of friends from England and had my foot dressed by a 50 Div. A.D.S. Got a grand mail two nights ago. 2 from P., one from Sandy, one from G. and one from N.Y. Also a good parcel from N.Y. yesterday. Sandy Leslie and Jimmy Fry are coming to dinner – at least I hope they are but Charles suddenly says I may have to go to Bn. tonight which is as usual unfair as I've done far more time up there than anybody else. He himself has done one night so far. I also have to attend a mine demonstration this afternoon at Brigade. I was hoping to have a bath today but this and a long nattering visit from the B.C. spoiled it, and this afternoon the demonstration. Damn Damn & Damn. I hope it'll be a quick one then maybe I can get back in time for a bath.

30 November

2215, at Bn. H.Q.: Magnificent party last night. Gavigan surpassed himself, and produced lovely soup, pork chops, roast potatoes, peas and apple sauce, roast chicken and for 'arters' tinned plums and cream. Then we had coffee and American fruit cake. A royal spread and we had a table cloth and china and everything. A most enjoyable evening. We now have an emergency exit called Exercise Deluge in case of enemy flooding. I hate to think of the shambles. Bad news: Joe Wright who'd been selected to go to England (he was D Coy. Comd.) and Charles Munro were both killed by V2 in Antwerp. Donald Beale and Sandy Leslie are both majors now. The latter has invited me to dinner on Saturday night. Wrote today to G., Bé, Sandy and Judy and someone else – I can't remember whom. Also started 10 pages to C. tonight which I'll finish tomorrow. There is mail at the Bty. tonight but I don't know whether there's one for me. 1 Dec. tomorrow – my god how the past year has gone – so much in it, so many killed or wounded – such changes of scenery. I wish it were over. Very wet still here with the water slowly but surely rising each day. Deluge? Findlay goes on compassionate leave to England on the 3rd. Great envy all round.

Incidentally I did my B. & A. yesterday after the demonstration which was not particularly impressive. But what can you do against a diabolical little contrivance like a Schumine?

1 December

2055, Bn. H.Q. now at Doodewaard: More bad news today. Gordon Smith Cunningham ambushed and captured in Opheusden. The Bn. has now moved up into there – two companies i.e., and we are putting an O.P. in there tomorrow. Five chaps had legs or feet removed by schumines when A Coy. moved in this evening. Finished my letter – 20 pages – to C. and sent Bé's kids a cheque for Xmas. I am wondering if I'll have to establish the O.P. tomorrow and I do hope not as I'm invited to dinner with Sandy Leslie tomorrow evening. He is now a Major. Chalky White the Sigs. officer is a captain. The water is still rising steadily and large portions of the road are now under water – in places about 6 inches deep. Letter from C. this morning.

2 December

1600, gunline: Miserable day; overcast and cold with a cutting wind and intermittent rain. Everything as regards the O.P. went as I'd hoped and I took Stewart up there at 0730 over the roads now 9 inches deep in places for big stretches. Got him established in one of the usual semi-pranged houses and went back in and got breakfast about 10. Tonight – god, I suddenly realised it's Saturday – I'm going up to have dinner with Sandy Leslie – pipers and all.

I'm looking forward to it; a roast suckling pig is to feature on the menu. Wrote to Dorothy this afternoon and Happy fell into a dyke but swam most proficiently out. Amusing incident yesterday. Gavigan, all tarted up for Nijmegen, yelled out 'Smithy' and up trotted Smith and carried Gavigan piggyback all the way to the truck to keep his shoes clean.

4 December

a.m.: Days of flap and frayed tempers. Yesterday I was given half an hour to get a battery harbour party ready and go to Mill, about 26 miles from here and south of the river, to recce new areas in case we are flooded out. It was needless to say raining hard. When we got there the area was already occupied (by a Canadian Mobile Laundry!) and quite impossible, so having reported this I was given exactly half an hour to recce another before darkness. This I just managed – having been told in the meantime that the Regt. was on the move – when we were told to come back in pitch darkness and slashing rain, and we all arrived back browned off and very wet. This morning we are having one of those maybe-we-shall-maybe-we-shan't days so typical of our completely inefficient R.H.Q. It is raining again and everybody is furiously winching stuff out in the mud and flood we live in. The new area is lousy and anyway occupied by somebody else. Letters from Dad, Mrs McPherson's father (had already written) and the bank yesterday – latter telling me I have apparently 21.11.7 in post war credit. Something to do with Income Tax I understand. It is now 1.30 exactly half an hour after we were told we were to move.

5 December

Quiet (cold) day doing maintenance, painting guns, and arranging various other domestic details. Current topics:

1. Home leave which starts on 1 Jan.
2. How long we'll be here (general trend of rumour is that it may be for some little while).

I am due for the next Antwerp vacancy which may be this month. Bill Carney was due back last night but hasn't yet appeared. Wrote tonight home, Bank, Joan-Mary and Mrs McPherson. Last night to C. There is mail tonight but I don't yet know whom for. I see I've not mentioned the journey here which went more or less according to plan, and everybody is now reasonably comfortably billeted. In our farm we've given the farmer tomorrow's chocolate ration (21 bars) for his ten children, it being St Nicholas, the dutch Xmas. In return we get milk and a few eggs and quite a bit of good will. At first he was inclined to be a bit cold, but as is nearly always the case in Holland, the people have accepted us. I don't really like to dwell too much on home leave. It's one of those impossibly good things

one hardly dares imagine. And first in any case one has to survive. Took Happy
for a walk on his lead today which he seemed to enjoy. He is really a most
amusing dog and is growing very handsome and not unintelligent. Winter
clothing is coming in much better now, also tentage. Particularly gumboots
(reconditioned) and leather jerkins. Letters tonight from C. and the bank.

7 December

Nothing much disturbs us now except cleaning and painting guns, truck
inspections etc. and wondering if we'll be back in the line before Xmas; also the
prospects of home leave in the New Year. I've written a large number of letters in
the last day or two, but received none. More rain last night and today. Alan
Moorehead reports in the *Daily Express* that war-correspondents are becoming
unpopular and 'received here and there with cynical laughter.' Too true. Bloody
Court of Inquiry of which I'm to be President any time I fix, and a Court Martial
(of the despicable gunner who fled near the River Dives) on the 9th at which
I'm a witness. I hope to go to the A.D.S. at Nijmegen and have my foot dressed.
In the last 2 or 3 weeks I've attended to every damn detail that's come into
this battery. Ate a very tough chicken with Steve last night, and some very
tender pig today.

8 December

The day after tomorrow I am to go on a four day leave to Antwerp. I don't
particularly want to go, chiefly because I've not laid on to go with any of my
friends – at least I had more or less arranged to go with the Adjutant or I.O. of
the 5 B.W. but I don't know when they'll be going now. However I may meet
them. Still it will be rather pleasant to have a hot bath and sleep in a real bed.
Also I'll be able to buy a few presents. Recent moan: having to pay £4.10 for an
'officers mess' Radio – listened to by H.Q. officers about 90% of the time.
Unpleasant job tonight sending a bombardier and gunner away to the Infantry.
Usual interview wanting to know 'why ME.' Party at 491 last night when we all
got vaguely drunk and sang songs from Ball of Kirriemuir to Hark the Herald
Angels Sing. (Largely provoked by absence of Wagstaff.) No mail yesterday or
today. Damn. Today's 'bag' from the other side of the flood included a pig,
4 chickens, 3 geese and two turkeys. Didn't get to the A.D.S. and my foot has
started to hurt again. View leave with less relish each minute.

9 December

1940: Woke up with awful gippy tummy and have felt like death all day. Not
going on leave tomorrow after all. Letters from C. and Dorothy. Wrote to C. Going
to bed now.

11 December

This afternoon the order came in 'Prepare for a quick move,' and the harbour parties did actually leave, but came back with the information that the area had already been allotted to somebody else so the move is probably off for 2 days.

Letters from C. and Joan yesterday, otherwise not much to report except that Happy had his operation yesterday and behaved quite well. He's now recovering quite well and so am I. I am likely to get Antwerp leave on the 15th. Wrote to C. last night, also Admiral Cochrane, Hylda and Donald, and June and Godfrey.

13 December

1930, 's Hertogenbosch: Two pretty bloody days. Yesterday we moved after the usual order and counter order in a blinding rainstorm to Helvoit where we arrived after dark to find the whole Regt. billetted in a monastery surrounded by a sea of mud. No fires, no heating, no light, no water. Not many of us were sorry when we were once more thrown out this morning and came here where we are billeted all over the town but not too badly off. My gippy started up again very severely today and I doubt if I'll go to Antwerp if it's like this. The M.O. wants me to go to hospital but I'm doing all I can to avoid that. It makes you worse, all that evacuation.

Last night there was a short letter from C. I would write back but I feel so done up I think I'll just go to bed instead. Parcel from home on the 12th containing good things such as Condensed milk, tea, Veganin etc. Had rather a pathetic letter from Mrs McPherson saying she couldn't understand how her husband had been killed as he'd always promised to be so careful. Also a letter from Bé and one from Dorothy.

20 December

Beers, near Grave: Eventually I went on leave on the 15th being partially recovered from my gippy. I can't say I enjoyed my leave. All these leave towns are the same; a mass of sex-starved officers and men with little to console them and a good chance of V.D. from anything that will. So they go round drinking a lot of bad liquor at worse prices and come back with a hangover. Also there was a succession of V1 and V2 banging and crashing about the place all day long. One hit the Rex Cinema to which I was actually going but decided at the last minute to skip. Rather luckily as the casualty figures were estimated at 600 killed and 300 wounded.* They were still digging blackened corpses when I left, 3 days after the incident. Shopping was good but fabulously expensive. I bought a good selection of perfume for C., mom and Mackie my cousin, also some stockings, and a pair of little gloves for Jane for her birthday at the end of the year. I stayed at the Excelsior after one night at the Century which I didn't much like. The former is Naafi/Efi run entirely for officers

*Actually, 900 were killed in this cinema.

and really quite good. The HD officers club was also very well run and the food was first class. They had a dance the first night, to which a proportion of 'nice' Belgian girls were invited. The club and also the O.R.'s club is now closed and Antwerp is discontinued as a rest camp. I forgot to mention that the Battery S/Major is among the missing from the cinema incident.* V2 comes without any warning at all, and is I think preferable to V1 for that reason. You've either had it or you haven't. However when I got back to 's Hertogenbosch rather tired and irritable, more was to follow. We were about to move – out of our lovely billet with its charming people, and to the area from which I am writing now. The story was continued rest and training for 6 weeks. We drove about 30–40 miles in the foggy darkness and arrived at this awful area which is dirty and uncomfortable, and finally prepared to sleep. Our room in a farm contained a filthy carpet, a canary which sang discordantly, a dog, rats, and a cat which made a revolting mess by my bed. I threw the cat a good 10 yards into outer darkness and tried to sleep. It was then about 0200 and Steve began to be consumed by an obsession that he was becoming lousy. I was trying not to notice what the cat had done. Eventually we fell asleep to be woken at 10 to 3 by Charles and Stewart bearing the tidings that the brigade was moving into Belgium in the morning on account of the German counter offensive which is making unpleasantly rapid headway round Liège. We are now waiting to move about 1600 to Hasselt where we don't quite know <u>what</u> awaits us. I have to travel the 60 odd miles in a 15 cwt as my Jeep was lent to the Rest Camp for a week's duty while I was away. Butcher my Ack is also away and all my personal food was stolen from my carrier last night such as the condensed milk etc. I was saving it for Xmas, but Xmas looks like being so bloody anyway it doesn't much matter. The Bty's farewell from 's H. was tearful and amorous (as V1s flew overhead) and we'd all been invited there for Xmas Day. But now what? I think the Boche must be trying to reach the coast NW of Antwerp and cut both it and Brussels off. This would be very serious obviously, but I doubt if he'll ever manage it. He has about 18 Divisions employed it would seem. The funny thing is that Monty told some of our people quite categorically the other day that the enemy is quite incapable of mounting an offensive again. For this reason I believe this one will be held but 20 miles into Belgium on a 60 mile front is no joke. Letters on my return from Mrs R.-T., Joan (Xmas card), Debroy (d.o.) and airgraph from Buthy in Cairo, A.M.L.C. from George Long in hospital and a letter from Mom, but even today's post has brought me nothing from C. to whom I wrote from Antwerp. Also visited Georges Pouvern, a friend of Dad's while there. Why nothing from C? It's about a week since I heard anything from her and a letter from her is about the only thing which <u>would</u> cheer me up at the moment.

---

* B.S.M.'s body was found later. He was due for the first leave party.

Letters have just come in from Findlay and Dad but – hell – nothing from C. Mail <u>has</u> been bad lately. Grey miserable day and I am low in spirits. Roll on Victory! Merry Xmas! – hell's bells . . .

21 December

2115, near Louvain: 77 miles we moved last night, arriving about midnight in the icy, foggy darkness in a village near Hasselt. This morning we were told we were coming to take up positions with a view to defending Brussels and Antwerp from here. However this has since been changed and the probability is that we go to the Aachen Salient early tomorrow morning. Tonight's move of 35 miles took from 1530 – after 2000 – roads crammed and still misty. News on the situation is vague but nobody seems unduly worried. The Boche is still pushing on slowly but apparently losing momentum. However the BBC just said the official view was that the push won't be stopped by Xmas. Xmas in fact, qua Xmas, looks like being something of a flop! The men are taking all this very well and seem remarkably cheerful. If only the weather clears a bit the Air Forces should make a delightful mess of Von Rundestedt and his swine.

22 December

2200, near Maastricht: 65 miles today, the first part in rain but with a clearing sky. The attack is slowing and large portions of the 21 Army Gp. are taking over the Aachen Salient. We are alleged to be moving into action tomorrow. No mail in or out for the last day or two.

Just having a brew of coffee with Steve. Morale still good with an undercurrent of browned-off-ness.

23 December

2245, near Sittard: Moved this morning in bitter cold into action. There had been a frost last night, but there is a much harder one tonight. You can hear the guns rumbling and booming at Geilenkirchen a mile or two to the east. We are attached to 12 Corps as a sort of Agra here and may stay for a while as the northern German thrust has been halted though the southern is still progressing slowly. However their objective of Antwerp in 5 days has signally failed and <u>our</u> push – when it comes – may follow them right back and end the war quicker than we expected. Several flying bombs while we were in Belgium. Generally an atmosphere of great confidence is about, specially as Monty has been given command of all the armies north of Luxembourg.

Letter and Xmas card from C. tonight – first mail for days. Busy making arrangements to try and give the men the best Xmas possible. We all have billets here actually on the position which is a very good thing. The moon is rising.

XMAS DAY

Noon: The worst ever. We are waiting to move! Back into Belgium where the enemy is apparently penetrating around Liège. The situation is in fact pretty serious, but even on top of a hangover from last night, morale is good all round. We had Xmas dinner, a tree, and everything laid on but all that has had to be scrapped now, though we are doing our best to get the meal out by Troops. At first one couldn't believe it as we'd almost been guaranteed Xmas. Still, it's no use grumbling. Heavy frost, sunshine, and bitter cold today. 2 letters from C. last night which cheered me up a lot – also we had a good booze up and I am (almost cheerfully) resigned to whatever may happen now. This must have spoiled Xmas at home. Remembered to think of C. at noon – I wonder if she did the same. Steve has just announced that he has the 'Supreme hangover'. Am now going to serve the men with their Xmas dinner. Life is indeed real and earnest.

2030, south of Liège – Strivay: Drive of 40 miles in icy weather. Tremendous welcome in Liège where we were the first British column ever into the city. We are going to have an Xmas dinner soon.

27 December

We had an Xmas dinner after all, and all got fairly tiddly as did most of the Regt. Last night – in fact from noon yesterday – we did the same and a huge mail arrived at night; a letter from C. and a parcel containing a new lead for Happy 'from Jane'. Also letters from Bé and Donald and cigarettes from Mrs. K. – some tobacco – obviously by mistake – and a <u>huge</u> parcel from Dorothy which I haven't opened yet, but it seems to have everything on earth inside it from cigarettes to sherry. We are likely to move today into action somewhere. There isn't much news but the radio reports the Germans were 4 miles from the Meuse on Xmas day. Everybody complete with hangovers is opening parcels of food etc. and the sun is shining but it's freezing still.

Had a troop collection for the cook which realised about 60 guilders, which must have been rather a pleasant surprise for him. Ronnie Taylor – the B.C. – has been quite a revelation this Xmas as he's been more human than ever before. We've had a new officer – on Xmas day – and John is coming back to the Tp. which will be a good thing. Forgot to mention quite a number of V1s and a few ordinary bombs – only a few casualties, none in the battery.

28 December

From 0400 we had a constant procession of flying bombs droning and crashing around the neighbourhood. News is good though, telling of an American armoured attack near La Roche. No news yet of any move. Posted letters to C., Bé, Dorothy, Mrs. K. etc. yesterday and wrote two more to C. last night.

Later: Well, by some miracle we haven't moved again yet and nothing more disturbing than a few flying bombs has interrupted a quiet day. Heavy mist – fog really, outside and a promise of more snow tonight.

29 December

1100: No further movement yet. Arnhem radio has reported that 'The most dangerous German thrust to the Meuse has been blunted and thrown back 3 miles by the crack British 51st Division, famed since the African Campaign and veterans of the Normandy battles . . .' This is distinctly news to us; thank the Lord it's not true! Flying bombs still come over at regular intervals but have ceased to interest anybody very much. Final documents were completed last night in my case against B.S.M. Renow who is being removed shortly. Mail last night was parcels only and I got a pair of brown shoes from Dorothy which puzzled me as I'd asked for boots. Wrote again to C. last night and went with Chas and Bill to 491 for a drink. Waggy is on a course and the atmosphere was pleasant.

30 December

Snow. Game of Net-ball-quoits this afternoon and the officers team won a knock out competition. I scored once and Stewart got the rest. My rib – bruised in a drunken moment on boxing day – has further been dented; I can hardly breathe now! Mail: a letter from Mrs Parry but nothing from C. Hell. My jeep is still away in Antwerp. Been playing quite a lot of bridge lately. German attack halted.

31 December

My Jeep returns.

1 January 1945, New Year's Day

Waiting as usual to move – this time towards Marche. It is cold and sunny and the roads are covered with ice and frost, so that all trucks which have chains are using them. Very drunk last night, together with nearly all the other officers in the Regt. Letters from C. (from Dutch House), Sister Spencer, and Judy, and the day before from Mrs Parry. We've had a large number of flying bombs during the last day or two, some of them quite close. Findlay came back last night which was pleasing though I think it may only be a matter of time before he gets a home posting. Steve is on leave in Brussels till tomorrow. Americans are now counter attacking in strength and the Boche are, it seems, being pushed back gradually, though it's on the cards that he may have another crack before he's finally had it.

2 January

Crupet: Bloody awful column taking nearly 7 hours to cover 40 miles. Icy roads and the weather freezing viciously. We are in rather a pleasant village and living in a chateau surrounded by a moat – now entirely icebound. The tactical situation has placed the Brigade in a reserve counter attack role. Meantime we rest and train. Had fun with Bill, the B.C. and the C.O. using a ladder as a toboggan down the icy hill outside our battery area leading to R.H.Q. It was very amusing. Mail today brought a letter from G. and rather a nice letter as a matter of fact – but nothing from C. It's very hard to write this in the mess, as also it is to write intelligent letters (sent 3 – home, C., and Judy tonight) and it isn't any good going to the room I share with Steve and John as it's so damn cold you can't hold a pencil. I kept waking up last night. Tonight I shall wear my fleece trenchcoat over my pyjamas. In the mess there is an enormous fireplace on which we burn huge logs, but the room is so cold it is only warm in a relatively small circle round the fire. Happy and Max (Bill's alsatian pup) are lying in front of it wrapped round each other in a mass of paws and ears. Am reading a book by H.E. Bates called *Fair Stood the Wind for France.* Rather good.

3 January

1730: Just as we were settling mentally and physically for a bit of a stay here as guaranteed by the C.O. and everybody else, the word suddenly came over the phone 'Prepare to move at very short notice in support of 53 Div.' The usual outburst of cynical despair, ranging from mild and indiscriminate cursing of 'them' to the picture of Stewart sitting in a chair, his head in his hands, saying in a broken voice 'I feel as if I've just done 10 rounds with Joe Louis.'

We are now waiting to see if, when, how, and why. Here goes the phone – false alarm, B.S.M. My own B.S.M. Freeman came back today and I've had a strenuous day climbing all the local hills laying out anti-parachute defences. Everybody is bloody well browned off.

4 January

1815, Marche: But worse was to follow, soon afterwards a phone call came for an L.O. to go to H.Q.R.A. at Baillonville about 20 miles away, taking a relay carrier, and to collect orders. Bill and I tossed and I lost so off I set about 7.30, both wirelesses going, and out into the cold snowy night. I placed the relay and pushed on, reaching the place about 2130 in snowy sleet and thick dark-ness broken only by gunflashes. The C.O. with an advanced Recce arrived about half an hour later, and took things over. I then spent till 0300 mucking around with wireless sets etc. and with great difficulty getting a kitchen for me and my four chaps. Slept clothed till 0645 when I had a cup of tea, brewed on the Primus, and after a wash and shave went back to H.Q.R.A. for non-existent instructions.

Set off for Regt. after breakfast in a blinding snowstorm. Awful position in the open, and it has snowed all day. Managed to wheedle a (rather good) mess out of 53 Div, where I am now writing. Early bed indicated if only we don't move tonight. Have just changed soaking boots and socks and feel more civilised. A meal at 1915 will complete the process. The allied offensive is going well and a brilliant southern thrust by the Americans threatens to encircle the Germans in the tip of their western push. Two letters today. One from home and a lovely one from C. just about to leave Farnborough after a happy Xmas with Bé. I am about to write back now. Hell I'm tired. One further anecdote of the great freeze: John Clark's brylcreem froze in his hair while he slept. Steve, doubtless benighted all over Belgium, has not yet returned to base. I think it seems to be getting colder again, and the snow blankets out the landscape.

6 January

Awful blow fell just after the 9 o'clock news when – as I was gloating over the prospect of a long night's sleep – I was suddenly informed I had to go out as a rep to the H.L.I. to be there at 0700. Followed much laying on of everything, and this morning out into the icy cold with light snow falling. The roads were pure glass and the carrier slid all over the road. When I got there I found I wasn't wanted, so I came back again for breakfast. The enemy counter-attacked 53 last night, causing one battalion to give ground. He is strong and aggressive in defence of the high ground protecting the road to La Roche. Radio last night announced the participation of British tps. in current battle, adding that German radio had claimed 51 were in action.

Bill has had to go out as Rep tomorrow. Has been told it is a small scale attack. Pertinent remark by Steve: 'what do they mean – there's no such thing as a small scale attack when you yourself are involved.' Very true. Letters from C. and Bé.

7 January

On the 9th the 153 attacks to try and get some high ground at present ferociously and tenaciously defended by the 116 Panzer Div. The country is ice bound and even carriers can make no headway – it looks as though F.O.O.ing will be largely on foot – and I am F.O.O. Bad luck as the last party was a bastard too. No wonder people took to alcohol in the last war. Short letter from C. Wrote to her – my 5th this year – I am numbering them as a check. Stewart went off on leave today. Hell I'd give a lot to get home to England now. A (German) woman with a gloriously mellow voice is singing Schubert's serenade on the wireless and outside the guns crash and crash as the snow falls on the already icy road – the temp. hasn't risen above freezing point today. Bill came back in the afternoon. B.C. got a couple of ducks for supper tonight; one walked all round the mess floor quacking loudly and indignantly. C.O. was in here predicting a 'sticky party' as our right flank is exposed. I was not surprised to hear the Div. is coming up; 53 were making a pretty good bog up and they always call us in to do what others can't.

8 January

Frantic work today. Five hours recceing in deep snow and ice in the mountains where hardly a vehicle can move. Eventually found an O.P. for tomorrow's attack (if it still comes off; at present not certain) right up in the mountains in the snow etc. miles from anywhere but overlooking the village we are due to take. I am going with a Jeep and a quad with a carrying party as you can only get within about a mile of the O.P. Problems like water, cooking and bedding just have to be discussed under 'what one can do in the circs.' Not much I fear, but we have at least got bivvy tents to keep the worst off. I shan't take this with me, it all means extra to carry. But I may leave it with the Quad. Everything is now just about laid on. A few German stiffs lie almost buried by snow and a few <u>very</u> bedraggled prisoners came back looking completely browned off – and not surprising. Very heavy fall (about 2–3 inches) of snow last night and it looks like more tonight. B.C. and Bill are going with Bn. H.Q. – only Jeeps and Weasels being used – even carriers haven't a hope.

10 January

1300, Wavizy: Nightmare day yesterday. We set out at 0800 and eventually after much ditching, sliding and cursing reached our mountainous O.P. The snow was knee deep but at first, visibility was clear and we had a fine view. Later it began to snow, and we got wireless orders that the plan of attack had been changed and we were to come down and make for here. It took us a good time to do this, but we did finally reach Verdenne, the start point – full of knocked out Panther tanks and a few bodies, and at this point my wireless went dis. The main axis was not a road at all; it was a path bulldozed through the hills and valleys, full of snow and ice. On the right a few German tanks threw high velocity shells about the place. Some miles on I ran clean out of oil. I managed to get some more. Later I ran nearly out of water after boiling up several times. Took 40 minutes to get more water and by then night had fallen though the artificial moonlight cast a glow over the snowy wilderness and dark patches of Christmas trees. We pushed on; twice we got ditched, and twenty times nearly ditched. I was driving (the Jeep) and had Butcher and Allen with me. We still hadn't eaten or brewed since 0730. The track was bloodier every minute. We reached here about 2200 and found all the wirelesses dis. too. By borrowing a power unit, mine got through. Then Ronnie's half track turned up, and soon after midnight we had a meal – the first for 17 hours. Bill had to go out to a nearby hill at first light in case of a Panzer attack, but nothing came off and he's in now. The Bn. is waiting to enter La Roche to which we've sent patrols, and we expect to move this afternoon. Charles has suddenly gone to England on a course which shows how one's fortunes can change from day to day. Last night's sleep was very blissful though rather short as we got up at 0730. There are a good many problems attached to this winter warfare. For example it isn't possible to carry any water as it freezes in the can. Even your bedding roll won't unroll as it freezes hard in the vehicle. Vehicles just won't move without chains, and one false move and you're in the ditch. Touching metal is almost painful.

14 January

1330, Hubermont (Bastogne front): We spent the 11th at Wavizy and in the night of the 11th got orders to advance on the 12th – this being the objective. Up at 0500 and the advance began, in the hilly roads and tracks beyond ruined La Roche. Snow was falling and it was very cold. There were a lot of mines and we soon lost a Recce armoured car. Ronnie and I were in Jeep O.P.s, Steve being with main Bn. H.Q., myself being with A Coy. forward. Some shelling in the morning but during the afternoon we ran up against a detachment of 2 Panther tanks, 140 men and spandaus and a 2 in. mortar team. Some panic as our own tanks were held up further back. I was on foot myself. The 3 tanks who came up headed by my Jeep were not a success. One had a jammed gun and engine failure; another was brewed up, and the third could not get to us. All this time we were getting a pleasant reception from over the way. I managed to get some orders back lying under my jeep with A.P. shells whizzing over the top and a few bursts of m.g. fire. Very unpleasant. I got in some shelling, both 25 pds. and medium, which seemed to quieten things down. We had about 7 wounded, and one chap we had to leave out wounded, died. So there we were pinned down and B Coy. went round. Nothing to eat since 0600 and we got nothing till next 0300. It was bitterly cold – 32 degrees of frost, and some people collapsed. Everybody's feet were agony and our teeth chattered and we shivered violently in the bitter cold. Not a building in sight. About 0530 we reached the farm area which had been holding us up and advanced again soon after dawn. The C.O. was so tired he went to sleep talking to David Macintyre the adjutant.

At this village we met the tanks again in the village on the ridge beyond. They knocked out one of our S.P.s (killing 3 and wounding one) and three or four Shermans which blazed in the snow. From the left flank two more tanks – one a Tiger – shelled us incessantly. There were more casualties, and Bill Fraser, the Pioneer officer, was killed by a splinter in the belly. My O.P. was (and is) in the attic of a small house. Excellent view. Eventually I found the Panthers and got a medium Regt. on them – or rather on one of them. Got some extremely close rounds – one seemed almost a direct hit, and the tank scurried away. Enemy continued to shell the village until after dark when 1 Gordons went through us, and soon after 8 I went to sleep, absolutely all in. So was Steve and also Ronnie. Agonising chilblains and twinges of rheumatism. Steve had a hot time when he got in here, missing an enemy half track by 50 yards! Last night he said he wouldn't take a troop if they put a pip <u>and</u> a crown in with it! Up about 0800 today and have been manning, but apart from fleets of Forts above (one shot down nearby) not much to see on the snowbound landscape except the bursts of shells on the left, where the Americans are advancing. The C.O. came up and said (1) we have met the yanks coming up from Bastogne (2) the Div. is getting a fortnight's rest. This, I think, has been the hardest battle I've ever seen, conditions being appalling. Had my first wash and shave for 3 days today and was horrified by my face in the mirror!

No mail since the 9th from C. Ronnie's really been excellent. He should get an M.C. soon.

15 January

Same place: Rested yesterday and went with the C.O. to where I shelled my tank. Found about a dozen rounds within 100 yards, and one actually 4 yards away. Very pleasing – the C.O. tickled pink. Ronnie left this a.m., also my carrier, and I've been with B Coy. most of the day. I'm staying here for the moment as Rep. but the Bn. expects to leave any day for a fortnight's rest; us too I hope. No mail; I hope today will bring some. And I also haven't written to C. since the 8th. Shall try and do so today. Found I inflicted casualties – dead and wounded – on the people who held up A Coy. (from civilian source). Also that the force was 1 Panther and 2 S.P. guns – one of which we captured intact in this village. Terrific frost this a.m. – steering frozen, even fanbelts and brake drums. The snow is covered with tiny droplets like white coffee sugar, but it is lovely weather out – very crisp and pleasant. The sun on the snow makes you quite blind when you come indoors again. Everybody in great form as they always are after a successful action – and there's no doubt the Div. has acquired considerable merit by this latest attack. I shan't forget for a long time the red blood on the white snow, and the tanks splattered with blood where the A.P. shot had riddled them. Or the night of agonising cold and fear with the battle loud and angry on all sides as 'ignorant armies clashed by night' – the numbness and pain of the feet, the drenching tiredness, the twinges of fear, and the night sky lit by flashes, and the whistle of shells nearby as one crouched in the snowy ditch, soaked, and tired beyond belief.

16 January

Petit-Halleoux, Bty Posn: Back again this morning. Small village and rather uncomfortable, but at least covered, though no fires alas. Have put Allen in for a M.M. and Butch for a mention. More or less on Ronnie's suggestion. He is in for an M.C. I am almost sure. Letter from C. this morning. I wrote No. 7 to her yesterday and No. 8 today.

1830: Recce parties – or rather harbour parties – leave tomorrow for the Herenthals area where we are allegedly to have a fortnight's rest. After that another (big) operation seems to be in the wind. A V1 just went over making the devil of a row on the wireless set, which is the first time I remember hearing this. I'm afraid Happy is going to have to be shot as his stomach has gone septic.

17 January

2040, Rumpst, near Lierre: Moved off in Ronnie's jeep this morning at 0730, after his becoming 2 i/c last night had put Bill in command of the Bty. and myself Bty. Captain. K2 (my temporary Jeep) followed us out, and the Recce party followed half an hour behind. Very cold and light snow falling, and it took us about 5 hours to cover 120 miles to Lierre. Saw Alistair C. there. We then mucked about from suburb to suburb and I eventually got most of the billeting done but I'll have all tomorrow to get it done anyway, as the Regt. won't arrive till at least late tomorrow evening. The country is flat again here – a tremendous contrast after the snowy hills of the Ardennes with their enormous pine trees and winding roads. It is much warmer here too, though tonight there's a frost. One buzzbomb cut out nearby tonight and landed with a loud bang not far away. My teeth are very bad. I simply MUST go to a dentist while I'm here.

19 January

2055: The Regiment arrived in a 'shambolic' state, the last portion of the battery arriving at about 0400 today. Eleven vehicles were missing but I think they're all in by now. Findlay has gone sick to hospital and I'm having persistent and nagging toothache which is bloody. Cold blizzardy weather with a gusty high wind. Did all the billeting forms today.

Awfully good mail – 3 letters from C. and a parcel, and one from Dorothy. I am doing some writing tonight if I can concentrate – toothache making this rather difficult. Sandy Kinnaird returned.

20 January

p.m.: Damn and blast and bloody everything! Prepare to move – to Buxtel – miles and miles and miles away. On top of this I am just waiting to go to the dentist for the second time today, as the filling he put in has failed to stop the aching.

Everything else is wrong too. My primus essential part is lost, I am changing battledresses – oh everything is all to hell. I'm hoping to get a bath when I get back from the dentist – I'm dreading the visit incredibly – I <u>hate</u> having teeth pulled out.

2045: Went off after writing the above in a mood of black despair, and had my offending tooth plucked out, to the accompaniment of 4 injections. Very sore afterwards but now thank god the pain has ceased, though there are so many more to be stopped or pulled out. When I got back I had a bath in a canvas bucket and changed all my clothes, and when I got down stairs blessings on all, the harbour parties suddenly got stand down on tomorrow. I shall write a short letter to Clare and then go to bed.

21 January

2200, 's Hertogenbosch: Last night, soon after going to bed with what seemed every tooth in my mouth aching, news came that harbour parties <u>were</u> after all wanted this morning. The usual story of order counter order etc. We set off this morning in deep snow and heavy fog at 0900 and were 2 hours late at Turnhout where we were redirected to Helvont. I had a rotten night. My mouth ached and ached and was still aching this morning . . . I sat up for hours with Veganin and a small flask of whisky. I don't know if it's after effects or what but it's wearing me to a shadow. After dealing with billets – which are <u>very</u> poor – at Helvont, I came with Laurence Geller to our old friends (Steve's and mine) here in den Bosch, where we are going to sleep the night. Tomorrow I shall try and go to the dentist again. The Regt. is not apparently moving till Tuesday – if this is the case we'll probably stay here tomorrow night too. Nobody quite knows what's in the wind. The Russians, doing their steady 25 miles a day, are now a little over 200 miles from Berlin. It's magnificent. Perhaps they'll win the war <u>for</u> us. Got a marvellous welcome here where we were very far from forgotten. Rather pleasing.

22 January

Had quite a good dope-induced sleep till about half past six this morning. A few V1s still growl over loudly but I only heard one in the night. I woke with toothache and went to the dentist this morning at the 8 Canadian General Hospital. The dentist – a small voluble French Canadian – failed to find anything which could be causing the ache other than general chill (in particular the feet) caught in the Ardennes. He gave me a good whack of codeine tablets to keep the pain away. But I think there is already a slight improvement; I've only had 4 tablets all day today. The battery arrives tomorrow – I should think in the late afternoon. Cold today and the Jeep froze, but I got it into a

Canadian L.A.D. and in addition to thawing it they filled it with anti-freeze mixture which is going to be useful. Funnily enough, a few days before I got here, they'd seen Mom's name in Vrij Nederland as organiser of the bazaar in London which brought in £1650 for the Dutch Relief Fund. They guessed who she was. As usual we've given the people of the house here heaps of Buck from sweets and chocolate and cigarettes to food. Luckily B.S.M. Nicoll managed a big ration scoop today so we've given them a great boxful of everything. Great pleasure all round; we've eaten all our meals here with them. Wrote letter No. 12 to C.

23 January

Helvont: Came back here in the afternoon. It's very cold. The bty arrived soon after dark; i.e. that part of the battery which arrived as we've so much off the road at the moment. Already the C.P.O. has to go on recce near Grave tomorrow. How soon do we go into action? Nobody knows; everything is Top Secret at the moment but it appears to be some sort of large scale deception movement. Ronnie has gone to hospital, apparently for a small nose operation. Bad, this. Excellent mail of delayed letters. One from Dad, one from C., both dated 10 Jan. and one from New York dated 13 Jan. – amazingly quick. Have written, and am going to write no. 13 to C. tonight. Also my new diary – a duplicate of this – arrived tonight. My toothache is much better today – I've only taken two Codeine tablets all day. A bottle of whisky and a bottle of gin each has arrived – very welcome in this weather. The thermos I bought in Malines has broken before ever being used, and Findlay has lost the top cone of my precious primus, thereby rendering it unserviceable. Maddening! Poor Happy has been shot. Poor Happy . . .

25 January

0915: Yesterday was fairly inactive. Laurence went on his (highly secret) recce yesterday with all signs covered on men and vehicles and officers only to see the place. He isn't even allowed to tell <u>us</u> anything. Conjecture (strictly forbidden by Div. orders) speaks of an attack in a week or two supported by 1000 guns, and heavily camouflaged dumping begins in a few days. Apparently we have once more lost the toss and are completely in the open – tents will again be the order of the day. Bloody. Steve and I went to our old friends the Troupins in 's Hertogenbosch and had a very pleasant evening.

Am going to Boxtel this morning to get money from the field cashier. We are supposed (I mention this purely formally) to be staying here for a fortnight or so which may mean anything or nothing but in any case it looks as though something big is in the wind. Very big.

26 January

p.m.: Uneventful day. the V1s continue to grind over us, and the night temperature is about 10 °F. Parcel from C. yesterday with more notepaper and an outfit for repairing and re-flinting my lighter. Have written to George Long and also Nos. 15 and 16 to C. Tomorrow I have to go to a lecture at Boxtel on V.T. fuses, our new and highly secret fuse which explodes in the proximity of a solid object. Incidentally Debroy should be at Boxtel in a day or two as 30 Corps H.Q. is there. At present he is away doing (of all things) A.D.C. to the C.C.R.A. who is temporarily commanding 43 Div. Steve and I are going to the Troupins this evening. The farmer's wife here has 5 kids, the youngest of which is 14 days old. They are actually small fiends in human guise and rush shrieking about the house all day long in noisy clogs. This room has 6 doors and a stone floor and is constantly exposed to piercing draughts left by these small demons. Also the fire is dis. and it is most <u>bloodily</u> cold. Hope there's some mail today anyway.

28 January

A couple of bad days for D Troop for when I came back on the evening of 26th I found that the George Truck had been burned out complete, also all cookhouse equipment. And the next day came a report that my carrier on the road at Poppel had also been burned to a cinder. So that's the majority of my troop equipment gone with the wind. Went to the first lecture at Boxtel; most interesting. Unfortunately the Germans have already captured the fuse from the Americans in the Ardennes. But it is said it will take him at least a year (the Americans say two) to copy it. I sincerely hope so. Went with Steve to the Troupins again last night. It's grand going there – just like home and we are certainly part of the family by now. Heavy snow the last two days and again today. No mail for two days – the last I got was two nights ago with letters from Judy and Joan. The demon-children are still as shocking as ever, and nearly drive us crazy. Stewart Watts came back yesterday and is still slowly recovering from the delights of leave. I think I have now discovered all I need about the new attack (now known as the 'battle to end the war . . .') but for security reasons – just in case I do lose this diary – I'll put nothing in here. However it looks like being a pretty considerable job.

30 January

The days crawl reasonably uneventfully by – uneventfully is O.K. with me as the weather is appalling with snow and ice and very sharp winds. Letter from C. the day before yesterday. I get very curious dreams these nights; nearly always about some strange and violent battle, though two nights ago I dreamt I was part of a Lancaster crew and we got a direct hit from a V1. I remember seeing the darn thing swoop down on us with its flaming tail! (We are getting plenty of V1s over us here. Last night about midnight, quite the lowest and loudest one I've heard came hurtling over the rooftops.) Then last night I dreamed I was first a diving champion – and eventually I dived down an enormous flight of stairs onto a carpet. And later I was doing an exhibition dance with my mother. Went to the Troupins again last night which was Steve's birthday, and they gave him presents which was awfully nice and unexpected of them. The amazing Russians, now within 95 miles of Berlin, continue to press on. If our own offensive is a success (and the withdrawal of troops from West to East should help) the end of the war may come much sooner than any of us could have hoped when Rundstedt stormed into the Ardennes 6 weeks ago. There isn't much to enter in here nowadays as very little is going on to outward view. In fact of course quite a lot is happening in the way of dumping ammo. etc. but it is all being done under a curtain of very great security. As we are going into a Canadian area, all HD signs have been removed by recce parties and so on, and many of the guns which will take part are only moving in the night before things start. I believe the Div. Comd. is holding a conference on Wednesday. From that point on, things usually have a habit of happening.

31 January

Worse perhaps even than the numbing snow, now comes the rain – slashing down and turning the snow carpet into muddy brown and green fields. Driving on the roads last night was damn dangerous as they were nothing but sheet ice and the car shot all over the road as soon as one touched the accelerator let alone the brakes. A lot of replacements for stores lost in the fire have started coming in including all the wireless sets – five to be precise. No mail from C. yesterday or today; I've an uneasy feeling something is wrong, that she's ill or something. I wrote no. 19 away today. Teeth have started giving me hell again. Tomorrow I am definitely going to the dentist.

1 February

And go I did. Chiefly because after getting back and going to bed last night I couldn't go to sleep till about 0345 on account of the most devilish pain from a big top tooth. Codeine and whisky eventually did the trick (assisted by the *Reader's Digest*!). But I woke up with a tooth which was quite untouchable even by the tongue. Therefore no breakfast. Anyway off I went in the Jeep, was duly examined by one of our own (very nice) dentists and having watched a 128 officer have one of his pulled out (by which time my anaesthetic had worked) into the chair and out the damn thing came. The relief from pain was heavenly. What I hate is the preliminary test for numbness when the dentist shoves a pointed probe a good 1/4 inch into the gums and although it doesn't hurt you know it's going right in – it makes me feel rather sick. Masses of traffic on the road – i.e. the main road to Nijmegen; Churchill tanks, Ducks, guns, everything. And I rather wonder if the Germans have cottoned on as we are getting many more V1s, some of them flying very low, and others exploding fairly near; we had one 200 yards from the fitters shop this morning. They really are most unpleasant things.

Stewart is back from a night at Lierre and has fetched me a Thermos – a most useful article. Apparently the man who owns the shop where he got it, said he'd sold 600 in the last fortnight so the cold weather helped somebody anyway. Parcel mail only yesterday, in which I was not included.

Ronnie Taylor is still in hospital where he's been having an operation for Antrum trouble, but is going on a course and leave first to England and doesn't expect to be back until 5 March. Lucky sod! Meanwhile Bill French, a 'floating' major from 59 Agra who came to the Regt. recently as a replacement for such occasions, is coming to us. He's a very nice chap – I went with him to that V.T. fuse lecture the other day. He's now commanded both the other batteries and been 2nd i/c as well, so he should be getting to know the Regt. pretty well. I'd rather hoped to have seen Debroy by now, but he's not turned up. I hope he does, it's as good an opportunity as we'll get.

2 February

Good night's sleep last night thank god and today 3 letters – one from C., one from Dorothy and one from Roger Andrews (now a major at Staff College in Haifa). Gale with rain and blustering rain with the thaw turning everything to a sea of sticky mud. Had two inoculations – one in each arm – TetTox and typhus this morning. Arms still rather sore. Am going to see the Troupins this evening but coming in early.

3 February

We had a particularly trying journey back last night; first the Jeep would not go properly owing to a short circuit in the coil, and when (about midnight) we did finally get onto the road there was a whole brigade of Churchill tanks coming the other way, with no lights. But the final blow came when we got in to discover the Regt. is moving today or rather by darkness tonight with no lights to the area East of Grave Bridge – completely in the open where we shall be for about 5 or 6 days before the battle starts. All Div. signs to be removed from selves and vehicles. I have as yet no replacement for my carrier, of course, nor quite a lot of other articles, among which, incidentally, is my tin hat. However I didn't have that for the Ardennes battle either and didn't particularly miss it. But it is something of a moral support if nothing else. Incidentally it was rather a good one of the light variety which I certainly won't acquire again. There is utter secrecy about this op. which it is said will take about 2 months and should finish the war for good. Presumably the attack will take place along the entire Western Front and should by all accounts be about the biggest build up of the war – anyway in the Western theatre. Bill Carney is going on leave on the 12th so I hope he doesn't even have to start the battle as it would be a bloody prospect with leave so near. On the other hand it's going to mean that I, as Senior Tp. Comd. carry the greater burden of the O.P. work, specially as I don't think Stuart will be terribly good. Oh hell – there is little enough to look forward to these days. Only the prospect of a great battle in bloody conditions and (it is said) with no cover for at least the first 20 miles of our advance. After that presumably booby trapped houses. Security or not, it is easy to see that everything we've got is being mustered for this great final (we hope) blow. In a way I shall be glad when it does start, for though battle is fearful and full of its own sort of terror, it is worse to lie in bed 2 nights – and then one night – before; thinking of the awful wounds we may get, of the hideous crashing of enemy shells and mortars, the singing bullets – and ahead in the darkness the hostile darkness and the enemy – and the ground teeming with every sort of devilish mine. And you lie there sweating, your brain ticking over feverishly and you just can't sleep and you think oh God let it start, then at least it will finish . . . However, once in battle I am not particularly worried by such things. The danger is tangible. One crouches cringing from splinters and bullets – but there it is – if you're hit you're hit and you never think you will be anyway. Funny how you don't. However enough speculation. I must go away and work.

2115, same night: We sit in the mess waiting to leave – at 2315. The night is dark but not too cold. Certain details of the forthcoming operation have been given. We seem to be playing a fairly important part with the 5 B.W. having some particularly sticky objective which (it <u>would</u>) 'will make an absolutely perfect O.P.' A letter from C., also one from Bé and 200 cigarettes from Dad. Have sent no. 21 to C. this evening.

Great increase in German night fighter activity lately but as I believe I mentioned earlier, convoys all travel in full darkness, even the leader only being allowed sidelights.

Berlin suffered a tremendous raid by 1000 Flying Forts today; the fighter escort flew on to the Oder where they could see the Germans firing at the Russians who have now reached the river.

4 February

Mook, near Grave: Awful move all last night in severe cold with no lights. Started badly by getting several trucks bogged at the S.P. so I started one and a half hours late – ie. at 0300. Got an awful headache during the night and arrived shortly before dawn. Then went round and supervised the camouflage by first light. It started to rain and has been doing so ever since. My spare carrier has also given up the ghost now – so they'll have to get a move on for the next battle which incidentally is going to be fought in Jeeps. We are also going to use the pipes – which will I believe be the first time since Alamein – by our brigade anyway. Everybody is in the open here but the officers are not too bad, being in a loft of the station master's house. We are all in here for sleeping and eating but it could be so infinitely worse.

5 February

Today we have been briefed. Roughly we and the Americans are pinching out the Ruhr and it is described as being the biggest thing the Army has ever done, 'even bigger' as Guy Lambert the acting C.O. said 'than Alamein, as Monty is being reluctantly forced to admit.' 1,000 guns are in support and god knows how many planes etc. Part of the operation order reads 'On the night of D D + 1 —— [names of five towns] to be destroyed.' It is said that if all goes well, this should finish the war in about two months. A tremendous pile up of stuff is taking place in this area, tanks and guns everywhere, but everything very carefully hidden and heavily camouflaged. However it is fairly obvious by now that the Boche has got wind of something as he sends so many recce planes and also we've had orders to expect a raid tonight. Mail today was one letter from Sheila H. who told me she's sending cigarettes, which is really rather nice of her. No sign of a replacement for my carrier so I'm using Charlie troop's – not a very good one but better than nothing I suppose; and anyway we're in Jeep O.P.s. Incidentally, Stuart Watts is doing C Tp. O.P., but I am doing F.O.O. for the first phase anyway.

6 February

2230: Today we have spent preparing everything for D day – 8 Feb. It is amazing how much one has to do – specially with the hundreds of maps one always receives before an operation of this magnitude. This op. is known as 'Veritable'. I can't quite decide in my own mind how stiff enemy opposition is going to be, but somehow I don't see how the boche can gather <u>very</u> much armour anyway, having lost so much in the Ardennes, and transferring stuff hastily to the Eastern Front. However we shall see soon enough. No mail today – so nothing from C. – but I sent no. 24 off to her today. Incidentally I don't think I mentioned that our infantry have priority for houses which involves in this case turning out some of a searchlight unit in whose billet we are ourselves billeted. Great indignation among the searchlights and officers heard exclaiming 'After all <u>we're</u> an operational unit'! Steve has a book in which he collects all such sayings under the title of 'Poor Buggers.' Classic is the R.A.S.C. officer who bought a leather jerkin at the officers' shop as it was so cold going to work in the tram of a morning. We got this one in Belgium so it was fairly well received. Another was the Staff Sgt. in 's Hertogenbosch who went home bomb-happy – from V1s! A V1 came over today flying very low – I think it was the best view I've had of one. We join the Black Watch tomorrow. Col. Bill is away and George Dunn the 2 i/c is commanding. Incidentally, Bill French, our acting B.C. is a very nice chap and most easy to get on with. Guy Lambert is commanding the Regt. – the C.O. being on blighty leave. Leave among senior officers is inclined to be a bit of a racket – but after all they bear the major responsibility so I for one don't grudge them it. Much noise of tanks rolling up tonight. Security seems more or less to have been eased up on now; presumably it is impossible to hide our intentions any longer. The U.S. 9th Army starts an offensive on D + 2. The 1st and 3rd are already pushing forward into the Siegfried line and there is just a breath of a suggestion that the boche is pulling back over the Rhine. However I treat this with considerable reserve.

7 February

2230, Beers: A little time ago the heavies went over and in the distance we saw the flashes and flares and the pink sky as one of the towns I mentioned was destroyed. I only hope the weather holds for tomorrow. Today it has rained heavily and tonight is still patchy. Final arrangements today and we joined 'the Watch' this afternoon. I have two jeeps for this job and am with A Coy. where I now am, sleeping on a kitchen floor. I was greeted by Eric Matthew the Coy. Comd. with 'Oh good, I hoped it'd be you', which is a pleasant greeting. Had dinner and a good bit to drink with Sandy at B Coy. and attended a final O Gp. at 2000. We _have_ to get on, whatever the state of ground or weather, even if we can't get tank support. Messages from Monty and the Army Commander – 'Knock out blow', 'final battle', 'good hunting' etc. etc. – all beginning to get a little stale now. Russians over the Oder and going great guns, and the big 3 are in conference. I don't know when I'll enter this up again as I'm not taking it forward with me, but leaving it with Stewart Watts. We start at the respectable hour of 0945. No sense of the greatness of the hour – or wondering what will happen; even the largest battles are becoming routine it seems. We hope to pick up mail en route for the F.U.P. and F.A.A. (Forward Assembly Area) tomorrow morning. There goes 11 o'clock. I must sleep – anyway till 0500 when 1000 guns play the opening bars of the coming symphony of battle.

In case anything should happen . . .

[here faint pencil markings are covered with the words:
'DULY RUBBED OUT 20 FEB']

. . . till it's safe to rub this out again.

10 February

p.m. Schielberg (on the Maas): The story so far:

Five o'clock on D day – and nearly every window in Beers was well and truly broken by the sudden crash of gunfire. It has been going on ever since. Well, we pushed on up the axis as planned, in bad weather – rain and cold – and didn't get up to the Reichswald forest till dusk, the 5/7 Gordons having had quite some difficulty. The track was appalling tho' nothing like as bad as it was to become. Had several nearish things from mortars and spandaus which have been particularly active in this show so far. I was behind A Coy. and eventually we took all our objectives by about 2300. The arty. support was really good, and the concentrations were enormous and very effective. Nothing to eat all D day and by night time I was too tired to take anything but some Self Heating (self propelled everybody calls it) soup. Some mail met us on our way up, mine being a letter from C., one from Dad, one from Ronnie Taylor and one from the bank. Also a very useful parcel from C. with Trentabs and Dettol Ointment, and a parcel from Norman Carter containing some new boots. At night the forest was damned uncanny by the artificial moonlight, with crashes and crumps and the whole skyline aflame with gunflashes, and bullets whizzing about the place from pockets of enemy holding out. We got to a Jerry strongpoint first and collected some useful items: 2 pairs of binoculars for 'Butch', a small hurricane, a machine pistol for me, and 2 automatics, one of which I gave to Bill French. Also oddments. The Churchills were up with us doing valuable work demoralising the Boche who was in no sort of state at all being quite bomb happy after our guns had finished with him. We got some intermittent sleep; it was raining. In the morning, George Dunn decided to attack southwards towards the Maas and try and cut the Gennep road. I was F.O.O. again. Had a hell of a job getting to the S.P., only managing after a weasel had towed me there – shearing my brakes as it did so, so I had no brakes. We had to attack over 2½ thousand yards of open country, quite flat with our left flank open, and the part where I had to leave the forest over a little bridge was heavily mortared by the boche. After the infantry went up under smoke from us and heavy medium shoot from 10 Regts, I took my brakeless jeep up the road. It was a bad moment waiting there but on we went flat out, closely followed and preceded by Spandau bullets from our right flank. They whistled overhead and at the road in front, but we got there and reached C Coy. Some time later they attacked for which I provided an H.E. stonk followed by a really most effective smoke screen. I went with the Coy. Comd. (Graham Pilcher) and Butch drove the jeep. We got there – quite good shooting at houses with the Piat gun was a feature – and I established an O.P. in the church steeple which I'd persuaded the Piat to spare! Excellent view and I got some grand shooting on the Maas bank where we got about 100 Germans all retreating from 1 Gordons on our right. We were by then right behind them. The shells broke up what looked like a possible counter attack and then good old B Coy. came up to the road – a hundred yards in front of me. We were again mortared and machine gunned. So far nothing to eat since breakfast of tea and bread and jam but had some bacon at 1600. Icy wind in the church tower. At dark I came in and joined Sandy Leslie in a good cellar and had some good if broken sleep after Bill F. had come up about 2200 with the D.F.s. This morning we all washed and shaved (he and I and Gordon Taylor his 2 i/c) with the aid of my primus and shaving gear and I went out with the B.S.M. to the river and collected a good (German) jeep trailer and found a couple of chaps I'd killed yesterday afternoon. Took a watch from one, which I've sent back to Findlay to replace the one he lost. The 5/7 went through us this morning but are held up by the blown bridge at Gennep over the river Viers. This we are assaulting tonight. When that and Goch (now being approached by 43 Div. who have passed through 15 – successful in their attack on Cleve –) the guards Armoured Div. go through us here. All is going very well. Our casualties have been light and the Brigade has taken about 1000 prisoners. And soon certain (British) troops assault at Venlo and link up with us and the Americans who are coming up from the South. We are slowly turning the Northern hinge of the Siegfried Line.

11 February

2300, Bn. C.P. Gennep: Continuing: ——

Today's battle has been a nasty one. We've had quite a few casualties, including Colonel Bradford's driver, Cpl. Robertshaw, a very stout chap. The day started early when I joined Bn. H.Q. and was ordered to get across the river Viers by 'Duck' with a walkie talkie as there were no gunners there yet, and the Alligators which were to take essential stores and vehicles, wouldn't be ready for some time. I'd had a few snatched hours of sleep but was feeling fairly fresh. The Duck was too long arriving so I got the party into an assault boat and we paddled across. We then had about a mile and a half to march. As we approached Gennep the shelling came in, and later when we'd established an O.P. in the badly damaged church, became very heavy. Also considerable mortar and spandau fire most of which was directed at the blown bridge about 150 yards to our left. It was cold and uncomfortable. I got some shooting onto enemy m.g. and S.P. gun positions. The Sappers did good work getting the bailey bridge up under fire, so that it is expected for use by 0500 tomorrow. Bill French is just about all in so I am on duty here till 0400 while he gets some sleep. I am pretty tired myself actually, and so is everybody else. A Coy. were counter attacked during this evening but they drove it off assisted by D.F. fire from us. Further advance tomorrow but Stuart is coming up to do it and I should get a little sleep I think. Did I mention I got two more letters yesterday from C.? I'm going to write to her during the night. It is very dark tonight and it has been snowing. Every so often an enemy m.g. crackles in front and some shells crash down into the town. We are all in cellars so shelling is innocuous enough, but one begins to get a little jumpy with fatigue. One's eyes become bleary, one's hair dirty, there is no time to shave.

12 February

2115, Gennep, a cellar: Came off duty at 0415 and stayed horizontal till 1615 but it was rather cold in this little cellar in which my complete O.P. party (Smith with the spare jeep and Shepherd with the carrier having come up today) is housed. But tonight we lugged in a stove from another part of the town and some chimney piping, and it is now glowing cheerfully as the chimney puffs away at pavement level. Tonight – over 110 hours since I put them on – I am about to remove my boots and socks from my tired feet. I shall also undress. The spandau fire which has made the last two days hideous has died down now as our advance pushed southwards, and it is silent in rainy, ruined Gennep except for the occasional crash of an enemy shell – and there are some big ones coming over – evidently from heavy guns in the Siegfried Line. The bn. did a further advance today, but we've had more casualties including Donald Beale, D Coy. Commander killed and 'Mac' (Macdonald) a platoon comd. in B. Coy. also dead. Ted Shirley an A Coy. Subaltern was also shot in the stomach. It's been a noisy day with a lot of enemy shelling as traffic (under a continuous smoke screen) poured over the bridge which was finished early this morning. The guards are due to go through soon, too, and vehicles with the watching eye sign have appeared in the town today. Stuart is unfortunately unable to take this life and is being sent back tomorrow and replaced by Steve.

The whole O.P. party has been talking over this and other battles with that hilarious reaction that follows a sticky job. They're becoming a cynical bunch (and bloody good under fire). Eg. a shell just landed fairly near –

'Butch' –   'God how can human beings stand it!'
Allen –   'Hell that was a close one.'
Foster –   'My nerves are shattered!'

This is alleged 'basewallah' conversation which enjoys a great vogue with Steve and me.

Bill French is excellent to work with and has made a very good first impression all round.

This diary is now approaching its closing pages, but Diary 7 arrived from the gunline with Charles Jones today, so I can go straight onto that when the time comes. The water can on my jeep was holed by a shell splinter and we are having a job replacing it.

We seem to have fetched nearly all the mattresses in Gennep into this cellar! I have a very big grey one to myself, and I made my bed up ready tonight. By the way one _very_ useful find in this battle has been an English _rubber_ hot water bottle, a loss I've been bemoaning ever since my own was stolen from my truck in Eindhoven. And now – bed . . .

14 February

0950, 6 (Can) General Hospital, Vucht: At about 1600 on 13 Feb. – 2 years to the day since Jock was killed – I was wounded. My whole crew and I were packing the carrier in the street as I'd decided to send my jeep back for an overhaul, and there'd been quite a lot of shelling nearby. All of a sudden (and I didn't even hear it coming) there was a blinding flash the other side of the road and I felt a sharp pain (no it was really hardly a pain so much as the stab you get from an injection) in my right leg, and down I went. The others, all except Shepherd, were in the cellar, but Shepherd fell in the road with about 8 wounds. I got the others up and we hauled him in and shell dressed him, and I gave him a shot of morphia. One of his fingers was hanging off, he was hit in both legs – one broken below the knee, neck, and back. Luckily Steve was there as I'd just phoned him a few minutes before asking him to come up and discuss an advance scheduled for that evening and he and the lads helped a lot. Turning to my own leg I was rather shaken to find the blood was not oozing but squirting, a small artery having been hit, but Steve quickly got a home made tourniquet onto it and the bleeding died down. Then they got us on stretchers to the 5 Bn. R.A.P. nearby where the M.O. gave me some morphia too and so we travelled back through the night in jolting ambulances along the bumpy roads round Nijmegen till, in the middle of the night, we got here. They put some of us in the pre-op room but the Canadian doctor decided to leave my piece in, anyway for the time being, as it is a very small one. However my leg is pretty stiff. I've been sleeping for hours here with an opium sedative inside me and no clothes at all. A good pair of b.-d. trousers had to be cut to ribbons to get them off me. Much devotion by Shepherd who begged all the doctors to be allowed to stay with me and embarrassed me a lot by saying publicly how he'd never forget how I'd treated him first! I'm not altogether sorry to get a short rest as I was getting tired – and 5$^{1}/_{2}$ months was a good run as F.O.O. without a scratch. However, I expect I'll be back soon.

Nearly all Canadians evacuated with me. Letter from C. yesterday which I read only a few minutes before getting hit. Our own doc. got to the C.C.P. to see me, which was rather decent of him I thought. As last July, I noticed how good everybody is to the sick and wounded. Wonderful soft weather today with sun and a gentle breeze. I've been told I'm likely to be evacuated to a base hospital today. The amount of stuff they put into you is extraordinary – morphia, opium, penicillin, sulphanillamide, TetTox etc. Medical attention couldn't be better – and you also drink enough hot sweet tea to float yourself. I'm still filthy dirty with blood all over my hands and finger nails and I itch enough to be lousy though I'm sure I'm not. I wish this didn't mean one of those bloody telegrams home; I know it will be a bad moment for them – also for C. when they ring her up. And so I've now finished Diary 6 – a thing which I had doubts of doing at one time. A V1 just exploded! You can't get away from it!

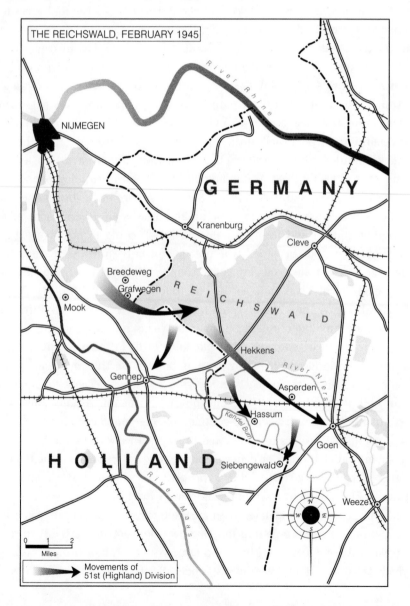

 PART FOUR

15 February – 21 August 1945

A s the Red Army drove westwards to meet the Americans and ourselves, it became possible to believe in victory – and the end of the war. The Highland Division had since before D-Day been led by a new and unknown general (relieved before long of his command). It sometimes adjusted with difficulty to the very different demands of European operations: the Normandy bocage, the fighting along roads, in forests, in towns. In some quarters, its reputation suffered; but respect was gradually restored as we struggled with the mud and snow of the winter. Lord Moran, Churchill's personal physician, suggested in *The Anatomy of Courage* that a man's reserve does gradually get used up. This was almost certainly true of soldiers in the former Eighth Army as we faced the crossing of the Rhine and the hostile fatherland on the other side.

So the Allied armies advanced and met. The fearful crimes of Auschwitz, Belsen and the other camps were uncovered. The major villains died or were captured. And – at last – the war in Europe ended.

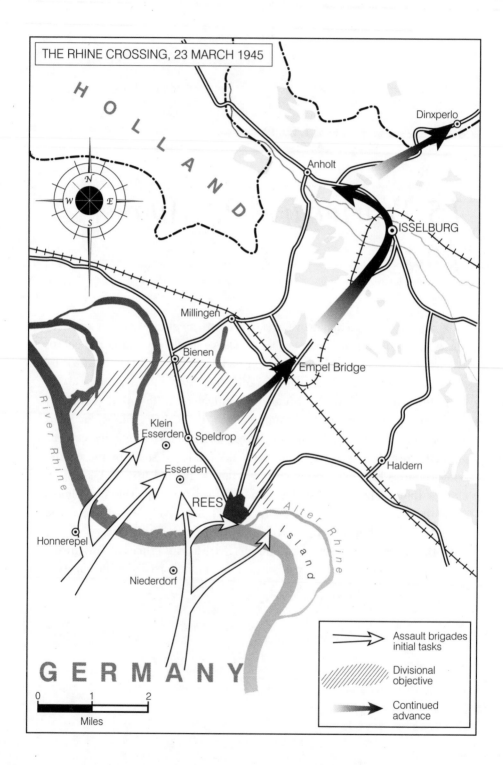

THE RHINE CROSSING, 23 MARCH 1945

HOLLAND

Dinxperlo

Anholt

ISSELBURG

Millingen

Bienen

Empel Bridge

Klein
Esserden   Speldrop

Esserden

Haldern

REES

River Rhine

Alter Rhine

Island

Honnerepel

Niederdorf

GERMANY

Assault brigades
initial tasks

Divisional
objective

Continued
advance

0   1   2
Miles

15 February 1945

a.m., 8 (Br.) Gen. Hospital, Brussels: I lie here in a warm bed. Against my naked belly lies a hot water bottle. A rather nice blue blanket covers my bed which actually has sheets. We left Vucht yesterday and were driven to 's Hertogenbosch station, where as a last gesture of ill will the Germans from across the Maas shelled the hospital train and hit it, wounding one of the orderlies. The wounded reacted better than I expected though underlying the jocular suggestions that we should 'get the fuck out of here' there was an undertone of uneasiness.

The train took seven long hours to reach Brussels, getting in after midnight, and I was very tired. One more ambulance and then we were at the hospital, into a warm bed and at last sleep claimed me. I am in a ward with two other officers – a captain who is an A.L.O. and a Lieut. from 52 Div. The former has a cartilage, the latter a bullet wound through the leg. The Col-Surgeon saw me today but he isn't operating for a day or two. My knee is rather sore as a matter of fact.

Later this morning they took me upstairs to be X-rayed which involved lying on a bloody cold plank for some time – nobody having yet provided me with any pyjama trousers. Also the Red Cross came round distributing 20 cigarettes each and books and, as a matter of fact, anything else one wanted. All I wanted was some hankies and a comb and I still want them! A lot of the Red Cross work is done by Belgian women, girl guides, and boy scouts, who actually are rather efficient. The nurses are quite pleasant and seem quite good at their job and there are some male orderlies who could be a lot worse. Even so, this hospital life is wearing and already, having slept extensively, I am rather tired of it. The place is no Queen Elizabeth Birmingham. Nor, for that matter, is mine a blighty one. My two companions are; the 52 Div. chap is a platoon comd. and had an artery severed, and the other bloke is terrified to go home in case he loses his cushy job and has been going through awful indecisions all day having been given the choice by the M.O. As his job will take 3 months I think he's a bloody fool if he stays here. He hurt his leg slipping on the icy snow near Mill! C'est dur, la guerre. Have written a few letters including one to C. telling them my war effort is temporarily suspended. My damned leg is sore. In today's paper I read that at Hommersun they took 60 prisoners; that's the place I was packing up ready to attack on the night of the 13th.

16 February

2115: As far as I know, nothing has happened today. You don't get much news of the outer world in here, but my thoughts never stray far from the rest of them struggling on there in the mud and scattered bricks which were houses and towns. Still, I suppose I'll be back there myself soon enough, and now I haven't even got a decent driver as poor Shepherd has certainly had it as far as warfare goes. I've slept nearly all day but wrote to the C.O. and Steve. The ligament bloke – rather a nancy with curly 'Airforce' hair – is after all going back to England.

17 February

Rather curious; the M.O. came around this evening and told me that nothing was showing on the X-ray. Yet something is definitely in there so what can it be? Anyway it begins to look as if I shall be back in the line again rather sooner than I expected. I can't say I face the prospect with any relish. It's so pleasant and comfortable here with nothing shooting at you, and I am getting rather tired of soldiering after all this time. I am to get up for a while tomorrow to see how the knee feels.

19 February

p.m.: To my delight, today (in response to a note I'd sent him) in rolled old Roden Parry, my best friend for years and one I've only seen once since the war. He is now a major R.A. at Rear H.Q. 21 A.G. and hasn't changed at all. He told me his father died at the end of Dec. as well as 2 of his 3 brothers killed in action. Also that George Russ, the third member of our trio known as the old firm at school, works just near him and will also come and see me. He's also buying me some clothes from the officers shop. Leg feels pain only when walking on it. It still aches like hell down the back. Wrote C. a long letter yesterday. Revised opinion of the A.L.O. – he's really very pleasant and amusing and the other lad's also very good fun. He's called John Lawson and was in Rep. before the war. One meets strange and unexpected people in the army.

Same night: It's a reflection on modern life in a big city that I've quite omitted to mention that we frequently get air raid sirens and even the odd V1 on Brussels. Not that it's of any importance.

The head Red Cross woman bought me 6 (very luscious) eggs in the Black Market today. No hope of mail for several days yet. A week tomorrow since I came out of the line, but I hadn't been in the gunline of course since the 7th. I wonder if old Findlay misses me – tho' of course I probably shouldn't have been back to the guns yet anyway – one can hardly be sure without knowing what the Brigade is doing. Goch has fallen.

Must try and look up George Baker whilst I'm in Brussels.

20 February

a.m.: Tomorrow I become an 'up' patient – at least I do if the Lieut Q.M. in these parts can supply me with a pair of b.d. trousers – which, incidentally, look like being the first pair I've had to pay for during the last 5½ years. I don't know how long I shall stay after that. I'd thought of asking George Baker to get me some sort of staff job because I'm really beginning to wonder how much more front line I can stand, and yet each time I think of it I feel I should be betraying something – myself and my friends (Jock perhaps) and everything I admire, and so I suppose I shall steam off back and get wounded again or killed or just by some stroke of luck survive completely. I do so hate these base-wallahs – not the genuine ones, but the stacks of cowards and incompetents who hide down here and let others do the work. I don't think I could be happy with such people after over 2 years in my Regiment. So there it is. I wish I were a bit more of a realist and I've no doubt I'd get myself some sort of quite interesting job down here and be done with it. But I don't think I am, so I must start steeling myself mentally for a return to the mud and general bloodiness of a troop commander's lot.

21 February

No news today except that I got some kit at the Q.M. below the hospital. Also Roden called with some more clothes – very nice of him to bother. Yet when I suggested that it was maybe too much trouble to come daily, he just said 'what – for you?' and left it at that. I felt quite humble. Georgie Russ is also coming up. My leg is not so good today – it swelled up and hurt quite a lot. Some talk of another X-ray. Sent C. no. 29 last night, and wrote today to Bé and Roger. Hart, the A.L.O., left for England yesterday.

Got one of the local ward-women to wash my clothes today. Rather annoyingly the leg of my only pair of pants is soaked in blood, and my right boot is also heavily caked. Even the sole is deeply stained. Also my sheepskin has bloodstains all over it – I suppose from when I lay on the floor after fixing Shepherd up and when I was beginning to black out a bit. Anyway there's more blood about than I thought. Also I've lost 3 out of 4 socks and 1 garter! Still, Roden brought me 2 damn good new pairs. Sent C. no. 30.

22 February

Exceedingly irritated today which is all the sillier as the weather outside is so lovely. Lawson left this morning by air which was rather a blow as he was good company. In his place I have an awful little tick from the medical side, who came in for tonsils (and looks it) and then developed a blister or something on his heel. I am dressed today. My officers shop shirt is not a success, being about 3 sizes too large around the neck. Tomorrow I can begin to hope for some mail from C. – and I hope it comes soon because I may not be here so very long myself. The M.O. had a look at my leg today and said it was clearing up; it is still rather swollen and hurts a bit, but I think it is really pretty well better. The lounge is almost empty – an elderly queen (R.A.S.C. 21 A.G.P.) sits reading *Captain Moonlight* by Ethel Mannin as he waits for the invariable visit paid him each afternoon by a rather awful blonde tart, whose hats make me shudder. The day sister doesn't seem to like me tho' I'm not sure just why. She is a big woman of about 40 with black hair, a long nose, huge hips and a general air of surly pugnacity. If the water's hot I shall have a bath after tea.

23 February

a.m.: I've just been censoring letters – a job we share each morning and which is exceedingly boring – the standards of letter writing being appallingly low. A third member of the room came in last night – a very pleasant Major from the Essex Bn. of 49 Div. He was wounded in the arm but has actually recovered from that and now has conjunctivitis. I am wondering how long I shall stay here and where I go from here. I'd rather like a day or two at a convalescent home but I suppose that's rather too much to hope for; such places seem to be reserved for members of the Chairborne Division with ingrowing toenails. However, you never know your luck.

Duly had a superb bath after tea last night. The hot water has taken much of the stiffness out of my leg. Today is the Commandant's weekly inspection. Everything has to be 'tidy' – tidiness being the law and god of any military (or civilian) hospital. Last week I was asleep when the Colonel came around. I am given to understand he's a pretty shocking individual. Dull, gloomy weather today, though the sun seems to be coming through. The C.O. has just made his rounds. I am wearing a scarf pending changing my shirt for something which fits. The C.O. said to me 'Bad throat?' 'No Sir,' I replied, '– no shirt.' Everybody for no reason I could see rather amused. C.O. not very amused!

24 February

1900: I am going away on Monday to the Conv. Home at Waterloo for a week. This is said to be a very pleasant place and I am quite pleased with the prospect. Today I went out for the first time. I went to Roden's office and he gave me a taxi – 21 A.G. have chartered a small fleet of their own! – and I went to the officers shop to buy some shoes etc. I couldn't change my shirt as they haven't a smaller size. Brussels is altogether too big, full and bewildering for somebody from the line. All the shops, people, lipstick and silk stockings rather daze one. And everywhere is that damned 21 A.G. badge – 'the red badge of courage' as we usually call it.* Had a haircut and washed it myself tonight. A letter came from Dad which was very pleasing. I hope something from C. arrives soon. Actually I understand the C.H. collects daily by D.R. so maybe it won't all get lost after all.

Sent C. no. 32.

---

* Better nickname later established: 'The Cross of Shame.'

25 February

1900: Rather varied day. No. 1 disappointment is no mail for me, and I had so hoped there'd be something from C. today. I may not be leaving tomorrow after all as the M.O. told me today my name would have to go on the waiting list so I may be here for another day or two. The U.S. 9th have at last attacked and are steadily driving on Cologne. Our own thrust is very slow (and I suspect fairly heavy in casualties). This afternoon I went down to see Roden again and George Russ came over – our first reunion since 1936. Yet neither of them seems to have changed at all. We had tea at Roden's mess which was rather nice. I went in to see George Baker, but he was out, so I left him a note. I'll try and get down tomorrow if I'm still here. A group of mending females in the hospital basement are fixing my shirt collar for me. Lovely bath again this evening for the 4th running. Had it very hot and felt quite weak when I emerged. Major Douglas 2 i/c of 128 came in with burst eardrums a couple of days ago. His Honey tank hit a mine on Recce. Having played bridge all the way to Sicily with him I resisted last night's invitation. Very nice Lt. Col. R.A.M.C. of Guards Armoured Div. here with same complaint was a friend of Dennis Pullin and I've had quite a lot of conversations with him. Also in, a magnificent nancy from Ensa ballet – he has flu. Wrote home after lunch. Went into the ops. room at H.Q.; a wonderful place and most interesting. Maps, charts, and graphs of everything from arms expenditure to V.D. rate which at one time was as high as 8%. I see my brigade is SW of Goch which is just about where I'd expected them to be. Saw my own name on the Casualty List, also that of Capt. Preece, the chap who came to us just after I got D Troop and was then posted to 126. He was wounded.

26 February

2100, Con. Home, Waterloo. In bed: Great joy; a letter from C. today which I got just before coming here. Also one from Bé. Came here in an ambulance during the afternoon. The place is quite pleasant; full of rather bored, rather browned off officers of course but the food – so far – is O.K. and generally the place is like a rather clean, quiet hotel. My companion coming here – and also sharing my room – is the same elderly queen I mentioned on 22 Feb. Actually he's not a bad chap at all and not a queen either apparently, being married. I'm a very bad judge of people on first appearances. The room I'm in has had the floor creosoted or something and smells <u>terrible</u>. It's giving me quite a headache. I am lying in lovely clean sheets, having had a very hot bath, and soon I shall go to sleep. Oddly enough I feel rather lonely tonight – perhaps the effect of C.'s letter (sent her no. 33 by the way). That's the worst of the army; you never stay anywhere for long. The pyjamas I have on are a gift of the Newfoundland Red Cross and are soft wool and very comfortable. I have to see the M.O. in the morning and then I must write to the Regt. to try and get a truck to come and pick me up here.

28 February

0930: Yesterday I did practically nothing all day which is a very pleasant thing to do from time to time. I saw the M.O. in the morning with a result that I've written to the Regt. asking them to collect me here on the 7 March, and should they not arrive here by the 8th I shall leave here and hitchhike up to the line. I think if it's at all possible, though, that they will in fact send a truck. Today I am going into Brussels, where I hope to see George Baker and do a little shopping. There are some pretty grave types in this place; it seems to be a failing of the Canadians that when talking at meals they are quite impossible to keep off their personal achievements even tho' they only involve activity since June 1944. Also it's surprising how few frontline officers are here and how many L. of C. there are.

The war is going well – advances all along the Western Front, with the U.S. 9th going great guns. Our own 1st 'Canadian' Army advanced 5 miles the other day, carrying them beyond Uderu. A lot of armour seems to be involved. Sent C. no. 34 yesterday – or rather, I wrote it yesterday but it won't go until today.

2 March

a.m.: Yesterday a great packet of mail arrived from the Regt., which as a matter of fact rather surprised me as I'd left a message telling them to keep it for me. Anyway there it all was – 14 letters and 4 parcels including 4 letters from C. (to whom I sent 35 and 36 yesterday). Letters were from Mackie, Dorothy, Steve, Bill French, Admiral Cochrane, 2 or 3 from Bé, Mom, one from N.Y., and a scoff parcel, a parcel and some magazines from Bé and a parcel of books from Dad. All very pleasing.

On 1 March I went into Brussels. I saw Roden and had a very pleasant lunch with George Baker – very resplendent as a full Colonel but wishing he was back with the Regiment. How good if he could be. I didn't ask for a staff job – I really don't think I'd enjoy the life even if he could fix it. Then I went around trying to do some shopping, but I could not find what I wanted. Eventually I dropped into a bar quite aimlessly and got pretty sozzled. Quite an attractive girl came in and sat with me (a hostess or something) and gradually got extremely amorous and begged me to sleep with her, gave me her address, declared she 'loffed' me etc. etc. She passed out after about 4 hours steady drinking and I walked a little unsteadily out, found a tram and got back here and fell into bed, spending all yesterday with a rather severe hangover. Rather a curious little adventure really. I've heard of such things happening but they don't often happen to me! I must say I was vaguely embarrassed when the girl started tearing off portions of clothing, but I maintained a dead pan and assured myself mentally that this was the continent etc. etc! Anyway no harm done.

Bill's letter was rather nice and sent a message from the C.O.* telling me that

* Letter from the C.O. on 3rd March.

however long I was away my place would be kept warm for me, which is rather a comfortable thought. It's rather pleasant to have been long enough in a regiment to have some value to them. Ronnie Taylor's course has been postponed, it would seem, and I think he'll be back by the time I get back. I hope the Regt. will send a truck; things will be so much easier that way. Curious coincidence. My room-mate (Kiernander is his name) lives at 212A Nell Gwynn House. The war goes well. Gladbach has fallen and we took over 70,000 prisoners in Feb. 'Bitter resistance' on the British front, however. The Div. (I discovered at 21 A.G.) was taken out of the line and relieved by 52 a few days ago. About time. Alec Brodie* who took Donald Beale's coy. after the former was killed, was wounded after performing some incredibly heroic deeds. Steve has also done very well according to Bill French.

3 March

It is snowing. The ground is white outside.

4 March

Sunday, a.m.: I was already asleep last night when a hand shook my shoulder and a voice kept saying 'Come on Jack, there's an O Gp., we're doing an attack tomorrow' and there of all people was Steve – on a 48 in Brussels. He sat down and we talked for about 2 hours (he was rather drunk!) and eventually he found a bed somewhere in the home and I went off to sleep. Rather a good day all round, yesterday. I went into Brussels in the morning and got some shopping – got 3 bottles of Eau de Cologne for Clare, her mother and Hylda. Lunch with Ronnie and an afternoon spent rather luxuriously having a haircut, oil shampoo and manicure. Then I came back here to find 7 letters – Joan B., Dorothy, Charles Jones, 2 from C., one from G., and one from Gerard Tallack. And Steve brought me one from home and another from C.

The battle west of the Rhine is virtually over and the Siegfried Line is smashed. How long now till the end of the war, I wonder. If only we can cross the Rhine quickly and in strength, we should reach Berlin before the Russians yet. It's 300 miles once over the river. Now at last it is no longer a mere figure of speech to say the end is in sight.

6 March

a.m. It is raining and tomorrow I am going. Tonight I shall have my last hot bath and lie in clean linen for the last time for – how long? Yesterday I did practically nothing all day. I played a bit of bridge in the afternoon, chiefly interesting on account of bidding a small slam vulnerable and making a grand slam. Went to

* Alec has been recommended for the V.C. – 4th March – And got the D.S.O.

bed rather early with an absolutely blazing headache. The one I originally so incorrectly diagnosed as a queen left yesterday. I was quite sorry as he turned out to be rather good company in the end, and I now have a <u>very</u> dim R.E.M.E. captain in with me. He must be quite old for his hair is quite grey. From what I hear, I expect to find the Div. out of the line when I come back which isn't such a bad thing, as I don't <u>think</u> we shall be used as assault troops for the Rhine crossing or crossings. However it wouldn't surprise me; we've done so many things now we could do that too if we had to I suppose.

Getting wounded certainly rather shocks one's nerve. I can't say I look forward to the hazards of war at all now. Still, as always, I suppose one will get used to it quickly enough, once back.

Evening: Rather an amazing day. Went into town and I met Nick, Gordon Taylor, and the M.O. all from 5 B.W., the latter two just returning from a 48 and Nick in hospital to have an old shrapnel wound re-operated. Had tea with him and Roden. Came back to find 1100 cigarettes in parcels, also a book from C. for my birthday, and a smashing new pair of sheepskin gauntlets. Also a letter from B.B. – somebody written up very fully in Diary 1 – at last home from Turkey. When I met her on the boat to Egypt in 1942 she'd just come from Tokyo where she'd been interned. She's now in hospital near Warminster, with malaria, or the remains thereof. 500 of the cigarettes were from C. I think as I know she was going to send them – and that means they'll be Churchman No. 1. Good. Remainder from Pa and Sheila H. Some talk of an M.C. for me from Nick today but I'm not allowing my hopes to go up, knowing what these things are. Sandy Leslie's got his M.C. which is awfully good. No sign of a truck for me yet incidentally. I hope the damn thing turns up tomorrow. It's going to be a nuisance getting back on the thumb, even tho' I'll have a Jeep as far as Eindhoven. To final bath and final bed now.

8 March

0015. Room 618, Plaza Hotel (British Officers Club), Brussels: Not so final after all. Today Harry Cable (of all people) called for me as he's on a 48 with Butch, Peters and another gunner and they're not going back till tomorrow so I go with them. So I got onto Roden who with influence fixed me up in this utterly palatial suite. Two beds, bathroom attached etc. To give you an idea, there are 10 lights in here alone. Heaven knows what this cost in peacetime. It's cost me 4/6 a night which is really absurd. Harry told me two things: one, that the Div. is moving and two, that Bubbly Burnett the C.O. has either left or is leaving for the Far East. I'm rather sorry really; he's been with us since D day and he's never any sort of bother as far as bull is concerned. The new C.O. is rumoured to come from A/Tank. Pottered round in a mildly inebriated state most of the day, and wound up at the Atlanta where I met George Armstrong (just over from Italy) whom I'd not seen since Oxford days except just once at O.C.T.U. There was a floor show and the little dancer was a nice looking child so I sent her a note asking her to have a cup of tea with me which she did. Rather pleasant, Russian, called Natacha, 21, engaged to an English Sgt., and spoke a little English. She went off to home and Mamma and I came back here. I like meeting new people, it's interesting. I met a couple of press blokes earlier, throwing back whisky fast and I had half a dozen on their expenses sheet. We leave here tomorrow and shall spend a night in 's Hertogenbosch. Lovely bath. Now for lovely sleep.

Sent C. no. 41 last night and wrote to B.

9 March

0015, 's Hertogenbosch: We left Brussels about 1230. I'd met Bob Gillman in the morning, who told me – I don't know how accurately – that the Regt. were moving today down into Belgium, but we came on up here. I drove the last 70 miles – fast. Harry's not a bad driver but murders the gearbox. He and two of the others have gone off to Mill and Butch is staying with some other friends here. How well I know the old road now – 'Maple Leaf Up' – and how many times I've crossed the border on that long straight road with the Christmas tree woods each side. Very good welcome as always. The Americans have established a bridgehead E of the Rhine about 25 miles South of Cologne, which rather relieved me as it's essential to get a quick crossing if we're going to keep the enemy on the wrong foot – more so as he's got a good bit of heavy equipment back owing to bad flying weather. There is still some shelling here though not close, and a procession of V1s Antwerp (presumably) bound. Sent C. no. 42 this morning and bought her a Schiaperelli lipstick at what I considered the rather excessive price of 25/-. I only hope the colour is right! I chose it with considerable care and I think it is. Future of Div. and Regt. still in the speculative stages. Nothing too violent I hope . . .

Later, Meerwen: Impossible to write – we're all talking too much!

10 March

p.m.: Last night, when I wrote the above entry, finally – and inevitably – developed into something of a tippling party which made it impossible to do any more about this. Reached here yesterday afternoon – and gosh it was good to see everybody again. Findlay had kept all my kit in decent order but somebody had stolen my Jeep! Also I have a new armoured O.P. – another carrier, but this time a new one, full of quite pleasing modifications. I also have acquired a new driver called Quartermaine who seems a good type and knows the job. I've been round seeing everybody in the Regt. which has been rather pleasant. We had a new C.O.

yesterday but he's left us already and we're getting another – the present C.O. of the Div. A/T Regt. Letter from P. and books from N.Y. Also some letters from home. We are doing the Rhine assault which is a blow, but oddly enough I don't particularly care. Bill French is still with us and more popular daily. Ronnie expected soon. Sent the parcel to C. today.

11 March

Sunday: For some reason quite unknown, I am most awfully tired tonight, so I expect this will be a short entry. Just been doing routine work today, chiefly on the new carrier which is having all sorts of ideas incorporated into it and is now a really first class effort. Butcher had a letter from Shepherd and I enclosed a note for him in a letter from Foster today. Also today I had a letter from Dorothy – one from N.Y. and 2 from C. No. 45 tonight. Played bridge yesterday and today with Bill, Charles and Lawrence and lost 12/6 a time! Must go to bed, I am dropping. Incidentally I saw the new C.O. today. First impression bad – a small peppery little man who looks rather like a groom or something. Went to tea at 49 yesterday. I believe Peter Dawson's in for an M.C. – and Sandy Cowie told me Ronnie recommended one for me after the Ardennes but it didn't go up. But I'm rather glad to know it somehow.

12 March

Ronnie came back this afternoon, very cheerful, and with a suspicious aura of keenness! Had some fun with my Luger today, firing nearly 100 rounds in all, at various tin cans and things. Work is going on well in the new carrier. The guns are going to Lounel to calibrate. I am booked for F.O.O. for the Rhine crossing, as it's a carrier party and the B.C. is borrowing Bill's carrier. So that leaves none, as my spare one is going to be used by the C.O. There is an O Gp. at 5 B.W. headquarters tomorrow, and I believe I have to go to it. Also a boating practice on the 14th I think. It looks as though things are cooking up a bit swiftly. Bloody nuisance.

13 March

Went over to the B.W. today just in time to bid George Dunn farewell as he is going to command 2nd Seaforth. He was piped out by a full pipe band in dress kilts. Tomorrow we have a river crossing exercise south of Roermond, and the day after, there is a night exercise. Unfortunately I have to leave my carrier there over that period, when there is work we still have to do on it. Today we painted it and it looks damn good. By the way I am doing F.O.O. for the Rhine assault. It's curious really how one gets so used to these things that one doesn't even feel terribly worried at this stage. But I shall have a couple of bad nights just before, I expect. Unfortunately this damn night exercise looks like being on my birthday. Beware the Ides of March!

We have to get up at some positively obscure hour tomorrow in order to leave at 0700. Still it might have been very much worse!

14 March

2200: Today's practice turned out rather abortive as most of us never got across the Maas at all. However, it was an interesting day. I am damn tired so I don't propose to write any more now. My birthday tomorrow – one that at one time I didn't really expect to see. Lovely spring weather today though this morning was cold with a heavy frost. And we didn't up till nearly seven after all. The new carrier is most satisfactory and goes like a gem so far.

THE IDES OF MARCH

Today has been an infinitely dull birthday devoid of even the stimulus of danger – something to be thankful for really. There was one letter from C. and apart from that I've been doing purely routine jobs and continuing the good work on the carrier. I've been trying to remember my other wartime birthdays. Last year I was at Gerards Cross with Clare who had a cake made with 26 little candles. 1943 – in the Mareth Line. 1942 – can't remember but I think I was at Grindle Court near Sherborne. 1941 – undoubtedly in Aldershot and a party in fact at the Officers Club and I met a girl called Susan Lyon – daughter of a retired General who lived at Farnham where I visited her home once or twice. She was very thin, but quite attractive and intelligent. In 1940 I was a gunner at Dover and we all got drunk, and those are my six wartime birthdays, and this one has perhaps been the dullest of the lot. Can't make up my mind about prospects for the next battle; sometimes I think it'll be a reasonably easy crossing followed by a stiff battle and then a large-scale armoured breakout and then quickly on to the end of the war.* At other times I can't see how the war will ever end at all. However, speculation is rather idle I suppose. Monty came to see us at practice yesterday and stayed for quite a time. Latest Monty story:

Churchill said to Monty on his recent visit over here. 'You know I think this war's going to end soon' and Monty replied 'yes – it'll be grand to get back into uniform.'

Bubbly Burnett, our recently departed C.O., has just been awarded the D.S.O. Our new chap is not particularly popular – it's all part of the 'Seniority' racket I suppose, that he, an A/T.K. man, gets a field regt., but he's got an M.C. so I suppose he must be reasonably good. Or must he?!

* Not bad!

18 March

Sunday morning: Quite a lot of things have been happening during the last day or two. Firstly Ronnie is leaving to take some sort of job at Larkhill – rather against his will as a matter of fact. This means that tho' we lose one good B.C. we shall get Bill French in his place, who will also undoubtedly be absolutely first class. An orgy of cleaning and inspecting has been going on. 'The New C.O. likes ——' all webbing <u>white</u> and gleaming like the C.M.P. One method of getting it this way is to use Milton etc. toothpaste. This has led to a large notice in Charlie Troop lines: 'Have you McCleaned your webbing today?' The O.P. vehicles now wear (as a battle honour! by special permission of Bill Bradford) a small 60 sign on a green ground – the Div. Serial of the 5 B.W. as well as our 43 sign! A good deal of derision on account of this, but actually it's quite a good idea. I forgot to mention that Bill French is on a course in England (and leave) so he'll be away for 3 or 4 weeks leaving Charles in comd. when Ronnie leaves, which I think is tomorrow.

Last night Steve, Bill and I went to Brussels to get drunk, in which we succeeded reasonably well. We went the rounds of all the most fearful little 'clubs' and 'cabarets' and drank everything – champagne, beer, whisky, cherry brandy, brandy and various proprietary brands such as an exceedingly evil cocktail known as 'Baisy Baisy'. We got back here in the very small hours, still rather squiffy. It was quite a good evening's entertainment – and very expensive one incidentally. Letters in the last few days from Shep., 2 from C., and one from home. Also rather a good book from Dorothy called *Night and Day* – a sort of anthology. Am reading *Elizabeth and Leicester* – interesting as it's a period on which I'm far too scantily informed.

Australian objection to the Americans in the continent summed up as '5 Overs' – 'Overdressed, Overpaid, Overdecorated, Oversexed and Over Here.'

19 March

Almost imperceptibly the signs of impending battle steal upon us. Top Secret documents, serials on vehicles, conferences, wireless silence. And of such the day has been.

Last night we saw Ronnie off in appropriate fashion. Graduating from gin we went onto brandy and finished on rum in an orgy of maudlin confidences about 0200 by which time Ronnie was very nearly paralysed so he went off to bed. Today we are all feeling the effects but it has been warm and sunny and the afternoon sky full of Forts, Thunderbolts and Lightnings – great fleets of them. A 20 page letter from C. which was a pleasant surprise. McVey has come over from 49, to do G.P.O. for me as Steve is now commanding C. Tp. Among drunken confidences from Ronnie emerged the fact that D Tp. when I arrived was considered the worst in the

Regt., and C the best. D is now better than C. Also that he Ronnie had given me a very good character with the C.R.A. – for what it's worth.

20 March

This evening closed so peacefully after such a beautiful day, that, looking at the long line of slim guns and stubby trucks with the last rays of sunshine glinting on their barrels and windscreens, it was quite difficult to realise that in three days time about the biggest slice of hell the boche has so far encountered is going to be let loose on him. The warm sun has dried the ground, and trucks move with a dust screen in their wake – how long, it seems, since one saw that. And in the hedges the bare branches are putting out small green buds. The grass is a vivid green. And this evening I saw two small lambs skipping about the place. And again all day in the bright sky the bombers have sailed slowly towards Germany, and the fighters weaved their wispy trails against the blue and the sunshine.

Today we were briefed. I'm not going into details but it looks like being a crashing success and everything we have is being put into it, including a deadly secret airborne landing. Ourselves and 15th Scottish are once more the assaulting division but there is plenty of ammo. in behind us to exploit when they can get across. The planning and the paper involved in this business is stupendous – the only possible word for it. The things that have to be thought of for a large scale river assault are innumerable – right down to marking ferry routes by night, and so on. A letter today from Roger Andrews, also one from George in Antwerp, otherwise mail has been meagre. Sent C. no. 51 which I started last night but I was so tired I went to bed and finished it today. The Regt. leaves here on the 22 but Charles' present plan is for us to leave here on the morning of the 23 and go straight to the Black Watch. I expect to land in Germany on the morning of the 24th March. And the powers that be expect this <u>really</u> to be the *coup de grâce*. I hope they are right. It's time they were right about something!

21 March

Slowly preparations move towards the climax. Maps – hundreds of maps – photos by the score – codes, rations, water, ammo., and all the other scores of jobs one has by now learned to associate with the build up which precedes a large scale attack. War has become so miserably complicated nowadays. It is now likely that the Regiment will move tomorrow, and the O.P. parties in a body, are moving with, but in rear of, the main body of the Regiment. We then join our battalions on the next day – on the night of which the battle starts. News from the 'I' Summary was not quite so cheerily nonchalant today. The first Paratroop Army is evidently defending our sector and a hundred guns are mustered on the very bit we attack – north of Rees. It begins to look like rather a tough job. Our own gunline incidentally, is about 600 yards from the river, which makes their opening targets about 1200 yards – an almost unprecedented thing.

Wonderful weather again today. I wonder if it will stay fine for the party – it's time we had really good luck with the weather.

23 March

1815, Marienbaum, Germany: The guns are pounding in the setting sun. In less than 3 hours the first waves of the greatest river assault in the world's history will be on the water. All along the Rhine from Emmerich to Duisberg, men stand waiting, or moving up to battle stations, touching up final jobs to be done, looking over engines, cleaning weapons, thick in the dust which lies heavy everywhere now – just like Normandy all over again. Today, Monty has been among us again, preceded by the usual flotilla of highly polished military policemen. Spent all yesterday on the road but got a good run through via Venlo (very badly damaged but hung with flags) and had a pretty good night's sleep in the wagon lines. This morning we joined the B.W. and I had an excellent tea with Sandy over at B Coy. Plus champagne. This attack is a magnificent thing. The 9th army is doing another 2-Div. attack South of us, and 5 battalions of commandos are to swarm over and take Wesel after an intensive bombing of the town. And tomorrow, an airborne Corps drops in front of us. Official verdict: four or five days stiff fighting followed by a general breakthrough. What a boon the unexpected Remagen bridgehead has been. I go over in the first 2 hours by Buffalo. I must admit I feel my usual nervousness, specially as the banks have already been fairly heavily shelled and mortared by the enemy. The Regimental gun position looks as though it may turn out an unhealthy spot before this battle's over.* I am now sitting with David Macintyre, the Adjutant, waiting for probably another two hours before we get the word to move up towards the river.

I shall delete this as usual if I come through alright.

[DULY DELETED]

The guns grow louder, and the evening mist creeps up slowly from the river, mingling with the cordite plumes, and the smoke screen. Everything is prepared. Only the battle remains.

24 March

0830, over the Rhine!: I sit in a smashed attic of the smashed German village of Esserden. The guns across the river pound so that the whole skeleton of the

---

* It did.

farmhouse trembles. Everywhere the ground is pitted with shell holes and every inhabited place is in ruins. Over it all, the sun rises calm and warm. The sky is full of planes. After the biggest artillery preparation I've ever heard, the river was successfully stormed last night. Enemy opposition was only moderate and we've already taken many prisoners. Their morale is completely broken. Patton has made a surprise crossing and the Russians are on the move – 33 miles from Berlin. Surely this must be the beginning of the end?

I and my crew crossed the glassy Rhine in the first shimmer of the dawn, after waiting all night in Vehicle Waiting Park, Vehicle Loading Park etc. – all superbly organised and signposted day and night! Shells are dropping around the farm. I am too tired to find out exactly where. They missed; what else matters? The Airborne should be over in about an hour. All this has been so easy so far – this enormous Rhine river – that one can't help feeling it's got to get hard soon. Or are the enemy really broken? Could that be?

Same evening: A day of heavy mortaring and some shelling – a lot of it close. Tonight the brigade attacks again, chiefly with a view to clearing Rees completely, while in the north, 152 abandons an attack, and the Canadians ease into their position. As I write, heavy mortaring is going on, but it's just far enough away to have no mental or physical strain at all (immediate anyway). (As I wrote the last sentence a mortar bomb landed within 25 yards showering dirt all over me, so I've moved into the carrier, which is a safer spot.) Moaning minnies and spandau bullets have also been in evidence all day. Stuff is now once more falling damn close all around. Another of the day's incidents was when Bill Bradford decided to hold an O Gp. at about 5 and a mortar bomb landed slap next door to Bn. H.Q. setting it and the adjoining farm on very vigorous fire. The boche then mortared and shelled the fire for about an hour while we held an improvised O Gp. in a house a few doors away. Rees, which we can see very clearly about a mile away, looks ruined and is on fire in many places. The garrison there is surrounded so we should get a good bag of prisoners. The Germans here – such few as have remained – are servile and distracted. It is difficult to be as hard hearted as one would like at the sight of these wretched old men and women and children watching even the ruins of their houses burned down by their own shelling. But plenty of old and young have wept because of the Germans during the last few years – it is good that they should taste now, for the first time, the bitter medicine they have forced down the throat of Europe for the past 5$\frac{1}{2}$ years. The whirligig of time does bring in his revenges after all.

Incidentally, Steve has not yet got over the Rhine.

26 March

1900, north corner of Rees: At nine o'clock (pm) on the 24th we attacked once more, moving up slowly over the mine-strewn roads amid occasional mortar stonks and the odd bomb from enemy a/c which growled about throwing flares and even coming down with machine guns and rockets. All objectives were taken during the night and I was in to an O.P. with B Coy. by first light. Got some shooting straight away at escaping enemy infantry and went on shooting hard all day as plenty of targets cropped up. The weather was still fine. I was damnably tired and my lips were cracked and sore from the dust and the wind. The O.P. was a ruined attic which presented a good view. Almost everywhere the countryside was in flames with great smoke pyres rising skywards – including on our lines. Before this attack started, J— As I started that sentence, four shells landed plumb outside this H.Q. with 4 sudden crashes – 2 wounded, one pretty badly – I was going to write Jerry gave us a most savage pasting with mortars and A.P. shot. He got 3 almost direct hits on us and the roof came tumbling in. Same thing most of yesterday with a lot of rifle and machine gun sniping. The enemy was very close all round the posn. and in the afternoon the tanks with a platoon of B Coy. blasted and winkled them out, collecting about 50 prisoners. Came down to B Coy. H.Q. and had 8$^{1}/_{2}$ hours sleep and was it welcome!

Up to the O.P. again this morning but stood down about midday as the battle had more or less passed beyond us. However at odd intervals during the day – and still – mortars and shells come crashing down. One of our wounded chaps referred to, died at the R.A.P. His brother was killed recently and his wife had a baby a few days ago. Hell.

The C.O. came up and visited me this morning, and was pretty affable. I forgot to mention I had some rifle shooting from this O.P. but unfortunately missed my prospective victim. Jerry a/c are active tonight, strafing the gunline and the road outside. It is terribly noisy – the guns have been firing for hours in support of 43 Div. (now across) and 154 Brigade. They (the guns) are now across the river and we visited them this afternoon. They are very full of the stuff thrown at them the other night on the West bank, but casualties were very light.

Went also with Sandy to the bank this afternoon; and saw the class 15 bridge which is open, and the class 40 not yet completed. We went across in a Duck and walked back over the bridge which, like all our bridges, bears the name of its makers, corps sign or whatever they choose. This one has 'Lambeth Bridge, opened 25 March 1945' and has the 30 Corps, R.E., and I believe 2nd Army sign. It is a fine bridge.

Wireless news – which has mentioned Divs. by name right from the start for the first time – is tremendous, with Patton at Frankfurt – Frankfurt! and the first army burst slap out of its bridgehead today with 2 armoured columns making advances of 20 and 15 miles. I don't see how the Germans can hold out for more than two or three weeks now. Unfortunately the main force – 3 Para Divs. and a Panzer Grenadier Div. – are concentrated on this Northern sector; we always seem to come in for it. Morale is simply tremendous all round with tails right in the air. Churchill and Monty came over the Rhine today but not to this sector of it. Nor would it be a good idea for them to come here. The guns still crash and thump – for hours now they've been steadily firing – the gunners are all dead tired and practically loading in their sleep. My new carrier was baptised today when several shell splinters went through the back. Also we had quite a bit of rain today for the first time for days, but in the sunny morning the Typhoons continued to pour down rockets and bullets, turning the countryside into a series of bonfires. Odd bits of loot collected this time include another automatic – a Browning this time, a thermos to replace the one I lost the other night, and a typewriter which I've given to Sandy Leslie.

And finally – as far as I know – Steve is still not over the river!

27 March

All goes well. 43 Div. are pushing on, and we go in tonight – probably for Isselberg.

28 March

I am exhausted, my eyes are heavy and a great weariness steals over my limbs. I haven't slept now since I last wrote this up, and last night's battle, though the opposition was unexpectedly light, was trying, owing to the damp mist and rather heavy artillery and mortar concentrations by the enemy firing north of flaming Isselberg, whose bridge we captured early this morning, and 152 went through at dawn to take the town. I joined B Coy. at about 0330 and established an O.P. in a mined housetop at dawn. A very noisy day, with lots of mortar and artillery fire coming back, particularly some very savage and accurate airburst eightyeight. Tonight we move on into the town, and 152 go forward to capture Anholt. The news continues superb with the enemy crumbling in front of 7th Armoured Div.'s thrust in the centre of the bridgehead. Our own armour – the 11th and Guard's Divs. – are expected to come through very soon. Close in front of us here, the Typhoons have been doing deadly work and I've been watching infantry groups cleaning houses, closely supported by tanks. Letters yesterday from C., Dad, Dick, Gerard, G. and Dorothy. Heaven knows when I'll get time to answer them. Sandy told me today that Col. Bradford wants to put me in for an M.C.* – which even if I don't ever get the thing is nice to know as he's a man I admire immensely and I'm glad he's got a reasonable opinion of me.

Meanwhile I am deadly tired. We are hoping to come out for a day or two soon; but even as a smaller picture I do hope to God I get some sleep tonight. I've not had my clothes off since the attack started, which counting D-1 is 6 days by the

* He did.

end of tonight. A huge pall of smoke hangs over Isselberg, started by enemy shelling about an hour ago, and the devastated countryside is pinpointed with small bonfires which a week ago were people's houses. The civilians are cowed but not particularly hostile and the white flag is prompt and universal. I dislike this servility in the German more than his arrogance.

29 March

a.m.: Damn good night's sleep. This morning we are still just waiting around the place while in front of us the advance goes slowly on under cover of heavy artillery fire. Rain during the night and heavy mist this morning. Special message to the Div. from Monty last night, on the strength of which I am trying to collect an M.M. for Butcher. Letter from home yesterday. Steve got wounded this morning but only a couple of scratches and it seems he hasn't even got to go back. Rumour has it that we may come out for 3 or 4 days shortly. On our right, 3 British took Halden and Werth last night.

1 April

Gunline: Spent the days of the 30 and 31 in delightful idleness with B Coy. – rudely shattered yesterday when the Colonel recalled all O.P. parties to the gun position to ginger up cleaning and maintenance. Northing much was going on at B Coy. The guards Armd. Div. went pouring through us in an apparently endless procession of tanks and trucks, by day and night. Enemy activity died down to sporadic shelling – one of which nearly got Butcher and me when we were caught out in the open. An unpleasant five minutes. Among other items much in evidence are huge oil portraits of Hitler. I remember seeing one propped up against a road block on our way up to Isselberg, across which was written in chalk by some Jock 'You've had it you bastard.' This caused much amusement. Deep into Central Germany the advance continues; the 7th are past Munster and the 11th on the line of the Dortmund Ems canal. We expect to follow as a flank guard in a day or two. The position here is dirty, battered and crowded. We eat in a tent and live – four of us – in one room down at the waggon lines. It is raining and cold and last night our room leaked profusely all over our beds. Yesterday I used my new Browning to shoot a wounded horse. Killed it immediately with a shot in the brain. Everybody is discussing when the war will end. I think the next fortnight will tell us whether it's likely to drag on for a few more months or is actually going to end by then. Letters – three, I believe, from C. in the last day or two.

2 April

Evening: Last night the clocks went on an hour with the inevitable result that we were all called an hour late this morning – and this evening after a conference this afternoon assuring us that we shouldn't be moving for two or three days, we've suddenly received an S.O.S. from 3 Div. with the result that we are to move at 0730 tomorrow morning as a Div. Arty. Oh hell! Another letter from C. today which was nice to get. The parcel I sent from Brussels has arrived. Today the new General (General Rennie was killed some days ago but I didn't mention it for security reasons) visited us. We lined up in the pouring rain and he shook us by the hand. Looks an awfully nice chap with a C.B., C.B.E., D.S.O., M.C. and 2 bars. Comes from 49 Div.

3 April

Midday: The move was finally cancelled late last night, and today preparations have gone ahead for our own move as spearhead brigade of the Divisional move directed on Bremen. We are likely to move off tomorrow and if so, we join the Bn. this evening. The Bn. is being split into two groups – Charles and Steve are with the left hand one, I am with the right, commanded by the C.O.2. It involves having a jeep as well as a carrier, for recce work. Very Aprilish weather today – rain and sun in turns but it poured all through the night and the ground is waterlogged this morning. The C.R.A. is meant to be coming round this afternoon.

4 April

Yesterday came a further message 'No move till 5 April' and this afternoon, normal recce parties are leaving for the Enscheide area. No real details are known. Osnabruck has been reached and passed and the wireless 'Security black out' lifted. Meanwhile some say we are to be Corps reserve. The C.R.A. came round yesterday afternoon and gave quite a good pep talk to the gunners. He revealed that we had more casualties in the breakout from the Reichswald than for the whole campaign in Sicily and said the Div. had, if possible, added new glory to its name. This I can believe. Message just in that Bde. Gp. will move some time tomorrow. Weather very typically April. Played bridge with Laurence V., Charles and Steve till very late last night. Ended 1000 points up. Wonder when I'll go on leave. I still hope the first fortnight in May but it may be a bit later now.

6 April

Daybreak. Belfry in Schutdorf, Germany: Below me – far below me – in the ruined town the sappers are working furiously on a bailey bridge to span one of the largest craters I've ever seen. Near them, the town's remaining civilians are trying to remove a road block composed of logs bound round cement, and very heavy. They can however be shot to pieces by tank guns. (Making me realise how futile our own 1940 efforts were.) Plans changed on the night of the 4th and it was decided we should go straight into action instead of harbouring at Enscheide. Chas went off ahead so I led the regiment and arrived without incident during the afternoon. It rained most of the way, about 65 miles. During the journey Steve's $^1/_2$ track broke down and as my own carrier was with a separate Bde. column, I had to push on here from Bentheim (where the guns are) in X car – the B.C.'s $^1/_2$ track. The factory O.P. which Chas had recced wasn't satisfactory so we got into this immensely high belfry where I can see for miles towards the Ems river and canal which we are supposed to reach and cross today. The enemy left here at 0400 yesterday morning and is not in evidence at all at the moment. The town has been pretty thoroughly sacked by the Gds. Armd. – many of the houses having been left almost full. We slept in quite a comfortable one ourselves last night. (Every so often the huge bell in this tower goes off with an enormous clang which makes me nearly jump out of my skin with shock!) Most of yesterday's trip was through Holland – well decked with red white and blue flags and orange banners – the enemy is pulling out of North Holland so I hope they may be liberated without smashing the place up too badly. The German border near Oldenzaal is almost unmarked except for a sign of our own saying 'This is Germany' and leaving the mines and bogged tanks just over the border to say the rest for themselves. The greatest problem of this war is how to treat the beaten German who, except for avowed Nazis, persists that he was never one, hates the fuhrer, is tired of the war etc. I entirely agree with non-fraternisation. The one thing that always stuck in the German gullet was the war guilt of the Versailles treaty, and it is becoming clear that they heartily dislike being sent, as it were, to Coventry. At the moment it is fairly easy to enforce, but a pretty face soon equalises good and evil as far as most of the men are concerned.

Letter from Joan B. yesterday.

Night – with B Coy: A too-exciting day. Suddenly and unexpectedly moved off up the main axis towards Emsburen with C Coy. at about 1230. Only two vehicles preceded my carrier over the bridge – the C.O.'s jeep and Charles's jeep. We shoved on up the road till we came to a small blown bridge where the fun started. We were mortared, shelled and machine gunned. Had 6 casualties. There were also A.P. mines. I walked on with the Coy. with a 38 set working to the carrier and I got some good shooting – about 250 rounds in all after which the enemy shut up and retired, followed by the 5/7 Gordons who came through us. Then we came back home here, Steve to C Coy. and I am back with B. No word of a move tomorrow, and everybody very cheerful and loaded with booty of various kinds from motorcars to Benedictine. Had a rather pleasant drink with Bill Bradford at Bn. H.Q. tonight; I believe he was a bit whistled!

8 April

1930, near Emsburen: Moved out this morning and came up to the regiment which is moving itself over the Dortmund Ems Canal late tonight, but we – Chas, Steve and I – are staying in this area till the Bde. moves again which I think will be in a couple of days, maybe less. Got a little drunk last night and played bridge. Today's weather has been superb – hot sunshine. Letters from Joan-Mary and Clare awaited me at the battery. The newspapers were also included in today's mail – they're an amazing boost to morale! You don't realise how well you're doing until the *Daily Mail* tells you! However, we seem to have reached or bypassed Hannover and the Zuyder Zee, and rocket attacks have almost ceased at home.

10 April

a.m., near Laxten: Yesterday morning we received orders that all O.P.s were to rejoin the regiment over the Ems which, as the bridge had collapsed, involved making a long trip round and using the bridge at Lingen. It took us four hours to reach here, in brilliant sunshine with dust rising from the roads as we passed through the usual redbricked-farm littered countryside and the occasional battered town with white flags hanging from most of the houses. Having drunk between four of us (the C.O. came to play bridge) a bottle of whisky and a bottle of alleged gin the night before, we weren't feeling too good and went to bed about 10. I discovered I'd left my personal haversack behind when I reached here and was in an awful spin as it contains so many valuable and personal items. I sent Bdr. Reid my sigs. N.C.O. back for it and he arrived back here after 0700 this morning. An advance is likely this afternoon – we are now in support of 154 Brigade. A thing I've noticed is the astonishingly large number of children everywhere round the countryside. Personally I hate the sight of them – their nasty little blonde polls seem to typify these false racial creeds which have brought us to this present pass. Another order – one of a series lately – has come in forbidding fraternisation – quite rightly, but the men are so incredibly stupid; already one or two have been caught feeding chocolate to German children. We never seem to learn. Among the pleasant little habits used by German saboteurs is to offer you a light from a lighter with a poisoned pellet beneath the wick. This kills you in about half an hour. At Isselburg arsenic was put in the water supply. Generally the news continues very good, though resistance is stiffening, particularly on our own sector where the 7th Armd. are within 5 miles of Bremen. Hannover is being surrounded and all Holland has now been cut off by another paratroop landing. The Russians are well into Vienna.

11 April

2045, south of Quackenbruck: As we were mentally contemplating a good night's rest last night, the word came from R.H.Q. of an early move this morning. So up we got and the Recce went away at 0530, and then the column of guns turned onto the dust road at about 0800. Lovely countryside; almond and cherry trees in their first blossoming already dusty from the convoys, the trees budding – last year they were budding at Melford and we still had D day in store for us, and all the other days, D and otherwise – yet even the budding of the trees holds a menace here, deep in Germany, for the forests are still sheltering deserters, saboteurs and other dangers. We went into 3 positions today, reaching this one towards sunset, following the rapid advance of the 154th Brigade through dusty lanes, avenues of tall trees and past single houses or hamlets nearly all bedecked with white flags, and back into the coolness of the forest (for the sun has been scorchingly hot). Past the old folk with their disillusioned expressions and the young children – the girls with flaxen pigtails and the tough-looking little boys. There seem to be so many children in Germany in these villages – it makes me nervous to see them – seeing in them the seeds of another war; and we don't seem to have enough children in England. How lovely England would be looking now . . . the bluebells in the woods and the quiet villages and little streams, and the swallows coming back and 'hearts at peace under an English heaven . . .'

But here it is the long, dusty cobbles and the fumes of petrol and grinding of tracks and the occasional violently dead man or animal, blood already coagulating in the dust. One is hungry and tired by nightfall, but we look like moving again fairly early tomorrow pushing on always for Bremen now only 4 miles from our leading troops. And Hannover has fallen; the advance to the Elbe continues, Koningsberg has been taken, Vienna is tottering. Soon, East and West will meet.

Letter from Ronnie and a book for N.Y. last night – the *Bedside Book* – a good collection of stories and articles.

Forgot one interesting item from the C.O. He says the Div. is bound for Denmark which will be a relief after the non-fraternisation now in force and tho' undoubtedly correct, a strain on everybody for we are a friendly army.

Friday 13 April

1830, near Goldenstadt: We moved on yesterday afternoon after the return of Bill French to the command of the battery – a very pleasing thing – and carried on till after dark, finally dropping into action west of Vechta. The only enemy activity was one medium S.P. gun which sent the occasional shell whistling and crashing somewhere not very far away. We got our meal about 2300 and then turned in until about 0800 today when we were woken with 'Prepare to Move'. We did so after lunch and although harassed by this same gun, came into action here during the afternoon. A little firing. I have picked up a rather nice Mercedes Benz 14 h.p. drophead coupe which is a handy thing to have about the place as my jeep is lost. It's a very good little car and goes well. One very good thing today was <u>2</u> lovely long letters from C. It had been rather a long time since I'd had one, so the two came as a special surprise. I must try and write back tonight. C.'s letter makes waiting for leave an absolute fever of anxiety.

Later: Our own brigade has come up the road and we are putting out O.P.s tomorrow morning. Actually I am being left with the battery for the moment and Bill is going out. Apparently there is no real prospect of anything in the way of a battle, just taking over ground. I can't say I like being left back here. However, it'll be a change.

Yesterday I got a book (returned by Ronnie) from his wife, also 3 *Tatlers* which gave rise to the usual cynical outbursts in the mess. Another lovely day. Summer seems to be coming early – and 'Apple blossom fills the air' – though that was Spring, of course. Sent C. no. 59.

14 April

2010, Wildenhaussen: Moved here today and the Div. are behind us. Ahead, the town is being mortared occasionally but generally speaking things are pretty quiet. The 2 Bills have gone off to 5 B.W. I am being left out of this next battle – if there is a battle. Went to see Sandy L. this evening to show him my car. Drank too much schnapps and reached 90 k.p.h. coming back.

16 April

Each day leave grows nearer and each day it seems to grow further away. The thought of going into battle grows more repugnant as the time for going to England grows closer. We stayed here all yesterday and are leaving late this afternoon. Weather still lovely but sounds of gunfire etc. have greatly increased. Over the Elbe where the Americans have 2 bridgeheads, one has been eliminated by heavy and persistent counter attack. On our own front the 15, 43 and 11 Amd. have also been counter attacked by German Marine Divisions. Evidently the war is not over yet. Roosevelt died suddenly last Thursday which is the hell of a blow to the allies. I should think he's almost the person we could least have spared and his successor seems a pretty ineffectual type. A depressing event. Chas came back yesterday afternoon from Guards and Armd. Div. where he'd been doing C.R.A.'s rep. Letters from home and H. yesterday. Replied to the former. The car is going exceptionally well and excites admiring comment.

Night – nearer Bremen: I am in a tent. From the nearby tent in which we have a small Mess come strains of Drink to Me Only. Overhead the bombers drone northwards. I was called up to the B.W. quite suddenly at midday and got up there to find the 115 Panzer Grenadiers being troublesome. Several s.p. guns and mortars were dropping stuff about the place, also some light flak guns. We've had some bad losses. An A Coy. sub. killed; two more wounded. Aldo Campbell wounded, Graham Pilcher badly wounded, and this afternoon, a few minutes after he'd been joking with me, Sandy L. got himself hit in 3 places, tho' thank heavens not seriously. Sgt. Hinchcliff (D.C.M.) another B Coy. friend of mine, was also hit by a bullet in each leg. The Gordons came through us and the Bde. has finished for the time being so Bill French sent me back. The Div. is rumoured to be scheduled to attack Bremen, which doesn't look like being so funny. I wish leave weren't so near; it doesn't do one's fighting spirit much good! Sent C. no. 60 today. Sandy Cowie's Croix de Guerre – an issue to Regts. and Bns. – has come through. He was wearing it and it did look quite nice. Great rumble of bombs from the north – softening them up I hope. 154 do an attack tomorrow.

17 April

Hot afternoon; the heat shimmers from the fields and red tiles of farm buildings. The road, winding through the green woods, is covered with a pall of dust as the ceaseless traffic rumbles down it towards Bremen. Overhead, the growl of fighters. Down here the occasional incredibly vicious crack as our guns fire on the slowly retreating enemy. We are moving up towards Delmondhorst this afternoon. Whether or not we assault Bremen is not yet known though it seems probable.

18 April

1900, Ippener: An enormous thunderstorm accompanied by hailstones about the size of a shilling burst on us yesterday afternoon and cleared the air, which had become very oppressive. This morning we moved again and got into action here before lunch. The weather is again fine. 152 are doing an attack tonight and 153 the day after tomorrow. It is thought that Delmondhorst is the objective, and it'll probably be no easy one. The enemy is fighting a very stiff rearguard round these parts and it's costing us fairly heavy casualties. I must say I don't look forward to the next attack – leave is too near, and life is too precious. Just the wrong frame of mind in which to enter a battle! Mail from Dorothy and home yesterday. Replied to both. Some more in tonight – not yet seen. (no luck)

19 April

Dusk, nearer Bremen: We came up here and joined the 5 B.W. this morning rather suddenly. The Bn. in turn has relieved 1 B.W. out of 154 Brigade. Still lovely weather and in the fading sun the enemy shells and mortars come crashing and crumping down in front of us where 152 advanced last night and this morning. We attack – the Bde. that is (the other two Bns. are still back somewhere or other) – tomorrow evening, Delmondhorst being the objective – I believe it is the Div. objective. A Bde. seems an awfully small force to employ – I feel considerable misgivings about the whole business – I hope they are misplaced. There go the heavy guns booming from Bremen . . . I am with C Coy., now commanded by a Major Fotheringham – quite a pleasant kind with an M.C. won in 1940 in France, since when he has been in England till the last week or two. Aldo Campbell, the 2nd i/c is also missing from the last do. He lost a testicle which must have upset him but reports say he'll still be normal on the sex side. Graham Pilcher is still on the danger list, and of Sandy there is no fresh news. The general news is still very good – particularly as read in the *Daily Telegraph*. We are quartered here in a large farm building with several outhouses, and quite comfortable. I've scrounged a nice little mattress to take the cold out of the floor tonight.

Bill French has gone back to the Bty. to collect mail. I hope there's something for me this evening. (There wasn't.)

20 April

1630, Delmondhorst: While the big shots sat round the conference table this morning, puzzling how to take this place, we were all suddenly electrified by the announcement that the Recce had found it clear. So I went with D Coy. (in carriers) and was therefore almost first to enter the town, which seems to have been declared open on account of the large number of casualties in it. It teems with civilians and is nearly undamaged. At the entrance to the town we got an ecstatic welcome from a large crowd of slave workers, throwing flowers at us and cheering. Quite a good moment. I am now perched in the tower of the Nord-Deutscher Wool Company's factory on the eastern end of the town. Bremen lies sprawled before us, and occasionally erupts into a column of smoke as another bridge is blown. It doesn't look particularly damaged from here. The Russians are 20 miles from Berlin. We are 7 from Hamburg. Noisy night last night; enemy mediums pounding the area just in front of us. Himmler visited Bremen two days ago to give them a pep-talk.

21 April

a.m.: I have a cold, a snuffly, irritating cold, and until a few minutes ago it has been raining furiously. Most annoying. The weather seems to have broken. Had a very good night's sleep; the only enemy activity apparent to us was an occasional clump of medium shells, but not near enough to cause any alarm and despondency. This morning I am going from C (where I spent last night) over to B – the left flank company, but visibility doesn't look much use at the moment. There is no form – it seems that Bremen will be attacked from the other side of the river and not by us which is good news. It is horribly cold by comparison with the recent summery weather.

Same night: Moved to B Coy. when the rain stopped. It is now commanded by rather a nice chap called Simon Ramsay – prospective Conservative M.P. for somewhere or other. Was in the desert and has an M.C. But I miss Sandy. Gordon Taylor came back from a booze gathering swan round France. He is also replaced by Jimmy Forbes, a thoroughly nice bloke who recently returned to comd. S Coy. Gordon told me some time back he was going to ask the C.O. to change his job as he feels a bit past it, and he may be going to take over S Coy. now. Heavy rain showers. Mail today, but once more absolutely nothing for me. Very disappointing.

There is a camp right in our Coy. area here containing 300 Russian slave workers. They look pretty moronic but hate the Germans heartily enough, and have even pinched a spandau from somewhere, and are mounting a voluntary guard. However, the danger of infiltrating German agents is considerable and we've cause to believe that's exactly what is happening. Harassing fire on both sides as darkness falls.

23 April

a.m., same place: Spent all yesterday here. It was uneventful except that 760 heavy bombers came and plastered an area beyond Bremen at five o'clock in the evening. My cold is still very snuffly and my head weighs about 25 lbs. A letter from C. last night. Heard that Peter Dawson's M.C. has come through. Can't help being secretly rather bitter as he got it for his first O.P. job and not being in line for promotion, hasn't even the prospect of further F.O.O.ing. And yet some of us have been on the job for 7 or 8 months without so much as a Mention.* All rather unworthy of me – but this medal business is becoming a bit of a racket. Wrote C. no. 63 last night and shall post it today.

Later: at the gunline: A bad day it's been. In the afternoon I was feeling pretty done up with this cold and a tooth had been bothering me last night, so I went to the dentist and had two of my (precious) remaining teeth out – very painfully as they both had an abscess on them – only to discover that the eye tooth uncovered thereby had another large hole in it and is also in danger. Oh hell. So when Bill French offered to let me come in and Bill C. come out, I accepted gratefully and I shall go to bed for a day or so I think. I have to return to the torture chamber on Wednesday – a prospect which I dread very much. Steve leaves us tomorrow. I shall miss him a lot. I have acquired another pair of binoculars – my own were 10 x 50 but these are of the same strength, and Zeiss glasses with more clarity and a bigger range. They are wonderful glasses.

Apart from my own petty worries, the war goes well. The Russians are fighting in Berlin, the assault on Bremen from the East has started, the 5th and 8th have reached the river Po, and the American 3rd and 7th armies are 50 miles from Munich. Hitler is said by the Germans to be in Berlin. Everybody has been horrified by pictures in the paper of German horror camps at Belsen and Buchenwald.

---

* Mine arrived later.

24 April

Evening: A bad night last night. The soporific dope tablets I took before bed-time ran out in the small hours and I woke up several times with an aching mouth. Today my mouth is still aching rather, but I'm hoping it doesn't augur any more immediate horrors. Tomorrow will tell to some extent. Letters from Dorothy and B. Sunny weather with a blue sky but much cloud. I stayed in bed until 1500. Still no release of any leave date, which is damned annoying as one simply can't make any arrangements till one has some idea of the date.

Night: I'm going to bed in a few minutes. My jaw is aching but won't for long with a good stiff dose of Veganin inside me. Sent no. 65 to C. and wrote back to Dorothy. Am dreading tomorrow afternoon's performance as much as I always do. Still, I must get it over. Bill F. came down and we had a few rubbers of bridge. What a grand chap he is. Charles borrowed a radio for the evening as our own was being repaired. He is an inveterate fiddler and is never happier than when going in a series of squeaks and squeals from station to station. As he says, Joan (his wife) would never let him do it at home! He got on a station this evening when on a rather a pleasant programme and said: 'this wireless really is excellent. You can almost ignore it!' 400 guns are shelling Bremen, and 52 Div. are attacking from the East while 3 and 43 and 2 Cdn. converge from South and West. We are holding only. I somehow think Hamburg may be in store for us; a somewhat toughish nut to crack I should think. Patton is driving down on Munich and the Bavarian redoubt. The 8th have crossed the Po. The Russians hold 1/3 of Berlin. Modena, Ferrara and Spezia are ours. One is apt to forget in these moments of triumph, the heavy price we've had to pay for them. The lonely graves in lonely places, the little groups of crosses in Holland and Belgium, with Spring flowers put on them every day, and far away under the bright desert stars lie those who have helped to make it all possible and will not share it. I don't forget those often and I am glad I don't.

25 April

Evening: My visit turned out less horrifying than I expected after all. Admittedly after he had drilled two large holes in my left eye tooth he found another even bigger in my right, but when, after a 40 minute session I lay back with sweaty palms and damp forehead, I felt: Thank the Lord I've had <u>those</u> done (for they're jobs I've been summoning up courage to do for some time). The scene of the earlier battles is still very sore but less so than yesterday. I hope by tomorrow (when I have to go again) it will be almost better. Another book from N.Y. arrived today, also a parcel of envelopes from C. but no letter. All things being equal, I expect to go back up to the O.P. (now nearer Bremen) tomorrow afternoon when I get back.

26 April

Evening, Huchting Rly. Stn, the O.P.: The O.P. is just this side of one of those large stretches of flood water which lie around Bremen. Two miles away, the city lies smouldering and burning in the evening sunshine. Seen from close up, there is far more damage than was apparent from my O.P. at the wool factory. Nearly all the big buildings seem to be in ruins, and the church towers and factory towers are mere shells. There is little or no movement. To all outward view Bremen is a dead city. Tomorrow we are moving towards Hamburg, leaguering at a place called Scharnhorst. I am going independently by car. I went again to the dentist and had all my teeth cleaned up. Bremen is almost clear – expected clear by tonight, I understand. I believe the Div. is to attend to the Weser Estuary. Letter from B. today.

27 April

1730, north of Volkersen: Almost it goes without saying that two or three changes of orders have taken place since I last wrote, but briefly I left this morning, came on independently and have now arrived in the middle of a huge wooded marsh, with not so much as a tent to protect us. By way of emphasis, it has been raining since daybreak. The Regt. is expected about 2130.

On the way up here I called at long last on Debroy who is very well and living in stinking luxury in 'L' Mess Main 30 Corps where he receives both field allowance and 5/- a day for swanning vaguely round in Jeep or staff car 'contacting' people. A wonderful war this is. Excellent mail before I left from Bé, C. and home. The question now is: where to sleep tonight? . . .

28 April

2115, Attken: Still have an aching mouth so will just note briefly that we shared a bit of B.W. room last night and slept from 0100 to 0700. Then we advanced unopposed all today and the guns came up alongside this evening.

The leave situation is still not certain. I am hoping for 6 May but for one reason and another it's all proving very difficult, but I'll go on trying all I can. Germany is breaking up. Himmler's offer of unconditional surrender to the Western Allies only has been refused. The Russians and Americans have joined up. Mussolini has been captured – for what he's worth. Very bad weather but it changed in the afternoon. The Italian front is crumbling.*

---

* Alec Brodie came back this day but was shot in the leg and arm by his pillion rider on 4 May and is away to hospital again – this is reputed to be his 47th time wounded.

30 April

Same place, with C Coy: Yesterday Jerry Shiel our C.R.A. was killed by a mine. It's a terrible loss to the Div. and the Div. Arty., and what utterly bloody luck on a man who'd come all the way from Alamein without a scratch. What good people we are losing in these final stages.

Today it is cold and raining, just as it was most of yesterday. Miserable weather, and I feel pretty low. My mouth was painful all day yesterday once more and is aching slightly today. I believe the infection is taking rather a time to disperse or something. I've got some permanganate from the M.O. to wash my mouth out. He says this will help. I hope it does. However, I've left my really good news: I should be in England on the 8th of May – leaving the battery on the 5th. Instead of going to Osnabruck in transport, I shall go by car to Gennep and catch the boat train to Calais from there. Sent C. no. 68 last night telling her. I am from this point L.O.B. (Left out of Battle – a military expression dating, I believe, from Africa where I heard it first). Meantime the war continues well. Mussolini caught and shot by partisans, Milan and Venice taken, the Russians and ourselves converging on Lübeck, Hitler reportedly dying of a stroke, Berlin almost taken. But the weather is lousy, as April goes out in a gust of cold rain.

2 May

a.m., gunline, near Bevern: Last night the radio announced that Hitler had died at the chancellory in Berlin and that Admiral Raeder had been appointed his successor. The same day saw the Red Flag flying over the Reichstag, the link up of 8th Army with Tito, the allies advancing towards Innsbruck and the Brenner pass, and British tanks 18 miles from Lübeck on the Baltic. There can be no question that the war is nearing its end. As a local picture, the Div., spearheaded by the Guards and with 43 on the left, is driving for Bremerhaven and Wesermunde. The weather is still very poor. May is starting as badly as April started well. My mouth is still sore, but less so. Won £3.10. at poker two nights ago and £1 here last night at bridge when I was Bill French's partner v Charles and Bill Masson from 491.

I went over to 491 myself for tea and had the usual gossip. Incidentally, Sandy C. told me a few days ago in the deadliest secrecy (which I haven't violated) that Waggy is likely to be sent to India as a 2nd i/c. Also I find my own Age and Service Gp. is 26 now, which puts me in danger of Far East service. Hell, I don't think I could stand another campaign, though I suppose if I had to go I would. But what a prospect after so long. All I can really think of at the moment is going on leave. I go away from here on the 5th – only 3 days but how long it seems. Two letters (27 and 28 April) from C. yesterday. Move imminent to acquire range.

3 May

0100, Bremervoerde: We moved late in the afternoon, and had a very nasty reception. Namely a shower of moaning minnies followed by an unpleasantly close dozen airburst just over the road I was standing on. Two killed, one wounded. I am now sitting waiting for the Mess lorry to arrive, as we had to send back for it. I found rather a good house here; there are a dozen terrified women, children and old people in the cellar but I've told them they'll have to get out in the morning. Every now and then a nearby Medium battery crashes out with a most startling explosion, otherwise the night is fairly quiet. Spandaus are talking out in front where the Black Watch are busy. The 2 Bills joined them this evening, and we passed them on the way up. The sun came out this afternoon, and the weather looks like clearing up – just as well as there is already a 24 hours postponement for leave which means I don't get home till the 9th. What an incredibly wonderful thought. Late this evening the news came through that the Germans in Italy and Austria had surrendered unconditionally. I don't think the end can be delayed by more than weeks – perhaps even days – now.

Letter from Dorothy. I sent C. no. 71 (our old unit Serial No. in Africa – so what?!)

Same evening, same place: The afternoon was livened up by attacks by about a dozen Jerry fighter bombers – the first we've seen for ages. The sky filled with flak and the crackle of Oerlikon guns. No bombs fell very near: This is the last corner of Germany in which resistance continues except for a small patch on the Baltic, for the 7th armoured entered Hamburg, which surrendered at 1800 this evening. The only really large enemy pocket (except Norway and Denmark) now left in Europe, is in Czechoslovakia.

A large enemy coast (?) gun is firing somewhere up forward and a huge crump shakes the ground as the shells land. Yesterday we took 1000 prisoners or more up here, some of them looked literally 14 years old, and today droves more have been coming in. There has also been a constant procession up the road towards Bremerhaven – tanks (mostly 8th Armoured Bde.), flame throwers (chiefly crocodiles), and every conceivable type of M.T. And, towards evening, the 154 Bde. mounted in Kangaroos. Mail brought me nothing but this evening I sent C. no. 72. Can hardly wait for tomorrow to be over.

4 May

Over the wireless a quarter of an hour ago came the voice of the announcer – 'All German forces in NW Germany, Holland, Denmark and Heligoland have surrendered to Field Marshal Montgomery's 21st Army Gp.' All over the village, Brens are firing into the air, flares are going up and even the Germans are out on the street as the word spreads rapidly around which really marks the end of the journey begun when Mr. Churchill told the Germans in those long dark days – 'We shall never surrender!' It seems strange to think that I may (repeat MAY) never have to risk my life in battle again.

Sent C. no. 73.

6 May

Afternoon, 's Hertogenbosch: Started at 0830 yesterday and arrived here at 2045 with two half hour halts for repairs. Distance exactly 310 miles. The evening before, Debroy had come in and we'd all had a few drinks and then I went round the troop where everybody was loosing off bren guns, stens, pistols and Very lights; as far as the eye could see the sky was green and red, orange, mauve and white and the cheers and rattle of small arms made the night full of noise. I was reminded of Benghazi in 1942.

Yesterday's long trip here was full of interest, particularly the heavily battered towns of the Rhineland – all names which we've written in blood – picturesque Cleve, perched on a hillside, Xanten with its noble ruined church tower, Wesch, in which I think no single house is left standing, and all the ghostly trenches, ammo. dumps, shattered trees and lonely graves over the flat lands leading to the Rhine. When I got here the city was all out on the streets celebrating the capitulation in the N.W. Flags and orange banners everywhere, and crowds going wild with joy, singing and dancing in the rain. The war has indeed passed 's Hertogenbosch. Even the L of C consider it a back area now. The car went pretty badly most of the way, having oil pressure, carburettor and general petrol trouble. Heaven knows how they'll get it back to Bremerhaven! Last night the Troupins, my friends here, invited me over to a party where we all drank cognac and Benedictine till a late hour so I didn't get up till 1100 today. And tomorrow I go to Gennep to get the train to Calais – and England . . . Am getting some cigars here for Pa, and I hope some French perfume for C. and Mom and probably a bottle for B. too. I really can't believe I shall be home in a day or two.

Got the cigars (£2.15!).

7 May

1830, Telen, Belgium: The war is over – we got this news in Tilburg as the train passed through. Now we are halted in a small village in the hot evening sunshine. The church bell is ringing and the apple blossom is out and everything is so very peaceful. All through Holland and Belgium we've been greeted by waves and V signs and cheers. Holland is a mass of flags. I can hardly wait to get home; equally I can hardly understand that for Europe it is over, at long last, almost 5 years to the day since the Germans attacked the neutrals and set the Western front alight. And how many good lives it's cost us to put things right again.

I wish they could all be here to see what they have made possible. A gloomy note for 'V.E.' day and peace, but let's hope we don't forget that side of things.

8 May 1945 – V.E. Day

0900, Calais: Today is V.E. day after all – not yesterday as we originally supposed. Mr. Churchill is speaking at 1500 and the King at 2100. I should be sailing for Folkestone at 1245 and therefore be in London by this afternoon. It was a long journey yesterday. All through Belgium we were cheered and saluted; I've never seen so many smiling faces in my life (I wonder if they were smiling in La Roche . . .). At 2330 we reached Lille and changed Engines and got out for an hour for a cup of tea and sausage roll. The streets were brightly lighted and plenty of people were lit up too. After that I slept for two or three hours till we reached Calais at 0330 and after changing currency I went to bed till about 0800. Then up and shaved and washed, and now we have several dreary hours to fill in before going. Last time I saw Calais was when we attacked it last year, and I remember standing on the obstacle studded beach near Gris Nez and seeing the white cliffs in the sunshine – so near it seemed and yet how many dangerous weeks have gone by before – today – I can look on them again.

29 May

Bevern, near Bremervoerde: I haven't often left this as long as three weeks before, but I felt so dispirited when I got back from leave on the 24th that it's taken me a few days to make my mind up to write it again. Well – passing over leave (just like that) – I came to the night of the 21st when with a gloomy crowd of leave-expired men, I reported to Victoria Stn. to return to the Continent. The Station was jammed with a great crowd of both sexes, ranging from riotously drunk to gloomily sober (these included me) and eventually I got in a train and down to Folkestone we went, where we really spent quite a comfortable night in Princes Hotel, which is now a transit camp. Left again next morning on quite a choppy sea, and I was quite glad when we went into Calais harbour which, on the return trip looked exceedingly drab and bleak and bombed and our depression increased when on our march to the transit camp we saw the chaps marching the other way towards the boat – and home. Still, we thought, we were the first lot to have 11 days so we musn't grumble. (Actually I took a little 'buck' – the first time I've ever done so – so I had least moan of all.) Into the transit camp to find our train left for Gennep about 10 o'clock that night and with nothing to do till then, except sit in the Nissen hut containing the bar and drink beer. Some humorist has called this bar 'Ye Way Back Inn' and it was well patronised (specially by the vociferous and boastful Canadians over from Italy full of themselves and their heroic deeds). The train left that night and took exactly 12 hours to reach Gennep where we had breakfast, packed into

T.C.V.s and drove for 7 hours to Osnabruck where 2nd Army Transit camp is located (the railway reached O. a few days later).

Next morning we got into Div. transport and leaving about 0900 reached Main Div. at 1500. One more trip to Bremervoerde bridge where I was picked up* by a 304 truck (I'd phoned from Div.) and I arrived back at the Bty. rather tired out. The first unwelcome discovery I made was that Findlay was away on 11 days compassionate leave, so Bill Carney's batman, Winder, undertook to look after me too. Secondly that anything over A & S Gp. 25 might go to the Far East (not 27 and over as originally announced). Being Gp. 26 this has considerably shaken me. There are several moans at this in the bty. which I record here:

Under Scheme 'Python' anybody with 3 years service overseas (Excluding B.L.A.) came home. This means that chaps from India or Gib. etc. who have never fired a shot in anger come home whereas (as among so many of our chaps) blokes who've done Africa, Sicily and the whole campaign in Europe may have to fight the Japs too. To the commonsense eye this is preposterous. Not that the Army could be expected to understand that. You also revert to war substantive rank which would wave goodbye to my third pip if I go. Another blow is that the Army newspaper talk of 25 Gps. out by the end of 1945 also appears to be balls and the earliest Gp. 26 can hope for is about April 1946. Making $6^{1}/_{2}$ years war service at that date.

The programme at the moment is chiefly sport, P.T., education and games. Softball – the popular sport – is a kind of debased but ferociously energetic baseball – we played the 491 officers the other night and were soundly beaten. Also at bridge later in the evening. The snag about education is that there are no books, and won't be till the end of the year. We are moving in a week or two to Verden to a big barracks where the C.O. can attain his heart's desire – a Regtl. Mess – he being the only officer in the Regt. who wants one — however 'twas ever thus. Today the 2 Bills and Chas and I are going to look over the place which is at present full of Poles. It has already been rejected by Div. H.Q. and is therefore eminently suitable for us. We are also having to house Ambulance and Middlesex people. It sounds bloody. It probably will be. We are pretty comfortable here anyway though the flies are bad and Typhus has broken out two villages away.

Incidentally on my way here, I think I saw the worst bomb-damage I've ever seen – in Münster, which is absolutely flattened. I suppose that in the central district not one per cent of the houses are habitable. If this is a sample (and Bremerhaven which I saw yesterday is similar) it will take at least 20 years to rebuild Germany.

High summer is coming in, with the odd thunderstorm breaking days full of sunshine and soft airs. Everything is green.

Must leave now. I'll add more later.

---

* So was Himmler, by the way. We have a most stringent guard on the place.

31 May

The days pass pleasantly enough with harmless unwarlike activities such as route marches and games. Yesterday we did one in the morning and in the afternoon watched the battery beat 301 two nil at Soccer. After tea, Charles, Bill and I armed with shotguns went out in the fields and woods. We shot one hare and missed another but there wasn't really much wildlife about the place. Had a letter from C. yesterday – in fact I've had one every day since I've been back – also one from B. There have also been sundry parcels of food and books from America. We went down to Verden the other day to look at the new quarters – an enormous ex-cavalry barracks which may, as a matter of fact, be fairly comfortable, being lavishly fitted with showers and ablutions in general, also central heating and electric light. If only the C.O. didn't insist on a Regtl. officers mess one could be fairly happy there. Also very good riding facilities if we can get hold of some horses and riding gear in general. We are said to be moving there not earlier than 10 June. The C.O. has been away with Sandy Cowie for the last 3 or 4 days, getting sports kit in Brussels. Sandy is likely to become adjutant and Bill Ovenstone suddenly left to have his appendix removed. There has been that pleasantly relaxed atmosphere that creeps in when you know the C.O. isn't going to come snooping about the place. The present C.O. isn't particularly popular anyway with his devotion to rather bad manners, and mania for white webbing (which, incidentally has been over-ruled anyway by H.Q.R.A.). The Far East worry is no nearer solution than before. Anybody over A & S Gp. 25 is definitely in the running but one hopes the Africa Star will help. In the Regt., only one Tp. Comd. (Peter McCarthy) has a higher number than me, and he is 32. Matt Simm is 29 but he's going to the J.A.G. Side. Bill is 25, so is Ian Kidd and Jimmy Gegan's about 23. Typhus is rampaging about 4 or 5 miles away and everybody has to have a re-inoculation. Also it was announced yesterday that 96% of the women in Bremervoerde have V.D. – a figure I find it hard to believe. Incidentally – items of vocabulary arising from our travels include one from non-fraternisation, by which a girl is known as a piece of 'Frat'. Another, from the cries from people in Holland and Germany is 'Allus Kaput.' Also 'Nix in der Winkel allus in der Kelder' – a reference to the German habit of hiding stuff in the cellar. They also used to bury it in the garden, but our chaps got wise to that and used to prod with anti-schumine prodders with occasional quite spectacular results. 'Having no clue' or 'clueless' is another expression meaning somebody who hasn't much idea what's going on. Also 'Seek' (sick) is the reply if you don't want to carry out some detail. Tonight we are playing a return match with 491 at softball and bridge.

2 June

Curious development in the Regimental scene. The C.O. can't get an adjutant. Bill Carney said he'd rather go to Burma and Sandy Cowie has somehow got out of it, so last night C.O. went to 301 and told Frank, Neil was to do it. This, the latter refused point blank to do, and Peter Macarthy who would have to go to 491 to replace Matt Simm (who goes to J.A.G. Branch tomorrow) refused to do that. Waggy in turn refused point blank to have Kiddo (even with £100 thrown in). At this point my name which had been hovering nervously on the outskirts for some little time, definitely came in when the other two B.C.s descended on Bill French last night. So I in my turn also refused. The situation remains therefore somewhat tense and completely as before – i.e. we have no adjutant.

Today I had to go to Corps to what had been described as a lecture of admin. I came away after a four hour course as one of the four officers in the Div. with a warrant to hold Summary Courts of Justice, with maximum powers of 12 months or ten thousand marks fine.

In my absence there was a 'mess meeting' behind which democratic facade, the C.O. lays down his wishes. These include a Mess Sec. (poor Bill Carney!), a Wine Sec., a Catering Sec, a Newspapers Officer – and he even wanted a gardening officer but didn't quite get away with it. Also a levy of £20 from each battery and £3 a head for rather inferior wine. Vive la Paix! Also insisted on: mess waiters with white jackets and gunner buttons!

They say:

– The Americans are striking an Ardennes medal for which we qualify. I also should get 4 more of the British issue.
– We are moving soon.
– We are losing all guns and equipment.

Good news: Only 27 and over for the Far East. This was collected by Sandy direct from O2E when he was in Brussels. He bought me a bottle of perfume for 800 francs which a few months ago cost (only a rather prettier bottle) 330. Welcome Liberators . . .

Good news: Butcher's M.M. came through this evening. Thank god somebody gets the medals anyway!

Rain stopped play the other evening when we were well ahead of 491. I have wrenched a groin muscle and am ordered no exercise for 3 weeks by the M.O. but I think it may take less. Local outbreak of Typhus has given rise to re-inoculations all round.

They say:

– No 2nd leaves to start till August. Reason:
– Too much work with demobbing.

Letters coming regularly from C. I sent her no. 84 yesterday.

4 June

304 and 491 officers last night played the Rest and beat them 7–3 at soccer. Bill C. and I couldn't play owing to sprained muscles. During the game the C.O. and Bob Mackay pulled the same ones. It always seems to be the big thigh muscle which goes first. Sandy Cowie has taken adjutant after all. Went to Bremervoerde this morning and laid on to use the courtroom next Thursday morning. So far there are no cases in this district but I suppose some may crop up. News re. the move is still vague. Apparently the Poles don't want to leave the barracks and some 21 A.G. engineering school wants to go into it. Latest verdict: we may move there even if we have to move again afterwards. Crass stupidity this as we're perfectly comfortable here. (No Regimental Mess here, however, which automatically condemns it in the eyes of the C.O. The C.O. is now known variously* as 'The groom' [my nickname which has a goodish following], 'Pig Face' [301's contribution] or 'The Non-entity' – which, though pleasing, is, I suspect not all that accurate. He is definitely not very popular.)

Findlay has been located at Gennep and so should be back here soon. Good. Also I want to know if he's wearing my best shirt which has mysteriously disappeared – I <u>think</u> on Findlay's body! Current joke is still 'Mr. Justice Swaab' accompanied by cries of 'the Court will Rise' when I come in the room etc. etc. etc. – Sent 85 and 86 to C. No mail for me yesterday at all.

7 June

a.m.: Yesterday being the anniversary of Der Tag we had a whole holiday, culminating in a 'Battery Social' in the evening. The barn in which the men's dining room is situated was splendidly decorated, a piano was obtained, and the cooks surpassed themselves, making a great buffet with cakes, sandwiches etc. There were 2 barrels of beer, a bottle of red wine per man, and a quadruple issue of rum. I wrote a duet which Bill C. and I were to perform. By about half past seven however we were very considerably lit up, and arriving to find the whole battery feeling the same, we had great difficulty putting the song over, though the audience sang the chorus lustily enough! By about 10 (I'm told) the few drunken survivors were scattering. I don't remember much more than that. I only know I woke up this morning with a splitting head, and Bill was violently sick into a bucket which somebody had conveniently left by his head. And is still prostrate in bed.

This morning's Court in Bremervoerde was spoiled by the non-appearance of the prisoner!** I helped on another court instead. The place was well attended by civvies.

---

* Also 'Porky' – I believe this originated in R.H.Q.: finally and universally known as 'Walnut' – also my invention – taken from the size (alleged) of his brain.

** Finally remanded by me the following Monday and executed in the first week in August.

The move to Verden is to be to civvy billets as the barracks are not available. Later, I understand, we shall move into some other barracks at present occupied by D.P.s. No mail today – the A.P.O. must have had a holiday too. Also none yesterday. My mail has been very poor lately.

8 June

An Ensa show came yesterday. I've never yet been to an Ensa show so I didn't start last night. We gave the company tea, and, after the last performance, drinks. Laurence and I went to tea but 'the gels' were making up and only one appeared. A self-possessed blonde of about 24, quite pleasant when she could forget her inferiority complex. 'From the Windmill', her act is described on the poster, and frankly I think that if you only had 3 words to use you couldn't find 3 that did the job more adequately.

The weather is curious here. The mornings are bright and sunny, but in the afternoons it starts to cloud over and very often in the evenings it rains and thunders. Sent C. no. 91.

10 June

Sunday: I seem to be getting more infrequent and less interesting where entries in this book are concerned. Chiefly I think because life is less interesting nowadays. There is awfully little to do and when the weather is as unsettled as it has been lately, you can't even play games much. The prospect of another year or even longer in these conditions, depresses everybody, for unless they find more for us to do, people are going to become awfully discontented. There is no doubt also that non-fraternisation though (I think) an excellent policy is proving a considerable strain on the men particularly. The only ones who are tempted to break the rules in private, run a very good chance of getting V.D. and one or two have got it already. It is made more difficult by the women who, generally speaking, go out of their way to be tempting both in dress and manner, and in summer dresses that can be quite tempting for somebody with no other ties. However, anyway on the face of it, non-fraternisation is being very faithfully carried out.

We move to Verden on Wednesday. This also is a bone of much contention for although we are going into billets till some fearful barracks is cleared of D.P.s, vermin etc., the C.O. insists on a Regimental Mess. The absolute pigheadedness of this is indicated by the fact that we have to go a mile to the Mess for each meal, and 301 a mile and a half. I think only two officers in the Regiment want a Mess – the C.O. and the C.O.2. The rest are solidly against it. So we are having one. Danger! Democracy at work! (Not, actually, that one really expects or even wants democracy in an army, but common sense at least would be welcome.) Moreover, it seems our quarters won't be vacated by the guards till about the 16th so we have the prospect of a night or two in tents, and as Bill Carney put it: 'Everyone knows we CAN manage in tents – but why the HELL SHOULD WE?' – Unfortunate perhaps that General Horrocks, the Corps Commander, should have proclaimed so loudly and publicly his intention that the fighting troops should have first claim to every comfort, for so far we seem to be in line for none, and we don't forget those broken promises. No wonder the prevalent mood in the army ever since I've been in it, has been one of cynical disbelief where promises of better things have been concerned.

The fruit is coming on well on all the local trees and bushes. This evening for supper we had some delicious fresh strawberries – the best treat we've had for ages. Sent C. no. 93 today, also a souvenir in the shape of a memorial service card for the end of hostilities in NW Europe. On the front was the 2nd Army sign surrounded by every Corps, Div. and Independent Brigade Sign which made it up, and done in colour and really rather impressive. Findlay still isn't back – and Dante (the favourite) won the Derby. And now I'm going to sleep.

13 June

Afternoon, Verden: We left Bevern this morning in pouring rain which continued intermittently throughout the journey, and reached this end in 3 hours, which was two less than the powers that be had 'estimated'. The quarters at this end are pretty good; a bit crowded at the moment, till the Guards clear out on Friday but comfortable enough.* One supreme luxury as far as our own mess is concerned is a bath – rather antiquated it's true, and worked by a sort of boiler, but long enough to lie down in and the water will be hot. My wireless is plugged in now, for we have electricity and proper lighting and everything. We are getting rather spectacular results these days – Ankara, Cairo, Italy, and a Japanese station speaking in English, and the short wave is positively hotching with stations every night. We'd been promised a double letter mail today, but all I got was a letter from B. This house of ours is very old (1670) and high and narrow with sloping floors which I remember C. told me are signs of authenticity in houses. But it's pretty comfortable. I am sharing a room with Laurence Geller. Bill French says second leave is starting up again almost immediately.

15 June

This morning, the Guards finally went away, leaving the area very dirty and mucked about, and so we have now taken over all our quarters complete. It's a good area. On the large leafy green beside the cathedral, all the guns and vehicles in the battery are drawn up in meticulous lines, looking very smart. The billets are also very reasonable all round, containing running water, electrical light, and

---

* I forgot to mention that the Guards left our area, and all the bty. areas, absolutely filthy. Bill French wrote rather a well-worded note on the subject to the C.O.

similar amenities. Non-frat is still being strictly carried out. In my opinion, for what it's worth, this grows easier with time. Admittedly I've no particular desire to fraternise, which perhaps makes it easier, but I really don't think it's as difficult as some people make out, particularly as we are not living in conditions of great want. However, I've heard it said that food is getting increasingly short around these parts. Yesterday afternoon I had an awful attack of migraine, which absolutely flattened me out for the rest of the day. This afternoon we had the Regimental Sports at the local stadium which is now under our control. 491 won the sport by a narrow margin from R.H.Q. of all people, with us a very comfortable last! Jimmy Gegan and I acted as time keepers. I have to attend a course at Div. H.Q. at Stade, starting on Monday and lasting, I believe, a week. I am sharing a room with Bill Carney in these new quarters which are very comfortable. We even have beds; no mattresses it is true, but very springy springs. Latest 'Crasshood' is by the C.R.A. – as follows: the vehicles in the Regiment could hardly be better but apparently the C.R.A. told the Colonel that he wanted to see them varnished! Varnished! The army in peace time . . .

17 June

2220. Div. H.Q. Harsefeld: Left Verden rather regretfully about 1315 as it was nice sunny weather and all the others were scything the lawn and everything was peaceful and pleasant. And it will mean no more strawberries for supper; which we've been getting with monotonous regularity lately – if you can imagine strawberries getting monotonous. Anyway off we set; I was driving the 15 cwt. and Jimmy Low in front with me. We reached here without incident or losing our way. (Zeugma I believe they call that.) The mail had come in just before I left, bringing me one from C. to whom I've just written no. 100. Div. is where I left it the other day and is not worthy of any particular comment. We are in 'X' Mess where the food anyway is very good. We are billetted out on some Germans who seem quite well-behaved and who own a large cherry tree from which in their usual way they have just given us a large bowl of fruit. Thus are the strawberries avenged! The course starts at a nearby cinema tomorrow morning at the civilised hour of 1100–1600 daily. This could be much worse. Considerable local female attraction with non-frat at Div. H.Q. less observed than elsewhere.

21 June

In the lunch hour at Horneburg: This is the fourth day of the course, which ends on Saturday morning. I find it rather a dull course myself. From 11 till 1 we are lectured with a break at twenty to 12 for syndicates to discuss the subject matter and return half an hour later for joint discussion. Most of the stuff is on rather a high, rather a theatrical level, not of much value when it comes to putting it over to the men. I feel it's well meant but not quite hitting the nail on the head. Yesterday we had an ex-Moderator of the Church of Scotland who gave quite a good, rather sermonic address. He had the ability to repeat a sentence 3 times using different words. This morning we had a thing called 'Open Forum'. 1 member of each of the four syndicates had to get up and make a twenty minute speech. Nobody in mine would do it, so in the end I did, under the vague title of News and the Public. I don't think it was too dull.

Generally the routine of our day is pretty similar. When the course ends at 4 we go back by 126 truck (Bob Roote and 'Tiny', two chaps I know, are attending from 126) and have tea in the mess which is only about 15 minutes from here by truck. After tea, we usually walk to the billet and lie on our beds till supper. I've been doing some writing during these spells and I'm in the middle of a second short story at the moment. It's nice to have the leisure to do it. We usually fill ourselves with cherries or strawberries at this time – given us by the house family. We give cigarettes in exchange – rather weakly perhaps but I don't like raping the countries (even Germany) we overrun. After dinner we follow a similar routine and write letters. Yesterday some mail came from the Regt., including a letter from C. I sent her No. 103 today.

The village of Harsefeld is full of rather lovely girls in summer dresses causing the problem of 'fratting' to be widely discussed. It is now semi-officially allowed with children up to 8 years old, which I think myself is a mistake. A good deal of promiscuous poking goes on in the woods of an evening, so Findlay tells me. A discarded (used) french letter was lying on the pavement this morning outside the German Staff Officer's quarters. I've just heard an officer say 'I think the form is to take a stroll and look at the frat', which more or less typifies the rather repressed state most officers are living in at the moment. I suppose really it is rather tantalising to see so much and nothing else. I personally am not inclined to do more, but if you have no ties and no scruples, they must constitute an irritating influence.

It's been hot and sunny all the week and maddening to have to sit indoors all day long. I look forward to getting back to the battery – Regimental Mess or not.

23 June

2245, *Verden:* The truck which was to have fetched us today, failed to arrive, so by about 4 we decided to borrow a truck from Div. This we managed to do and we left about 5.10. I was driving. We got here in two hours. I was tired and had a headache from the glare. Four letters when I got back. 1 from D., 2 from C. and one from home. Also a book parcel from N.Y. containing two new books. I wrote two short stories at Div. and am in the middle of a third. I'm anxious to get started on a novel, but it's not a particularly easy thing to do, I find. Sent C. 106 this evening. News this end is chiefly of rage at a set of orders at the Regtl. mess, which if it weren't so wearyingly stupid would indeed be insulting. Bill French is out fishing with the C.O. Everybody else is here – Bill Carney suffering from alcoholic remorse again as the result of another jag the other night. I find it good to be back, comfortable though it was at Div. This is the nearest approach to home. Latest rumours say new ribbons imminent and 24 groups out by the end of the year. I wonder; it would be good going.

25 June

2220: Yesterday I decided after a very pleasant swim in the local river on a small private 'Kraft durch freude' programme. Actually I'd more or less decided on it before going on my course but yesterday I decided definitely. Starting today, I run half a mile* before breakfast and swim if possible these sunny afternoons. I went again today. The river here is deep, fairly wide – say 50 yards – and has a swift current. The banks and the bottom are sandy. The form is to swim as nearly straight across as possible and then walk up stream (yesterday about 1/2 a mile) and swim back. The river banks, except for our own private section, swarm with frat – some of it quite presentable. Also stacks of naked blond children of excellent physique. Two letters from C. yesterday. I sent no. 103 to her today. Went to the local flickhouse last night to see *The Uninvited* – quite a convincing thriller. The Regtl. Mess is a washout; by 9 o'clock there's nobody left in it except the C.O. and C.O.2 and sometimes Sandy Cowie – now irrevocably committed as adjutant! The food is good though. Am depressed this evening so I'll go to bed now I think.

27 June

1800: Good weather yesterday with a glorious bathe in the afternoon, but this morning it was raining lightly so that I got a bit wet on my early morning run, and during the day it has rained hard and constantly. No bathing today and it has been very dull and stagnant. A short letter from C. I sent off no. 110 today. The new D Tp. sign went up the other day accompanied by ribald comments from the other troops as it is very large. It's got a great HD in the centre with a gun crest on top, a 43 and a Q and a scroll with D Tp. down each side. It has five more scrolls and one more underneath, containing the troop's battle honours – Alamein, Tripoli, Mareth, Wadi Akarit, Enfidaville, Sicily, Normandy, Havre, Boulogne and Calais, Holland, Ardennes, Reichswald, the Rhine and Germany.

There is talk of moving the Regtl. mess to another very palatial house in the centre of the town. At the moment it is deserted except for meals.

Chas went home for a course and leave yesterday and I've taken over battery captain for a month, while retaining Don. Troop.

* Nearer ¾ of a mile.

Much play among certain regimental officers for the 6 Ensa girls who play what is known as 'good music' of an evening in the local theatre. They are known as the 6 Good Girls. At one time Ensa had a sort of H.Q. in this town, but now only passing companies stay at the Hannoversche Hof, the local hotel where the H.Q. used to be.

I'm having a hot bath this evening and then I'll go to bed and I hope finish my third story called 'White Xmas' – a story of a battle in the Ardennes which is nearly finished. I think it'll work out at about 3,000 words like the other two. Then I'll type them on the rather good portable I bought for £10 – which it would have cost in peacetime I think. It's a good model and almost new. Interest is fairly large in the general election. We found today that Eric Harben, one time B.C. of 491 and a bad type, is standing as Liberal candidate for Watford. I don't think he's got a hope. I hope not. The first reel of photos from my little camera were not very good because as I'd feared there is a small hole in the bellows which lets in a bit of light, so about half the prints are spoiled. Those that have come out show it to be quite a decent little toy. It has after all, a 2.8 lens and a 1/300 shutter, so it ought to be fairly good. I don't think I ever mentioned that my S.D. arrived from C. (sent to Harry Cates who brought it back from leave with him) on the 17th so I've been able to grace dinner nights correctly dressed.

30 June

Chief event today was a sport meeting at our local stadium against 86th Field Regiment – the Hertfordshire Yeomanry. They were well and truly beaten to the tune of 93 points to 30. Otherwise, the days have been rather monotonous with almost continuous heavy rain and thunderstorms which have precluded bathing – annoying as it's one of the biggest pleasures of a normal summer. Sent C. no. 112 this evening, making 29 letters I've sent her in June – more than in any month since I started writing. My early morning running – now by way of a regimental joke – is going on rather well. I am now doing $7/8$ of a mile each time, and as soon as I reach the stage of doing a mile, I'm going to start doing it with a stopwatch to see how long it takes me. In fact I think I'll probably attempt a mile tomorrow morning. At the moment I should think I'm taking nearly 7 minutes, but that's only a guess – it may be less than that. But not much less I'm sure! I've been typing out the stories I've finished; so far I've done nearly two of them. It's rather laborious work for I'm a slow typer. Beeston (Charles' batman) bought me a pair of swimming trunks in Antwerp, and I've also got hold of a pair of riding breeches – more accurately Don R. breeches, but quite adequate for riding. However, I want to find a quiet horse first! I've not ridden for about 6 years and anything with any fire would probably run away with me.

Played bridge last night with Bill French, Laurence, and Bob Gillman. I lost. One of our friends here is a Polish officer by the name of Morarvice. He snoops round the town trying to find things for us, and is on the trail of a Retina camera for me. This would be a good find if he could. He is anti-Russian government and I've not found any Poles outside Poland who are anything but anti-Russian. It is a very difficult problem, this one of Poland.

1 July

1830: More torrential rainstorms today and a few peals of thunder from time to time. So no bathing. And I didn't even do a run this morning as I woke up feeling bloody. The mess has moved into a rather more comfortable building – the ex-H.Q. of the local gestapo. Finished my typing of three stories today, and sent them off to S.G. for (I imagine) inevitable destruction. No letter from C. today for the third day running, but one did arrive from Dorothy. Also my voting papers from Chelsea. I've voted for the Conservative candidate – a naval Commander, with an impressive string of decorations. I think the Conservatives will win this election but not too easily. Sent C. no. 113 this evening. The sergeants have invited us over to their mess after supper; they're giving a farewell party for B.S.M. Lawbridge and Sgt. Baxter – both leaving for the Far East tomorrow. I rather doubt whether I shall go; I'm not feeling much in the mood for such festivity.

2 July

A day of some incident. Just as I was leaving the mess after breakfast, the CO. said 'I want to see you for a moment' and told me Guy Lambert is getting a regiment, and that he is trying to put Sandy Cowie as 491 B.C. and I've to be adjutant. I'm not a bit keen on the idea, but it's a detail so if things go as the C.O. wants, I shall become adjutant. Went to the Sergeants' mess after all but stayed relatively sober and this morning did what I thought was a mile, by stopwatch. I discovered later I'd done a mile and a quarter as the circuit is 276 yards, not 210, so my time is (for the mile) about 6 mins 50 secs; however, I can improve on that, I'm certain. I've had a headache all day from the heavy, thundery weather, and it's rained about once an hour as usual. Motored to Nienburg this morning to draw cash. The usual Corp H.Q. set up – masses of bull, black and white paint, sumptuous quarters etc. Everybody up there sweating on getting Russian decorations. Saw Debroy, Matt Simm and 2 other chaps with whom I went out in 1942. Debroy is in for a Croix de Guerre. Matt and I had a good grouse about our lack of a gong – disappointed troop commanders! A parcel from C. but not letter. 4th day without one. I begin to get worried. Sent her 114 and wrote to Dorothy.

This majority, if it stays in the Regt., is likely to cause some heartburning, as Chas Jones is 2 years senior to Sandy in their present rank and was, I know, expecting to get the next battery. As, in fact, he really had every right to do so.

I wish the bloody weather would improve a bit. It's absolutely shocking at the moment, and everybody is feeling distinctly depressed including me.

4 July

a.m.: Nothing is happening except that the weather is appallingly cold with heavy rainstorms almost hourly throughout the day. Yesterday for the fifth day running, there was no letter from C. I sent off rather a panicky letter in the afternoon as I'm getting rather worried. Let's hope there's something today. Latest story is that the Regiment is to lose 8 officers for S.E.A.C. which is a pretty heavy loss if true. No further developments of the Adjutant situation. I hope I don't have to do the bloody job – specially with Waggy as second i/c.

Did my morning mile in 6.15 yesterday morning and twisted my foot in the effort so that this morning I had to stop after doing 440. In the evening went to the flicks with the 2 Bills, Laurence, and Bob and saw Ginger Rogers in *Lady in the Dark* – rather good if one wasn't in too critical a mood, which I'm not as far as picture going is concerned – nowadays. Tonight there is a farewell dinner for Guy to which a dozen guests from the various infantry bns. and gunner regts. of the Div. are coming. We are expecting David Macintyre from 5 B.W., who will stay the night with us here at 304 if he does come. It'll be nice to see him again.

6 July

I am now adjutant – for better or for worse. Actually, the job may prove fairly interesting, and it is bound to be useful experience. Also, one always knows what is going on, which is a thing that appeals to me. I found out one very interesting thing from the honours and awards file today. Frank Philip and I have both been shoved in for the M.C. – a sort of 'final allotment' which went in about 3 weeks ago. I got two citations – one from Bill Bradford, and they were in such glowing terms that I find it hard to suppress my hopefulness. I am also in for a Mention in Despatches, so it's not unreasonable to hope one or the other will come through – but it's that ribbon I want! Well I'll just have to wait and see. Today we had our Div. Arty. sports at the local stadium. The Regiment did extremely well to win the meeting from 5 other regiments. It was a most exciting afternoon. The camera venture fell through.

I see I've forgotten to mention Guy's farewell dinner which went more or less according to the usual form. Actually it was more sober than usual, and relatively few glasses etc. were broken. David Mac. came and spent the night with us, and gave us all the gossip about our friends in the 5th. He slept in Charles' room. Letter today from C. I got one on the 5th – no two – which had already expelled my anxieties. Sent her no. 118 today. Incidentally the Goya perfume I sent her duly arrived, but it certainly took a hell of a time. I wonder if the duty-free label is responsible, for the ordinary parcels I sent at the same time arrived about four times as quickly. Weather still lousy. This is a rotten Summer we're having – last year I was at home having malaria and able to telephone Clare. How long ago it all seems. Another letter today came from Ronnie Taylor, still at Larkhill. One of the reasons I'm so sorry to leave 304 is because Bill F. is such a first class B.C. I really think it would be hard to find a nicer, fairer man anywhere. No wonder he's so popular with the men. Surprising compliment when John Lawry, the Signal officer, said that as a connoisseur of adjutants, he was delighted they'd chosen me! Waggy also seems exceedingly pleased. Odd, really, considering we were once very definite enemies. I think Waggy respects my vitriolic tongue, and our present friendly relations may have been built up on that rather queer foundation. Poor old Findlay is not very pleased about the move – it's less than a year since we left 491; however he's raised no objections this time – a thing which I was rather fearing might happen. I suppose he feels he's rather too much a part of me at this stage ($2^1/2$ years together) to start breaking away. Anyway he knows it's only for another year or less, and he'll be pretty well off up at the Regimental Mess, where I'll now have to live. Hell! Secretly I do rather hope I get that M.C! Also I'm glad Frank is in. He's richly deserved one if ever anybody has, and been unlucky not to get one before.

8 July

Sunday: A quiet weekend. The C.O. has been away fishing – his ruling passion – along with bridge, booze and horses – and Waggy's had a hangover after entertaining most of the Ensa girls most of last night. I'm getting the hang of my new job. You have to know every single thing that happens in the Regiment – that's what it boils down to. Frank Philip came back from Course and leave last night, and he and most of the 301 officers came round to us at 304 and drank a lot of whisky until a late hour.

I am now in The Regtl Officers mess in my own bedroom – Guy Lambert's old one – very comfortable with large windows looking towards the sunset. Findlay has installed me most expertly with everything in its own place. Tomorrow I am hoping to get the camera I mentioned the other day. The original deal fell through but a Leica is now up for barter, and I've managed to scratch together the various necessaries. Tomorrow the second 304 wireless is ready, so I'll be able to get my own set up here by my bedside which will be very pleasant. How I'll ever get all this kit home when the time comes, God knows!

Letter from Dick (who nearly got himself drowned the other day in Alex harbour) and home. Sent reply home and a letter of condolence to Chas Jones. Also 119 to C.

9 July

Got my Leica today. And bathed. River cold; weather hot. Letter from C. Sent 120.

10 July

Today is the second anniversary of our Sicily landing, yet I'd have forgotten it completely but for the fact that a rum issue was authorised for the occasion. Busy day but got a bathe in the afternoon. Lovely weather and the river much warmer. A piano plays *Warsaw Concerto* nearby and it grows dark. I am tired. With my Leica yesterday I achieved the 3rd of my 'Major War Aims' – a Luger, a Leica, and Zeiss Binoculars!

12 July

Chief event yesterday a visit by the C.R.A. which went without any hitches from this department. In the afternoon rather a good bathe, tho' it clouded over and was very muggy in the evening. Saw an excellent film, *Madame Curie*, which was admirably adapted to deal with the dignity and immensity of the subject. I was considerably moved by the whole thing; shall write home for the book which should contain more detail. Letter from C. I sent her 122 to Primrose Hill where she'll arrive on the 15th. I am quite liking my job. There's no doubt it gives me a certain status within and outside the Regt., for there is only one adjutant and it really is quite a responsible job. There is nothing insuperably difficult about it but you have to keep your finger on a very large number of buttons at the same time.

14 July

Saturday: Non-frat lifted today. Glorious swim. Am going riding tomorrow morning as the C.O. is away fishing and he wants somebody to take his horse. It's a huge stallion and I should think it'll throw me for certain. Bill Carney back from Brussels last night with Alec Cowan who's gone off to hospital with dip. today. Went to hear Margery Lawrence sing tonight – very good.

16 July

A distinctly energetic day yesterday. Duly went riding in the morning without any disasters, though after so long, my riding doubtless left much to be desired. As it's the first time I've ever ridden a large and energetic thoroughbred racehorse it wasn't *too* disgraceful. In the afternoon a glorious swim in quite the best weather we've had yet. In the evening, played bridge with Laurence; we beat Bob Mackay and Jim Cowper – chiefly – through getting better cards. Terribly hot all night and lay sweating for a long time before getting to sleep. Sent C. 125.

18 July

You get a curious assortment of jobs in the Adjutant's office. Everything from moaning civilians to people wanting to borrow the Regimental Steamroller! The other day I had a woman who looked exactly like Elsie the cow in the Borden's milk ad. I managed to fix her trouble and two days later she returned beaming and presented me with a bunch of flowers and an exceedingly evil cigar which I gave to the C.O! Lousy overcast weather again today – but yesterday afternoon wasn't bad, and I got in quite a good bathe with Frank Philip. We've been discussing our gong chances – the citations have been away a month now, though it may of course take much longer for them to come through – if they DO come through at all. Sent C. 127 yesterday but nothing from her since last Friday. The Poles are being moved rapidly out of our barracks so it looks as though we may move into them sooner than expected – not popular with anybody. C.O. is fanatical about V.D. and probably would have got into trouble if he'd published the order in Regt. Orders giving all names. However, I quietly filed it and said nothing. We have 21 cases in the Regt.

20 July

Today I had to prosecute in a court martial over at Hannover – another of the Adjutant's jobs which I am slowly finding out day by day. The thing started badly for we all went to Osnabruck by mistake – the name of the barracks being the same! So off we set on the 111 miles to Hannover and the Court finally got cracking at 1500. I'd taken the C.O.2's staff car which made things less arduous. I won both my cases – one was a walkover. The second took four hours. I was up at 0530 today after a poor night's sleep broken up by a tremendous electric storm in the small hours – I was woken by the lightning flashing in my face and the frightening crash of a nearby thunderbolt. There was very heavy rain. Other items of news include: two days ago the C.O. broke his arm while driving his jeep (very drunk) with kids in it coming back from Nienburg. This was hushed up and even now I am about the only one to know the facts of the case. Jack Peach has been promoted A/Capt. in place of Alec Cowan. The W.O.s and N.C.O.s are giving a big dinner for all officers next Friday. I have to reply for the guests! Letters from C. today and yesterday. Sent her 130 tonight.

25 July

a.m.: The days pass rather uneventfully one way and another. This morning the results of the Court Martial I mentioned the other day came through. One chap got 40 days detention, the other was reduced to the ranks plus 28 days detention – a pretty stiff sentence. Weather's been awful lately, today is the first decent day – so far – since I made my last entry. Borrowed *The Razor's Edge* by Somerset

Maugham from L/Bdr. Spencer of 491 – a book I've been trying to get for ages. It is as beautifully written as all his stuff. On Friday the Regtl. Sergeant's Mess is having a big dinner for all officers at which I have unfortunately to make a speech. A bad piece of news this morning – we are losing our guns at the end of the month. The guns of a Regt. means so much to it, it is rather like losing a limb. Also, preparations are going ahead for our move to Nampeal barracks, possibly by the end of August. The barracks are absolutely filthy – the departing Poles have left it in a foul condition with excreta all over the floors, smashed furniture, broken windows and nearly all electric light fittings and bulbs removed. It is going to be weeks before the place is fit for habitation. The move itself is exceedingly unpopular all round, and even if we keep our present mess, it's going to mean a trip of a mile and a quarter from there to the barracks. Not a good thing in Winter. Mail not terribly good lately; sent C. 134 yesterday. Had two from her in the last 3 or 4 days. No news at all of any awards. Even old Frank is rather restless about them. Infuriating if some basewallah in England turns them down after all this time.

28 July

Last night we had a tremendous dinner for all the officers, W.O.s, and Sergeants in the Regt., in the Hannover Hotel. It went the way of all parties, getting more and more riotous till eventually the few survivors (about 10% I suppose) had a very excellent game of rugger – officers v. the Regt. – at about 0200 – with a potted palm tree. Considering the amount of broken glass etc. lying around, it's surprising there weren't more casualties. I staggered home with (a very drunken) C.O. at about three o'clock and woke up this morning feeling definitely frail. Letter from C. yesterday and I sent her 136. Recited my poem – a parody of Kipling's 'If' – after my speech last night and it went over very well really. Charles Jones arrived back in the middle of the party. Very good to see him again.

31 July

Funny that the above should have been my last sentence because I've had rather a row with him. He thinks I pulled a fast one in the matter of the camera I acquired, by getting help from a Polish officer who'd been trying to get one for Charles without success. As the contact was of my own finding and in view of the amount of work I put in, I don't feel I've robbed him in any way. At first I was so surprised I nearly gave him the bloody thing (which he wouldn't have taken anyway as a matter of fact) and then I thought No, why the hell should I after all, so I'm keeping it. I can quite see Charles is disappointed about it but it's rather small-minded of him to go on so about it. Nothing much happening.

The weather has been godawful, and there is a railway strike in the U.K. which has provided ammunition for Tory guns in the mess. The left wing is headed by Sandy Cowie, Jimmy Gegan, Peter Jackson, John Bentley and the M.O. The C.O. is the sort of bigoted Tory who won the election for Labour. But he's really easy enough to work with and we get on well enough together. Bill Ovenstone the adjutant before Sandy returned yesterday and has been put in the education and entertainment. Letters from C. and Dorothy yesterday. Sent C. no. 138.

7 August

a.m.: I see I've not written anything in this book for a week, which seems rather slack. As a matter of fact I don't get an awful lot of time for writing up a diary these days, specially as lack of any real news destroys much inclination to do so anyway. The main world news at the moment (apart from the 4th Test at Lords!) is the dropping of the first Atomic Bomb on Japan. This bomb has the equivalent bursting power of a 20,000 ton H.E. bomb, and on its trials in America knocked flat a man standing 10,000 yards away. It could be a great power for peace held by the right people but if it gets about the place I can see the world blowing itself to pieces in another 25 or 50 years. 'Harnessing the power of the Universe' is one description of this horrible weapon. Let's hope it will shorten the Jap war. The inclination to go and find some far corner of the earth (is there one now?) to go and live for the rest of one's days, is very strong. (Away from all That–omic.)

Other news is scanty. We are preparing hard for the H.D. games to be held at our stadium early in September, and have hopes of a place, if not a win. Unfortunately, while we have a few star performers, our teams have rather a poor tail. On Friday I'm going to a party at 5 B.W. with Bill French. Bill Bradford and some of the other officers came over the other day to watch 5 B.W. defeated in the semifinals of the Div. football by 4–3. It was a most thrilling game, and a draw would have been the fairest result. Last night we had a bridge Tournament. I played with Laurence, and apart from one good hand in which we made a small slam doubled and vulnerable, we had bad cards all the evening. However we only ended 2 down after 4 rubbers. Our game has much improved lately.

Campaign ribbons are expected any day now. I'm told they're a bit of an eyesore. The C.O. goes on leave today, and Waggy (back on Sunday full of almost inhuman energy) assumes command of the Regiment. Long faces all round. Our 100 German P.W. have arrived and started work on Nampeal barracks, and we expect to move in by 1 September. More long faces.

Jimmy Law and Bob Mackay back up to Captain. Also John Lawry the sigs officer. Incidentally all our phonelines are now on a civvy exchange and you dial the number you want. Sent C. no. 144 yesterday and have been hearing from her regularly too. Also wrote (or typed rather) to America yesterday. Leo is sending me some stockings for C. I hope they arrive before I go on leave. Weather has been very poor lately but better today and yesterday. Quarrel with Chas was made up (not in so many words) two or three days later, but it obviously still rankles.

10 August

Another atomic bomb has been dropped – this time on Nagasaki. The Russians have declared war on Japan and advanced 14 miles into Manchuria. Truman has told the Japs that if they don't pack in their cities will be disintegrated by atomic bombs. The pope has protested against the use of the weapon, which is to be kept secret by U.S. and G.B. until some means of controlling it can be laid on. A good thing that. The phenomenal cost of the research leading to discovery of the bomb was £500 million. And its warhead weighs about eight pounds. When you consider that bomb weight has multiplied itself about 20 times in this war, you are faced with the possibility of a future bomb with a blast power of 500,000 lbs of H.E. This presumably could destroy any city yet built – and probably the plane that dropped it. In fact it would start a small earthquake. There are a good few articles in the paper explaining the meaning of atomic energy, but even when you've grasped the principles the thing remains in the realms of pure science.

Yesterday it rained nearly all day. We are expecting to send all our S.E.A.C. officers – 9 of them – away any day now. Letter from Dorothy yesterday to which I replied. Also sent C. no. 147. Had a curious dream about a sort of Vivien Leigh-ish creature – who also had those indefinable dream qualities of other women I've known – last night and was woken by toothache at about 0400. Slept fitfully for the rest of the night. I shall have to have this tooth out (left lower molar) within a day or two at latest. Damn. Am going to 5 B.W. guest night with Bill French tonight. Hope the tooth doesn't ruin things.

12 August

Sunday: Japan has virtually surrendered, which doesn't surprise me for I hear the estimated death toll for Hiroshima is 250,000 out of 300,000. I also heard on the wireless that the Atomic bomb could be stepped up by 2000 times, giving a bomb of <u>2,000,000 tons of H.E.</u> I imagine this might easily start general disintegration and destroy mankind. Excellent party the other night with my tooth apparently deadened by alcohol! I had it out with gas this morning by a <u>very</u> pleasant dentist over at the 3 C.C.S. at Rotenburg. Nasty big brute with a chronic abscess in the end.

Main discussion now is on the prospect of a speeded up demob. I think 25 groups by the end of the year should be easily possible. The problems of civvy street loom large and rather menacing. No house, no job, no prospects, little money. Millions must be feeling the same. Letter from C. today – first for nearly a week. Sent her no. 150. Have sent her eighty one letters since the 20th May. Another Bridge tournament tonight. Am playing with Laurence again. Today it is pouring with rain for the third successive day. Also thundering wildly. All our S.E.A.C. drafts have been cancelled pro-tem.

15 August

Today is 'V.J.' day – 3 months after the end of the war in Europe, which is better than anybody ever dared hope for – certainly not myself. No official celebrations here thank god. We are having two days holiday tomorrow and Friday but I'm afraid it won't affect my own particular routine very much. Particularly as I have to sit on a Mil gov. general court on Friday. Col. Morris of 128 Fd is the president, and we have to try about 9 Poles on charges of concealing arms, robbery etc. It means the death sentence if they are found guilty. Kiddo – amazing creature – told me in heavy confidence today that he sneaked away to Berlin the other day to get a Leica. He did – for 1000 cigarettes and 1500 marks. Apparently the Black Market there is incredible. Cigarettes are 100 marks (£2.10) for 20. A Russian bought his watch for £100.

Been feeling lousy since Sunday but better today. A sliver of that tooth I had out is still in. I hope it doesn't mean more hacking and scraping. The ex local mil. gov. commander is in for a court martial for smuggling stuff out of Germany. I knew they were on his trail. He is Lt. Col. Hallesworth and a <u>very</u> bad type. He has to live with us for a couple of days while a summary of evidence is taken. Letters from C. and B. Sent C. 154 today. But mail in general has been very bad. Like the weather; it has rained heavily almost every day for a week. Summer . . .

20 August

Last Friday a General Military Court sat in Verden on 9 Poles, accused of various offences from concealment of arms to armed robbery – a practice which is rather prevalent in the neighbourhood. Col. Morris of 128 was President, a legal Major and I were members. We passed 2 sentences of 17 years, one of 15 and six of 10, which I must say I found pretty harsh. These D.P.s – many of them were youths when they were hauled into Germany – have not learned any better. And even if they had, I'm all for giving the Germans a taste of their own medicine. However – Law and Order must be maintained, and while I'm by no means sure these repressive sentences are the best way of doing it, one must make it clear that highwayman tactics just don't pay in an occupation zone. The rest of the trouble is of course that insufficient attention is being paid to D.P. welfare in general. That again is not a problem of ours.

Current topic is demob. speed up. The *Daily Mail* is particularly pernicious with its promises of 32 Groups out this year etc. I don't think they'll get more than 23 or 24 groups out myself. Campaign ribbons have arrived and everybody goes around looking very colourful. It's a pity the Italy and F/Germany stars come together in many cases, as they don't look good side by side. Separated they are O.K. Got drunk on Saturday night – very pleasantly, and went to sleep with the wireless going. Woke up in the middle of the night and it was still going.

Wrote to B., Dorothy and C. (157) yesterday. Mail has been very poor again lately. No news of the periodic decorations – just over 2 months now since they went in. These things are always absurdly slow, and knowing the ponderous army machinery, it doesn't surprise me in the least. Another Court Martial on Friday, at which I've got to prosecute again. It's an easy case. One of the most moronic gunners in the world went beserk in a small way, in a German house in the small hours, discharging among other things a .765 pistol.

21 August

At the close of play in the 5th Victory Test at Old Trafford on Saturday Australia were all out for 173 and England 162 for 5.

POSTCRIPT

After VJ Day I stopped waking in the night and thinking about a possible sixth campaign, and my diary ended . . . fifty* summers ago. It was as though there was nothing left to say.

Eight months of service remained, marked by a slow but perceptible reversal of our previous way of life. 'Bull' – that arch-enemy of us all – increased; discipline decreased. (No longer was it permissible – indeed desirable – to go, carrier-borne, to Bren-gun a wild pig for Sunday lunch!)

Eight months of pleasurable idleness they must have been, but already marked by the uneasy realisation that, at twenty-seven, one had a living to earn. On our 'liberated' horses, I galloped recklessly across the frosty heath in the winter dawns, attended increasingly meaningless parades, played endless bridge, and drank too much too often.

Finally, on 1 May 1946, six years and eight months after I enlisted, I was demobilised. It was not a happy return. Within three weeks, I stood by my father's deathbed. On New Year's Eve, I watched my younger brother lie dying – knocked down by a speeding car. He had joined up under age and come safely through. Then, during 1947, Clare began to indicate that her future would be complete without me. There was a painful parting, and by the time she changed her mind, so had I. In this process I was much helped by meeting a lady from the far west of Canada, whom I had the good sense to wean from her other suitors, and marry on the third anniversary of VE Day. Seven years and four miscarriages later (and after we had firmly decided not to try again) my first son was born. Three years later, without a whisper of trouble, my second. Now they tend to beat us regularly at bridge, having long since beaten us at every other scholastic achievement open to them.

Before the war, I had been for a short time a reporter, but in August 1946 (having discovered too late that what I really wanted to be was a doctor) I went into advertising. This much-maligned trade sharpened my wits and brought me into contact with some of my dearest friends, and – inevitably – a few

* Now sixty (2005).

particularly unsavoury individuals. It also brought me half a million miles of air travel and a chance to see much of the world, little of which disappointed me, and much (such as the Orient) which turned out to be all I expected, and more.

I started this life in advertising as 'P.A. to the Managing Director' of a newly founded agency in Mayfair. He, an American, interviewed me and gave me the job as he lay in his bath, and – as an ex-adjutant! – I rapidly became proficient in working the switchboard, acting as his chauffeur, bribing the Post Office engineers (with nylons) to produce 'non-existent' telephones, organising the office furniture from Stockholm. Eventually via copy writing I became overseas manager and my travels began. It was a hectic life (starting at £6 per week) and in 1952 I got T.B. In spite of Maugham-inspired visions of despair and haemorrhage, and thanks to newly available streptomycin, I emerged from my sanatorium fit and bronzed, a mere ten months after I took to my bed; and twenty-eight pounds heavier at that.

In 1958, lured by ambition and money, I joined another agency, where I remained for eight most successful and enjoyable years. By then I had become joint Managing Director, but disaster struck when three clients went bust. It became clear that the doctrine of collective cabinet responsibility was not one which had any appeal for my colleagues, and after much heart searching I resigned.

An unhappy few months followed as director of a new Anglo-American agency, which was shut down overnight and the staff all fired. So, approaching fifty (long since 'dead' in advertising terms) I found myself on the dole. The wheel had indeed come full circle.

Job-hunting, well into middle age and on the dole, is a disagreeable and demoralising experience. Happily, by Christmas, I was walking somewhat taller in one of the world's largest companies, and there I remained until retirement.

But it took me a long time to regain my self-confidence. After all, I used to tell myself, your war effort, if no epic, was very adequate. You have battled your way to somewhere near the top of an ultra-competitive industry. You have met with Triumph and Disaster, and if you haven't treated those Two Imposters just the same, they haven't finished you off either!

It was by my past, by that fundamental self-respect, gained in so many isolated O.P.s, that I was finally sustained. The years had not been wasted. And now, from my Observation Post of incipient old age, it is 'Time to turn back and descend the stair, with a bald spot' (albeit a small one) 'in the middle of my hair.'

Time to advance once more, for another battle is ending, but the war is not over yet.

March 2005

GLOSSARY

Abbreviations used in the text

A/T	Anti-Tank	D.F.	Defensive Fire
Anzacs	Australian and New Zealand Army Corps	Div. Arty.	Divisional Artillery
A.C.P.O.	Assistant Command Post Officer	E Tp. - G.P.O.	E Troop Gun Position Officer
A.C.I.	Army Council Instruction	E.T.A.	Estimated Time of
A.M.L.C.	Airmail Letter Card		Arrival
A.L. 63	Flea Powder		
A.A.	Anti-Aircraft	F.O.O.	Forward Observation
A.G.	Airgunner		Officer
A.L.O.	Army Liaison Officer	F. Tp.	F Troop
21 A.G.P.	21st Army Group	F.U.P.	Forming Up Place
A.P.	Armour Piercing	F.D.L.S.	Forward Defence Lines
		F.D.S.	Field Dressing Station
B.C.	Battery Commander		
Bty.	Battery	GS	General Service
B.Q.M.	Battery Quartermaster	G.P.O.	Gun Position Officers
B.H.Q.	Battery Headquarters	G.O.C.	General Officer
Bn. H.Q.	Battalion Headquarters		Commanding
B.S.M.	Battery Sergeant Major	Gp.	Group
Bdr.	Bombardier		
B.M.R.A.	Brigade Major, R.A.	H.D.	Highland Division
Bde.	Brigade	H.Q.R.A.	Headquarters Royal Artillery
C.P.O.	Command Post Officer	H.L.I.	Highland Light Infantry
C.O.	Commanding Officer		
C.P.	Command Post	I/C	In Charge Of
C.R.A.	Commander Royal Artillery	I.O.	Intelligence Officer
C.C.S.	Casualty Clearing Station	L/Bdr.	Lance Bombardier

L.O.	Liaison Officer
L.S.T.	Landing Ship Tank
L.C.	Letter Card
L.C.T.	Landing Craft Tank
M.T.	Motor transport
M.O.	Medical Officer
M.L.	Mine Layer
M.T.B.	Motor Torpedo Boat
N.A.	SS Niew Amsterdam
N.C.O.	Non-Commissioned Officer
N.Z.E.F.	New Zealand Expeditionary Force
Naafi/NAAFI	Navy, Army, and Air Force Institute
O.T.C.	Officer Training Corps
O.C.T.U.	Officer Cadet Training Unit
O.P.	Observation Post
O.R.	Other Ranks
O. Gp.	Observation Group
P. - Force	Pi Force: unit in Persia
Q.M.	Quartermaster
R.E.	Royal Engineers
R.H.Q.	Regimental Headquarters
R.A.F.	Royal Air Force
R.H.A.	Royal Horse Artillery
R.A.S.C.	Royal Army Service Corps
R.D.F.	Radio Direction Finder (Radar)
R.A.M.C.	Royal Army Medical Corps
R.N.V.R.	Royal Navy Volunteer Reserve
R.Q.M.S.	Regimental Quartermaster
R.S.M.	Regimental Sergeant Major
R.A.P.	Regimental Aid Post
S.A.	South Africa
S.E.A.C.	South East Asia Command
Tp. Comd.	Troop Command
Tp. C.P.	Troop Command Post
W.A.A.F.	Women's Auxiliary Air Force

INDEX

Note: Jack Swaab is abbreviated to JS. Page numbers in italics refer to maps. Major entries are in chronological order, where appropriate.